W0079704

# Beginning JSP™ 2 API: From Novice to Professional

PETER DEN HAAN, LANCE LAVANDOWSKA,
SATHYA NARAYANA PANDURANGA,
AND KRISHNARAJ PERRUMAL

EDITED BY MATTHEW MOODIE

APress Media, LLC

Beginning JSP™ 2 API: From Novice to Professional

ISBN 978-1-59059-339-4 ISBN 978-1-4302-0693-4 (eBook)
DOI 10.1007/978-1-4302-0693-4



Lead Editor: Matthew Moodie

Technical Reviewers: Scott Davis and Matthew Moodie

Editorial Board: Steve Anglin, Dan Appleman, Gary Cornell, James Cox, Tony Davis, John Franklin, Chris Mills, Steve Rycroft, Dominic Shakeshaft, Julian Skinner, Jim Sumser, Karen Watterson, Gavin Wray, John Zukowski

Project Manager: Sofia Marchant

Copy Manager: Nicole LeClerc

Copy Editor: Kim Wimpsett

Production Manager: Kari Brooks

Production Editor: Laura Cheu

Compositor: Kinetic Publishing Services, LLC

Proofreader: Liz Welch

Indexer: Michael Brinkman

Artist: Kinetic Publishing Services, LLC

Cover Designer: Kurt Krames

Manufacturing Manager: Tom Debolski

In the United States: phone 1-800-SPRINGER, e-mail orders@springer-ny.com, or visit http://www.springer-ny.com. Outside the United States: fax +49 6221 345229, e-mail orders@springer.de, or visit http://www.springer.de.

For information on translations, please contact Apress directly at 2560 Ninth Street, Suite 219, Berkeley, CA 94710. Phone 510-549-5930, fax 510-549-5939, e-mail info@apress.com, or visit http://www.apress.com.



The source code for this book is available to readers at http://www.apress.com in the Source Code section.

# Contents at a Glance

# Contents

# About the Authors

## *Peter den Haan*

**Peter den Haan** is a senior systems engineer at Objectivity Ltd., a UK-based systems integration company. He started out programming at 13 on a RadioShack TRS-80 model I with 16KB of memory, but he has progressed since to become a J2EE systems architect and lead developer for Internet and intranet projects for customers ranging from the UK Football Association Premier League to Shell Finance.

Peter has previously written the security and cryptography chapters for *Beginning Java Networking*. He's a Sun Certified Java 2 developer, a JavaRanch bartender, a self-confessed geek; he has a doctorate degree in theoretical physics and plays bass in the local worship band. You can reach him at `bjsp@peterdenhaan.info`.

## *Lance Lavandowska*

**Lance Lavandowska** has been working with JSP since 1998. He has contributed to several Apache Jakarta projects, the Castor project, and the Roller Weblogger project. Lance has also served as a technical reviewer on several JSP books and was a coauthor on *Professional JSP Site Design*.

## *Sathya Narayana Panduranga*

**Sathya Narayana Panduranga** is a software design engineer living in Bangalore, the Software Capital of India. He has expertise in Microsoft and Java technologies and has worked in the domains of Internet, telecom, and convergence. His favorite areas of interest are distributed and component-based application architectures and object-oriented analysis and design. Contributing to a range of technical articles and books is a hobby that gives him the immense satisfaction of sharing his knowledge. You can contact him at `sathyanp@hotmail.com`.

## Krishnaraj Perrumal

**Krishnaraj Perrumal** is founder and director of Adarsh Softech. He has successfully developed and managed a number of software projects and e-projects, and his programming experience spans the past 15 years. He regularly gives presentations on Java technology, XML, information systems security, and audits.

He's a Sun Certified Java Programmer, a Certified Novell NetWare Engineer, and a Certified Information Systems Auditor. Currently he spends most of his time providing consultancy and solutions for computer security, in addition to Web development. He loves to spend all his free time with children, but being tech savvy, information technology constitutes both his profession and his hobby. You can contact Krishnaraj at `adasoft@sancharnet.in`.

# About the Editor

## *Matthew Moodie*

**Matthew Moodie** enjoys a life of fun in Glasgow, Scotland. He's a keen novice gardener with a houseful of plants. He'd like to thank Laura for her love and friendship.

# About the Technical Reviewer

**Scott Davis** is a senior software engineer and instructor in the Denver, Colorado, area. He has worked on a variety of Java platforms, from J2EE to J2SE to J2ME (sometimes all on the same project). He's a frequent presenter at national conferences and local user groups. Most recently, he was the president of the Denver Java Users Group (`http://www.denverjug.org`).

# Introduction

**Welcome to** *Beginning JSP 2: From Novice to Professional.* This book is for novices and teaches JavaServer Pages (JSP) 2 using basic principles. You don't need to know any Java to use this book because JSP 2 is a significant development of the JSP technology that has greatly reduced JSP's reliance on Java knowledge. However, to get the most out of supporting technologies and maximize your JSP applications, you need to know some basic Java techniques. We'll teach you these techniques and show you when and where to use the Java language.

The JSP 2 specification is the biggest revision of JSP since its creation. It's now easier for nonprogrammers to build powerful, dynamic Web applications. The authors of this book realize that JSP 2 is a tremendously powerful tool but that it's also a daunting prospect for many nonprogrammers. In response to this, the authors have written an easily accessible guide for those who are beginning their career in Web programming. This book introduces all the important concepts without fuss or overcomplication and always keeps the readers' best interests at heart.

Chapter 1 takes you through the Java and JSP installation processes so you're ready for the rest of the book. Chapter 2 is a Hypertext Markup Language (HTML) recap, which will act as a useful reference for those who already know a little HTML. After running through the basics, the book moves through simple JSP pages in Chapter 3 to working with data in Chapter 4, probably the most common and important task you'll have to undertake when using JSP. After all, what's the point of using dynamic Web pages if you have no dynamic data on which to work?

Chapters 5 and 6 introduce your first Java and show you how to use simple Java utility code to enhance your JSP pages. The emphasis is always on JSP and how Java fits into the new JSP 2 framework. Throughout these chapters you'll slowly build and incrementally improve an application that uses HTML forms, databases, and validation. The book explains each stage and introduces good practice as you learn new techniques.

Chapters 7 and 8 introduce more advanced JSP techniques and use the newly incorporated JSP Tag Library (JSTL) tags to work with dates, times, and formatting. Chapter 8 introduces Extensible Markup Language (XML), the ubiquitous data description specification, and JSP's tools for dealing with it. XML is such an important part of modern Web applications that it's essential in any beginner's handbook. You'll soon find that XML is an inescapable part of today's Web.

Chapters 9 and 10 cover topics that will ensure your applications are well designed and flexible. Specifically, Chapter 9 covers servlets and filters, both of which are Java classes that run alongside JSP pages and add robust functionality to any Web application. Chapter 10 introduces the Model-View-Controller design concept and the Struts framework, which implements it for JSP pages. By using Struts you instantly add good design and flexibility without any of the hard work usually associated with scalable Web applications.

By the time you've finished the book, you'll have an example Web application for taking data, validating it, storing it in a database, and reporting back to the user. However, the real benefit will be in the design under the covers. Your application will use good practice throughout and can form the basis for many similar applications in the future.

I hope you enjoy reading this work and that you have every success in the future.

Matthew Moodie, Editor

CHAPTER 1

# Creating Your First JSP Page

**Welcome!** In recent years, Java has risen to become one of the dominant development platforms for the Web, and knowledge of Java and often JavaServer Pages (JSP) is required for a wide variety of situations throughout the industry. You probably already knew that, and that's why you're reading this book right now.

In this book, we set out to make it easy for anyone of only modest computing skills to learn enough about Java and JSP to create Web applications using the latest technologies in this arena, such as JSP 2.0 and Tomcat 5.0 (you'll learn what these are in just a few paragraphs).

The goal of this first chapter is to install all the tools on your machine that you'll need to develop JSP Web applications. We'll walk through the process of writing a simple Web application and discuss some fundamental principles of the Web itself, covering the role that Java and related technologies have to play.

Subsequent chapters of this book will gradually ramp up your knowledge of JSP and of Java as it pertains to JSP applications. By the end of the book, you'll be confident enough to start writing your own JSP Web applications.

## Installing the Software

Fortunately, all the software you'll use throughout this book is available without charge. In this chapter, you'll install the essentials for creating Java Web applications:

**Java 2 Standard Edition Software Development Kit (J2SE SDK)**: Software developers use three different versions of Java: Java 2 Micro Edition (J2ME), Java 2 Standard Edition (J2SE), and Java 2 Enterprise Edition (J2EE). J2ME is used for developing applications for small devices such as phones or personal digital assistants (PDAs). It's a stripped-down version that's highly optimized for these devices' limited capabilities. J2SE is the standard version of Java for developing everything else from games to business applications. J2EE is built on top of J2SE, adding a plethora of features geared toward applications for large businesses (so-called enterprises). All the extras included with J2EE can be downloaded separately and used with J2SE.

**Apache Jakarta Tomcat**: Tomcat is what's known as a *servlet container*. In the Java world, a servlet container is responsible for receiving Web requests and passing them to Java Web applications. We'll discuss servlet containers and Tomcat in greater detail later in the "Java and the Web" section.

We'll provide instructions for installing these applications on Windows 2000/XP and Red Hat Linux. If you're using a different version of Windows or a different distribution of Linux and you can't figure out what's going on from the instructions given, don't panic; both of these applications come with their own installation instructions. In a pinch, you can simply refer to them.

## Downloading Java Standard Edition

Sun Microsystems, the creator and maintainer of Java, makes Java available for download from its Web site. At the time of this writing, the latest version is 1.4.2, which you can find at the following uniform resource locator (URL):

```
http://java.sun.com/j2se/1.4.2/download.html
```

This URL takes you to a page offering the various flavors available depending on the platform you use. You also have a choice between the Java Runtime Environment (JRE) and the SDK. The JRE is for folks who want to run Java applications but aren't developing Java software, so you'll want the SDK.

If you're on Linux, download the RPM in the self-extracting file.

> **NOTE** *Be sure to download the J2SE SDK, not the JRE.*

Because Web sites are subject to change, and books sadly don't change after they've been printed, these links may no longer work. In that event, visit `http://java.sun.com` and download the latest version of Java for your operating system that you can find. Sun does a pretty good job of providing help and instructions to get you this far.

## Installing Java on Windows

The file you've downloaded is a self-extracting EXE file, so double-click it once it has been downloaded. You then need to enter the name of the folder where Java is to be installed. Choose something such as `C:\java\jdk1.4`, but if you install to somewhere else, be sure to note the location for future use. Now finish the installation, leaving any options at their default values.

> **NOTE** *If possible, you should avoid using directory names that contain spaces (for example,* `C:\Program Files`*). This can cause subtle, difficult-to-troubleshoot errors in the future.*

## *Installing Java on Red Hat Linux*

The Red Hat Package Manager (RPM) file you downloaded is wrapped in a self-extracting binary format that you'll need to execute before installation. Open a shell prompt to the location you've downloaded Java, and type the following:

```
chmod a+x  j2sdk-1_4_2_02-linux-i586-rpm.bin
./j2sdk-1_4_2_02-linux-i586-rpm.bin
```

You'll then see a long license. Read it carefully (wink), and then agree to it, at which point an RPM file will be extracted into the same directory. Before you can install it, you must become the `root` user by typing the following:

```
su
```

Once you've entered the `root` password at the prompt, you can then install Java by typing this:

```
rpm -U  j2sdk-1_4_2_02-linux-i586-rpm
```

Of course, if you've downloaded a different version of Java, you'll need to use that filename in place of the one shown here.

The RPM will install Java to the following path: `/usr/java/j2sdk1.4.2_02`.

## *Downloading Tomcat*

This book has been written for the latest incarnation of the Apache Foundation's Tomcat Web server, which is version 5.0. However, Tomcat 5.0 wasn't quite ready for release at the time of this writing, so we can't provide a definitive URL for downloading it. A good place to start is at the following URL:

```
http://jakarta.apache.org/site/binindex.cgi
```

This URL should open a page with (among other things) assorted links under the headings of Release Builds, Milestone Builds, and Nightly Builds. Look for anything starting with *Tomcat 5* in the Release Builds section, and click it. In the event that there's no release build of Tomcat 5, download the latest Tomcat 5 release under the Milestone Builds heading or try the following URL:

```
http://www.apache.org/dist/jakarta/tomcat-5/v5.0.16/
```

The Tomcat 5 link takes you to a screen that begins with a file listing. Click the folder marked `bin`, and from the list of files that then appear, Windows users should select the latest version of Tomcat 5 that ends with `.exe`, and Linux users should download the latest version ending with `.tar.gz`.

> **NOTE** *Don't download any files that have* `LE` *in the filename because this indicates the Light Edition of Tomcat. Although the Light Edition avoids downloading duplicate copies of libraries that are now included in the 1.4 version of J2SE, it also excludes two libraries, JavaMail and the Java Activation Framework, that you'll use later in this book.*

## Installing Tomcat on Windows

Just as with Java, all you need to do to install Tomcat is double-click the file you've downloaded. You'll need to select a directory for the installation, such as `C:\java\tomcat50`. As with Java, you'll need to remember this location for later use. Don't click the NT Service checkbox if you see it. This option means that Windows will start Tomcat automatically every time the system boots up and stop it when Windows shuts down. This is really only useful when Web applications are finished, rather than when applications are being created, as in this book.

## Installing Tomcat on Linux

To install Tomcat, you'll need to create a suitable directory with the `mkdir` command and extract Tomcat into that directory with the following command (assuming you're in the same directory where you downloaded Tomcat):

```
tar -xzf jakarta-tomcat-5.0.16.tar.gz -C /usr/local/java/tomcat50
```

Of course, change the names of the file and directory as appropriate.

## Configuring Your Environment

The final step of the installation is to set some environment variables that applications can use to find components required for proper operation. Tomcat needs you to set two environment variables, and you'll also modify the PATH variable so that the Java and Tomcat files are accessible from any other folder.

### Windows 2000/XP

To configure Windows 2000/XP, follow these steps:

1. Open the System item in Control Panel, and select the Advanced tab.

2. Click the Environment Variables button to open the Environment Variables dialog box. You should see a window like the one shown in Figure 1-1.

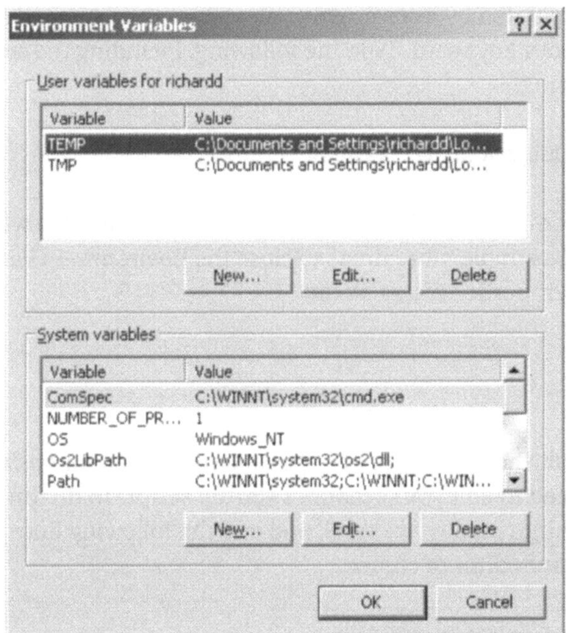


*Figure 1-1. The Environment Variables dialog box*

3. Click the New button in the lower System Variables section. When the New System Variable dialog box appears, enter a name of **JAVA_HOME** and enter the full path to your JDK (such as **C:\java\jdk1.4**) for the value.

4. Repeat step 3 to create another variable; call it **CATALINA_HOME**, the value of which specifies the location of your Tomcat installation (such as `C:\java\tomcat50`).

5. Create one last variable by following the same process. Call it **CLASSPATH**, and give it a value of **%CATALINA_HOME%\common\lib\servlet.jar;.**

> **NOTE** *If you already have an environment variable called* CLASSPATH, *place the previous value at the end of the existing value, with a semicolon (;) at the end of the old value and before the value given in step 5.*

6. Locate the variable named Path in the System Variables list, and double-click it or click the Edit button to open the Edit System Variable dialog box.

   Chances are, a few different paths are already given for this variable, each path separated by a semicolon. Select the value box, and press the End key on your keyboard. Type the following, including the semicolon at the beginning:

   ```
   ;%JAVA_HOME%\bin;%CATALINA_HOME%\bin
   ```

7. Once you're done, click OK to close the Edit System Variable window, and click OK a couple more times to close the Environment Variables and System Properties dialog boxes.

### Red Hat Linux

Red Hat Linux's default shell is the popular Bourne Again Shell (or *bash*). If this is your shell, you'll need to edit your account's startup script. To do this, log in under your own account (usually *not* `root`), and add the following lines to the `~/.bashrc` file using your editor of choice:

```
export JAVA_HOME=/usr/java/j2sdk1.4.1_01
export CATALINA_HOME=/usr/local/java/tomcat50
export PATH=$PATH:$JAVA_HOME/bin:$CATALINA_HOME/bin
export CLASSPATH=$CLASSPATH:$CATALINA_HOME\common\lib\servlet.jar:.
```

If by chance you're using the TC Shell (tcsh), you'll need to edit `~/.tcshrc` by adding the following lines:

```
setenv JAVA_HOME /usr/java/j2sdk1.4.1_01
setenv CATALINA_HOME /usr/local/java/tomcat50
setenv PATH ${PATH}:${JAVA_HOME}/bin:${CATALINA_HOME}/bin
setenv CLASSPATH ${CLASSPATH}:${CATALINA_HOME}\common\lib\servlet.jar:.
```

Again, if you've chosen different directories for the previous installation, change them as necessary; if you're not sure which shell you're using, type **echo $SHELL** to find out.

You're all done with installing—time to try out Tomcat!

### *Trying It Out: Testing Tomcat*

To test that Tomcat is working, follow these steps:

1. On Windows, the installer created a group in your Start menu, probably called Apache Tomcat 5.0. To run Tomcat, select the Start Tomcat item in this menu. Alternately, if you prefer the Windows command line, you can execute the following command:

   ```
   > %CATALINA_HOME%\bin\startup
   ```

   However, because you've added `%CATALINA_HOME%\bin` to the path, you can just type **startup**, and it'll work.

   On Linux, you can start Tomcat by executing the following script:

   ```
   /usr/local/java/tomcat50/startup.sh
   ```

   Because you've added Tomcat to the `PATH` variable, you can simply type **startup.sh**.

2. Once Tomcat is up and running, open your favorite Web browser and navigate to `http://localhost:8080`. You should see a page something like the one shown in Figure 1-2.

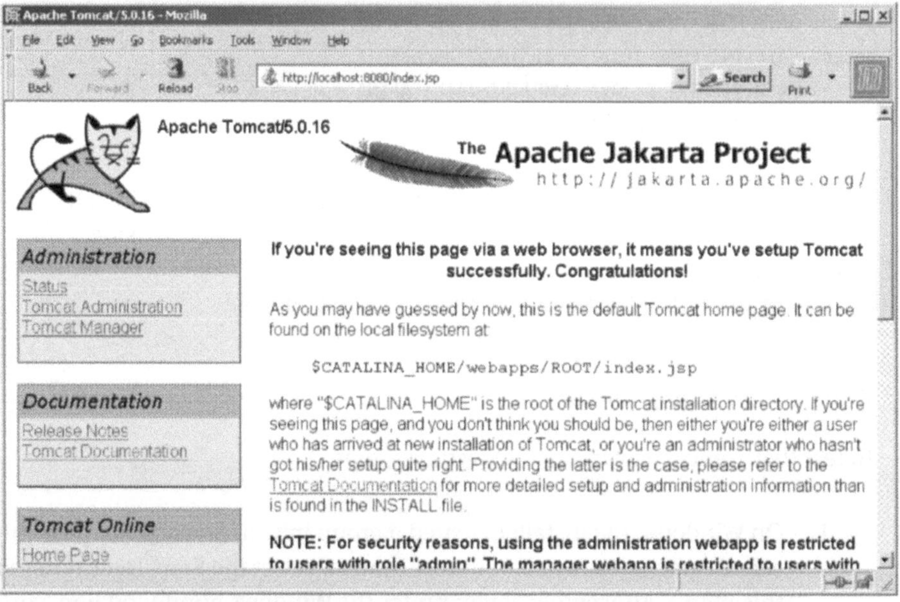


*Figure 1-2. Tomcat's default welcome page*

3. Scroll to the Examples box on the left side, click the JSP Examples link, and try out a couple of the sample programs to verify that everything is working properly. If you can't get the examples to work, double-check that you've correctly followed the previous instructions.

4. At some point, you'll want to shut Tomcat down. On Windows, you can do this by clicking the Stop Tomcat item in the Start menu. The command-line version of this is `%CATALINA_HOME%\bin\shutdown`, or just `shutdown`. Normally, you should avoid simply closing the Tomcat window because that may result in losing data.

   On Linux, execute the script `shutdown.sh`.

### *How It Works: When Things Go Wrong*

If Tomcat didn't start like it was supposed to, try the following suggestions to figure out where things went wrong:

1. On Windows, open a command prompt (look for Command Prompt in the Start menu or type **cmd** or **command** in the Run option given on the Start menu). Type the command **cd %CATALINA_HOME%**. On Linux, type **cd $CATALINA_HOME**. Verify that you're now in the directory where you installed Tomcat. If not, repeat the step for creating that environment variable in the previous "Configuring Your Environment" section.

2. Repeat the same process using **%JAVA_HOME%** or **$JAVA_HOME**. If you're not in the correct location, make sure you set up this variable correctly in the "Configuring Your Environment" section.

3. From the Windows command line, type **java** and press Enter. If you see a message starting with "'java' is not recognized as," try typing **%JAVA_HOME%\bin\java** and pressing Enter. If that still produces the same error message, it indicates that Java wasn't properly installed for some reason.

   Verify that you properly followed the instructions for installing Java, and check the `http://java.sun.com` Web site for help. If the first command failed but the second one succeeded, repeat the instructions for setting the `PATH` variable in the "Configuring Your Environment" section.

   The same applies to Linux users, but you'll need to use `$JAVA_HOME` in place of `%JAVA_HOME%` in the previous instructions. Also note that Windows uses a backslash (\) for its paths whereas Linux uses a forward slash (/).

4. If you've made it this far, check and see if Tomcat was properly installed at the path you selected. If not, reinstall it, referring to the `http://jakarta.apache.org/tomcat` Web site for any special guidance.

## Creating Your First Web Application

Okay, you've got Java, you've got Tomcat: Now you're ready to write a little Web application. This example will be your first look at JSP technology, which mixes Java code with standard Hypertext Markup Language (HTML), and what could be better for your first application than a version of the timeless "Hello World" program? Far be it from us to break from long-standing tradition. To add a dynamic touch, you'll make it perform some hard-core number crunching.

*Trying It Out: Building a Simple Web Application*

To build a simple Web application, follow these steps:

1. You'll start by creating a new Web application called `helloJSP`. To do this, create a new folder with that name in the `webapps` subdirectory off the Tomcat installation folder. This will create the directory structure shown in Figure 1-3.

*Figure 1-3. Tomcat's directory structure*

2. Inside this folder, you need to create another folder. You won't actually *use* it in this chapter, but it must be present for Tomcat to recognize your Web application.

   Inside the `helloJSP` folder you just created, create a folder called `WEB-INF` (on Linux, this directory name must be ALL CAPS). As you'll see in later chapters, this folder is the location for essential files for the Web application.

   You can now place all sorts of resources in the `helloJSP` Web application folder that form part of the Web application itself. This might include HTML files and JSP pages, which can be placed directly inside the `helloJSP` folder, and you could view them by navigating in your Web browser to a URL such as `http://localhost:8080/helloJSP/filename.html`.

3. You're going to create a JSP page, which can include Java code that's run *by the Web server* (in other words, by Tomcat) to alter what's sent to the browser. It's important to be clear that the code is running on the server—although, as you run examples in this book, you'll probably have the browser running on the same machine as the Web server, that's not the case for applications that have been deployed.

Create a new text file in your `helloJSP` folder, and call it `index.jsp`. When writing code files, be they JSP or Java, you'll need to use a text editor such as Notepad or emacs rather than a word processor such as Microsoft Word that would insert special formatting characters that would render your code useless.

4. Open the new `index.jsp` file, and add the following code:

```
<html>
  <head>
    <title>My First JSP</title>
  </head>
  <body>
    Hello, world!
    <p/>
    2 + 2 is ${2 + 2} and 4 * 4 is ${4 * 4}
  </body>
</html>
```

Save the file, and you're done.

5. Now, you'll check to see how your JSP page appears in a Web browser. Start Tomcat (if it's still running from earlier, you'll need to shut it down and restart it so it'll recognize your new `helloJSP` Web application), and then navigate to `http://localhost:8080/helloJSP/index.jsp` in your browser. You should see a screen that looks something like the one in Figure 1-4.

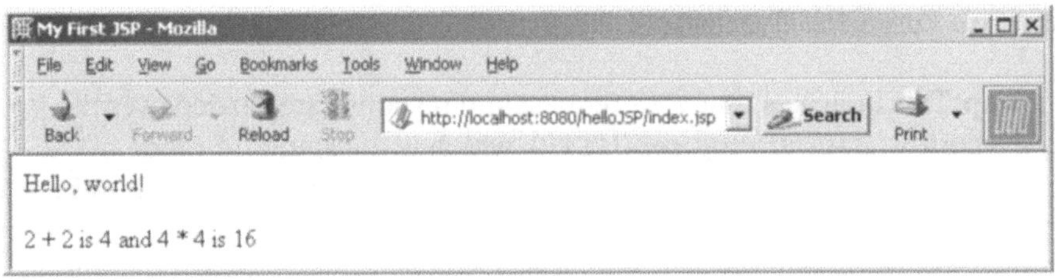


*Figure 1-4. A first JSP*

Congratulations! You've created your first JSP page, and you're on your way to a larger world of Java fun. If all this still seems a bit hazy at the moment, don't worry because things will become clearer as you progress through the book.

If it didn't work for you, make sure that Tomcat is running and that you have capitalized the URL just as the `index.jsp` file and `helloJSP` folder are capitalized on your hard disk.

*How It Works*

If you've done any work with HTML, the JSP you wrote should look familiar to you. In fact, the only JSP-centric code you wrote was this line:

```
2 + 2 is ${2 + 2} and 4 * 4 is ${4 * 4}
```

JSP uses the `${ ... }` special notation to distinguish itself from normal HTML. The servlet container (that is, Tomcat) will then attempt to evaluate the expression within those tags.

In this case, you've created code that completes two simple mathematical expressions: 2 + 2 and 4 * 4. Of course, you'll soon learn how to do much more than simple arithmetic.

While you're here, select View ➤ Source in your browser to see exactly what HTML the browser received. Notice that it's entirely HTML: The JSP code elements have been replaced with the result of the contained expressions, and the Java code was run *on the server* and never made it as far as the browser:

```
<html>
    <head>
        <title>My First JSP</title>
    </head>
    <body>
        Hello, world!
        <p/>
        2 + 2 is 4 and 4 * 4 is 16
    </body>
</html>
```

The URL you used to request the page, `http://localhost:8080/helloJSP/index.jsp`, comprises five distinct parts:

**http**: This indicates that your request and response are carried over the Hypertext Transfer Protocol (HTTP), which is the standard mode of communication between browsers and servers on the World Wide Web.

**localhost**: This is the name of the Web server. `localhost` is a reserved name to indicate the local machine—that is, the machine on which the browser is running. Normally, a Web browser will access a server somewhere else in the world, in which case this part would be replaced with the domain where you're making the application available, such as `www.myJSP.com`. During development and testing, however, pages are often accessed from a browser running on the same machine as the Web server, in which case the `localhost` shortcut can be used.

Technically, `localhost` is an alias for the IP address 127.0.0.1, sometimes called the *loopback* address, which indicates the local machine.

**8080**: This is the port number on which the Web server is listening. A computer can have various server programs each waiting for clients (such as Web browsers) to connect to them. To avoid clashing, each server program must have a unique port number. Normally Web servers use port 80, so Tomcat uses port 8080 by default to coexist with any other Web server that may be running on the same machine.

**helloJSP**: This is the name of the Web application you created, and it tells Tomcat which subfolder of `webapps` contains the resources for this application.

**index.jsp**: This is the name of the actual document you requested. The `.jsp` extension tells Tomcat to treat the file as a JSP file and execute any Java code it contains. Files that have the `.html` extension are left untouched and sent directly to the browser.

You can also create subfolders in your `helloJSP` folder to hold other Web resources, such as images. Such subfolders don't become Web applications in their own right, though—only folders directly within Tomcat's `webapps` folder are Web applications.

## Exploring a Brief History of Java and the Web

For the curious, the following sections summarize the history of the Web and the role that Java plays in it. Feel free to skip to the next chapter if you'd rather just get down to business.

### The Web

Back in the 1960s, as computers began their prolific distribution, the U.S. military constructed a computer network called ARPANET, which was designed to link key computers across the nation. The network was based on a peer-to-peer model; that is, instead of a single machine acting as the server, all computers on the network passed along messages. The idea was that this made the network resistant to disruption caused by a nuclear attack on the United States knocking out key computers.

Fortunately, this resistance to nuclear attack was never tested, but the network's well-designed and robust architecture ensured its survival. As well as the military, the academic community was connected to it, and soon the network became primarily used for scientific research and collaboration. It was renamed the *Internet* because it linked up many local-area and wide-area networks.

In the early days of the Internet, few people outside the scientific disciplines were even aware that it existed, and fewer still had access to it. Ease of use wasn't a priority, and the first generation of Internet users worked with command-line utilities such as Telnet, File Transfer Protocol (FTP), and Gopher to get anything useful done.

The seeds of a more user-friendly Internet, and hence one that was open for more widespread use, were sown in 1989 when Tim Berners-Lee, a computer scientist working for the European Organization for Nuclear Research (CERN), came up with the concept of the World Wide Web. Berners-Lee envisaged an interactive hypertext system on top of the existing Internet to facilitate communication in the world community of physicists. *Hypertext* refers to any system where certain words function as links to other documents or sections of a document; Macintosh users might remember the classic HyperCard, which was the first hypertext application used by many.

The Web began to gain momentum and by 1993 comprised around 50 Web servers. At this time an event occurred that would light the fuse of the Internet skyrocket: the National Center for Supercomputing Applications (NCSA) at the University of Illinois released the first version of the Mosaic Web browser for Unix, PC, and Macintosh systems. Prior to Mosaic, the only fully featured browser available was on the NeXT platform.

With the Mosaic foundation in place, 1994 saw the emergence of the Web into popular culture, and members of the general public began to explore the Internet for themselves. In the same year, a small Silicon Valley company, which would eventually become Netscape, was founded by some of the same folks who had created Mosaic. The so-called New Economy consisting of e-land grabs and irrationally overvalued companies was just around the corner. And the rest is, well, history.

**NOTE** *For more information about the history of the Internet, see* `http://www.isoc.org/internet/history/`. *For more information about the history of the Web, see* `http://www.w3.org/History.html`.

## How the Web Works

There can be confusion as to what exactly the Internet is and how it's different from the Web. The Internet is the physical computer network that links computers around the world. The Web, on the other hand, is a service that sits on the foundation of the Internet. The Web allows computers to communicate with each other. The Web is one of many different services that utilize the Internet; others include e-mail, streaming video, and multiplayer games.

As a service, the Web defines how two parties—a Web client (generally a Web browser) and a Web server—use the Internet to communicate. When you visit a Web site, you create a relationship between your browser and the Web site server. In this relationship, the browser and server communicate through the exchange of messages. First, your browser sends a message to the Web server *requesting* the particular Web page you've asked for, and the Web server *responds* with an appropriate message containing the HTML for the page if it's available. For each additional page that's viewed, the Web browser sends additional requests to the Web server, which likewise responds with the appropriate messages.

This type of relationship is called a *request-response* model. The requests and responses travel over the Web using HTTP. Just as a diplomatic protocol dictates how two governmental parties should conduct discussions, HTTP defines what messages should be exchanged when two computers communicate remotely. The request the client sends to the server is the HTTP request, and the response sent by the server back to the client is the HTTP response.

### *The Responsive Web*

The Web today doesn't consist solely of static pages that return an identical document to every user, and many pages contain content that's generated independently for each viewer. Although static files still have their place, the most useful and appealing pages are dynamically created in response to the users' preferences.

The Common Gateway Interface (CGI) provided the original mechanism by which Web users could actually execute programs on Web servers, not just request HTML pages. Under the CGI model, the following happens:

1. The Web browser sends a request just as it would for an HTML page.
2. The Web server recognizes that the requested resource corresponds to an external program.
3. The Web server executes the external program, passing it the HTTP request that it received from the browser.
4. The external program does its work and sends its results to the server.
5. The Web server passes the program's output back to the browser as an HTTP response.

CGI was enormously popular in the early days of the Web as a means of generating Web pages on the fly. Almost every programming language imaginable has been used to implement some kind of CGI-based solution, but Perl is perhaps the most popular language for CGI development.

However, as the Web grew in popularity and the traffic demands placed on Web sites increased, CGI wasn't efficient enough to keep up. This is because, with CGI, each time a request is received, the Web server must start running a new copy of the external program.

If only a handful of users request a CGI program simultaneously, this doesn't present too much of a problem, but it's a different story if hundreds or thousands of users request the resource at the same time. Each copy of the program requires its own share of processing time and memory, and the server's resources are rapidly used up. The situation is even bleaker when CGI programs are written in interpreted languages such as Perl, which result in the launch of large run-time interpreters with each request.

### Alternatives to CGI

Over the years, many alternative solutions to CGI have surfaced. The more successful of these provide an environment that exists *inside* an existing Web server or even functions as a Web server on its own.

Many such CGI replacements have been built on top of the popular open-source Apache Web server (`http://www.apache.org`). This is because of Apache's popular modular application programming interface (API), which allows developers to extend Apache's functionality with persistent programs. The modules are loaded in memory when Apache starts, and Apache passes the appropriate HTTP requests to these in-memory modules and passes the HTTP responses back out to the browser. This means that the cost of loading an interpreter into memory is removed, and scripts can begin executing faster.

Although few developers actually create modules themselves (because they're relatively difficult to develop), many third-party modules exist that provide a basis for developers to create applications that are much more efficient than normal CGI. These are a few examples:

- **mod_perl**: This maintains the Perl interpreter in memory, thus freeing Perl scripts from the overhead of loading a new copy of the Perl interpreter for each request. This module is very popular.
- **mod_php4**: This module speeds up code in the popular PHP language in the same way that mod_perl speeds up Perl.
- **mod_fastcgi**: This is similar to plain-vanilla CGI, but it enables programs to stay resident in memory rather than terminating when each request is completed.

> **NOTE** *Although the Apache name originally referred only to the Apache Web server, a legion of open-source programs have been developed under the auspices of the Apache Project, including the Tomcat server, which you're using in this book.*

One CGI replacement technology you may well have already heard of is Microsoft's Active Server Pages (ASP). Initially, Microsoft attempted to create an interface to its Internet Information Services (IIS) Web server, called Internet Server Application Programming Interface (ISAPI). This didn't spawn the large following that Apache's equivalent API did, but it's nevertheless a high-performance API that many businesses use, including eBay (you can visit `http://www.netcraft.com` to see which Web server any site on the Internet is using). However, because of its complexity, ISAPI is rarely suited to the beginning developer. Microsoft's IIS Web server itself, however, is widely used, largely because it comes free with many versions of Windows. Incidentally, you can configure IIS to work with Tomcat.

Microsoft followed up ISAPI with its ASP technology, which lets you embed programming code, typically VBScript, into standard HTML pages. This model has proved extremely successful and was the catalyst driving the development of Java Web technology, which we'll discuss shortly.

## Java and the Web

At last we come to Java. Java was initially released in the mid-1990s as a way to liven up dull, static Web pages. It was platform-independent (the same Java code can run on computers running a variety of different operating systems rather than being tied to just one), and it allowed developers to have their programs execute in the Web browser. Many an industry sage prognosticated that these Java applets (*applet* being a "mini-application" that executes within another application—the browser) would catch on, making the Web more exciting and interactive and changing the way people bought computers, reducing all the various operating systems into mere platforms for Web browsers (see Figure 1-5).

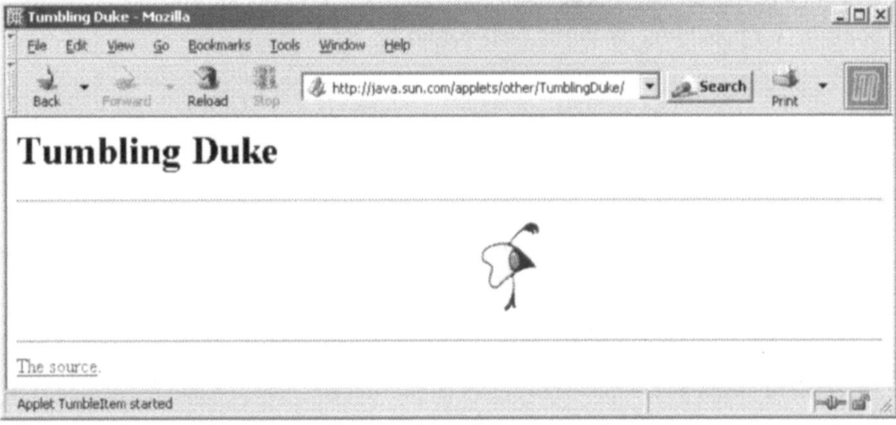


*Figure 1-5. A Java applet in action*

**NOTE** *Figure 1-5 shows one of many applets available at* `http://java.sun.com/applets/`. *If you enter the URL shown in Figure 1-5, don't forget to capitalize it as it appears.*

However, Java applets never really caught on to the degree people predicted, and other technologies such as Macromedia Flash became more popular ways of creating interactive Web sites. However, Java isn't just good for applets: You can also use it for creating stand-alone platform-independent applications. Although these too could threaten the monopolies of entrenched incompatible operating systems, Java applications haven't really caught on yet either. This is probably because Java's support for creating graphical user interface (GUI) applications—applications with windows, icons, buttons, and so on—has until recently been quite poor and slow. This situation is changing; in fact, today's versions of Java enable developers to create cutting-edge GUI applications.

But like a prizefighter who won't stay down, those innovative Java architects kept on fighting, releasing Java servlets into the arena. *Servlets* ("mini-servers") are another alternative technology to CGI. Servlets aren't stand-alone applications, and they must be loaded into memory by a servlet container. The servlet container then functions as a Web server, receiving HTTP requests from Web browsers and passing them to servlets that generate the response, typically an HTML document. Alternatively, the servlet container can integrate with an existing Web server; for example, a popular Apache module, called a *connector* and found on the Tomcat Web site, integrates Apache with the Tomcat servlet container.

The simplicity of the Java programming language, its platform-independent nature, Sun's open-source and community-driven attitude toward Java, and the elegance of the servlet model itself have all made servlets an immensely popular solution for providing dynamic Web content.

### *JSP*

To make creating dynamic Web content even easier, Sun introduced JSP. Although writing servlets can require extensive knowledge of Java, a Java newbie can learn some pretty neat tricks in JSP in a snap. JSP represents a viable and attractive alternative to Microsoft's ASP.

**NOTE** *JSP technology is actually built on top of servlets. As you'll see later in the book, the two technologies actually work well together, and it's common to use both in the same Web application.*

### *More About Servlet Containers*

As mentioned earlier, JSP and servlets require a special kind of server to operate: a servlet container. Tomcat, which you installed earlier, is known as a reference implementation of a JSP servlet container, but this isn't to say it's not worthy of use in production systems. Indeed, many commercial installations use Tomcat, but many other servlet containers are available. These include Caucho Resin (`http://www.caucho.com`), which is very popular and somewhat faster than Tomcat but is a commercial product that must be purchased. Jetty (`http://jetty.mortbay.org`) is perhaps the most popular open-source competitor, and there are many alternatives.

### *The Java Community*

In fact, the multiplicity of servlet containers is another example of the biggest strength of the Java family of technology: choice. All the Java technologies are controlled by a community of developers and corporations who together form the Java Community Process (JCP). The JCP system enables anyone to contribute to the future of Java by participating in expert committees that shape new features of the language or simply by issuing feedback to Java's architects.

Through the JCP and the documents it publishes into the public domain, anybody can develop Java extensions and features as defined by the JCP. The JCP's main purpose is to prevent the Java language from degenerating into a chaos of incompatible, duplicated, and redundant functionality by setting standards. However, because of the freedom to create Java technology based on these standards, Java developers have a great deal of choice of development tools offered by a variety of competing vendors.

This philosophy is often referred to as "agree on standards, compete on implementation." It's in direct contradiction to Microsoft's philosophy embodied in such technologies as its .NET platform. Microsoft controls the standards used in .NET, and it creates most of the development tools associated with .NET. Considering the benefits and pitfalls of each model—Java's community-driven approach versus Microsoft's benevolent dictatorship approach—is a complex and often emotionally charged issue that we'll leave out of this book.

### *Web Applications*

To create a Web application of any significant utility, a developer usually creates many different JSP pages and/or servlets. Additionally, the developer may have a number of images and HTML pages they want to associate with the JSP pages and servlets, and there may be code libraries and other files that form part of the same application.

Keeping track of all of these files can be a bit difficult, and configuring a servlet container to know where to find them all can seem quite a nightmare. Hang on—actually, it's really rather easy. It turns out that there's a standard directory layout for Web applications. Furthermore, a standard configuration file for Web applications tells servlet containers how the Web application works. Both of these are regulated by the JCP as described previously.

By following this standard layout, Java developers don't have to worry about how to configure different servlet containers; it all happens automatically. Chapter 2 discusses this standard directory layout in greater detail.

### Application Servers

Servlet containers are only part of the Java story. Since the development of servlet and JSP technology, many additional Java technologies have been created that ease the development of large and complex business applications, either for use on the Internet or for use on private intranets. Examples of these technologies include Enterprise JavaBeans, which aims to make it easier for developers to distribute Java code onto many different servers (as opposed to having all of the code for an application on one server), and the Java Connector Architecture, which helps developers include older, pre-Java applications and data sources in their applications. These advanced technologies geared toward large businesses make up the J2EE standard, which was briefly mentioned at the start of this chapter.

A servlet container alone isn't sufficient to power J2EE applications. Instead, an application server is required. This supports all of the J2EE technologies, is usually much more feature-rich than a servlet container such as Tomcat, and often includes features that enable it to service many more users than a typical servlet container. However, because JSP and servlets compose a key part of the J2EE platform, application servers also must support the same features that a servlet container does—and often, an application server simply integrates with one of the existing servlet containers.

Although application servers can set you back tens of thousands of dollars, some free application servers are available, such as jBoss (`http://www.jboss.org`).

### JavaScript

In closing, we'll talk about JavaScript. JavaScript is a technology that enables Web pages to have some programmatic functionality *in the browser*. Java applets are isolated applications that are simply displayed on a Web page, but JavaScript works with and can manipulate the HTML page in which it's embedded.

Some folks, after coding some JavaScript code here and there, are under the impression they know Java and have programmed in Java, but this isn't really true. JavaScript isn't Java; it's an entirely distinct programming language that was developed about the same time Java was released.

Originally called *LiveScript*, the name was changed by Netscape to *JavaScript* because its syntax was similar to Java's and because those behind it wanted to capitalize on the exposure and popularity of the Java language. However, Microsoft introduced its own scripting language, JScript, and after a while a neutral standard was developed, with the decidedly less appealing name of *ECMAScript*. Today, JavaScript and JScript are based on this open standard (also called ECMA-262), but Netscape and Microsoft persist in using their proprietary names for their implementations.

To better understand the distinction between JavaScript and JSP, it may help you to remember that JavaScript code is generally executed by the Web client (browser) after the Web server sends the browser the HTTP response, and JSP code is executed by the Web server before the Web server sends the HTTP response. In fact, JSP is what creates the HTTP response. Thus, JavaScript is said to be a *client-side* technology, and it's code that can be viewed (and copied) by Web users; JSP is a *server-side* technology where the code isn't visible to Web users because it's processed by the Web server before reaching the client.

## Summary

In this chapter, we've tried to get you up and running as a budding Web developer. You've done the following:

- Installed the basic tools you need to create Java Web applications
- Created your first simple Web application
- Examined the history of the Web, the difference between static and dynamic Web content, the approaches to creating dynamic content, and the difference between client-side programming (such as JavaScript) and server-side programming (such as JSP or servlets)

In subsequent chapters, you'll build on this foundation to create increasingly complex and useful Web applications, and you'll also learn more details about how the Java language works.

CHAPTER 2

# Learning How HTML Works

**In Chapter 1,** you downloaded and set up the tools necessary to develop applications with JavaServer Pages (JSP). Chapter 1 also covered some background information that will help put that development into context. In this chapter, we'll carry on consolidating the foundation that you'll build upon as you establish your JSP career.

We'll start out with a quick rundown of Hypertext Markup Language (HTML), covering what makes up a simple HTML page. Once the HTML refresher is out of the way, we'll introduce JSP's major features so you get a feel for what's possible with JSP.

We'll conclude the chapter by demonstrating several key features of JSP through two examples.

## Summarizing HTML

JSP pages consist of normal HTML with additional JSP-specific code. For readers with HTML experience, this means that writing JSP pages will be a piece of cake—you simply add a few JSP elements to your existing HTML pages where you want JSP to create dynamic features, and you're good to go.

However, if you've never written HTML before, or are quite rusty, don't panic. In the following sections, we'll briefly introduce HTML. You won't be an HTML expert after this crash course, but you'll learn enough to lay a solid foundation upon which you can build with JSP.

### *Tags*

HTML consists of two basic elements: tags and text. To understand the relationship between the tags and the text, look at a snippet of HTML:

```
<h1>Header</h1>
Normal text.
```

This HTML would be displayed by a Web browser in a format similar to the following:

# Header

Normal text.

The <h1> tag, short for *header 1*, instructs Web browsers to display the text within it as a large header. The </h1> tag, which complements the <h1> tag, marks the end of text that should be formatted as a header.

You can extract a few key points from this example:

- HTML tags are enclosed in angle brackets, < and >. Examples of HTML tags are <h1>, <body>, and <table>.

- HTML tags have two types:

  Tags that contain text, such as <h1>text</h1> and <span>text</span>. Such tags should always have a matching beginning and ending tag.

  "Stand-alone" tags that don't contain text, such as <hr /> and <br />. Such tags should always end with />. Although the final /> wasn't a requirement in the past, it has been changed to comply with the rules of Extensible Markup Language (XML), and it also makes it clear if a tag is a container tag. This set of new rules is called Extensible HTML (XHTML). Although today's browsers support both formats, you're strongly encouraged to use /> where it's compatible.

- The primary purpose of tags is to modify the appearance and behavior of text. There are, however, some other uses, as you'll learn in the "Creating HTML Forms" section.

## *Important Principles*

There are 90 different HTML tags. However, an HTML page should contain at least two tags: <html> and <body>. The following example therefore represents the smallest possible HTML page:

```
<html>
  <body>
  </body>
</html>
```

Generally speaking, all of the content of the HTML page that's displayed by the Web browser should be nested in the <body> tag.

To actually display an HTML element's tag in a browser, you need to use *special characters*; otherwise, the browser would interpret the tag you want to display as the tag itself. The following example shows a situation where the browser interprets your intention and processes the example tag instead of displaying it as text:

```
<html>
  <body>
    The </body> tag is used to close the <body> tag.
  </body>
</html>
```

This results in *The tag is used to close the tag.* in the browser window. To solve this problem, you use < (the less-than symbol) and > (the greater-than symbol):

```
<html>
  <body>
    The &lt;/body&gt; tag is used to close the &lt;body&gt; tag.
  </body>
</html>
```

There are many other special characters in HTML, such as copyright symbols and specialist text symbols, as you'll see in the "Nonbreaking Spaces" section.

### *Attributes*

Most HTML tags can have various *attributes* set to alter their behavior or appearance in some way. Such attributes appear after the tag name, within the opening tag itself. For instance, the HTML <table> tag, which you use to organize output in the form of rows and columns, has the attribute border that can be set as follows:

```
<table border="1">
```

In this case, you've assigned border a value of 1, which indicates the size of the border to draw around the table and its cells.

Note that all values given to attributes should be enclosed in quotes (either single or double quotes, but they must match and be consistent throughout the page). Previous versions of HTML didn't require the quotes, and you may encounter code that doesn't use them, but in general you should avoid that style.

In this book, we'll introduce the attributes that are useful for the examples and case studies. You can obtain the complete list of HTML tags (elements) and their attributes at the following uniform resource locators (URLs):

```
http://www.w3.org/TR/REC-html40/index/elements.html
http://www.w3.org/TR/REC-html40/index/attributes.html
```

### Formatting HTML Output

One of the key concepts of HTML is that any sequence of whitespace is rendered on the browser screen as a single space. In other words, any line breaks or groups of more than one space character will appear on the screen as a single space. For example, the following three different HTML pages would all be displayed in the same way:

```
<html>
  <body>
    Hello
    World!
  </body>orl
</html>
<html><body>Hello        World!</body></html>
<html><body>Hello World!</body></html>
```

A browser would display all of these pages as this: Hello World!

### Preformatted Text

You can switch off this whitespace handling if you have text you want to display as is by wrapping the text in <pre> tags. The classic example is displaying formatted code in the browser:

```
<pre>
public class Servlet01 extends HttpServlet {

  public void doGet(HttpServletRequest req, HttpServletResponse res)
    throws ServletException, IOException {

    String reqErrorUri =
      (String) req.getAttribute("javax.servlet.error.request_uri");

  }
}
</pre>
```

This will be rendered in a fixed-width font much like the code font used in this book. Note that the newline after the beginning <pre> and immediately before the ending </pre> won't be rendered.

### *Line Breaks*

To display text on two or more different lines, you use the `<br />` tag to instruct the browser to insert a line break. The following code:

```
<html><body>Hello<br />World!</body></html>
```

would therefore be displayed as follows:

Hello
World!

### *Nonbreaking Spaces*

Browsers will wrap the lines of text on your Web page according to the margins in the current window, with the break at the most convenient whitespace. This may cause a problem if you want to keep two words or symbols on the same line. You solve this problem with the nonbreaking space character:

```
 
```

For example, if you want to display a date, using ` ` will ensure the entire date is displayed on one line:

```
The date of publication is the 29th March 2004.
```

### *Paragraphs*

Although the `<p>` tag is mainly a container tag (that is, `<p></p>`), the `<p />` form can separate two paragraphs of text. It's similar to the `<br />` tag, with an important difference: The `<p />` inserts space between two paragraphs whereas the `<br />` tag simply breaks the line.

The following HTML:

```
<html><body>Hello<p />World!</body></html>
```

would be displayed like so:

Hello

World!

### Phrases

All of the previous elements allow you to format and structure entire paragraphs of text. The next set of elements you'll see allows you to format phrases to make them stand out from the surrounding paragraph. For example, you may want to format a single Java command in a paragraph or cite a source for your quote.

This is a sample Web page showing a few phrase-formatting tags:

```
<html>
  <body>
    <p>
      Here is some <em>emphasized text</em>.
    </p>
    <p>
      Here is some <strong>strongly emphasized text</strong>.
    </p>
    <p>
      A line of code in a paragraph would look like this
      <code>System.out.println("Code text");</code>
    </p>
    <p>
    As the <cite>NY Times</cite> said in January...
    </p>
  </body>
</html>
```

### Tables

A great many HTML pages place text into tables as a simple yet robust means of formatting data. HTML tables are defined by the `<table>` tag, which contains a `<tr>` tag for each row in the table and a `<td>` tag for each cell in a row. Thus, the following code:

```
<html>
  <body>
    <table border="1">
      <tr>
        <td>
          Hello
        </td>
        <td>
          World!
        </td>
```

```
      </tr>
      <tr>
        <td>
          This is
        </td>
        <td>
          a table!
        </td>
      </tr>
    </table>
  </body>
</html>
```

would appear in a browser as shown in Figure 2-1.

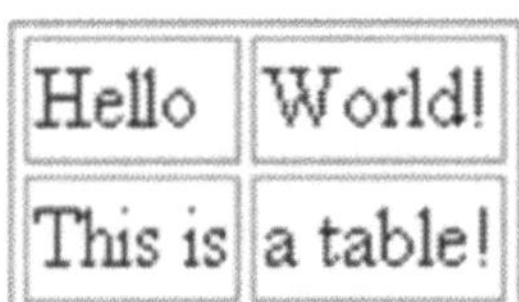

| Hello | World! |
| --- | --- |
| This is | a table! |

*Figure 2-1. Formatting tables*

Tables can also have column headings, which are added with the `<th>` element:

```
<html>
  <body>
    <table border="1">
      <tr><th>Course</th><th>Tutor</th></tr>
      <tr>
        <td>
          Introductory Linguistics
        </td>
        <td>
          Prof. Hurford
        </td>
      </tr>
      <tr>
        <td>
          Starting Prolog
        </td>
        <td>
```

```
          C.S. Mellish
        </td>
      </tr>
    </table>
  </body>
</html>
```

Each <th> element is equivalent to a bold <td> element and is placed in a <tr> element in the same way.

## A Little Style

So far you've learned about inserting line breaks and creating tables, but you haven't learned how to change other details about the appearance of your HTML, such as font size or color. There are a number of ways to achieve this, and we'll start with the basic syntax.

The style of HTML text is controlled by a special attribute that belongs to almost every tag: the `style` attribute. Some examples of the `style` attribute are as follows:

```
<html>
  <body>
    <p style="color: red">
      This text will be in red!
    </p>
    <p style="color: blue; font-size: 20pt">
      This big text will be in blue!
    </p>
  </body>
</html>
```

The preceding example if rendered would appear in a browser as shown in Figure 2-2.

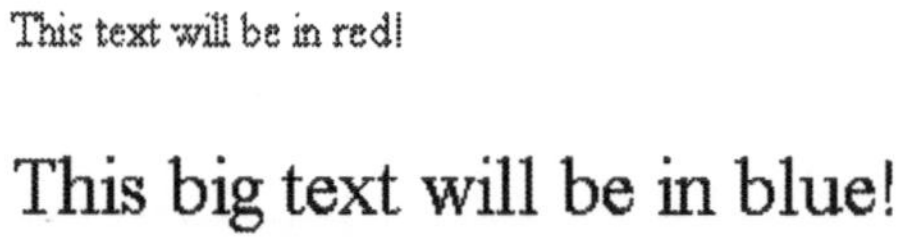

This text will be in red!

This big text will be in blue!

*Figure 2-2. Using the* `style` *attribute*

Note that you used the <p> tag as a container to apply its style to the text inside. Take a closer look at one of the `style` attributes you added to the <p> tags:

```
style="color: blue; font-size: 20pt"
```

The value of the `style` attribute—`"color: blue; font-size: 20pt"`—controls how the contents of the container tag are displayed using the style language called *Cascading Style Sheets* (CSS). CSS is a way of defining rules that modify how HTML tags are rendered. A CSS rule takes this form:

```
css_attribute: css_value
```

You can assign multiple CSS attributes to a tag's `style` attribute by joining them together with a semicolon, as shown in the previous example. Table 2-1 describes some examples of valid CSS attributes.

*Table 2-1. Valid CSS Attributes*

| **Attribute Name** | **Example(s)** | **Description** |
|---|---|---|
| `color` | `color: blue`<br>`color: white`<br>`color: #FFFFFF` | Controls the font color. Possible values for color include `aqua`, `black`, `blue`, `fuchsia`, `gray`, `green`, `lime`, `maroon`, `navy`, `olive`, `purple`, `red`, `silver`, `teal`, `white`, and `yellow`. You can provide either a name of a color (16 colors are supported by name) or an RGB value in hexadecimal format. The hexadecimal (hex) format starts with a # and then is composed of three groups of two characters. Each character can be 0–9 or A–F. Using the letter characters lets each character represent 16 values instead of just 10. For example, A represents 11, B is 12, and so on to F, which is 16. The first two characters determine the value for red, the second two for green, and the third two for blue. Thus, the hex color for pure red is #FF0000, blue is #0000FF, and white is #FFFFFF. |
| `background-color` | `background-color: black` | Determines the background color of a region. Like for the `color` attribute, this may be either a name or be a value. |
| `font-size` | `font-size: 12pt`<br>`font-size: 12px`<br>`font-size: smaller` | Controls the size of the font. The values can be given in either font point size (pt) or exact height in pixels (px) format. Relative font sizes are also possible with the words larger and smaller. |
| font-family | `font-family: Arial`<br>`font-family: Tahoma, sans-serif` | Sets the font to be used. |

That's enough CSS to get you started, but CSS enables you to do a lot more. If you're interested, visit `http://www.w3.org/Style/CSS/`.

### *Creating Style Classes*

If you want to apply the same style to multiple parts of your HTML document, it'd be rather tedious to repeat it all over the place, as in the following HTML fragment:

```
<p style="font-size: 20pt; color: blue; font-family: sans-serif">
    Paragraph 1 Text.
</p>
<p style="font-size: 20pt; color: blue; font-family: sans-serif">
    Paragraph 2 Text.
</p>
<p style="font-size: 20pt; color: blue; font-family: sans-serif">
    Paragraph 3 Text.
</p>
```

CSS enables you to create classes that consist of a set of style rules, defined in a `<style>` tag within the HTML `<head>` section. You can then associate these styles with HTML tags by setting the `class` attribute as shown in the following example:

```
<html>
  <head>
    <style type="text/css">
      .bigblue {
        font-size: 20pt;
        font-family: sans-serif;
        color: blue;
      }
    </style>
  </head>
  <body>
    <p class="bigblue">
        Paragraph 1 Text.
    </p>
    <p class="bigblue">
        Paragraph 2 Text.
    </p>
    <p class="bigblue">
        Paragraph 3 Text.
    </p>
  </body>
</html>
```

The <head> tag, which precedes the HTML <body>, is a special area of an HTML document called the HTML ***head section***. It contains tags that describe the HTML document (so-called meta information) or provide other information required for the document, such as the CSS class definitions in the previous example.

### *Trying It Out: Creating a Simple HTML Page*

To create a simple HTML page, follow these steps:

1. First, you need to set up folders in Tomcat's webapps directory to create a new JSP application. For this example, call it **PhoneBook** and create a folder inside it called **WEB-INF**.

   As you may remember from the first chapter, this folder must exist for Tomcat to recognize your files as a new Web application.

2. Save the following code as **phoneNumbers.html** in the PhoneBook folder:

```
<html>
  <head>
    <style type="text/css">
      BODY {
        font-family: sans-serif;
        font-size: 10pt;
        background-color: navy;
        color: white;
      }
      TABLE {
        border: 1px solid black;
        font-family: sans-serif;
        font-size: 10pt;
      }
      .row1 {
        background-color: gray;
        color: black;
      }
      .row2 {
        background-color: silver;
        color: black;
      }
```

```
    </style>
  </head>
  <body>
    These are some of my friends.
    <p />
    <table>
      <tr>
        <th>
          Name
        </th>
        <th>
          Phone
        </th>
      </tr>
      <tr class="row1">
        <td>
          Amy
        </td>
        <td>
          415-555-1212
        </td>
      </tr>
      <tr class="row2">
        <td>
          Geoff
        </td>
        <td>
          415-555-1213
        </td>
      </tr>
    </table>
  </body>
</html>
```

3. Start Tomcat, and view the file by navigating to the following URL in your browser:

   ```
   http://localhost:8080/PhoneBook/phoneNumbers.html
   ```

   If you've entered everything correctly, you should see a page similar to Figure 2-3.

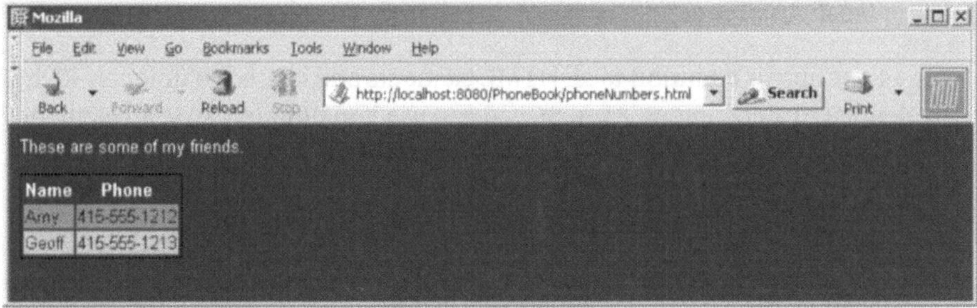


*Figure 2-3. CSS in action*

*How It Works*

This HTML file is a good example of the tags introduced earlier. You added a few new twists to the CSS in the `<style>` tag, such as the ability to redefine a tag's default style (the `BODY` and `TABLE` style names) and the `border` attribute.

It's important that you save the HTML file with a name that ends in `.html` or `.htm`, as you've done, so that the Web server (in this case, Tomcat) knows that the file contains HTML markup.

### *Specifying a Style for a Single Element*

The previous code uses the `.stylename` form to apply the style to all elements with that class. Sometimes, however, you'll want to be able to specify styles for individual elements, some of which may have identical names. For example, you may want to have a `<table>` element of class `red` and a `<td>` element of class `red`, each of which with a different property you want to alter.

In this case, you can use the `tag.stylename` form:

```
TABLE.red {
  border: 1px solid red;
}

TD.red {
  color: red;
}
```

These settings will override any general CSS settings for `<table>` or `<td>`. Therefore, you can think of CSS as hierarchical because you can specify a top-level setting for all elements of a certain type and then override these as you get more specific needs. So, in these examples, a `<table>` element of class `red` will have all the attributes from the `TABLE` entry, except `border`, which is specified with `TABLE.red`.

### *Using the id Attribute*

The id attribute is common to all HTML elements and is used to uniquely identify an element in a document. As such, you can use it to uniquely style an element in a document. Suppose you have the following HTML:

```
<tr id="grade"/>
```

You could style it using the following syntax:

```
#final_marks {
  background-color: red;
}
```

## *Styling an Application*

So far you've been adding style to a single document, but most Web sites consist of more than one document. If you wanted consistency of style across all the documents, you'd have to copy and paste all the style information from phoneNumbers.html into all the other documents. This is a time-consuming and error-prone process.

Luckily, CSS has an answer to this problem: You can move all your style information into an external file that can be shared by all pages in your Web site. For this you have to create a style sheet with the .css extension. This file contains the contents of the <style> element that you would have used across your Web site.

Open phoneNumbers.html, and copy the contents of the <style> element into a new file called format.css, which should be in the PhoneBook directory as follows:

```
BODY {
  font-family: sans-serif;
  font-size: 10pt;
  background-color: navy;
  color: white;
}
TABLE {
  border: 1px solid black;
  font-family: sans-serif;
  font-size: 10pt;
}
.row1 {
  background-color: gray;
  color: black;
}
```

```
.row2 {
  background-color: silver;
  color: black;
}
```

Delete the <style> element, and replace it with the following <link> element:

```
<head>
  <link rel="stylesheet" type="text/css" href="format.css" />
</head>
```

View `phoneNumbers.html` again. There should be no difference in the output, but it's now much easier for you to reuse style information.

## *<div> and <span>*

The `<div>` and `<span>` elements specify style information over blocks of text, irrespective of their underlying physical structure. Both these elements therefore add logical structure but not physical structure to a document. For example, a `<table>` element specifies how the data should be laid out on the screen whereas a `<div>` element specifies that the data represents overdue bills and so should be colored red.

A `<div>` element covers blocks of text, much like a `<p>` tag does, and a `<span>` tag is used inline, much like the `<em>` or `<cite>` tags. The logical structure is maintained with the `id` attribute. As with all the tags that provide a physical structure, you can use `class` and `style` attributes with `<div>` and `<span>`.

The following example highlights new code to the user. You'll apply the following stylesheet to a page that contains examples of code that are built up as the user progresses through a tutorial:

```
.newcode {
  background-color: silver;
  color: black;
}

.oldcode {
  background-color: white;
  color: gray;
}

.highlight {
  text-decoration: underline;
}
```

Here you're marking new code with a light-gray background and black text. Code the user has already seen is on a white background with gray text, and any variables or individual lines you want to highlight are underlined.

The following HTML page uses the <pre> tag to format the code, the <div> tag to partition the code into old code and new code, and the <span> tag to highlight the name of a variable because it's inline text:

```
<html>
  <head>
    <link rel="stylesheet" type="text/css" href="code.css" />
  </head>
  <body>
    <pre>
      <div class="oldcode">
public class Servlet01 extends HttpServlet {

  public void doGet(HttpServletRequest req, HttpServletResponse res)
    throws ServletException, IOException {
      </div>
      <div class="newcode">
    String reqErrorUri =
      (String) req.getAttribute("<span class="highlight">user</span>");
      </div>
      <div class="oldcode">
  }
}
      </div>
    </pre>
  </body>
</html>
```

Figure 2-4 shows the resulting page.

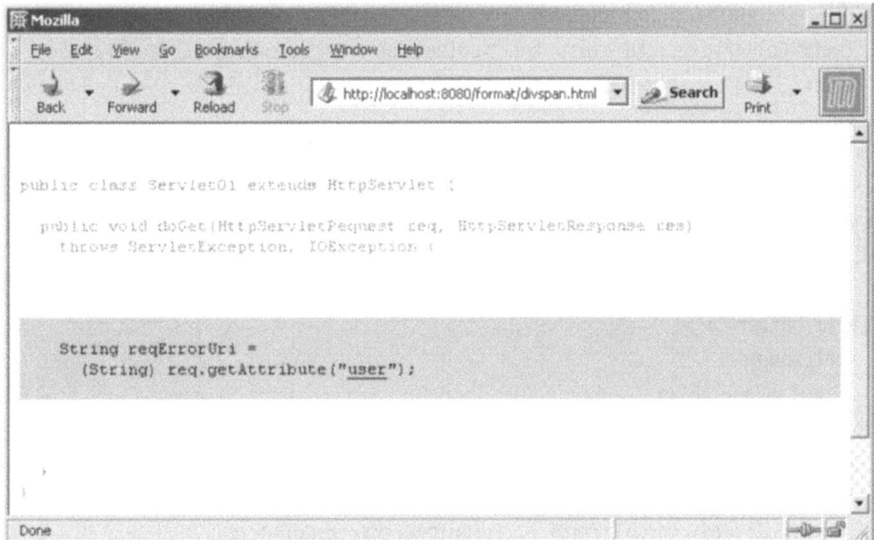

*Figure 2-4. Using* `<span>` *and* `<div>`

## Grouping Columns

Sometimes it's necessary to group the columns of a table together in the same way you grouped blocks of text together previously. All tables have an implicit group of columns; in other words, all the columns are treated as a group when attributes are applied, but you can change this by using the `<colgroup>` or `<col>` element.

The `<colgroup>` element is used to group columns structurally, but `<col>` doesn't imply any structural grouping—you can use it inside a `<colgroup>` or by itself. Both elements have `span` and `width` attributes, the first of which defines how many columns are included in the group and the second of which defines a default width for the columns in the group. The `width` attribute is slightly different from regular column `width` attributes in that it can take the special value of `0*`, which means that the column should be the minimum width required for its contents. You can override the `width` attribute of `<colgroup>` using the `width` attribute of `<col>`.

To start with, you'll see how `<colgroup>` could make a difference on a page. Consider a case where you want to highlight the final two columns of a 30-column table. Up until now you'd have to do the following:

```
<table border="1">
  <tr>
    <td>Col1</td>...<td class="red">Col29</td><td class="red">Col30</td>
  </tr>
```

```
  <tr>
    <td>Col1</td>...<td class="red">Col29</td><td class="red">Col30</td>
  </tr>
</table>
```

For a table that's more than a few rows deep, this is a major amount of work if you decide to change the format. Instead, you now can use `<colgroup>` to group all the columns in the table together and `<col>` to highlight the final two:

```
<table border="1">
  <colgroup>
    <col span="28"/>
    <col span="2" class="red"/>
  </colgroup>
  <tr>
    <td>Col1</td><td>Col2</td>...<td>Col29</td><td>Col30</td>
  </tr>
  <tr>
    <td>Col1</td><td>Col2</td>...<td>Col29</td><td>Col30</td>
  </tr>
</table>
```

In this case we're not implying any separation of the data; we're simply highlighting part of the data. In the following example, two sets of data are combined into the same table with the second set highlighted to compare and contrast:

```
<table border="1">
  <colgroup span="15" width="0*"/>
  <colgroup span="15" width="50" class="silver"/>
  <tr>
    <td>Col1</td><td>Col2</td>...<td>Col29</td><td>Col30</td>
  </tr>
  <tr>
    <td>Col1</td><td>Col2</td>...<td>Col29</td><td>Col30</td>
  </tr>
</table>
```

## Creating HTML Forms

HTML forms are the usual way of getting information from the client for use by a server-based Web application. The information that the user provides may be textual (for instance, the user's name), or it may be a selection from a number of options in drop-down lists, radio buttons, and so on. Once the form is complete, the user clicks a button to submit the data to the server.

HTML provides a number of different controls for requesting information from the user in a form. You'll meet these in the "Using HTML Elements" section; first you'll see the basic building block of any HTML form—the `<form>` element itself.

Forms on HTML pages are defined with the `<form>` tag, but note that the `<form>` element doesn't directly produce any visual effects in the browser. You need to place controls within the `<form>` element to provide information for the user and the means for them to input any information you require.

The `<form>` tag's attributes let you specify certain configurations for the form, and you'll look more closely at these attributes over the following pages.

## The action Attribute

The `action` attribute specifies what's to happen when the user has completed the form and submitted it. You can specify a server-side resource—for example, a JSP page—that processes the form data submitted by the user. This server-side resource may then produce an HTML page that's sent back to the client.

You indicate such resources using a URL as follows:

```
<form action="http://myServer.com/process.jsp"></form>
```

On form submission (for example, when the user clicks a submit button), the page will jump to the stated URL. For example, this could be the URL `http://myServer.com/process.jsp`.

Note that you can also supply URLs as *relative* paths based on the location of the page that contains the form:

```
<form action="process.jsp"></form>
```

In this case, `process.jsp` needs to be in the same folder as the page containing the form. For instance, if the current page were at `http://myServer.com/input.jsp`, the request would be sent to `http://myServer.com/process.jsp`.

Finally, if a form has no `action` attribute, the page that contains the form is reloaded when submitted, but you can have it take a different course of action than when it was first loaded.

## The name Attribute

When you pass data from the form, you can use the name specified in the form's `name` attribute to identify to which form or form control the data belongs. This is necessary because there may be more than one form on the page. You'll use this attribute in the examples to come.

## The method Attribute

As well as a choice of where to send the form data, you also have a choice of how to send it, which you specify using the `method` attribute. Two commonly used methods for sending the data are as follows:

- `GET` (the default)
- `POST`

When a form is submitted, the browser collates the data entered or selected by the user into name/value pairs, where the name corresponds to the `name` attribute of the control and where the value denotes the value chosen. The way the browser sends this information to the server differs according to the method used.

The `GET` method of transferring data appends data as a list of name/value pairs after the URL of the page to which you're sending the form. The list is separated from the URL itself by the `?` character, and any subsequent pairs begin with an ampersand (`&`), as in this example:

```
process.jsp?userName=John+Doe&tummy=large&head=square
```

Data appended to a URL like this is said to form a *query string*. The target page will then be able to get hold of these values by using the associated name.

As you may be thinking, placing name/value pairs in the URL is a rather public way of passing information. The `POST` method provides an alternative that sends the name/value pairs hidden inside the body of the HTTP request.

The main drawback of `POST` is that if the user bookmarks the page, the name/value pairs won't be stored in the bookmark, potentially causing problems. Also, be aware that although `POST` is more secure than `GET`, `POST` data isn't encrypted, and it wouldn't be difficult for someone to get hold of the data if they really wanted to do so.

## The target Attribute

As noted earlier, the server-side resource identified in the `action` attribute might produce an HTML page when the form is submitted. You can use the `target` attribute to identify a frame or window within the browser to which the resulting HTML page should be sent if it's different from the frame or window containing the form. This attribute may take one of the following values:

- **blank**: The resulting HTML page is sent to a new window.
- **parent**: The resulting HTML is sent to the parent of the current frame.
- **self**: The resulting HTML page overwrites the current page. This is the default value used when one isn't specified.
- **top**: The resulting HTML page will occupy the entire browser window, ignoring all the nested framesets.

Now that you know how to create a form, you'll find out how to fill it with elements.

## Using HTML Elements

You use HTML form controls for rendering the textboxes, drop-down lists, and checkboxes that forms use to get data from the user. You can use the following HTML elements:

- **<input>**: Renders controls such as textboxes, radio buttons, and checkboxes
- **<select>**: Renders multiselect listboxes and drop-down listboxes
- **<textarea>**: Renders multiline edit controls

The following sections review each of these elements in turn.

### *The <input> Element*

The HTML `<input>` element creates textboxes, radio buttons, or checkboxes, depending on the value of the `type` attribute. Other attributes set other properties, and you'll see the most common of these in the following sections.

#### *The type Attribute*

This is perhaps the most important attribute because it defines the type of control you want, according to the values given in Table 2-2.

*Table 2-2. Values for the* type *Attribute*

| Attribute Value | Description |
|---|---|
| text | Renders a textbox. This is the default if the attribute isn't specified. |
| password | Renders password controls. These are the same as textboxes, but input is represented on the screen by an asterisk character. |
| hidden | Defines hidden controls for storing information on the page that isn't to be displayed on the screen. These values typically store values used by the server across multiple requests. |
| checkbox | Renders checkboxes. |
| radio | Renders radio buttons. |
| reset | Renders a button control that resets the form controls to their original default values. |
| submit | Renders the button control that submits the form. |
| image | Uses an image for the button instead of the default look. |
| button | Renders a button control that may be linked to client-side script. |
| file | Renders a file control that allows the user to browse to and select files from their local file system to be uploaded to the server. |

This is an example that creates a textbox:

```
<input type="text"/>
```

### The name Attribute

After you've chosen the type of control you need, you must give it a name if the data the control contains is to be passed to the server on form submission. You do this using the name attribute:

```
<input type="text" name="address"/>
```

The previous code would create a textbox called address. Therefore, when you submit the form to the server, you can obtain the information in this textbox by using the name address.

### *The maxlength Attribute*

You can use the `maxlength` attribute only if the `type` attribute is either `text` or `password`. It specifies the maximum number of characters that may be entered into the control. For instance, you could impose a limit of 30 characters on the textbox you created earlier:

```
<input type="text" name="address" maxlength="30"/>
```

### *The size Attribute*

You can also use this attribute if the `type` attribute is either `text` or `password`. It sets the control's visible width in characters (note that `maxlength` doesn't change the actual width of a textbox, just the number of characters that will be accepted). So, you could define a width for the `address` textbox like this:

```
<input type="text" name="address" maxlength="30" size="30"/>
```

These attributes are enough for you to create a simple HTML form, so that's what you'll do now. You'll look at other attributes of the `<input>` element afterward.

#### *Trying It Out: Adding Textboxes to an HTML Form*

To add textboxes to an HTML form, follow these steps:

1. In this example and the next, you'll build a form that could be used to order a pizza over the Internet. Create a folder called **Pizza** in `webapps` and one called **WEB-INF** inside it.

2. Create a file called **pizza.html** in the `Pizza` folder. It starts off with the usual HTML for beginning a page:

```
<html>
  <head>
    <title>Take The Pizza</title>
    <style type="text/css">
      H1 {
        font-size: 12pt;
        font-weight: bold;
      }
```

```
    </style>
  </head>
  <body>
```

Notice that you're defining a default style here for HTML `<h1>` elements.

3. Now you have to add the HTML form that will get the information from the user. You'll set the form to submit its data to a page called `process.jsp` using HTTP `POST` (however, you won't actually process anything until Chapter 3):

```
<form action="process.jsp" method="post">
```

4. Once you've got the explanatory text in the form out of the way, you'll set up a table that contains a couple of textboxes for the user's name and address by adding the following code:

```
<p>
Welcome to Take the Pizza Online! We're eager to take your order
for pizza via our new web form.
</p>
<p>
Please fill out the fields below and click on "Place Order" when
you're done.
</p>
<h1>Your Information:</h1>
<table>
  <tr>
    <td>
      Name:
    </td>
    <td>
      <input type="text" name="name" size="30"/>
    </td>
  </tr>
  <tr>
    <td>
      Address:
    </td>
    <td>
      <input type="text" name="address" size="70"/>
    </td>
  </tr>
```

5. Now you just have to close all your HTML elements by adding the following code, and then save the page:

```
        </table>
      </form>
    </body>
</html>
```

6. Restart Tomcat, and navigate to `localhost:8080/Pizza/pizza.html`. You should see something similar to Figure 2-5.

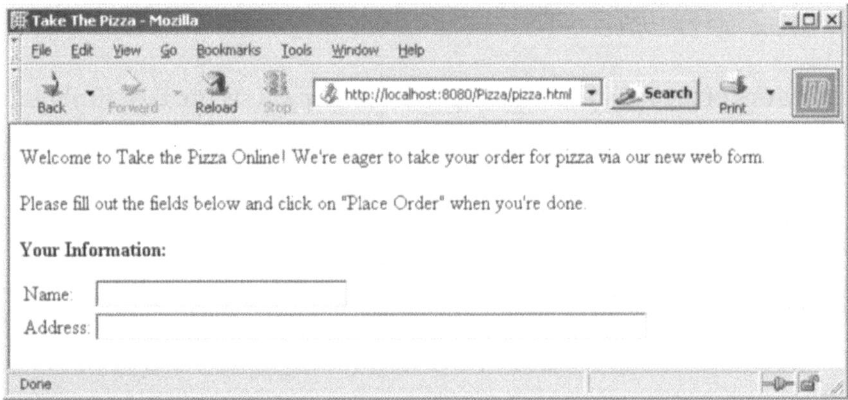


*Figure 2-5. Your first HTML form*

*How It Works*

As it stands, this page doesn't actually do much. Okay, the textboxes are there for your hungry user to enter their name and address, but there's no Place Order button yet. There's not even a way for them to let you know what type of pizza they want.

You can see, though, that creating textboxes on a form is easy. You simply have to place `<input>` elements at appropriate places, specifying a `type` attribute of `text` and a suitable value for the `name` attribute.

Note that because your first page didn't require any special JSP features, you simply used a normal HTML page. This is good practice because HTML pages have less overhead than a JSP page; the server does less to serve an HTML page to the user than with a JSP page. However, the pizza order page is still under construction; after all, you haven't given your client a choice of pizzas or even provided a submit button so that you can send the form data. Before you fix that, you'll see some more of the attributes of `<input>`.

### *The checked Attribute*

You can use this attribute on the <input> element if the type attribute is either radio or checkbox. If the attribute is present, the radio button or the checkbox is checked by default. For example:

```
<input type="radio" name="someValue" checked="true" />
```

This code would create a radio button called someValue that's checked by default.

### *The value Attribute*

The behavior of the value attribute depends on how you set the type attribute. Button controls display the contents of this attribute on the button. In other words, a button defined by this HTML:

```
<input type="button" name="bob" value="Press Me!" />
```

will appear in the browser as shown in Figure 2-6.

*Figure 2-6. Adding a Press Me button*

Along the same lines, this is an example of creating a submit button called dataSubmit with *Submit Form* as the button text:

```
<input type="submit" name="dataSubmit" value="Submit Form" />
```

For text and password controls, the value attribute supplies the default value to use for the control, as in this example:

```
<input type="text" name="marge" value="Pigsy" />
```

This creates a textbox called marge that contains the string *Pigsy* by default, as shown in Figure 2-7.

*Figure 2-7. Adding a Pigsy textbox*

Finally, for selectable controls such as radio buttons and checkboxes, this attribute defines the value that's sent as part of the name/value pair for the option represented by that particular radio button or checkbox.

Note that more than one control in a form might share the same value for the `name` attribute when you have a group of controls that you intend using together. For example, you might have a group of radio buttons for selecting one of a set of choices. Each choice would be represented by its own `<input>` element, but all the elements would have a `name` attribute with the same value:

```
<input type="radio" name="delivery" value="express" />
<input type="radio" name="delivery" value="surface" />
<input type="radio" name="delivery" value="pigeon" />
```

This would create three radio buttons, where only one may be selected at one time. If the first radio button is selected when the form is submitted, a name/value pair of `delivery=express` would be sent to the server. If the second radio button is selected, the name/value pair `delivery=surface` would be sent instead and similarly for the third button.

For other controls, which are grouped by sharing a `name` attribute, users may select any combination of them. In such scenarios, the key/value pairs sent to the server can contain duplicate values for the key. For instance:

```
<input type="checkbox" name="limbs" value="arms"/>
<input type="checkbox" name="limbs" value="legs"/>
```

Both these checkboxes could be checked at once, and if that's the case when the form is submitted, the name/value pairs `limbs=arms` and `limbs=legs` would both be sent to the server.

Now you'll incorporate some of these extras into the page you started earlier. You'll start with a pair of radio buttons that let the user specify whether they want the pizza delivered or whether they intend to drop in and pick it up themselves.

### *Trying It Out: Adding Buttons and Checkboxes to an HTML Form*

To add buttons and checkboxes to a form, follow these steps:

1. Open the `pizza.html` file, and add the following highlighted code immediately after the `<table>` element you've already got:

```
    ...
    </tr>
  </table>
```

```
        <h1>Order Type:</h1>
        <table>
          <tr>
            <td>
              <input type="radio" name="purchaseType"
                          value="Home Delivery"/>
            </td>
            <td>
              Home Delivery
            </td>
          </tr>
          <tr>
            <td>
              <input type="radio" name="purchaseType" value="Take Away"/>
            </td>
            <td>
              Take Away
            </td>
          </tr>
        </table>
      </form>
    </body>
  </html>
```

2. Next you'll add another table, this time creating a set of checkboxes for the user to choose the toppings they want. Place these lines after the table from step 1:

```
          </tr>
        </table>
        <h1>Please Select Any Additional Toppings:</h1>
        <table>
          <tr>
            <td>
              <input type="checkbox" name="peppers" value="Yes"/>
            </td>
            <td>
              Peppers
            </td>
          </tr>
          <tr>
            <td>
```

```
                <input type="checkbox" name="sweetcorn" value="Yes"/>
              </td>
              <td>
                Sweetcorn
              </td>
            </tr>
            <tr>
              <td>
                <input type="checkbox" name="mouse" value="Yes"/>
              </td>
              <td>
                Mouse Innards
              </td>
            </tr>
          </table>
        </form>
      </body>
    </html>
```

3. The last thing you'll add at this stage is a submit button that submits the form data containing the order to the `process.jsp` page:

```
            </tr>
          </table>
          <input type="submit" value="Place Order"/>
        </form>
      </body>
    </html>
```

4. Save the file, and navigate to `http://localhost:8080/Pizza/pizza.html`. You'll see something similar to Figure 2-8.

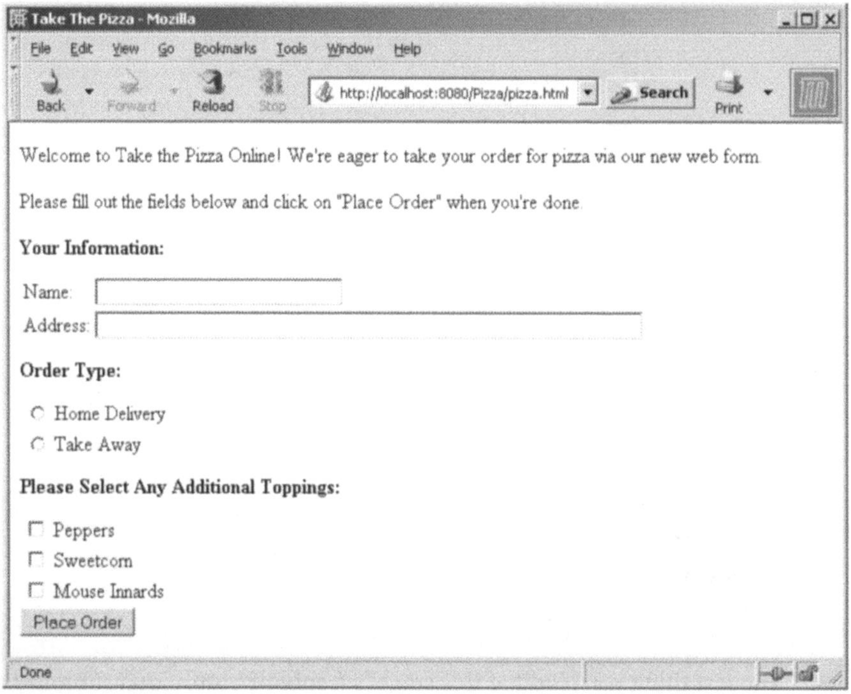

*Figure 2-8. The improved pizza form*

### *How It Works*

When you added the two radio buttons, you gave both the name `purchaseType` to ensure that only one of the two may be selected at any one time. The value to use for each radio button is given with the `value` attribute:

```
<input type="radio" name="purchaseType" value="Home Delivery"/>
<input type="radio" name="purchaseType" value="Take Away"/>
```

A description for each option is provided as straight text in the next cell on the row.

Next you'll see three checkboxes that offer a (rather limited) selection of toppings. Remember that the `value` attribute for a checkbox indicates the value that will be sent if that checkbox is checked:

```
<input type="checkbox" name="peppers" value="Yes"/>
<input type="checkbox" name="sweetcorn" value="Yes"/>
<input type="checkbox" name="mouse" value="Yes"/>
```

So you now have a form where the user can submit a range of information. You also have a submit button, but why should clicking it result in an error message?

The reason is that the page attempts to send the form data to `process.jsp`, which doesn't exist yet. You'll write that page in the next chapter.

## The <select> Element

The `<select>` element provides the means for rendering drop-down lists and multiselect listboxes within HTML forms. One such control is represented by a single `<select>` element, which contains an HTML `<option>` element for each item in the list as shown:

```
<select>
  <option>Item 1</option>
  <option>Item 2</option>
  ...
  <option>Item N</option>
</select>
```

You configure details of the control's appearance and behavior by setting attributes on the `<select>` and `<option>` elements.

You'll now review some of these attributes, starting with attributes for the `<select>` element.

### The name Attribute

As usual, the `name` attribute for a `<select>` element specifies the name in the name/value pair that's sent back to the server when the form is submitted.

### The size Attribute

If the value of the `size` attribute is `1`, the control is rendered as a drop-down listbox; if it's greater than `1`, the control is rendered as a listbox, and the value of the attribute indicates the number of items that are visible in the list at once. The default value is `1`.

### The multiple Attribute

If the `multiple` attribute is present, the control will allow multiple items in the listbox to be selected together. If a form is submitted with multiple items selected, all the selected values are sent as name/value pairs using the `name` defined for the `<select>` element.

Next, two attributes for the `<option>` element are particularly useful: `value` and `selected`.

### The value Attribute

If no `value` attribute is present, the data that appears between the start and end `<option>` tags is passed as the value when an option is selected. For instance:

```
<select name="caller">
  <option>Dobber</option>
  <option>Yasser</option>
  <option>Mio Mio</option>
</select>
```

If the user now selects the third option from this list and submits the form, the name/value pair `caller=Mio+Mio` would be sent.

In many cases, this wouldn't be suitable, and the `value` attribute lets you provide the value you'd rather use.

So you could change the previous example to return the caller's phone number rather than their name:

```
<select name="caller">
  <option value="212 421 5532">Dobber</option>
  <option value="212 336 7205">Yasser</option>
  <option value="431 771 8027">Mio Mio</option>
</select>
```

If you selected the last option this time, you'd now get `caller=431+771+8027`.

### The selected Attribute

If this attribute is set to `true` for an `<option>` element, the contents of this `<option>` are displayed in the control by default.

You'll now apply this knowledge to incorporate a listbox into your pizza application.

#### *Trying It Out: Adding Listboxes to HTML Forms*

To add listboxes to an HTML form, follow these steps:

1. You'll add a listbox that gives the customer three sizes of pizza from which to choose. As before, you'll place the control in an HTML table. Add this highlighted code to the end of `pizza.html`:

```
        ...
          <td>
            Mouse Innards
          </td>
        </tr>
      </table>

      <h1>Pizza Size:</h1>
      <table>
        <tr>
          <td>
            Size:
          </td>
          <td>
            <select name="size">
              <option>Small</option>
              <option selected="true">Medium</option>
              <option>Large</option>
            </select>
          </td>
        </tr>
      </table>
      <input type="submit" value="Place Order">
    </form>
  </body>
</html>
```

2. Save the file, and navigate to `http://localhost:8080/Pizza/pizza.html` in your browser. You will see something similar to Figure 2-9.

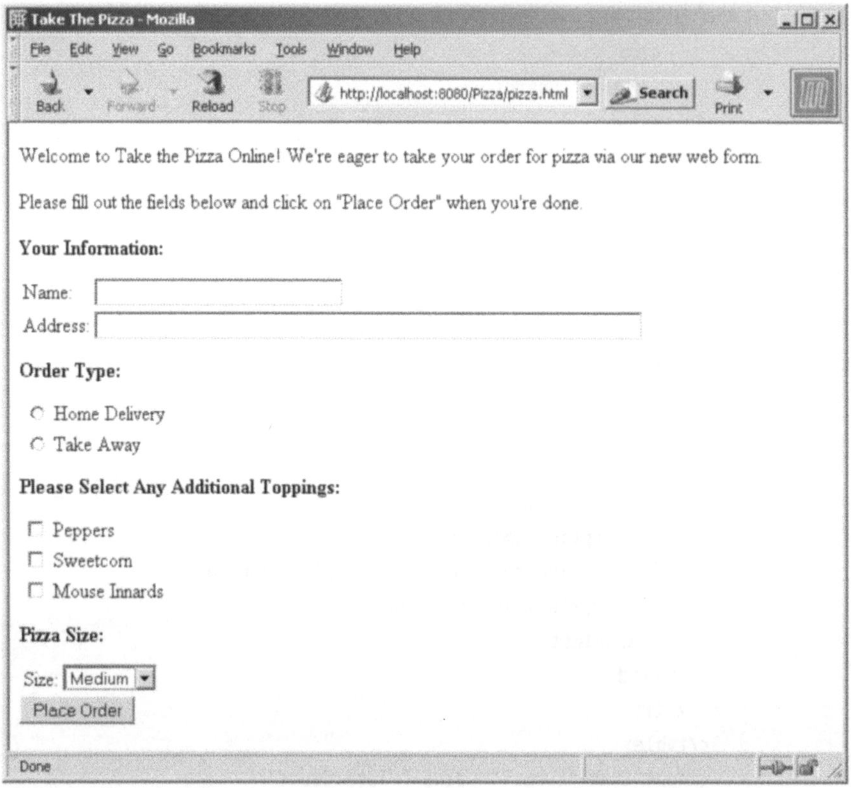

*Figure 2-9. Your form with its new select box*

### *How It Works*

You added a `<select>` element called `size` to create a listbox. It contains three `<option>` elements, one for each available size: `small`, `medium`, and `large`. The second of these, `medium`, is the option that's selected by default when the page loads:

```
<select name="size">
  <option>Small</option>
  <option selected="true">Medium</option>
  <option>Large</option>
</select>
```

You've nearly finished with the pizza order page now. You have just one minor modification left to make.

## *The <textarea> Element*

The `<textarea>` element is used in an HTML form to render multiline textboxes. All the text appearing between the start and end tags are displayed in the control:

```
<textarea>
line of text
another line of text
</textarea>
```

Note that unlike normal HTML, the `<textarea>` will preserve spaces and carriage returns. You'll look at the attributes of the `<textarea>` element.

### *The name Attribute*

As with the other controls, the `name` attribute sets the name in the name/value pair that's sent to the server when the form is submitted.

### *The rows and cols Attributes*

The `rows` attribute defines the number of rows of characters displayed in the control. Similarly, the `cols` attribute defines the width of the control in characters. The default value of these attributes varies with the browser and the operating system.

You'll now finish off the pizza example by incorporating a multiline textbox. The pizza order page looks pretty cool at the moment, but you could make one improvement. Because an address is composed of several lines of text, the Address textbox would be better as a multiline textbox.

#### *Trying It Out: Adding Multiline Textboxes to HTML Forms*

To add multiline textboxes to an HTML form, follow these steps:

1. Open `pizza.html`, and replace this line:

   ```
   <input type="text" name="address" size="70"/>
   ```

   with this one:

   ```
   <textarea rows="4" cols="40" name="address"></textarea>
   ```

2. Now save the file, and reload it in your browser once again. You'll see that the original one-line text field has now been replaced with a multiline textbox as in Figure 2-10.

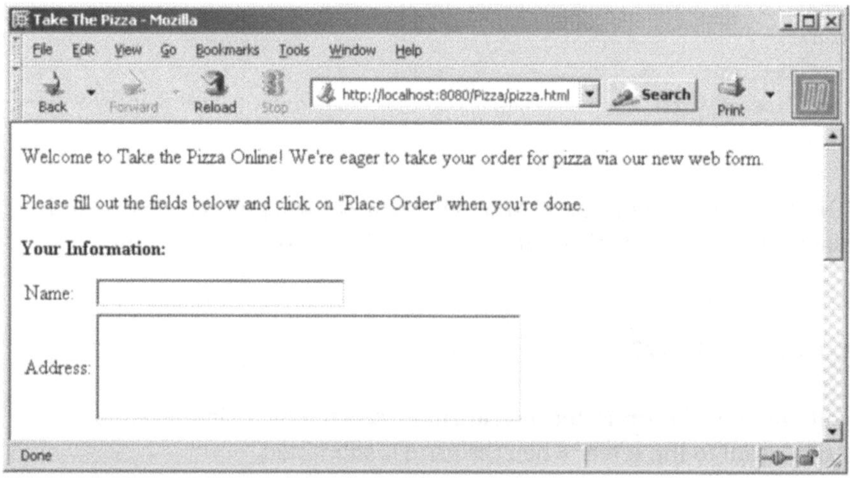


*Figure 2-10. A textarea for typing an address*

*How It Works*

Creating multiline textboxes in HTML isn't hard. Here, the `<textarea>` element specifies a textbox that has four rows and 40 columns. As an empty element, the textbox will appear without any text when the page first loads.

## Finding Further Resources

Well, this is a JSP book, not an HTML book, so we'll wrap up our brief introduction to HTML. If you'll interested in learning more about HTML and CSS, we recommend the following resources:

- "Getting Started with HTML" by Dave Raggett: `http://www.w3.org/MarkUp/Guide/`
- The Official HTML 4.01 Specification: `http://www.w3.org/TR/html401/`
- The Official CSS Specification: `http://www.w3.org/TR/REC-CSS1`
- The Official CSS-2 Specification (which adds more features to CSS): `http://www.w3.org/TR/REC-CSS2/`

## Summary

It's time to take a step back and review what you learned in this chapter:

- HTML consists of tags and text. Tags take the form `<tag>`. They're either container tags of the type `<tag></tag>` or stand-alone tags of the type `<tag />`.
- HTML tags typically modify how text appears on the screen.
- HTML tags may have attributes that affect their behavior and appearance.
- The `class` and `style` attributes may be used to further control the behavior of tags and the appearance of text.

## CHAPTER 3

# Introducing JSP

NOW IT'S TIME TO look at the JavaServer Pages (JSP) technology properly. Chapter 1 and Chapter 2 skimmed over it, but now you'll learn about its features and the additions you can make to it.

In the previous chapter, you looked at Hypertext Markup Language (HTML) and finished the chapter by creating a pizza order form. At the end of this chapter, you'll complete the pizza application using the JSP skills you learned in the chapter.

## Understanding the Available Object Scope

One of the most powerful features of JSP is that a JSP page can access, create, and modify data objects on the server. You can then make these objects visible to JSP pages. When an object is created, it defines or defaults to a given scope. The container creates some of these objects, and the JSP designer creates others.

The *scope* of an object describes how widely it's available and who has access to it. For example, if an object is defined to have page scope, then it's available only for the duration of the current request on that page before being destroyed by the container. In this case, only the current page has access to this data, and no one else can read it. At the other end of the scale, if an object has application scope, then any page may use the data because it lasts for the duration of the application, which means until the container is switched off.

You'll learn about each of the four scopes in turn.

### Page Scope

Objects with *page scope* are accessible only within the page in which they're created. The data is valid only during the processing of the current response; once the response is sent back to the browser, the data is no longer valid. If the request is forwarded to another page or the browser makes another request as a result of a redirect (more about this later in the "Processing Forms with the JSTL" section), the data is also lost.

### Request Scope

Objects with *request scope* are accessible from pages processing the same request in which they were created. Once the container has processed the request, the data is released. Even if the request is forwarded to another page, the data is still available though not if a redirect is required.

### Session Scope

Objects with *session scope* are accessible from pages processing requests that are in the same session as the one in which they were created. A *session* is the time users spend using the application, which ends when they close their browser, when they go to another Web site, or when the application designer wants (after a logout, for instance). So, for example, when users log in, their username could be stored in the session and displayed on every page they access. This data lasts until they leave the Web site or log out.

### Application Scope

Objects with *application scope* are accessible from JSP pages that reside in the same application. This creates a global object that's available to all pages.

Application scope uses a single namespace, which means all your pages should be careful not to duplicate the names of application scope objects or change the values when they're likely to be read by another page (this is called *thread safety*). Application scope variables are typically created and populated when an application starts and then used as read-only for the rest of the application. You'll learn more about this initial setup in Chapter 9.

## Understanding JSP Code Types

With JSP, as with many other programming tools, there's more than one way to carry out most tasks. Each has its own advantages and disadvantages. Don't worry if the different types seem confusing now; the distinctions between them will become clearer as you put them to use throughout this book. You'll quickly deal with each one in turn, and then you'll see the two most important in detail.

### Scriptlets

*Scriptlets* allow Java code to be embedded directly into JSP pages by placing the code within <% and %> delimiters. For illustration, you'll create a simple page containing a scriptlet that displays either *Good Morning* or *Good Afternoon* according to the time of day. Insert the following code in a file called **goodAfternoon.jsp** in the existing `helloJSP` folder:

```
<%@ page import="java.util.Calendar"%>
<html>
  <body>
    Good
    <%
      Calendar calendar = Calendar.getInstance();
      if (calendar.get(Calendar.AM_PM) == Calendar.AM) {
        out.print("Morning");
      } else {
        out.print("Afternoon");
      }
    %>
  </body>
</html>
```

When executed in the afternoon, this JSP will generate the following output:

```
<html>
  <body>
    Good
    Afternoon
  </body>
</html>
```

Although scriptlets are certainly powerful, their use is generally discouraged in professional Java development circles for two main reasons:

- Scriptlets result in JSP pages that are almost always horribly structured and difficult to maintain.
- Effective use of scriptlets requires an understanding of the Java programming language. Because the people who actually design pages are often not the people who add the code, a JSP littered with scriptlets would be difficult for a page designer to reformat.

This dim view of scriptlets is universally accepted, and JSP even allows scriptlet support to be disabled entirely. Throughout this book, you'll follow good design practice and refrain from using them.

## Expressions

A JSP *expression* is similar to a scriptlet except that instead of containing arbitrary amounts of Java code, it returns the result of a single Java expression. The syntax is also similar except that the opening delimiter finishes with an equals sign. The following simple expression displays the user-agent header:

```
<%= request.getHeader("user-agent") %>
```

When placed in a JSP page, the previous line would display code similar to the following for a Web client running Microsoft Internet Explorer 6.0 on Windows XP Professional:

```
Mozilla/4.0 (compatible; MSIE 6.0; Windows NT 5.1; .NET CLR 1.1.4322)
```

Expressions are primarily used to display values that are automatically provided by your servlet container or to display already existing values that have been created by other means in your Web application or JSP page. Contrast this with scriptlets, which are primarily used to create new values using custom Java code.

You should avoid expressions, like scriptlets, in favor of the JSP Expression Language (you'll learn about this language in the section "The Expression Language").

## JSP Tags

As you know, HTML consists of dozens of tags that page authors can use; JSP adds about a dozen new ones. The servlet container processes these special JSP tags (also called *standard actions*) before the page is sent to the browser. Consider the following example:

```
<html>
  <body>
    This is a JSP.<br />
    <jsp:include page="anotherPage.jsp" />
  </body>
</html>
```

In this code, <jsp:include> is a JSP tag that tells the servlet container to insert the page indicated by the page attribute, which is anotherPage.jsp. The page sent to the browser will then contain the contents of anotherPage.jsp in place of the <jsp:include> tag, as well as the contents of the containing JSP page. There's a little more to it than this, as you'll see in Chapter 4.

JSP tags are powerful for accomplishing a wide range of tasks, and as you proceed through the book, you'll come up against more of these tags as and when they're needed. Appendix A also lists them in full.

## The Expression Language

JSP has a special syntax for incorporating the results of simple expressions into a page. This syntax is the Expression Language (EL), new in JSP 2.0, and it uses the following syntax:

```
${EL_expression}
```

Be aware that unlike other ways of adding dynamic content to JSP pages, EL doesn't use standard Java but a syntax all its own; however, there's considerable overlap between the two.

The following EL fragment displays the `user-agent` value given in the header part of the Hypertext Transfer Protocol (HTTP) request that was sent by the browser when asking for the page:

```
${header["user-agent"]}
```

The `user-agent` value in the HTTP header specifies the type of browser that's making the request for the page. For example, Mozilla 1.5 running on Windows XP Professional would display the following:

```
Mozilla/5.0 (Windows; U; Windows NT 5.1; en-US; rv:1.5) Gecko/20031007
```

Prior to JSP 2.0, to retrieve a value from a `Map` in a JSP page, you'd have to use something such as the following:

```
<%= ((Map) pageContext.findAttribute("myMap")).get("someKey") %>
```

This isn't the prettiest code you're likely to see. We'll explain what's happening. The `pageContext` object, which is basically a container for various key JSP functions, has a method `findAttribute()` that searches the four object storage scopes (page, request, session, and application) for an object with the passed key. Once you obtain the object, you must cast it to its proper type, in this case a `Map`, and then execute the `get` method on the `Map` to obtain your object. That's quite a few steps!

If this seems tedious and rather complex to you, you're not alone. Many of the most experienced Java and JSP developers find this syntax somewhat opaque.

The EL equivalent of the previous example is as follows:

```
${myMap.someKey}
```

### EL Features

You can use EL expressions anywhere in a JSP page where HTML or text may appear. You can also use them as attribute values for JSP tags and custom tags if appropriate.

Now that you know where you can use the EL, you'll learn about what you can do with it. JSP's EL is actually rather simple. Its key features are as follows:

- Easy syntax for accessing variables
- Special support for collection objects and arrays
- Implicit objects
- Arithmetic

The following sections cover each of these in turn.

### *Easy Syntax for Accessing Variables*

When you use JavaBeans with JSP via the `<jsp:useBean>` tag, or other mechanisms that introduce variables into your environment, you must have a means of accessing those variables. With the EL, this is trivial. To access any object, just use the following syntax:

```
${object}
```

You learned earlier that JavaBeans and other objects will reside in one of four scopes (page, request, session, or application), and this syntax searches all four for any variable of the given name.

However, simply knowing how to reference an object isn't useful in itself, and you generally need to access its properties. The EL makes this easy, too. Recall that you can access properties of JavaBeans with the `<jsp:getProperty>` tag. For example:

```
<jsp:getProperty name="myBean" property="myProperty"/>
```

The EL equivalent of this tag is the following:

```
${myBean.myProperty}
```

### *Special Support for Collections*

Accessing simple properties, such as a number or a string, is fine, and you can easily accomplish this via the EL or with a more complex `<jsp:getProperty>` tag, as you've just seen. But what if the property is a `Map`, `List`, or array? Well, if you're using a `<jsp:getProperty>` tag, accessing a property that's a `Map` will display the following:

```
{key1=value1, key3=value3, key2=value2}
```

In other words, it'll display the contents of your `Map`. This is probably not something you want displayed. The following is what's displayed when `<jsp:getProperty>` is used on an array property:

```
[Ljava.lang.String;@b9b8d0
```

Now that is truly cryptic. In short, although `<jsp:getProperty>` and the EL are interchangeable for some properties, the EL enables access to other properties that can't be meaningfully accessed through `<jsp:getProperty>`.

### EL Map Support

To access the contents of a `Map`, you have two options:

```
${myMap.myKey}
${myMap["myKey"]}
```

Although the first of these two seems the simplest, the second has an advantage: It can be used at runtime, but the first can't be. For example, imagine you have a `Map` variable (`myMap`) and another (`myKeyVariable`), which corresponds to a key that you want to access. Further suppose that `myKeyVariable` contains the value `aFunKey`. The following syntax wouldn't work:

```
${myMap.myKeyVariable}
```

This doesn't work because the EL searches `myMap` for a key that's literally equal to `myKeyVariable`, which isn't what you intend. However, this will do the trick:

```
${myMap[myKeyVariable]}
```

Using a `Map` in JSP pages has never been simpler!

### List and Array Support

Recall that you can access both `List` objects and arrays via an index property. Using these with the EL is quite simple:

```
${anArrayOrList[0]}
```

where `0` is the index of the item you want to retrieve.

## Implicit Objects

Implicit objects are those objects that are always available to JSP developers. The EL gives JSP developers more implicit objects than they've ever had before, making it convenient to access all sorts of data. Table 3-1 describes these objects.

*Table 3-1. Implicit Objects*

| Implicit Object | Description |
|---|---|
| pageContext | The PageContext object. |
| pageScope | A Map of all the objects that have page scope. |
| requestScope | A Map of all the objects that have request scope. |
| sessionScope | A Map of all the objects that have session scope. |
| applicationScope | A Map of all the objects that have application scope. |
| param | A Map of all the form parameters that were passed to your JSP page (for example, the HTML <input name="myName" type="text"/> is passed to your JSP page as a form parameter). |
| paramValues | HTML allows for multiple values for a single form parameter. This is a Map of all the parameters, just like param, but in this object the values are an array containing all of the values for a given parameter in the event that there's more than one. |
| header | A Map of all the request headers. |
| headerValues | For the same reasons as paramValues, a headerValues object is provided. |
| cookie | A Map of all the cookies passed to your JSP. The value returned is a Cookie object. See the next section for an example of how to interact with this object. |
| initParam | A Map that maps context initialization parameter names to their parameter values (you'll learn more about these in Chapter 9). |

You'll now see some examples of how to use these objects:

```
${pageScope.myObject}
${param.firstName}
${paramValues.phoneNumber[0]}
${cookie.someCookie.value}
```

As you can see, all of these implicit objects follow the simple rules you've just finished reviewing.

### Cookie Class

By the way, you'll be dealing with the `Cookie` class in JSP pages. It's a simple, JavaBean-compliant class with the key properties shown in Table 3-2.

*Table 3-2.* `Cookie` *Properties*

| Property | Description |
|---|---|
| `name` | The name of the cookie. |
| `value` | The value of the cookie. |
| `domain` | The domain name of the cookie; it'll be sent only to servers in this domain (for example, `www.apress.com`). |
| `maxAge` | The length of time in seconds that the cookie will exist; `-1` indicates that the cookie will stick around until the browser quits. |
| `path` | Restricts the cookie to be sent only to the server when requesting uniform resource locators (URLs) from it that contain this path (for example, `/companyStore`). |
| `secure` | `true` or `false` indicating whether the cookie will be sent only when connecting via HTTPS (an encrypted form of HTTP). |

### Arithmetic

The final feature of EL you'll look at is its ability to evaluate various arithmetic expressions. The following is an example of some of the EL's arithmetic operators at work:

```
${((2 + myVar) * 16) % 5}
```

The EL supports the arithmetic operators shown in Table 3-3.

*Table 3-3. Arithmetic Operators*

| | |
|---|---|
| Addition | + |
| Subtraction | - |
| Multiplication | * |
| Division | / or "div" |
| Remainder (modulo) | % or mod |

Furthermore, EL supports relational operators to compare two values (see Table 3-4).

*Table 3-4. Relational Operators*

| | |
|---|---|
| Equals | == or eq |
| Not equals | != or ne |
| Less than | < or lt |
| Greater than | > or gt |
| Less than or equals | <= or le |
| Greater than or equals | >= or ge |

Finally, the EL also supports the standard logical operators (see Table 3-5).

*Table 3-5. Logical Operators*

| | |
|---|---|
| And | && or and |
| Or | \|\| or or |
| Not | ! or not |

### *Trying It Out: Using the EL with Your Pizza Form*

To demonstrate the EL's form-handling abilities, you'll use the pizza form you completed at the end of the previous chapter. If you remember, the form asked users to add their details to an HTML form, which was then submitted to a JSP page called `process.jsp`. In this section, you'll write `process.jsp` using the EL. Follow these steps:

1. Modify `pizza.html` as follows (this will demonstrate the EL's map-handling abilities):

```
<h1>Please Select Any Additional Toppings:</h1>
<table>
  <tr>
    <td>
      <input type="checkbox" name="topping" value="Peppers"/>
    </td>
    <td>
      Peppers
    </td>
  </tr>
  <tr>
    <td>
       <input type="checkbox" name="topping" value="Sweetcorn"/>
    </td>
    <td>
      Sweetcorn
    </td>
  </tr>
  <tr>
    <td>
      <input type="checkbox" name="topping" value="Mouse innards"/>
    </td>
    <td>
      Mouse Innards
    </td>
  </tr>
</table>
```

2. Create a file called **process.jsp** in the `Pizza` folder. This is your processing page:

```
<html>
  <head>
    <title>Your details</title>
    <style type="text/css">
      H1 {
        font-size: 12pt;
        font-weight: bold;
```

```
      }
    </style>
  </head>

  <body>
    <h1>Your Details</h1>

    <table>
      <tr>
        <td>Name: </td>
        <td>${param.name}</td>
      </tr>
      <tr>
        <td>Address:</td>
        <td>${param.address}</td>
      </tr>
      <tr>
        <td>Delivery type:</td>
        <td>${param.purchaseType}</td>
      </tr>
      <tr>
        <td>Toppings:</td>
        <td>${paramValues.topping[0]}</td>
      </tr>
      <tr>
        <td></td>
        <td>${paramValues.topping[1]}</td>
      </tr>
      <tr>
        <td></td>
        <td>${paramValues.topping[2]}</td>
      </tr>
      <tr>
        <td>Pizza size:</td>
        <td>${param["size"]}</td>
      </tr>
    </table>

    <p>Thank you for ordering.</p>

  </body>
</html>
```

3. Go to `http://localhost:8080/Pizza/pizza.html`, and fill in your details. Submit the form, and you should see something like Figure 3-1.

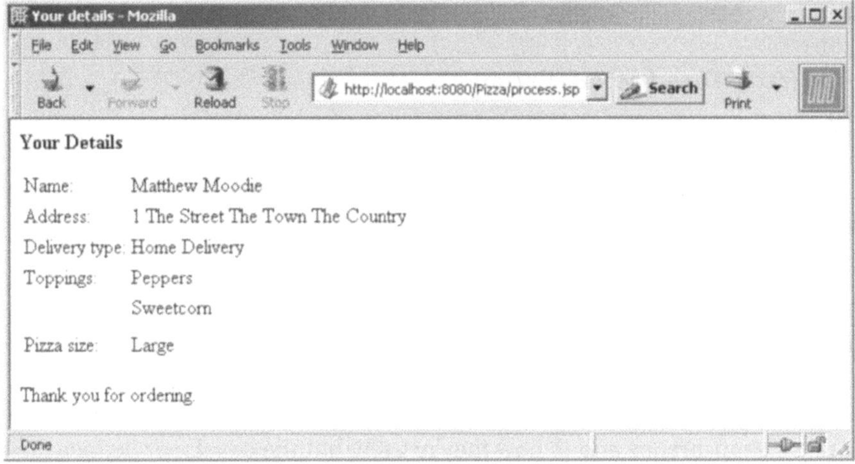


*Figure 3-1. Processing a form using the EL*

## *How It Works*

Retrieving the values of your unchanged input elements is simple with the EL. For example, the following retrieves the `address` parameter from the request and sends it to the browser:

```
<td>${param.address}</td>
```

The following does the same:

```
<td>${param["size"]}</td>
```

The new lines in `pizza.html` assign the name `topping` to each of the checkboxes, which bundles all the values of the checkbox into one parameter:

```
<input type="checkbox" name="topping" value="Peppers"/>
```

The values are retrieved using the `paramValues` object because they're made available as a `Map`:

```
<tr>
  <td>Toppings:</td>
  <td>${paramValues.topping[0]}</td>
</tr>
<tr>
  <td></td>
  <td>${paramValues.topping[1]}</td>
</tr>
```

```
<tr>
  <td></td>
  <td>${paramValues.topping[2]}</td>
</tr>
```

Each row in the table is empty if the Map doesn't contain a value at the index specified, so only those checkboxes chosen will be shown to the user.

### Custom Tags

JSP lets page authors define their own custom tags. These tags resemble regular JSP tags in appearance and in how they're used, but the developer defines their specific function.

Custom tags are a neat way of extending the standard functionality available through JSP, and they also provide an excellent means for sharing code with others. Dozens of custom tag libraries are floating around the Internet that you can download and use in your applications.

Chapter 6 discusses custom tags in detail.

## Using the Java Standard Tag Library (JSTL)

In addition to the regular JSP tags, the Java community has created a standard library of custom tags to be used in JSP pages. This collection is called, appropriately enough, the *JSP Standard Tag Library* (JSTL). JSTL is now officially included with JSP 2.0.

You'll use the JSTL extensively throughout this book, and you'll have a first go at using it in the "Trying It Out: Viewing Request Headers" section.

Now you'll see a couple of examples that put these JSP techniques into action. The first example will use the JSTL to display the information contained in the HTTP header section. As already mentioned, a browser sends an HTTP request to the server when the user wants to view a page held on that server. The HTTP request details which page the user wants to see, and the server sends the browser an HTTP response that contains the requested page (see Figure 3-2).

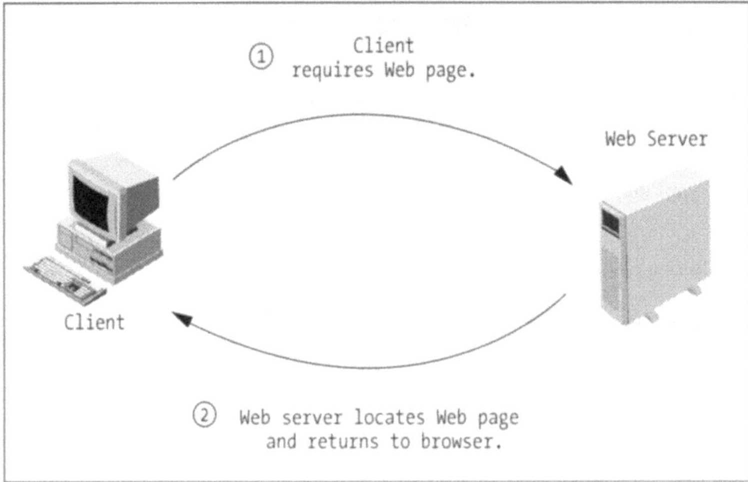


*Figure 3-2. The request-response process*

HTTP requests contain certain details about the browser in an initial section called the *HTTP header*, and it's these details that your first sample JSP will display. First, though, you need to download and install the JSTL.

## Downloading the JSTL

You can download the JSTL from the Apache Software Foundation, the same place you obtained Tomcat. Navigate to the following URL:

`http://www.apache.org/dist/jakarta/taglibs/standard-1.0/`

Download the latest version you see (click the Last Modified link at the top of the listing twice to order the files in descending order by date). Windows users should download the file ending in `.zip`, and Linux users should download the file ending in `.tar.gz`.

## Installing the JSTL on Windows

The JSTL is distributed as a ZIP file because this format allows multiple files to be included in a single, compressed package. You'll need to extract the files from the ZIP archive for use. Windows XP has built-in support for ZIP files, and just double-clicking the file will open it as if it were a folder in its own right. Other versions of Windows require a separate program to extract ZIPs, such as WinZip, which is available over the Internet as shareware (`http://www.winzip.com/`).

Extract the files to somewhere appropriate, such as `C:\java`. When you extract the files (or copy them if you're using Windows XP), a directory is created called `jakarta-taglibs` that contains the JSTL files in various subfolders.

### Installing the JSTL on Red Hat Linux

Once you've downloaded the JSTL, you must decompress it into a directory of your choice, say /usr/local/java/. The appropriate command is as follows:

```
tar -xzf jakarta-taglibs-standard.tar.gz -C /usr/local/java
```

*Trying It Out: Viewing Request Headers*

To view request headers, follow these steps:

1. Set up a new Tomcat Web application by creating a directory called **RequestHeaders** under webapps. As before, create a folder called **WEB-INF** within it and a folder called **lib** inside that.

2. To use the JSTL, you need to copy the JSTL files into your Web application's lib subdirectory. The files you need to copy are those within the lib folder off the standard directory within jakarta-taglibs.

3. Now create a file called **request.jsp**, which starts with this line:

   ```
   <%@ taglib uri="http://java.sun.com/jstl/core_rt" prefix="c" %>
   ```

   This is a *taglib directive*, and it tells Tomcat that tags that start with the letters given in the prefix attribute belong to the tag library specified by the uri attribute. You'll see this in action in a minute, when you use some JSTL tags.

4. The next few lines of the JSP are simple HTML tags to start a table:

   ```
   <html>
     <body>
       You sent the following request headers:
       <br />
       <table border="1">
         <tr>
           <th>
             Header
           </th>
           <th>
             Value
           </th>
         </tr>
   ```

5. This table will format the different request headers for display. You do this by looping through every header and inserting its name (entry.key) and value (entry.value) into a row of the table:

```
<c:forEach var="entry" items="${header}">
  <tr>
    <td>
      ${entry.key}
    </td>
    <td>
      ${entry.value}
    </td>
  </tr>
</c:forEach>
```

6. You perform the loop by using the `<c:forEach>` custom tag. Note the prefix `c:` indicating that this tag belongs to the JTSL library.

7. Finally, your JSP ends by closing the HTML tags and should be saved to the `RequestHeaders` folder:

```
    </table>
  </body>
</html>
```

8. Now restart Tomcat, open your Web browser, and navigate to `http://localhost:8080/ RequestHeaders/request.jsp`. You should see a screen similar to Figure 3-3.

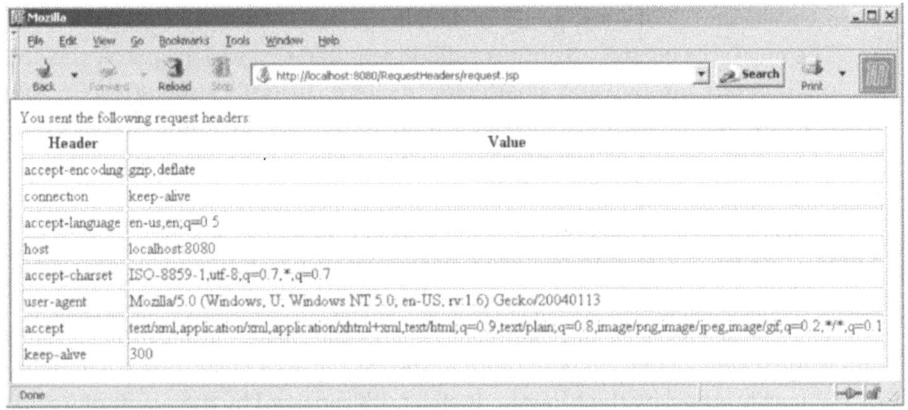


*Figure 3-3. The JSTL reading request headers*

You've created a table that lists the name and value of each request header that your browser sent to Tomcat (of course, your system may have different values than the ones shown). Most of these headers aren't values you're likely to be interested in as a developer, though, because they're more for the server's benefit. For example, the `connection` header's value is `keep-alive`, which tells the server that the browser wants to keep the connection open because subsequent requests are likely.

One header that's often used by JSP developers, as shown in earlier examples, is the `user-agent` header that specifies the type of Web browser in use. This enables a Web application to change its behavior according to the capabilities of the browser or to keep statistics about which browsers users have.

### *How It Works*

Take another look at the `taglib` directive:

```
<%@ taglib uri="http://java.sun.com/jstl/core_rt" prefix="c" %>
```

The `uri` attribute (which stands for *uniform resource identifier*) provides a unique name for the tag library. Although this takes the form of a regular Web address you might type into a browser, it doesn't necessarily correspond to a valid Web location, and it needs only to be a unique name to identify tags that belong to a particular library. Tomcat can then find the required tag library, not by visiting the URI but by searching all the files in the `lib` subdirectory of the current Web application for a tag library that matches this URI, which in this case will be the JSTL.

The `prefix` attribute sets the custom tags from this library to start with in order to distinguish them from other tags in the page. Here, the prefix is `c`, as shown in the JSTL `<forEach>` tag. This tag is what's known as an *iterator* tag. It iterates—or steps through—each item in a *collection*, applying the code inside the tag to each item. A collection can be any group of data items stored in a single place.

The `<forEach>` tag has attributes called `items` and `var`, which specify the collection to iterate through and a name for the item currently selected by the loop, respectively. In this example, you've used EL in the `items` attribute to make the loop cycle through the collection of request headers. You've set the `var` attribute so that you can access each header in turn by the identifier `entry`.

Items in the HTTP headers are stored as key/value pairs, where the key is a name that can be used to retrieve a particular value. In this case, you can access the value using `${entry.value}` and the key name using `${entry.key}`.

Thus, your `<forEach>` tag iterates through each header and prints its name and value inside a table. Note that the `<forEach>` tag, as a custom tag dealt with by JSP, isn't received by the browser. Instead, it's replaced by the result of its operation, which is a bunch of `<tr>` tags containing the header names and values, as you can see by viewing the source for your JSP in your browser.

There you have it—using EL and the JSTL in tandem lets you create JSP pages that are quite a bit more complicated (and useful) than the first example in Chapter 1.

## Processing Forms with the JSTL

Previously you used simple EL to display the results of the pizza form on the `process.jsp` page. However, you had no way of checking whether the user submitted any personal information. A pizza delivery order with no name and address isn't going to get very far. Now that you have access to the JSTL, you'll extend the pizza application to check the user's details.

### *Trying It Out: Using the JSTL with Your Pizza Form*

To use the JSTL with your pizza form, follow these steps:

1. You'll use the core library of the JSTL, so add the taglib declaration to `process.jsp`:

   ```
   <%@ taglib uri="http://java.sun.com/jstl/core_rt" prefix="c" %>
   ```

2. You'll deal with the validation logic first. So far you've seen a simple loop operator (the `<c:forEach>` tag), but now you'll use some of the JSTL's conditional operators to check the user's details. Change `process.jsp` as follows:

   ```
   ...
       <h1>Your Details</h1>

       <c:if test="${param.name eq '' or param.address eq ''}">

       </c:if>

       <table>
         <tr>
           <td>Name: </td>
           <td>${param.name}</td>
         </tr>
   ...
   ```

3. You'll eventually want to show the user the original form so they can correct any mistakes. It'd be better if you took some of the work away and filled in the details they did remember. For now this will be just the name and address; you can do the others on your own. You'll store the values they submitted in session scope so that all the pages the user sees can access them:

```
<c:if test="${param.name eq '' or param.address eq ''}">

  <c:set var="name" value="${param.name}" scope="session"/>
  <c:set var="address" value="${param.address}" scope="session"/>
```

4. Finally, you want to go back to the original form so the user can correct their details. You'll use the `<c:redirect>` JSTL tag to accomplish this. This tag tells the browser to send a new request to the specified URL (now a JSP page so you can work with the user's information). You can add request parameters to the new URL with the subelement `<c:param>`. These parameters are added only if the information is missing:

```
  <c:redirect url="pizza.jsp">

    <c:if test="${param.name eq ''}">
      <c:param name="name" value="missing"/>
    </c:if>

    <c:if test="${param.address eq ''}">
      <c:param name="address" value="missing"/>
    </c:if>

  </c:redirect>

</c:if>
```

5. The rest of the page is the same, but the user won't reach it if their name or address is missing.

6. Next you have to alter the form itself. This is where you'll tell the user about their missing information. The first step is to rename `pizza.html` to **pizza.jsp**. Tomcat will now process the page. Without this change you couldn't react to the user's missing details.

7. You need to declare the core JSTL:

```
<%@ taglib uri="http://java.sun.com/jstl/core_rt" prefix="c" %>
```

8. You need a style for the warning text:

```
.missing {
  color: red;
}
```

9. You need a paragraph informing the user of their mistake:

```
<p>
Please fill out the fields below and click on "Place Order" when
you're done.
</p>

<c:if test="${param.name eq 'missing' or param.address eq 'missing'}">
  <p class="missing">
    You forgot to fill in some details. Please fill in the
    marked sections.
  </p>
</c:if>

<h1>Your Information:</h1>
```

10. Next you need to show them which fields they missed and fill in the information they remembered (which is stored in session scope):

```
    <tr>
      <td>
        Name:
      </td>
      <td>
        <input type="text" name="name" size="30"
               value="${sessionScope.name}" />
        <c:if test="${param.name eq 'missing'}">
          <span class="missing">
            * Required field
          </span>
        </c:if>
      </td>
    </tr>
    <tr>
      <td>
        Address:
      </td>
      <td>
        <textarea rows="4" cols="40"
                  name="address">${sessionScope.address}</textarea>
        <c:if test="${param.address eq 'missing'}">
          <span class="missing">
            * Required field
          </span>
        </c:if>
```

```
            </td>
          </tr>
```

11. Your final change to `pizza.jsp` will save the user some work by checking the `purchaseType` radio button. Not all users will save time with this change, but a significant number will:

```
<input type="radio" name="purchaseType" value="Home Delivery"
       checked="true"/>
```

12. To test the new system, go to `http://localhost:8080/Pizza/pizza.jsp`. You will see the familiar form. Omit your address, and click Place Order. You should return to the form with a warning like the one shown in Figure 3-4.

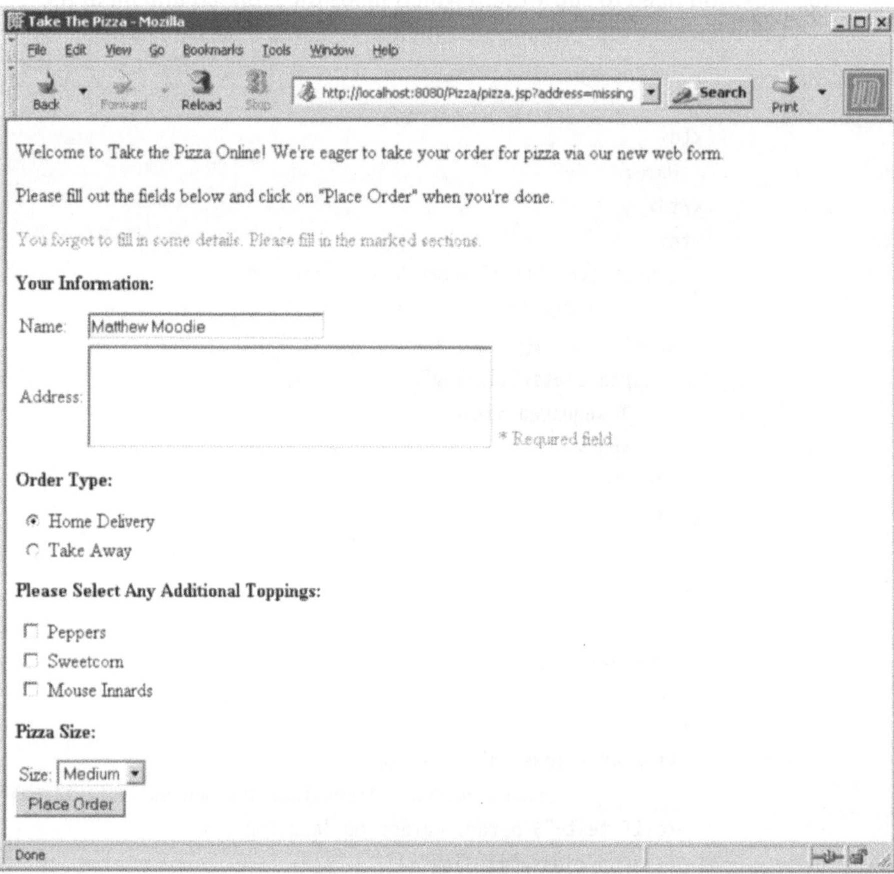


*Figure 3-4. The pizza application with a missing field*

*How It Works*

The core JSTL tags contain a number of tags to conditionally evaluate parts of a page. In other words, they can check a condition and, if that condition is true, send a section of HTML to the browser or process some JSP terms. In this example, you use the `<c:if>` tag to check if either the name or the address parameters sent from the form are blank and act accordingly:

```
<c:if test="${param.name eq '' or param.address eq ''}">
```

The EL expression in the `test` attribute will evaluate to `true` or `false`. If `test="true"`, the body of the tag will be evaluated.

If one or more of the parameters is missing, you'll return to the form. However, you don't want the user to repeat any typing, so any information they've already typed should be saved for use later:

```
<c:set var="name" value="${param.name}" scope="session"/>
<c:set var="address" value="${param.address}" scope="session"/>
```

The `<c:set>` tag can save information in the scopes described earlier: page, request, session, and application. The default is page, but you want to save the information for the duration of the user's visit—in other words, for the duration of their session. The `var` attribute is the name by which this information will be referenced later, and the `value` attribute is the information you want to save. It doesn't matter if the name or address is blank; each will be stored as a blank in the session and displayed as a blank on the form page. None of this affects the processing logic.

The `<c:redirect>` tag returns the user to the form to finish the order:

```
<c:redirect url="pizza.jsp">
```

The `url` attribute takes a relative path to a URL and instructs the browser to send a new request to the server. To add parameters to this URL, you use the `<c:param>` subelements, which you conditionally evaluate according to what information is missing:

```
<c:if test="${param.name eq ''}">
  <c:param name="name" value="missing"/>
</c:if>

<c:if test="${param.address eq ''}">
  <c:param name="address" value="missing"/>
</c:if>
```

The browser will use the resulting URL as a GET HTML request, so any sensitive information shouldn't be added in this way. It's better to use the session instead, as demonstrated previously. This way, no data is sent to the browser and back in plain text. Once the <c:redirect> tag is closed, the redirect takes place, and the rest of the page is discarded:

```
</c:redirect>
```

The new HTML page is reasonably similar to the processing page. It first checks whether any information was omitted when it was last submitted using a <c:if> tag:

```
<c:if test="${param.name eq 'missing' or param.address eq 'missing'}">
  <p class="missing">
    You forgot to fill in some details. Please fill in the
    marked sections.
  </p>
</c:if>
```

Note that the user can add these parameters when they type the form's URL, which demonstrates another downside to HTML GET. However, the form uses POST to submit the details, so no amount of URL typing will get around the processing logic.

The input fields now have a value attribute that's set to the value stored in the session (the sessionScope EL object). If the field was omitted originally, this value is blank. Any subsequent resubmission will still contain a blank value:

```
<td>
  <input type="text" name="name" size="30" value="${sessionScope.name}" />
  <c:if test="${param.name eq 'missing'}">
    <span class="missing">
      * Required field
    </span>
  </c:if>
</td>
```

The <c:if> tag again checks for the presence of the appropriate parameter indicating a missing value. Note the layout of the <textarea> element:

```
<textarea rows="4" cols="40"
                name="address">${sessionScope.address}</textarea>
```

Any extra spaces or carriage returns would introduce whitespace into the field's value. This would break the processing logic because it checks for completely blank fields, not whitespace. If you want to lay out your HTML neatly, make sure to check for the correct value in process.jsp.

Finally, adding `checked="true"` to the radio button relieves the user of the burden of checking it, unless of course they want to leave their couch and go down to the pizza shop for their pizza. Such throwbacks are rare, so you can safely make this change:

```
<input type="radio" name="purchaseType" value="Home Delivery"
       checked="true"/>
```

## Summary

You've learned the following key points about JSP:

- JSP page are similar to HTML pages but end in `.jsp`. JSP pages have access to a wealth of features not available to plain-vanilla HTML pages.
- JSP uses the following to achieve these extra features:
    - Scriptlets, which consist of embedded Java code in the JSP page. Scriptlets are viewed as poor programming practice and are generally avoided.
    - Expressions, which display data and values in the JSP.
    - EL expressions, which are a fast and efficient way to display data in a JSP page.
    - JSP tags, which are somewhat like normal HTML tags but produce JSP-specific functionality.

You also learned about the JSTL, which is a set of custom tags that grants you a wealth of functionality. Finally, you processed an HTML form using the EL and the JSTL.

CHAPTER 4

# Working with Data

**You can store data** in several ways, including in Extensible Markup Language (XML) files, plain-text files, relational databases, object databases, spreadsheets, or memory. This chapter will introduce you to relational databases, how to request data from them using their "native" language, and how you can use this knowledge in JavaServer Pages (JSP) pages.

Specifically, in this chapter you'll learn about the following:

- Relational databases
- Concepts associated with databases, such as normalization
- How to install MySQL
- The basics of Structured Query Language (SQL)
- How to use a JSP page to connect to a database and display information
- How to use a JSP page to add information to a database

The chapter starts by establishing what databases are and why you'd want to use them.

## Introducing Databases

Chapter 2 introduced some mechanisms for handling user input. For this input to be useful, it must be stored somewhere so it can be retrieved later; in the pizza example from the previous chapters, the pizza shop would need some way of looking up the order. Although it'd certainly be possible to store the information as plain-text files, it'd quickly become inadequate if your information became increasingly complex. Structured information, such as that found in an online shopping site or on a message board, usually necessitates the use of a database.

**NOTE** A database *is a collection of data organized so that its contents can be easily accessed and manipulated.*

To understand a database better, consider an example of an unsorted pile of papers. How do you find a particular page within the pile? You'd probably start from the top of the pile and work your way down until you found the page you wanted. This could be a time-consuming process if the pile was large and your page was near the bottom. This unorganized environment is analogous to data that's stored in a normal "flat" file on a computer, where data is held in no particular order and has to be searched from beginning to end (known as *sequential access*) to locate information relevant to a particular task.

Now, consider a library or bookshop. When you need a particular book, you might have to search through a card catalog. This is an example of a (nonelectronic) database. It's a well-organized system in which data is stored in specific locations, and because of its structure and organization, any data can be retrieved quickly and easily. This also allows both direct and random access to the information.

A software program for creating and modifying databases is called a *database management system* (DBMS). The DBMS removes the complexities of storing the database information in specific locations within the particular files, directories, and disk volumes used by the server. The server keeps track of where the data is stored, so as a database user you don't have to worry about it.

## Using Tables

One of the most common ways to organize data is to arrange it in *tables*. For instance, referring to the bookshop analogy, you could make a table of books. Each book's data (author, title, price, and so on) would fill a *row* (or *record*) of the table. Because you'd want to use the table to compare data from different books, you'd arrange the data you want to compare (say, the price) into a *column* (or *field*). Assuming the wise bookshop owner stocks Apress books, a portion of the Book table might look something like Table 4-1.

*Table 4-1. The* Book *Table*

| Title | Author(s) | Price |
|---|---|---|
| Beginning JSP 2.0 | Peter den Haan, Ben Galbraith, Lance Lavandowska, Sathya Narayana Panduranga, Krishnaraj Perrumal | $39.99 |
| Pro JSP, Third Edition | Simon Brown, Sam Dalton, Daniel Jepp, Dave Johnson, Sing Li, Matt Raible | $59.99 |

As you can see, the table groups the data about each book into a separate row and groups data about each attribute of a book into separate columns.

Now, if you were to construct a database to contain this data, you'd do the same thing—organize the data into a table. In fact, a database will probably contain more than one table, each holding data about a different *entity*—books, computers, movies, or whatever. These things are all different, so you wouldn't want them all jumbled together in one place.

> **NOTE** *An entity is a "thing" that a database holds information about. Usually, each entity you identify will have a table of its own in the database.*

Of course, the fact that you create tables to hold information about a particular entity implies that the records within the table share common attributes—in other words, the records within a table are related. After all, it makes no sense to store unrelated information, such as mixing up the information related to your movie collection with the information about the books in your bookstore. Although they all have titles, books have authors, movies have running time, and computers have processor speeds.

## Using Relational Databases

Think back to the `Book` table. Although it's perfectly logical to store related data about books in a table, this table isn't as efficient at storing this data as it may first appear.

Look at the way you're storing the information about the authors. You'll see that a couple of authors are listed for more than one book. If you wanted to look for books coauthored by a certain individual, you'd need to look through the author list for each book. Not only that, but by repeating this information in each book entry, you're introducing the possibility of typographical errors. For instance, if an author of an existing book releases a new book, there's a chance that whoever enters the new book's details into the database may misspell the author's name, and the new book wouldn't come up if someone searched for all books by that author.

If, on the other hand, you were to have a separate list of authors, you could link each book to authors in that list. This would eliminate the possibility of misspellings (well, outside the first time the name is entered), and you could more easily look for a particular author's books because they'll be explicitly linked to that author. A system that links data across more than one entity (table) is referred to as a *relational database management system* (RDBMS).

### Understanding Relationships Between Data

This second problem arises because of the nature of the relationships between attributes *within* the table. You have no problem storing data within a table when all of the attributes map *one-to-one* (1:1) or *one-to-many* (1:M). In a 1:1 relationship, each column involved in the relationship contains unique values. Say, for instance, a business has a separate table holding yearly orders for its customers. There would then be a 1:1 relationship between the customer table and the order table. This assumes that the business allows its customers one order per year (or that its product lasts only a year, as would be the case for diary makers). You should note that 1:1 relationships are pretty rare.

On the other hand, a more sensible approach for this business would be to allow more than one order per customer. Each customer in the customer table has a customer ID, which is used to reference orders in the order table. You can organize 1:M relationships within a table although you can encounter the data repetition problem discussed earlier.

The big problem comes when you encounter *many-to-many* (M:M) relationships. Such a relationship exists in the data between titles and authors because a book can have more than one author, and an author may have written more than one book. Organizing M:M relationships in a table is a difficult task, as you've seen, and one that reduces your ability to modify the table later.

### Understanding the Relational Model

One common way to solve the problems discussed previously is to break up any tables with M:M relationships into smaller ones that together hold the same data. This multitable approach is called the *relational model* because there are relationships between the data in different tables. Obviously, you need a way to preserve these relationships even though the data is now in separate tables. To do this, you share one attribute per table with another table; these attributes that are shared between tables are called *keys*.

For instance, you might choose to place information about authors in one table and data about books in another and then link the two tables using the author's name attribute as a key. In this case, if you looked up information on a particular book title in the `Book` table and then wanted to find out about the authors of that book, you'd note the names of the book authors and scan down the `Author` table until you found the correct records. Note that in this case, the author's name column of the `Author` table would have to contain unique values; otherwise you'd get confused when you tried to track down the record for a particular author. A key column such as this, which is allowed to contain only unique values, is called a *primary key*. The corresponding author name column in the `Book` table is called a *foreign key* because it refers to values from a key column in another table. Table 4-2 shows the `Book` table, and Table 4-3 shows the `Author` table.

*Table 4-2. The* Book *Table*

| Title | Author(s) | Price |
|---|---|---|
| Beginning JSP 2.0 | Peter den Haan, Ben Galbraith, Lance Lavandowska, Sathya Narayana Panduranga, Krishnaraj Perrumal | $39.99 |
| Pro JSP, Third Edition | Simon Brown, Sam Dalton, Daniel Jepp, Dave Johnson, Sing Li, Matt Raible | $59.99 |

*Table 4-3. The* Author *Table*

| Author | Book(s) |
|---|---|
| Peter den Haan | Beginning JSP 2.0 |
| Ben Galbraith | Beginning JSP 2.0, Pro JSP, Third Edition |
| ... | ... |

> **NOTE** A primary key *is a column in a table that has a unique value for each row and can thus be used to identify any one row unambiguously. A* foreign key *is a column in a table that itself refers to a primary key in another table. Foreign key values aren't necessarily unique—that is, several rows can refer to the same row in the related table.*

But how do you decide what attributes to use as keys? You need to follow a process that enables you to optimize your database table split. Luckily, this process exists and is called *normalization.*

## Understanding Normalization

The process toward database normalization progresses through a series of steps, typically known as *normal forms,* which is a concept that was introduced in the 1970s by a fellow named E. F. Codd.

Normalizing a database aims to do the following:

- Arrange data into logical groupings so that each group describes a small part of the whole.
- Minimize the amount of duplicate data stored in a database.

- Organize the data in such a way that, when you modify it, you make changes in only one place.
- Build a database in which you can access and manipulate the data quickly and efficiently without compromising the integrity of the data in storage.

> **NOTE** *Normalization minimizes redundancy in data by dividing a database into two or more tables and defining relationships between them. This allows for changes, additions, and deletions to fields to be made in just one table but to be reflected in the others via the relationships defined.*

The following three sets of rules apply to *database normalization*. If you observe the first set of rules, as follows, the database is said to be in *first normal form*. The following are the rules you should follow for converting the database to its first normal form:

- Eliminate repeating groups in individual tables.
- Create a separate table for each set of related data.
- Identify each set of related data with a primary key.

The book data would therefore change to that shown in Table 4-4 and Table 4-5. `Book_ID` and `Author_ID` are the primary keys in this instance. This is a convenient way of uniquely identifying the records.

*Table 4-4. The* `Book` *Table*

| Book_ID | Title | Price |
|---|---|---|
| 1 | Beginning JSP 2.0 | $39.99 |
| 2 | Pro JSP, Third Edition | $59.99 |

*Table 4-5. The* `Author` *Table*

| Author_ID | Author(s) |
|---|---|
| 1 | Peter den Haan, Ben Galbraith, Lance Lavandowska, Sathya Narayana Panduranga, Krishnaraj Perrumal |
| 2 | Simon Brown, Sam Dalton, Daniel Jepp, Dave Johnson, Sing Li, Matt Raible |

The following are the rules to convert the database to its *second normal form* (the database should already be in its first normal form):

- Create separate tables for sets of values that apply to multiple records.
- Relate these tables with a foreign key.

Table 4-6, Table 4-7, and Table 4-8 show the book data in second normal form.

*Table 4-6. The* `Book` *Table*

| Book_ID | Title |
|---|---|
| 1 | Beginning JSP 2.0 |
| 2 | Pro JSP, Third Edition |

*Table 4-7. The* `Price` *Table*

| Price_ID | Price |
|---|---|
| 1 | $39.99 |
| 2 | $59.99 |

*Table 4-8. The* `Author` *Table*

| Author_ID | Author(s) |
|---|---|
| 1 | Peter den Haan, Ben Galbraith, Lance Lavandowska, Sathya Narayana Panduranga, Krishnaraj Perrumal |
| 2 | Simon Brown, Sam Dalton, Daniel Jepp, Dave Johnson, Sing Li, Matt Raible |

Continuing on the quest for complete normalization of the database, the next step in the process would be to satisfy the rule of the *third normal form:* Eliminate transitive dependencies (where a nonkey attribute is dependent on another nonkey attribute). For example, say you have a `Contacts` table with names and addresses, and the `Author` table links to it using the name field. This would be a problem if the name in the `Contacts` table or `Author` table were changed because you'd break the link between the tables. A row's primary key should never be altered; thus, it isn't transitive.

Adhering to the third normal form, although theoretically desirable, isn't always practical. For instance, if you wanted to create a database of friends' addresses, you'd need to eliminate all possible interfield dependencies, creating separate tables for cities, ZIP codes, and so on. In theory, full normalization is worth pursuing. However, many small tables may degrade performance or exceed open file and memory capacities. It may be more feasible to apply third normal form only to data that changes frequently. If some dependent fields remain, design your application to require that the user verify all related fields when one changes.

Although normalization forms can go up to the fifth form, third normal form is considered the highest level necessary for most applications. As with many formal rules and specifications, real-world scenarios don't always allow for perfect compliance. If you decide to violate one of the first three rules of normalization, make sure your application anticipates any problems that could occur, such as redundant data and inconsistent dependencies. For this example, you won't be splitting out the price information as demonstrated previously. Creating a new table to hold one column of data creates more work (linking the tables) and complexity than you'd save by not repeating pricing information in each book row.

Given the guidance from the normalization process, you'll now split the `Book` table into the most efficient set of relational tables. As mentioned, you could split the table into `Book` and `Author` tables, but this still presents you with inefficiencies:

- Although this isn't the case at the moment, as you add new books to the table, you might encounter different authors with the same name and different books with the same title—so, it wouldn't be wise to use either of these columns as primary keys.

- Each title in the `Book` table can still have many authors, which makes it difficult to match entries in the author name column of the `Book` table with corresponding entries in the author name column in the `Author` table.

However, you can solve these problems. To get around the first problem, create another table to hold authors. This `Author` table will contain an author name column and another column that contains a unique ID for that author. You can then use this author ID column as the primary key for this table. Because author ID values rather than author names will be used by other tables, you're then free to modify an author's name without having to modify every record that belongs to this author.

Solving the last problem of multiauthor entries takes a bit more effort. One way to address it would be to create the concept of an "author contribution." You'll have a third table, the `Contribution` table, which simply consists of the author's ID, the ID of the book associated with that author, and a contribution ID (the primary key for this table).

Table 4-9 shows the structure of the database model.

*Table 4-9. The* Book *Table*

| Table | Column | Key |
|---|---|---|
| Book | ID | Primary key |
| | Title | Not a key field |
| | Price | Not a key field |
| Author | ID | Primary key |
| | Author_Name | Not a key field |
| Contribution | ID | Primary key |
| | Title_ID | Foreign key |
| | Author_ID | Foreign key |

Table 4-10, Table 4-11, and Table 4-12 show a partial example of how the data would look now.

*Table 4-10. The* Book *Table*

| Book_ID | Title | Price |
|---|---|---|
| 1 | Beginning JSP 2.0 | $39.99 |
| 2 | Pro JSP, Third Edition | $59.99 |

*Table 4-11. The* Author *Table*

| Author_ID | Author(s) |
|---|---|
| 110 | Peter den Haan |
| 120 | Ben Galbraith |
| 130 | Matt Raible |

*Table 4-12. The* BookAuthor *Table*

| ID | Book_ID | Author_ID |
|---|---|---|
| 1 | 1 | 110 |
| 2 | 1 | 120 |
| 3 | 2 | 130 |
| 4 | ... | ... |

You're now almost ready to implement this database structure (or *schema*) on your machines. However, there's one last aspect of relational databases you must consider: referential integrity.

## Understanding Referential Integrity

What happens when you start manipulating the records in your tables? You can edit the book information at will without any ill effects, but what would happen if you needed to delete a title? The entries in the `Contribution` table will still link to a nonexistent book. Clearly you can't have a contribution detail without the associated book title being present. So, you must have a means in place to enforce a corresponding book title for each contribution. This is the basis of enforcing *referential integrity*. You can enforce the validity of the data in this situation in two ways. One is by cascading deletions through the related tables; the other is by preventing deletions when related records exist.

> **NOTE** Referential integrity *prevents inconsistent data from being created in the database by ensuring that any data shared between tables remains consistent. To put it another way, it ensures that the soundness of the relationships remains intact.*

Database applications have several choices available for enforcing referential integrity, but if possible, you should let the database engine do its job and handle this for you. Database engines allow you to use declarative referential integrity. You specify a relationship between tables at design time, indicating if updates and deletes will cascade through related tables. If cascading updates are enabled, changes to the primary key in a table are propagated through related tables. If cascading deletes are enabled, deletions from a table are propagated through related tables.

Before you go ahead and enable cascading deletes on all your relationships, keep in mind that this can be a dangerous practice. If you define a relationship between the `Author` table and the `Title` table with cascading deletes enabled and then delete a record from `Author`, you'll delete all `Title` table records that come under this category. Be cautious, or you may accidentally lose important data.

## Introducing SQL

In a moment, you'll install an RDBMS so you can create and manipulate databases. First, however, you learn about the language used to communicate with relational databases in this book: Structured Query Language (SQL for short). A *query* is simply a statement you send to an RDBMS to retrieve and manipulate data.

There are actually three languages within SQL itself:

- **Data Definition Language (DDL)**: Used to create databases and tables
- **Data Maintenance Language (DML)**: Used to add, remove, and change data in tables
- **Data Query Language (DQL)**: Used to retrieve data from tables

As you'll see later, SQL resembles a human language and reads almost like a form of broken English (SQL originates from the Structured English Query Language of the 1970s, and although *English* has now been dropped from the acronym, SQL is still widely pronounced as *Sequel*). SQL itself is platform-independent, but each relational database management system usually has a few quirks in its SQL implementation. Many different RDBMSs are available with different capabilities—from simple systems with limited features to sophisticated databases capable of handling large numbers of concurrent users and offering advanced features such as distributed transactional support and powerful search algorithms. However, almost all use SQL as the data access language. The following are some common RDBMSs:

- Oracle
- Sybase
- Informix
- Microsoft SQL Server
- Microsoft Access
- MySQL

In addition to being easy to use and having great performance and reliability, the last RDBMS on that list, MySQL, has another feature that makes it popular: free availability under the terms of the GNU Public License (GPL). It's a feature that appeals to us, so we'll use it throughout this book. For more information about the GPL, or the GNU Project, visit `http://www.gnu.org`.

## Using MySQL

You'll now play a little with MySQL's command-line tool, `mysql`, located in the `C:\MySQL\bin\` folder. Open a command prompt window, change to the appropriate directory, and type **mysql**. The MySQL prompt should then appear:

```
mysql>
```

Note that when MySQL is installed on Windows, all local users have full privileges to all databases by default. Although you can skip it for the purposes of the samples in this book, production scenarios require MySQL to be more secure, and you should set an individual password for all MySQL users and remove the default record in the `mysql.user` table that has `Host='localhost'` and `User=''` using the following command:

```
mysql> USE mysql
mysql> DELETE FROM user WHERE Host='localhost' AND User='';
mysql> QUIT
```

The first command tells SQL to use the `mysql` database, and the second removes the appropriate record from the `user` table of that database (don't forget the final semicolon!). Lastly you exit the `mysql` tool using the `QUIT` command (alternatively, you can use `EXIT` if you want).

> **NOTE** *Note that SQL commands, such as* `DELETE`, `WHERE`, *and* `QUIT`, *aren't case-sensitive; however, according to convention, we'll capitalize them in this book. Be aware, though, that the names of SQL tables and columns, as well as values themselves, are case-sensitive, and they must use the casing applied at definition.*

Now, you should also add a password for the `root` user. The `root` user, also called the *admin user*, has full privileges to the database, so anyone logged into MySQL as `root` has the power to change the database however they please (or to make costly mistakes). To change the password, make sure you're in the `C:\MySQL\bin\` folder and use another command-line tool, `mysqladmin`:

```
> mysqladmin reload
> mysqladmin -u root password your_password
```

where `your_password` is the password you want to use. Make sure you type this correctly because you won't be asked to confirm it. Once the password is set, you then shut down the `mysql` server with the following command:

```
> mysqladmin --user=root --password=your_password shutdown
```

Now that you can get the MySQL server up and running securely, you can experiment with some basic database administration issues. For more help getting up to speed with MySQL, check out *MySQL* by Michael Kofler (Apress, 2001).

After you've connected successfully, you can disconnect at any time by typing `QUIT` at the prompt or by pressing Ctrl+D:

```
mysql> QUIT
Bye
```

## *Issuing SQL Commands*

Run the following simple command that requests the current date from the server:

```
mysql> SELECT CURRENT_DATE;
```

Note the semicolon that ends the SQL statement. It should produce output something like the following:

```
+--------------+
| CURRENT_DATE |
+--------------+
| 2003-11-21   |
+--------------+
1 row in set (0.07 sec)
```

This query illustrates several points about the `mysql` tool:

- A command normally consists of a SQL statement followed by a semicolon; however, there are cases where the semicolon isn't needed. `QUIT`, mentioned earlier, is one of them.

- When you issue a command, it's sent to the server for execution. Any results are displayed in the form of a grid. The first row typically shows the names of the columns, and results from the query appear below.

- `mysql` shows how many rows were returned and how long the query took to execute as a rough idea of server performance.

You've just entered is a single-line command consisting of a single SQL statement, but more complex commands can comprise multiple statements. You can either add all the statements on a single line one after the other or enter them on multiple lines by simply pressing Enter before the typing the final semicolon. `mysql` indicates what's expected next by changing the prompt to one shown in Table 4-13.

*Table 4-13. MySQL Prompts*

| Prompt | Meaning |
|---|---|
| `mysql>` | Ready for new command |
| `->` | Waiting for next line of multiple-line command |
| `'>` | Waiting for next line, collecting a string that begins with a single quote |
| `">` | Waiting for next line, collecting a string that begins with a double quote |

## Using SQL Data Types

When you create a database table in your database, you must define the data type for each column, along with the lengths of any strings where appropriate. The data types that MySQL supports for columns may be grouped into three categories:

- Numeric
- Date and time
- String

### Using Numeric Data Types

Table 4-14 shows the numeric data types.

*Table 4-14. Numeric Data Types*

| Data Types | Description | Range/Format |
|---|---|---|
| INT | Normal-sized integer | ($-2^{31}$ to $2^{31}$-1), or (0 to $2^{32}$ -1) if UNSIGNED |
| TINYINT | Very small integer | ($-2^{7}$ to $2^{7}$-1), or (0 to $2^{8}$ -1) if UNSIGNED |
| SMALLINT | Small integer | ($-2^{15}$ to $2^{15}$-1), or (0 to $2^{8}$ -1) if UNSIGNED |
| MEDIUMINT | Medium-sized integer | ($-2^{23}$ to $2^{23}$-1), or (0 to $2^{24}$ -1) if UNSIGNED |
| BIGINT | Large integer | ($-2^{63}$ to $2^{63}$-1), or (0 to $2^{64}$-1) if UNSIGNED |
| FLOAT | Single-precision floating-point number | Minimum nonzero $\pm1.176\times310^{-38}$; maximum nonzero $\pm3.403\times310^{+38}$ |
| DOUBLE/REAL | Double-precision floating-point number | Minimum nonzero $\pm2.225\times310^{-308}$; maximum nonzero $\pm1.798\times310^{+308}$ |
| DECIMAL | Float stored as string | Maximum range as DOUBLE |

Note that INT is an alias for INTEGER, and you can use them interchangeably.

### Using Date/Time Data Types

Table 4-15 shows the date/time data types.

*Table 4-15. Date/Time Data Types*

| Data Types | Description | Range/Format |
|---|---|---|
| DATE | A date | YYYY-MM-DD format. The range is from 1000-01-01 to 9999-12-31. |
| DATETIME | A date and time | YYYY-MM-DD hh:mm:ss format. The range is from 1000-01-01 00:00:00 to 9999-12-31 23:59:59. |
| TIMESTAMP | A time stamp | YYYYMMDDhhmmss format. The range is from 19700101000000 to sometime in 2037. |
| TIME | A time | hh:mm:ss format. The range is from -838:59:59 to 838:59:59. |
| YEAR | A year | YYYY format. The range is from 1900 to 2155. |

### *Using Character Data Types*

Table 4-16 shows the character data types.

*Table 4-16. Character Data Types*

| Data Types | Description | Range/Format |
|---|---|---|
| CHAR | Fixed-length string | 0–255 characters. |
| VARCHAR | Variable-length string | 0–255 characters. |
| BLOB | Binary Large Object (BLOB) | Binary data 0–65535 bytes long. |
| TINYBLOB | Small BLOB value | Binary data 0–255 bytes long. |
| MEDIUMBLOB | Medium-sized BLOB | Binary data 0–16777215 bytes long. |
| LONGBLOB | Large BLOB value | Binary data 0–4294967295 bytes long. |
| TEXT | Normal-sized text field | 0–65535 bytes. |
| TINYTEXT | Small text field | 0–255 bytes. |
| MEDIUMTEXT | Medium-sized text | 0–16777215 bytes. |
| LONGTEXT | Large text field | 0–4294967295 bytes. |
| ENUM | Enumeration | Column values are assigned one value from a set list. |
| SET | Set value(s) | Column values are assigned zero or more values from a set list. |

As Table 4-16 shows, MySQL offers two ways of storing strings, `CHAR` and `VARCHAR`. The difference between them is that `CHAR` is ***fixed-width***, and `VARCHAR` is ***variable-width***. Suppose you had two columns set to a size of 20 characters, `name1` and `name2`, of type `CHAR` and `VARCHAR`, respectively. If you entered the name *Bob* into both of them and then retrieved the values, `name2` would return exactly *Bob*—those three letters and nothing more. However, `name1` would return this string followed by 17 spaces: *Bob*                 . So, what are `TEXT` fields? Suffice to say that they behave like `VARCHAR`s except that they're specified in bytes instead of characters and have certain limitations when it comes to querying data.

## Using SQL Modifiers

You can apply certain modifiers to a column to further define its properties, a few of which are specific to MySQL. Table 4-17 shows the most common modifiers.

*Table 4-17. SQL Modifiers*

| Modifier | Description |
|---|---|
| AUTO_INCREMENT | Allows a numeric column to be automatically updated when records are added. Useful for creating a unique identification number for each row. |
| DEFAULT *value* | Specifies the default value for a column. |
| NULL | Specifies that a column may contain undefined, or NULL, values. |
| NOT NULL | Requires that the column must contain a non-NULL value. |
| PRIMARY KEY | Makes the column the primary key. It must also have a NOT NULL modifier. |

The next task is to use this information to create a MySQL database and tables. You'll first familiarize yourself with the necessary SQL statements.

## Creating Databases and Tables with SQL

You'll start with an example of creating a SQL database. You'll use the database you create here, publish, throughout the remainder of the book, so make sure you set it up as described here.

### *Trying It Out: Creating a Sample Database*

To create the sample database, follow these steps:

1. The CREATE DATABASE statement creates an entirely new empty database. You must be the administrative user (the root user) for MySQL to be able to use this statement. Open the mysql prompt, and run the following command to create the sample database, which is called publish:

```
mysql> CREATE DATABASE publish;
```

2. To check that you created the database successfully, list all of the databases in MySQL with the following command:

```
mysql> SHOW DATABASES;
```

You should see the following output:

```
+----------+
| Database |
+----------+
| mysql    |
| publish  |
| test     |
+----------+
3 rows in set (0.00 sec)
```

3. While you're here, you can remove a database using the `DROP DATABASE` command:

```
mysql> DROP DATABASE publish;
```

Feel free to try this, but if you do, make sure to re-create the `publish` database by running the `CREATE DATABASE` command again.

4. It isn't good practice to use your `root` account for general database access, so you'll create a new user named **publish** for use with these examples:

```
C:\mysql\bin>   mysql --user=root -password=your_password
mysql>      grant all privileges
mysql>      on publish.*
mysql>      to publishuser@localhost
mysql>      identified by 'secret';
```

5. Now you have a database, but it contains no tables as yet. Before you can add them, though, you have to tell `mysql` to work with your database using the `USE` command:

```
mysql> USE publish;
```

The *Database changed* message will tell you that your change was successful.

6. Now you use the `CREATE TABLE` statement to define the structure for new tables in the database. This statement consists of the name of the new table followed by the list of each column in the new table. The list provides the name of the column followed by its data type and then any modifiers (as described earlier). The definition for each column is separated from the next by a comma, and the whole list is enclosed in parentheses.

7. You'll create a text file (`book.sql`) for the table definition and then run it through MySQL. This allows you to create a table on your test machine and then transfer it to another machine. Now go ahead and create the file like so:

   ```
   CREATE TABLE book (
   ```

8. The first column you want is an `ID` field, which will be used as the primary key for the table, so it must be unique (and not null). This is an ideal candidate for the `AUTO_INCREMENT` modifier:

   ```
   id INTEGER NOT NULL AUTO_INCREMENT PRIMARY KEY,
   ```

9. Now you want a few strings for the title, author, and editor details. Only the title is required, so you use the `NOT NULL` modifier:

   ```
   title VARCHAR(50) NOT NULL,
     authors VARCHAR(50),
     editor VARCHAR(50),
   ```

10. Lastly, add some other fields you'll need later in this book:

    ```
    chapters TEXT,
     page_count INTEGER,
     status CHAR(1) NOT NULL);
    ```

    If you're wondering where the `price` field is, don't worry; you'll come to that in a moment.

11. To run the script, type the following at the `mysql` prompt (with the correct path to your `book.sql` script):

    ```
    mysql> \. ./book.sql
    ```

12. You can use the `SHOW TABLES` command to check that your `Book` table is in your database:

    ```
    mysql> SHOW TABLES;
    ```

You should see something like this:

```
+-------------------+
| Tables_in_publish |
+-------------------+
| book              |
+-------------------+
1 row in set (0.00 sec)
```

13. You can then see the structure of book with the following:

```
mysql> DESCRIBE book;
```

You should see the following:

```
+------------+-------------+------+-----+---------+----------------+
| Field      | Type        | Null | Key | Default | Extra          |
+------------+-------------+------+-----+---------+----------------+
| id         | int(11)     |      | PRI | NULL    | auto_increment |
| title      | varchar(50) |      |     |         |                |
| authors    | varchar(50) | YES  |     | NULL    |                |
| editor     | varchar(50) | YES  |     | NULL    |                |
| chapters   | text        | YES  |     | NULL    |                |
| page_count | int(11)     | YES  |     | NULL    |                |
| status     | char(1)     |      |     |         |                |
+------------+-------------+------+-----+---------+----------------+
7 rows in set (0.00 sec)
```

## Altering Tables

As you develop new applications, a fairly common requirement you'll encounter is the need to modify a table that has already been created by you—or by some other developer before you. You do so using the ALTER TABLE statement, which lets you add, change, rename, or remove columns from an existing table.

### *Trying It Out: Changing the Structure of an Existing Table*

To change the structure of the table, follow these steps:

1. First you'll add the price field to the table, using the ADD command and specifying the properties of the field:

```
mysql> ALTER TABLE book ADD (price INTEGER);
```

So here you've added a field called price that contains integer values.

2. Why would you represent price as an integer when a decimal would seem much more logical? Well, it was a deliberate mistake, so remove this field using the `DROP` command:

   ```
   mysql> ALTER TABLE book DROP price;
   ```

3. Now add the field again, but this time as a decimal field, with a maximum of five characters, two of which are after the decimal point:

   ```
   mysql> ALTER TABLE book ADD (prize DECIMAL(5,2));
   ```

4. Whoops, another boo-boo. This time, the data type of the field is correct (a decimal field), but the name of the field is wrong. Modify the field using the `CHANGE` command, rather than deleting it and creating a new one:

   ```
   mysql> ALTER TABLE book CHANGE prize price DECIMAL(5,2);
   ```

   At last, the field is just how you want it. Note that you had to specify all of the properties of the new field when you used the `CHANGE` command, even though you just wanted to change the field name.

5. You should know about a couple of other SQL commands used with `ALTER TABLE`. The first is the `ALTER` command for changing field definitions. For instance, if you wanted to set the `status` field to a default value of `P` for published, you could use the following:

   ```
   mysql> ALTER TABLE book ALTER status SET DEFAULT 'P';
   ```

6. The other command is `MODIFY`, which can change the entire definition of a particular field. Say, to be awkward, you wanted to change the `price` field back into an integer field. Then you could use the following:

   ```
   mysql> ALTER TABLE book MODIFY price INTEGER;
   ```

   If you try this last command, change the field back to a decimal afterward because you'll need it to be that type when you start inserting data.

## Manipulating the Database

You now have the database set up, but it's not that useful without any data, so you'll now move on to see how to add some records.

## Inserting Data into Tables

Now that you've created the table, you need to add the data about your books to it. To do this, you need to use the `INSERT INTO...VALUES` command.

This command inserts the column values given in parentheses after `VALUES` into the table named after `INTO`. You'll see it in action on your sample database.

### *Trying It Out: Inserting Data*

To insert data, follow these steps:

1. For example, to insert data for a book titled *Lord of the Things*, you'd enter the following:

   ```
   mysql> INSERT INTO book (title, price) VALUES
           -> ('Lord of the Things', 9.99);
   ```

   Note that you specify the fields (or columns) that are to be populated by this command after the table name and then list the values for these fields in the same order. All fields and values are separated by commas, and strings are delimited by single or double quotes.

2. To check that the data has been placed in your table correctly, run the following command:

   ```
   mysql> SELECT id, title, price, status FROM book;
   ```

   This should display something similar to this:

   ```
   +----+--------------------+-------+--------+
   | id | title              | price | status |
   +----+--------------------+-------+--------+
   |  1 | Lord of the Things |  9.99 |   P    |
   +----+--------------------+-------+--------+
   ```

   Notice that as an auto-increment field, the `id` column has automatically been set to `1` for this first record. Also, the `status` column has the value `P` because this is the default you set earlier.

3. Now you'll add details for another couple of books. You can insert more than one record at a time by giving more than one set of values, each separated by commas. Run the following SQL command:

```
mysql> INSERT INTO book (title, price) VALUES
    -> ('Mr Bunny\'s Guide to JDO', 14.99),
    -> ('Parachuting for You and Your Kangaroo', 19.99);
```

Notice that the first of these two books demonstrates a title string that contains a single quote character. You can't use a quote character as is because MySQL would assume that you're finishing the string at that point and return an error when it came to the rest of our string.

To get around this, you have to use *escape characters*, where you precede the quote with a backslash character (\) to make `\'`. Astute readers might be wondering what you'd do if your book title contained the sequence `\'`. You'd then need to use the `\\` escape character for the backslash, followed by the one for the single quote, to make `\\\'` altogether. Alternatively, you could simply change your string to use double quotes at either end because as long as the type of quotes (single or double) surrounding the string is different from those inside it, there won't be any confusion.

4. Check that all three books have been added as expected by running the same `SELECT` statement you used in step 2. Note how the `id` field is incremented for each new record.

## *Querying the Database*

As you were inserting data into your database, you checked that new records had been correctly using the SQL `SELECT` statement to query the database. You'll now have a closer look at the command you ran:

```
mysql> SELECT id, title, price, status FROM book;
```

Running this command produces output something like this:

```
+----+-----------------------------------------+-------+--------+
| id | title                                   | price | status |
+----+-----------------------------------------+-------+--------+
|  1 | Lord of the Things                      |  9.99 |   P    |
|  1 | Mr Bunny's Guide to JDO                 | 14.99 |   P    |
|  1 | Parachuting for You and Your Kangaroo   | 19.99 |   P    |
+----+-----------------------------------------+-------+--------+
3 rows in set (0.04 sec)
```

The command asks for the columns called id, title, price, and status for all rows in the Book table. The general form for a SELECT statement that retrieves all of the rows in the table is as follows:

```
> SELECT Column1Name, .... , ColumnXName FROM TableName;
```

There's also a special form that returns *all* columns from a table, without you having to type the name for every column:

```
> SELECT * FROM TableName;
```

If you run this, you'll see that other columns for which you didn't specify a value are set to NULL.

> **NOTE** *As a rule, you should avoid using* SELECT * FROM *except for testing or debugging purposes, unless you really do need every column from the table. Performance will be enhanced if you request only those fields you actually intend to use. Additionally,* SELECT * *offers no control over the order of the returned fields because they're returned in the order in which they were declared in the* CREATE TABLE *statement.*

When retrieving data with a SELECT query, you can order the returned rows by adding an ORDER BY clause to the command. The ORDER BY statement is followed by the column that you want to sort on, and finally you specify whether to order highest to lowest (a descending sort as indicated by DESC) or lowest to highest (an ascending sort, as indicated by ASC). ASC is the default sort, so it's assumed if neither DESC nor ASC is specified. For instance, the following command displays books in order of price, highest price first:

```
mysql> SELECT price, title FROM book
        -> ORDER BY price DESC;
```

You'll see something like this:

```
+-------+------------------------------------------+
| price | title                                    |
+-------+------------------------------------------+
|  9.99 | Lord of the Things                       |
| 14.99 | Mr Bunny's Guide to JDO                  |
| 19.99 | Parachuting for You and Your Kangaroo    |
+-------+------------------------------------------+
```

You'll see that the column order has changed because of how you've ordered the column names in the SELECT statement.

### *Modifying Data*

You've already seen how to modify the structure of existing tables, so now you'll look at modifying the data that your tables contain using the `UPDATE...SET` command. When using this syntax, you simply specify the table where you want to change column values after the `UPDATE` statement and specify which column or columns are to be affected after the `SET` statement.

Hence, you could change the `status` column for all books to `0` (for *out of stock*) using this command:

```
mysql> UPDATE book SET status = '0';
```

You should see a confirmation that all three rows in the table were affected by the command, and you can verify that by executing the `SELECT` statement you used earlier.

> **NOTE** *Likewise, you could use an* `UPDATE` *to modify the* `title` *or any other fields. Note that it isn't a good idea to modify the* `id` *field once you've set it. Changing a primary key field could impact other parts of your system that rely on the* `id` *keeping the same value, such as maintaining referential integrity.*

### *Using the WHERE Clause*

Although the `UPDATE` command you've just seen is a quick way to change all values for a given column or set of columns in a table, you generally want to change only certain rows. To specify criteria that rows must match for a command to be applied, you append a `WHERE` clause.

For instance, the following command would change the price of the book with an ID of `1` to $8.99:

```
mysql> UPDATE book SET price = 8.99 WHERE id = 1;
```

Run it now and see. Can you guess what SQL command you should use to retrieve the following information for just that book?

```
+----+---------------------------------------------+-------+
| id | title                                       | price |
+----+---------------------------------------------+-------+
|  1 | Lord of the Things                          |  8.99 |
+----+---------------------------------------------+-------+
```

You simply use the same WHERE clause on a SELECT statement:

```
mysql> SELECT id, title, price FROM book WHERE id = 1;
```

### Deleting Data

To delete a given row or set of rows, you use the DELETE FROM...WHERE command. For instance, you can delete the book called *Mr Bunny's Guide to JDO* with this command:

```
mysql> DELETE FROM book
         -> WHERE title = "Mr Bunny's Guide to JDO";
```

Now execute a SELECT command to retrieve all books from the table, and you'll see that the record for that book no longer appears:

```
+----+------------------------------------------+-------+
| id | title                                    | price |
+----+------------------------------------------+-------+
|  1 | Lord of the Things                       |  8.99 |
|  3 | Parachuting for You and Your Kangaroo    | 19.99 |
+----+------------------------------------------+-------+
```

**NOTE** *Be careful when using* DELETE *because once a row is removed, it's lost forever. Hence, be particularly wary when specifying a nonunique column in the* WHERE *clause, such as you have here. In your small database, you know that only a single row will be deleted, but in a real-world database, you can easily end up accidentally deleting a whole bunch of records if you use a badly thought-out* WHERE *clause. You can reduce the chances of this happening by specifying a* WHERE *clause on a uniquely valued field (such as a primary key).*

We've now covered enough of the basics of the SQL syntax to move on and show how you can use it to access databases in a JSP page.

## Displaying Data Using the JSTL SQL Tags

Chapter 2 introduced you to the JSP Standard Tag Library (JSTL). The JSTL is divided into four functional groupings, one of which is the SQL tag library for querying a database and performing inserts and updates. In the following sections, you'll apply what you've learned about SQL to a simple JSP page that displays the information in the `Book` table.

> **NOTE** *Placing SQL commands directly in your JSP code can be a maintenance nightmare in the long run. JSP pages that make direct SQL calls are useful for debugging and simple applications, but see Chapter 10 for information about the MVC pattern for a more robust way of associating databases, JSP pages, and servlets.*

### *Trying It Out: Querying Data with the JSTL*

To query data with the JSTL, follow these steps:

1. Create a new Web application folder called **DataAccess** inside Tomcat's `webapps` folder. Create a folder inside it named **WEB-INF**.

2. Next you need to give your Web application access to the JSTL by copying the JSTL `lib` folder into `WEB-INF`, just as you did in the previous chapter. Be sure to copy the entire `lib` folder, not just its contents.

3. You also need to make the MySQL JDBC classes available, which you can find at `http://www.mysql.com/downloads/api-jdbc-stable.html`. Once you've downloaded the file, unzip it and copy `mysql-connector-java-3.0.9-bin.jar` into your `webapps` folder's `WEB-INF/lib` directory (the filename may be slightly different if a newer version has been released).

4. Create the following JSP page in the `DataAccess` folder as **bookList.jsp**:

```
<%@ taglib prefix="c" uri="http://java.sun.com/jstl/core_rt" %>
<%@ taglib prefix="sql" uri="http://java.sun.com/jstl/sql_rt" %>

<sql:setDataSource var="datasource"
                driver="com.mysql.jdbc.Driver"
                   url="jdbc:mysql://localhost/publish"
                  user="publishuser" password="secret"/>

<sql:query var="books" dataSource="${datasource}">
  SELECT id, title, price FROM book
</sql:query>
```

```
<html>
  <head>
    <title>A First JSP Database</title
  </head>
  <body>
    <table border="1">
      <tr>
        <td>id</td><td>title</td><td>price</td>
      </tr>
<c:forEach items="${books.rows}" var="row">
      <tr>
        <td><c:out value="${row.id}" /></td>
        <td><c:out value="${row.title}" /></td>
        <td><c:out value="${row.price}" /></td>
      </tr>
</c:forEach>
    </table>
  </body>
</html>
```

5. **Start Tomcat.**

6. **Start a Web browser, and navigate to http://localhost:8080/DataAccess/bookList.jsp. You'll see a page like the one shown in Figure 4-1.**

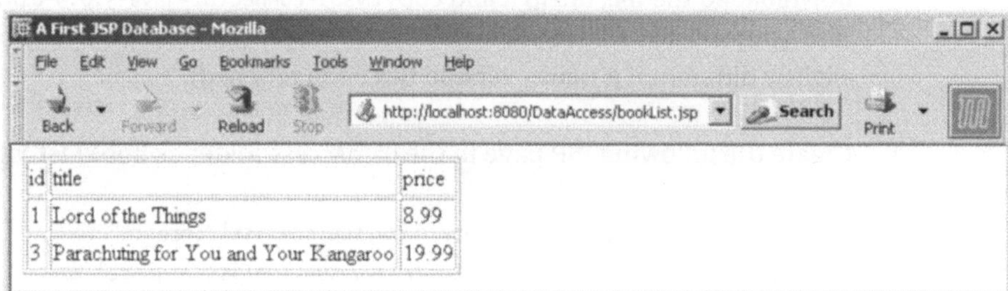


*Figure 4-1. Data access with JSP*

### How It Works

You first declared the core and sql libraries so they'll be available to you in the page. This should look familiar from the examples in Chapter 2.

Before you can issue a query, you'll need to make a connection to the database using <sql:setDataSource />. You declare the JDBC driver you're using, the url where the database is located, and your username and password combination.

The JDBC driver and uniform resource locator (URL) will be the same no matter where in your Java applications you use them (well, the URL could be different if your application isn't running on the same machine as the database). And, of course, you'll need to use a username and password that has read and write permissions. If your application won't do any inserts or updates, you should configure a user without these permissions and use this new user for your application:

```
mysql>     grant select
mysql>     on publish.*
mysql>     to publishuser@localhost
mysql>     identified by 'secret';
```

The resulting JDBC data source is assigned to the variable `var`, which you've named `datasource` (aptly enough). In JDBC, all queries (including inserts and updates) are performed against a data source. There are several ways to obtain a data source for use, and you'll see some other ways later in this book.

A familiar SQL query appears in the body of the `<sql:query />` tag. Because all queries must be performed against a data source, you assign the `dataSource` and declare that the resulting data be held by a variable `var`, named `books`. Unlike with the examples using the `mysql` command-line tool, you're responsible for handling the display of the data yourself.

> **NOTE** *JDBC queries return a resultset, a mechanism for holding each row of data returned by the query. If you're unfamiliar with the concept of looping (or iteration), consider it like flipping through a notepad where each page of the notepad represents a row from the database. Each page (or row) contains one set of data for that entry: In this example, the "page" contains an* `id`, `title`, `price`, *and the other fields that you're currently ignoring.*

Now that you've loaded your `Book` data, you can display the data using the JSTL core tags. The JSTL provides the `<c:forEach />` tag for looping over data, which requires two arguments: the set of data to loop over and the variable that will hold each row of data, represented as `items` and `var`, respectively (to be strictly accurate, these two arguments aren't required but are one possible set of options). Chapter 5 covers looping with the JSTL in more detail; for now, just rest assured that it's used to present each row of data. Once each row is assigned to the variable `row`, the fields of data can be accessed directly by column name as you see in the `<c:out />` tags.

Hold on to your hats because next you'll look at using JSTL tags to insert information into your database.

## Manipulating Data with JSTL SQL Tags

To create or edit data, you'll use another JSTL tag. As you saw previously, you edit data using an UPDATE query. Developers have a strange passion for granting objects the most obvious of names (well, good developers do), so the JSTL tag you'll use is the <sql:update> tag. That said, perhaps you're expecting to see <sql:insert> and <sql:delete> tags, but they don't exist; <sql:update> is used for all three operations. For example:

```
<sql:update>INSERT INTO book (title, price) VALUES (?, ?)
  <sql:param value="${param.title}" />
  <sql:param value="${param.price}" />
</sql:update>
```

If you've used SQL and JDBC in the past, the INSERT statement will look familiar. If not, you may be wondering about the question marks in the previous query. The <sql:update /> tag acts like a prepared statement, into which the <sql:param /> tags insert their values in order of appearance. Look again, and you'll see param.title and param.price specified in the same order as in the insert. You'll learn more about prepared statements later in Chapter 12.

The use of ${param.title} should be familiar to you from the previous chapter because it's the Expression Language syntax for getting the value for the new title from the request, which is then inserted into the stored procedure (and then into the database).

### *Trying It Out: Inserting Data with the JSTL*

You learned about HTML form handling in the previous chapter, so you'll create a form that will allow users to insert new books into your database. Follow these steps:

1. Create the following JSP page as **bookList2.jsp**:

```
<%@ taglib prefix="c" uri="http://java.sun.com/jstl/core_rt" %>
<%@ taglib prefix="sql" uri="http://java.sun.com/jstl/sql_rt" %>

<sql:setDataSource var="datasource"
     driver="com.mysql.jdbc.Driver"
     url="jdbc:mysql://localhost/publish"
     user="publishuser" password="secret" />
```

```
<c:if test="${param.title != null}">
    <sql:update dataSource="${datasource}">
      INSERT INTO book (title, price) VALUES(?, ?)
      <sql:param value="${param.title}" />
      <sql:param value="${param.price}" />
    </sql:update>
</c:if>

<sql:query var="books" dataSource="${datasource}">
  SELECT id, title, price FROM book
</sql:query>
<html>
  <head>
      <title>A First JSP Database</title
  </head>
  <body>
    <form method="post">
      <table border="1">
        <tr>
        <td>id</td><td>title</td><td>price</td>
        </tr>
<c:forEach var="row" items="${books.rows}">
        <tr>
          <td><c:out value="${row.id}" /></td>
          <td><c:out value="${row.title}" /></td>
          <td><c:out value="${row.price}" /></td>
        </tr>
</c:forEach>
        <tr>
          <td> </td>
          <td><input type="text" name="title" size="30" /></td>
          <td><input type="text" name="price" size="5" /></td>
        </tr>
        <tr>
          <td colspan="3" align="center">
          <input type="submit" value="Save New Book" />
          </td>
        </tr>
      </table>
    </form>
  </body>
</html>
```

2. In your Web browser, navigate to `http://localhost:8080/DataAccess/bookList2.jsp`. It looks pretty similar to how it did before, except the last row in the table now lets you add new book details, as shown in Figure 4-2.

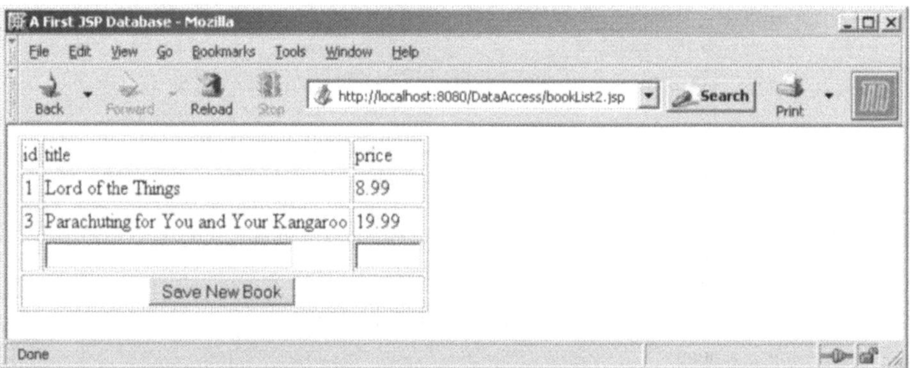

*Figure 4-2. A form to add a book*

3. Enter a title and price (including the decimal point), and click Save New Book. Notice that you don't have to explicitly set the ID of the new book because that field is set to `AUTO_INCREMENT`, so MySQL assigns the "next available" number as the value of the new row's `id` column.

4. Even though you've already deleted the row that had an ID of `2`, the database doesn't take the deleted record's ID as available. MySQL has kept track of the last value it assigned as a book's ID and considers the next available number to be `4`, as shown in Figure 4-3.

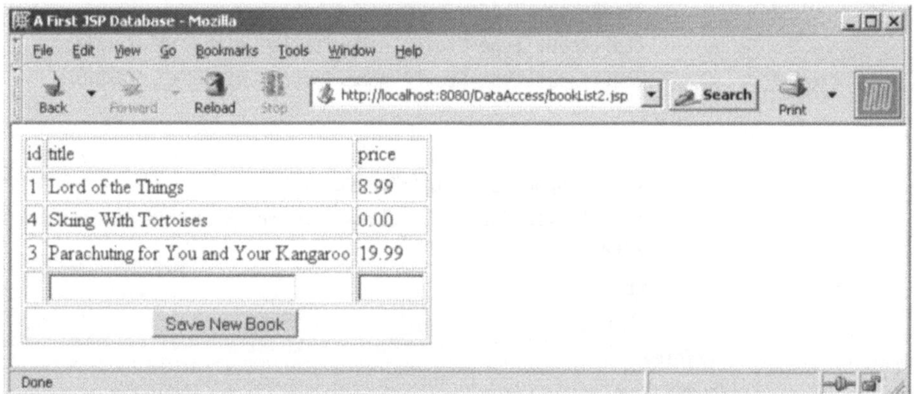

*Figure 4-3. A new book has been added.*

### *How It Works*

The `taglib` declaration should be familiar by now, and you saw the `<sql:setDataSource>` tag in the first example. You'll repeat that code here.

The `<c:if>` tag lets you apply the standard conditional logic: "If the test is true, then perform the following actions." Chapter 5 covers this in detail. You'll use it here to prevent the page from trying to `INSERT` a new record when someone is just viewing (that is, the submit button hasn't been clicked). This prevents the page from causing an error by attempting to insert "blank" entries into the `book` table because both of these fields are declared `NOT NULL` (meaning *some* value has to be entered).

Inside the `<c:if>` tag, you have the same `INSERT` code shown earlier. This checks the request, and if a title has been submitted, it creates an `INSERT` query to be executed.

Next you reload the books for display. Because this happens after the `INSERT` query, your new book should show up in the list.

Now add the HTML form tags (again, see Chapter 2) that allow the user to enter a title and price, and you've got the means by which to enter your new books.

Now you have the core of a library management system. You can view the books in your "library," and add more as you please—all by using a few simple JSP pages! The power of the JSTL should be readily apparent, and you've had but a taste. Thirsting for more?

## Revisiting the Pizza Application

Now that you can insert data into a database, you'll complete the pizza application. The pizza shop will need to see all the orders once they've been placed. The best place to store them is in a database.

### *Trying It Out: Creating a Backend for the Pizza Application*

You first need a sensible database design. Each order is fairly straightforward, but it may contain more than one topping. Including the whole order for each topping breaks the rules of normalization, as shown in Table 4-18 (other details are removed for clarity).

*Table 4-18. The Orders*

| Order_ID | Name | Address | Topping |
|---|---|---|---|
| 1 | Matt Moodie | 1 The Street | Peppers |
| 1 | Matt Moodie | 1 The Street | Sweetcorn |
| 2 | Ben Galbraith | 10 The Road | Peppers |

Because including the customer's details every time also breaks the rules of normalization, you'll use a `pizza.order` table, a `customer` table, and a `topping` table, as shown in Table 4-19, Table 4-20, and Table 4-21, respectively.

*Table 4-19. The* `pizza.order` *Table*

| Order_ID | Customer_ID |
|---|---|
| 1 | 1 |
| 2 | 2 |

*Table 4-20. The* `customer` *Table*

| Customer_ID | Name | Address |
|---|---|---|
| 1 | Matt Moodie | 1 The Street |
| 2 | Ben Galbraith | 1 The Road |

*Table 4-21. The* `topping` *Table*

| Order_ID | Topping |
|---|---|
| 1 | Peppers |
| 1 | Sweetcorn |
| 2 | Peppers |

So, follow these steps:

1. Create a new database called **pizza** with all permissions granted.

2. Create the `pizza.sql` file as follows:

```
CREATE TABLE pizza.order (
  order_id INTEGER NOT NULL AUTO_INCREMENT PRIMARY KEY,
  customer_id INTEGER NOT NULL,
  delivery VARCHAR(13),
  size VARCHAR(6),
  status CHAR(1) DEFAULT '0' NOT NULL);

CREATE TABLE customer (
  customer_id INTEGER NOT NULL AUTO_INCREMENT PRIMARY KEY,
  name VARCHAR(50) NOT NULL,
  address TEXT NOT NULL);

CREATE TABLE topping (
   order_id INTEGER NOT NULL,
   topping VARCHAR(13) NOT NULL,
   PRIMARY KEY (order_id, topping)
);
```

   You've used a compound primary key for the `topping` table to make sure every record is unique. The status of the order is `0` (for *open*) by default. Run this through MySQL using the `\. pizza.sql` command.

3. Modify `process.jsp` as follows. First you add the JSTL SQL tag library:

```
<%@ taglib uri="http://java.sun.com/jstl/core_rt" prefix="c" %>
<%@ taglib prefix="sql" uri="http://java.sun.com/jstl/sql_rt" %>
```

4. The `<sql:setDataSource>` tag is slightly different because this time you don't want to set the data source as a variable; you want to set it as the default for the whole page. You'll see why in step 6:

```
<sql:setDataSource
     driver="com.mysql.jdbc.Driver"
     url="jdbc:mysql://localhost/pizza"
     user="publishuser" password="secret" />
```

5. You now come to the SQL to insert your data into the database, which you want to do only if the form was submitted correctly:

```
...
<c:if test="${param.name eq '' or param.address eq ''}">
  ...
</c:if>
```

6. The sequence here is more complicated than you've seen before. You first start a transaction. A transaction allows you to have exclusive use of the database, and other processes must wait until you commit the transaction. Transactions are a large subject and best left for another book. For the moment, all you need to know is that no other orders can be written to the database while you're writing this one (they will wait until you finish so they're not lost). Note that a new data source can't be set during a transaction because you're already holding one for yourself. Therefore, you must use the default one as set previously:

```
<sql:transaction>
```

7. The first table you'll use is `customer`. You just insert the details of the customer. Remember that a new customer ID is created every time. A more realistic system would require the user to register and log in, so this step wouldn't be required every time:

```
<sql:update>
     INSERT INTO customer (name, address) VALUES(?, ?)
     <sql:param value="${param.name}" />
     <sql:param value="${param.address}" />
</sql:update>
```

8. Once the new customer has been created, you'd like to know their customer ID. You query the database to find out the highest customer ID because this corresponds to the user you just created. This is the reason for the transaction; if you allowed other orders to be placed, then you couldn't guarantee that the highest customer ID was the one for your order. The `MAX(column)` function returns the highest value in the specified `column`, and the `AS` keyword names the returned value appropriately. This makes your subsequent code more readable:

```
<sql:query var="customer_id" >
  SELECT MAX(customer_id) AS id FROM customer
</sql:query>
```

9. Now that you have the customer ID of this order, you can insert the order into the `pizza.order` table:

```
<sql:update >
  INSERT INTO pizza.order (customer_id, delivery, size) VALUES(?, ?, ?)
  <sql:param value="${customer_id.rows[0].id}" />
  <sql:param value="${param.purchaseType}" />
  <sql:param value="${param.size}" />
</sql:update>
```

10. You need the current order ID to complete the `topping` table, so you go through the same process as previously:

```
<sql:query var="order_id" >
  SELECT MAX(order_id) AS id FROM pizza.order
</sql:query>
```

11. You insert all the toppings chosen by the user into the `topping` table:

```
<c:forEach items="${paramValues.topping}" var="topping">
  <sql:update >
    INSERT INTO topping (order_id, topping) VALUES(?, ?)
    <sql:param value="${order_id.rows[0].id}" />
    <sql:param value="${topping}" />
  </sql:update>
</c:forEach>
```

12. Finally, you commit the transaction to complete all the changes. Other orders can now be inserted into the database:

```
</sql:transaction>
```

13. Restart Tomcat, point your browser to `http://localhost:8080/Pizza/pizza.html`, and fill in the form as before.

14. Now check the database to see the results using the following commands:

```
mysql> SELECT * FROM pizza.order;
mysql> SELECT * FROM customer;
mysql> SELECT * FROM topping;
```

It's a simple task to write a JSP page that displays all open orders for the pizza chefs. We'll leave that as an exercise for you.

---

## Why Not Try?

At this point you may be ready to try something a bit more complicated. The following are a few challenges to test what you've learned so far:

- How could you change the last example so that it can be used to close and order once it has been processed?

> **TIP** *You'll need to add a mechanism for selecting which order to close and use a* `DELETE` *query. Alternatively, you could use an* `UPDATE` *to change the status to allow closed orders to be examined later.*

- How could you revise the book example to allow users to update a book's title or price?

> **TIP** *You'll need to add a mechanism for selecting which book to edit and rewrite the SQL query as an update.*

- Change the book example to give each of the books an arbitrary value for `status` and show the `status` field on the HTML form, colored according to its value.

> **TIP** *You'll need to* `UPDATE` *each of your books with a status value. Then use the* `<tr>` *tag's* `color` *attribute to color each row dependent on each book's status value. You can make up your own status values and colors, or color* `P` *and* `O` *as "green" and "white," respectively.*

---

## Summary

This chapter has covered a lot of information; you first examined the fundamental concepts of relational databases, and then you installed and configured your own personal RDBMS—MySQL—and used it to create a books database. This demonstrated the basics of SQL queries, including how to add, remove, and read information from a database. Finally, you took a peek at how the JSTL provides a means to put that database to use in a JSP page.

CHAPTER 5

# Making Decisions, Decisions

**Only the most** simplistic JavaServer Pages (JSP) page can get away without needing to perform one of several actions according to some condition. These conditions control the flow that your code follows as it executes, and they do so through *control statements*. Such statements evaluate an expression to determine the condition and direct the flow of execution accordingly.

The kinds of program flow control you'll meet in this chapter are as follows:

- **Conditional statements**: Evaluating a condition in the program and executing code depending on whether the condition evaluates to "true" or "false"
- **Iterative statements**: Repeating (*looping* through) sections of code
- **Branching statements**: Transferring execution of the program to a particular section of the code

This chapter discusses the syntax Java provides for all of these and also presents the flow control constructs of the Java Standard Tag Library (JSTL). You'll also look at how Java lets you store and manipulate groups of variables of the same type using *arrays*. In short, the chapter covers the following:

- How to use arrays and when to use them
- How to compare values
- How to easily incorporate logic in your code
- The `if`, `if...else`, and `switch` statements
- The `while`, `do...while`, and `for` loops
- The `break`, `continue`, and `return` statements

In each case you'll learn about the standard Java techniques, followed by a JSTL example if appropriate.

## Introducing Arrays

Before learning about the important control statements, you'll look at how you can group variables of the same data type into arrays. This will allow you to see how combining control statements with arrays can make your code simpler and easier to manage.

So what exactly is an array? Well, imagine that your program needed a thousand `String` variables, each one storing a different value as follows:

```
String name1 = "Richmal";
String name2 = "Tobian";
String name3 = "Rozzle";
.
.
.
String name1000 = "Joey";
```

Remembering and managing them all would be troublesome to say the least! Also, there would more than likely be many situations where you'd need to perform the same action on every variable. Even something as simple as printing a list of all the names would require you to type the same code for each `String`:

```
myPrintMethod(name1);
myPrintMethod(name2);
myPrintMethod(name3);
.
.
.
myPrintMethod(name1000);
```

To address such situations, array variables allow many instances of a single data type to be grouped together, which greatly simplifies using groups of variables, as you'll see.

Arrays can contain groups of any of the basic primitive data types, such as `int`, `String`, `char`, and `float`, and they can also handle other data types such as user-defined objects. You can even have arrays of arrays (of arrays...)! Note, however, that you can't have an array of mixed data types—every element of an array must be of the same type.

### *Understanding Array Elements and Index Values*

Each variable in an array is known as an *element*. To be able to reference a particular element within the array, you use its *index*, which indicates the element's offset from the start of the array. The fact that array indices start at zero is a source of many programming errors, and you always need to remember that the first element has an index of zero (not one), the second has an index of one, the 15th has an index of 14, and so on.

## Creating Arrays

There are three steps when creating an array:

1. Declare.
2. Define.
3. Initialize.

The third step isn't always required, but the other two are necessary for an array to be usable.

### Declaring an Array

You declare an array by specifying the type of array elements followed by a pair of empty square brackets and finally the name of the array, like so:

```
int[] numbers;
```

The previous line declares an array of integers called `numbers`. However, you can place the square brackets after the array name, as in this example, which declares an array of strings called `names`:

```
String names[];
```

### Defining an Array

Before you can use an array you've declared, you need to *define* it by stating its size—the number of elements it'll contain. This step is necessary so that the correct amount of memory can be allocated for it. You use the `new` keyword to define an array, like so:

```
numbers = new int[4];
names = new String[1000];
```

Here, you've defined the `numbers` array as containing four elements and `names` as containing 1,000.

On definition, each of the elements in an array is set to the default value for that data type. The default value of any primitive data type (except boolean) in an array is zero, the default value for a boolean is false, and the default value for any `Object` type is `null`.

### Initializing and Resetting Array Values

The final step is to place initial values into your array elements. You can assign values to each of the elements individually, as follows:

```
numbers[0] = 39;
names[0] = "Chris";
```

The number between the brackets is the index of the element you want to populate.

You should note that you can *reset* the values contained by the elements in an array at any time during the array's lifetime in the same way. So if Chris changed his name to Kurt, you could reset the value of the second element of the `names` array using this:

```
names[0] = "Kurt";
```

### Creating an Array the Easy Way

There's no need to declare and define arrays in individual steps; you can perform all of these steps in a single line of code if you want. For instance, you can create an array of four integers with the values 39, 21, 8, and 93 with this line:

```
int[] numbers = {39, 21, 8, 93};
```

Note that Java uses the number of values provided as initialization to set the size of the array.

Finally, the easiest way to create a new array is to initialize it using an existing array. For instance, now that you've created the `numbers` array, you could use it to initialize a new array, `moreNumbers`:

```
int[] moreNumbers = numbers;
```

In this case, Java creates a new integer array, `moreNumbers`, that has the same number of elements as the `numbers` array, and each element of `moreNumbers` will contain the same value as the corresponding element of `numbers`.

On a JSP page, you could declare an array using this sort of code inside a scriptlet. Generally speaking, however, placing Java code in a JSP page is considered a "breach of contract." This "unwritten contract" states that JSP pages are for Hypertext Markup Language (HTML) and JSP tags, and Java objects are where code belongs. However, JSP actually provides you with arrays whenever data has been submitted to a page, whether using the `GET` or `POST` method (review Chapter 2), and the JSTL expression language provides a handy mechanism for getting these arrays, as you've already seen:

```
${ paramValues.book_id }
```

This will return a `String` array of the parameters called `book_id` that were submitted to the page. If there were only one `book_id` parameter, it'd be a `String` array whose size is one.

Now that you know about arrays, you can move on to control statements.

## Creating Multidimensional Arrays

So far, the arrays you've seen have had a single index value to access elements they contain. You can visualize them as simple lists of data items, where the index specifies the number of the required item in the list. Such arrays are known as *one-dimensional* because just one index can uniquely identify any one particular member (see Figure 5-1).

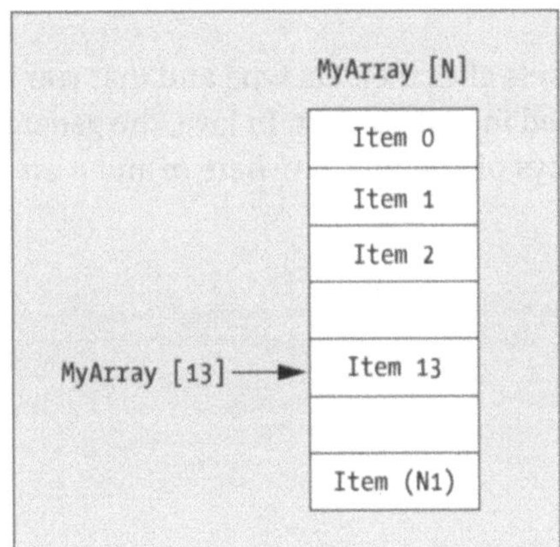


*Figure 5-1. A one-dimensional array*

However, arrays can have more than one dimension. For instance, a two-dimensional array has two indices. You can visualize such arrays as a set of pigeonholes, and to locate one specific pigeonhole, you need to know both how far from the left side it is, and how far down from the top it is (see Figure 5-2).

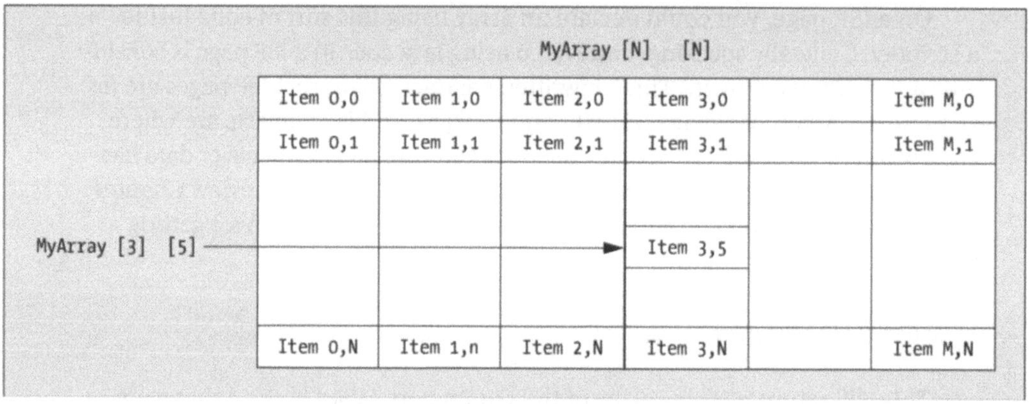

MyArray [N] [N]

| | | | | | | |
|---|---|---|---|---|---|---|
| | Item 0,0 | Item 1,0 | Item 2,0 | Item 3,0 | | Item M,0 |
| | Item 0,1 | Item 1,1 | Item 2,1 | Item 3,1 | | Item M,1 |
| MyArray [3] [5] → | | | | Item 3,5 | | |
| | Item 0,N | Item 1,n | Item 2,N | Item 3,N | | Item M,N |

*Figure 5-2. A two-dimensional array*

For instance, say you had two houses in your street, and each house had three occupants. You could store the names of the occupants in a two-dimensional `String` array, where the first index would indicate the house in question and the second one would indicate a particular occupant.

Creating a two-dimensional array is similar to creating an ordinary one-dimensional array:

```
String[][] houses = {
  { "Joey", "Tommy", "Podlington" },
  { "Pickles", "Scragg", "Floopy" },
};
```

Note that you need two empty brackets after the data type and that you initialize using a set of values each contained in curly braces. In Java, the general syntax for creating two-dimensional arrays of size $m \times n$ (where $m$ and $n$ are positive integers) is as follows:

```
DataType[][] array_variable_name = {
  { value1, value2, ..., valuen },
  { value1, value2, ..., valuen },
  .
  .
  .
  { value1, value2, ..., valuen }, // mth array of values
}
```

Referencing elements in a two-dimensional array is equally straightforward. For instance, you could find the name of the second member of the first house using `houses[0][1]` (don't forget that array indices always start at zero!). Also, you could indicate the whole of the first house using `houses[0]`. In other words, if you want to reference all occupants of the *m*th house, you'd use houses[*m*-*1*], and if you want to reference the *n*th occupant of the *m*th house, you'd use both indices: houses[*m*-*1*][*n*-*1*].

> **NOTE** *Another way to think of two-dimensional arrays is as an array of arrays—that is, as a one-dimensional array where each element is itself a one-dimensional array. Thus, when you access the array, the first index specifies which "subarray" to use, and the second index specifies the offset within that subarray.*

One thing to be aware of is that Java allows so-called jagged arrays. This is when the arrays within an array are of different length. For instance, if the two houses in the road had different numbers of occupants, you could use an array such as the following to store their names:

```
String[][] houses = {
  { "Joey", "Tommy", "Podlington" },
  { "Pickles", "Scragg", "Floopy", "Zuppo" },
};
```

As you can see, the first house has three occupants, and the second has four. In other words, houses[0].length will be three, and houses[1].length will be four.

As with one-dimensional arrays, you don't have to declare, define, and initialize an array at the same time. For example, you might not know how many occupants there are in the houses:

```
String[][] houses  = new String[2][];
```

Here, you've told Java that the first dimension of the newHouses array will contain two elements that will both be arrays. When you declare a two-dimensional array, you do have to declare at least the first (primary) array dimension. You can then specify the second index before use. Again, you can create jagged arrays in this fashion, as in the following example:

```
String[][] houses = new String[2][];
houses[0] = new String[3];

houses[0][0] = "Joey";
houses[0][1] = "Tommy";
houses[0][2] = "Podlington";

houses[1] = new String[4];
```

```
houses[1][0] = "Pickles";
houses[1][1] = "Scragg";
houses[1][2] = "Floopy";
houses[1][3] = "Zuppo";
```

Now, you'll finish the chapter by looking at a common task when working with arrays: sorting.

## Sorting Arrays

The standard Java package `java.util` contains a class called `Arrays` that provides a range of methods for array handling. It has methods for searching an array, for comparing arrays, and so on. One method of this class, `Arrays.sort()`, provides a way of sorting the elements of an array. For full details of this class, see the documentation at `http://java.sun.com/j2se/1.4.1/docs/api/java/util/Arrays.html`.

The `sort()` method sorts an array according to the ***natural ordering*** of the data type held in the array. Natural ordering is the name given to the default ordering for a particular data type. For example, the natural order for integers is ascending numerical order, and for strings, it's ascending alphabetic order.

For example, if you have an integer array containing five values:

```
int[] sortme = {25, 32, 19, 27, 24};
```

and you printed this array using a loop such as this:

```
for(int i = 0; i < sortme.length; i++)
  System.out.println(ages[i]);
```

then you'd expect to see the following:

25

32

19

27

24

However, if you first sort the array and then print it like this:

```
Arrays.sort(sortme);
for(int i = 0; i < sortme.length; i++)
  System.out.println(ages[i]);
```

then the values would appear lowest first:

19

24

25

27

32

So what if you need to sort something *un*naturally? The `java.util` package also contains an interface called `Comparator`. If you implement the `compare` and `equals` methods of this interface, you could use another `Arrays.sort()` method, `Arrays.sort(Object[] array, Comparator c)`, to order elements according to a different pattern. Implementing comparators is beyond the scope of this book, but if you want to find out more, you can find a good book at `http://www.apress.com/category.html?nID=32`.

## Comparing Data Values

The data values being compared are known as *operands*, and these operands can be variables, constants, or expressions. The basic syntax for comparing two data values is as follows:

```
operand1  <relational_operator>  operand2
```

where `relational_operator` is one of those shown in Table 5-1. The table also shows the JSTL equivalents. In a JSTL tag, you're free to use either form of operator.

*Table 5-1. Relational Operators*

| Operator | JSTL | Operator Name | Explanation |
|---|---|---|---|
| `<` | `lt` | Less Than | Evaluates to `true` if `operand1` is less than `operand2`; otherwise `false` |
| `<=` | `le` | Less Than or Equal To | Evaluates to `true` if `operand1` is less than or equal to `operand2`; otherwise `false` |
| `>` | `gt` | Greater Than | Evaluates to `true` if `operand1` is greater than `operand2`; otherwise `false` |

*Table 5-1. Relational Operators (continued)*

| Operator | JSTL | Operator Name | Explanation |
|---|---|---|---|
| >= | ge | Greater Than or Equal To | Evaluates to `true` if `operand1` is greater than or equal to `operand2`; otherwise `false` |
| == | eq | Equal To | Evaluates to `true` if `operand1` is equal to `operand2`; otherwise `false` |
| != | ne | Not Equal To | Evaluates to `true` if `operand1` isn't equal to `operand2`; otherwise `false` |

## Using Logical Operators

These relational operators form the basis of all logical tests, and they can be combined into more complex tests using the logical operators listed in Table 5-2 to construct more complex expressions that consist of two or more conditions. Remember that operands can be values, variables, or expressions.

*Table 5-2. Logical Operators*

| Operator | Syntax | Explanation |
|---|---|---|
| \|\| | *operand1* \|\| *operand2* | This is the logical OR operator, which returns `true` if `operand1` *or* `operand2` is `true`. It only returns `false` if both the operands are `false`. It evaluates `operand2` only if `operand1` is `false`. |
| && | *operand1* && *operand2* | This is the logical AND operator, which returns `true` if `operand1` *and* `operand2` are `true`. In other words, if any of the operands are `false`, it returns `false`. Note that `operand2` is evaluated only if `operand1` is `true`. |
| ! | !*operand1* | Returns `true` if `operand1` is `false`. Else if `operand1` is `true`, it returns `false`. |

As an example, say an online store offers free shipping to customers who purchase four or more items of total value greater than $100. If you have a couple of variables that indicate number of items bought and total cost—called `itemCount` and `totalCost`, respectively—then the following expression will determine whether shipping is free:

```
itemCount >= 4 && totalCost >= 100
```

If you're going to be using this expression regularly, you can store the result in a boolean variable, say `freeShipping`:

```
freeShipping = (itemCount >= 4 && totalCost >= 100);
```

So for instance, if a customer buys six items and pays $130, then `freeShipping` will be `true`. Now say the store changes its policy so customers need to meet only one of the criteria (buying four or more items or spending $100 or more) to qualify for free shipping. You could implement this by simply changing the logical operator in the expression:

```
freeShipping = ((itemCount >= 10) || (totalCost >= 100));
```

Another example demonstrates the use of the complement operator, `!`, applied to an integer, `n`:

```
!(n >= 0)
```

In this case, when `n` is negative, the part of the expression within parentheses results in `false`. The `!` operator takes the complement of that to give the result of the expression as a whole—in other words, `true` when `n` is negative. Conversely, if `n` is zero or greater, then the part in brackets will be `true`, so the whole expression will evaluate to `false`. This expression is in effect just a more convoluted way of writing this:

```
n < 0
```

## Making Decisions

The things you've learned thus far—how to compare values and how to use Boolean logic to create more complex expressions (or "decisions")—are the basic tools for controlling the flow of a program. There are many situations where such expressions are useful, and you'll find few programming problems that don't require them at one point or another.

Most often, such expressions are combined with *control statements*, which are statements that control the flow of program execution. There are three basic kinds of control statement:

- **Conditional statements**: Here the statement is evaluated, and the code block executed depends upon the value returned by the statement.
- **Iterative statements**: The same block of code is executed again and again (*iterated*).
- **Branching statements**: The statement moves execution to a particular point within the code.

The following sections examine each of these in turn.

## Introducing Conditional Statements

While writing programs you continually come across situations where you need to evaluate a condition and proceed according to the result. Java has two main types of conditional statement:

- The `if` statement (and its variations)
- The `switch` statement

The main difference between the two is that an `if` statement requires an expression that results in either `true` or `false`, and `switch` allows one of many blocks of code to be executed, depending on the outcome of the expression.

### *Using the if Statement*

The following is an example of an `if` statement:

```
if ( itemQuantity > 0 )
{
  System.out.println("The Quantity is greater than 0");
  System.out.println("No. of items : " + itemQuantity);
}
```

In English, what this basically means is this: If the value of `itemQuantity` is greater than zero, then display the following:

The Quantity is greater than 0

No. of items :

followed by the value of `itemQuantity`.

Note that this `if` statement follows the general form of `if` statements:

```
if (expression)
{
  Statement Block
}
```

You may recognize the correspondence with the JSTL `<if>` tag that you've already used in earlier chapters' examples:

```
<c:if test="expression">
  Statement Block
</c:if>
```

The expression is evaluated first, and if it evaluates to `true`, the statement block (which consists of one or more Java statements) is executed. In a JSP page the statement block could consist of other tags (HTML or JSP tags) or even plain text.

Be aware that here you see the syntax using a statement block, as denoted by enclosing curly braces. Java doesn't require that statement blocks be used, and if only a single line is to be executed if the expression evaluates to `true`, the braces can be omitted, as follows:

```
if (itemQuantity > 0)
  System.out.println("The Quantity is greater than 0");
```

This practice is frowned upon because mistakes can be made unwittingly. For example, the author doesn't always maintain the code (they may have left the company, or it may not be their job). So, if the previous code were given to somebody else, that person may want to exit the program if the quantity is greater than zero:

```
if (itemQuantity > 0)
  System.out.println("The Quantity is greater than 0");
  System.exit(1);
```

However, the previous code will actually exit the program no matter what value is stored in `itemQuantity`. Braces are much safer:

```
if (itemQuantity > 0) {
  System.out.println("The Quantity is greater than 0");
  System.exit(1);
}
```

This applies to all other Java constructs, as well as `if`, with the exception of `do...while` loops. Note that this doesn't apply to the JSTL. The JSTL's `<if>` tag, for instance, always requires a closing tag:

```
<c:if test="expression">Statement Block</c:if>
```

This requirement is the same as numerous HTML tags, which also require a closing tag, such as the table (`<table></table>`), heading (`<h1></h1>`), and font (`<font></font>`) tags. Although most Web browsers are lenient about this rule, JSP tags aren't: You must supply the closing tag.

### Understanding the if...else Statement

You'll often find the `if` statement used in conjunction with `else`, which allows you to specify code that should be executed when the expression doesn't evaluate to `true`:

```
if (expression)
{
  Statement Block 1
}
else
{
  Statement Block 2
}
```

As before, the expression is evaluated first and if it results in `true`, then the first statement block is executed. If the expression isn't `true`, then the second statement block is executed instead.

The following is an example of the `if...else` statement that evaluates whether you have four or more items to ship. If this is the case, the customer incurs no shipping costs. If you have fewer than four items, you find the shipping cost by multiplying the number of items to ship by the cost of shipping an item:

```
if (itemQuantity >= 4)
{
  shippingCost = 0.0;
}
else
{
  shippingCost = basicShippingCost * itemQuantity;
}
```

So for orders of four or more items, the shippingCost variable will be set to zero. For fewer items than that, the cost will depend on the value of basicShippingCost and the total number of items ordered.

### Understanding the if...else if Statement

Many situations are a little more involved, and you don't simply want to execute one of two options depending on whether a single condition is true or false. For instance, the online store might offer several levels of discount to customers, depending on how much they spend. There might be no discount for purchases less than $100, but between $100 and $500 the customer gets 10 percent off and greater than $500 they get 15 percent off.

You can quite easily code such behavior in Java by simply placing further if statements for each else keyword, as follows:

```
if (expression1)
{
  Statement Block 1
}
else if (expression2)
{

Statement Block 2
}
.
.
More else if Blocks !
.
.
```

Here, the only statement block that will be evaluated will be the first one where the associated expression evaluates to true (and all previous expressions have come up as false).

Consider the following code snippet, where you test the value of the integer variable n against several possible values. You first check to see if it is less than zero (negative), then check if it's equal to zero, and finally check if it's greater than zero (positive):

```
int n = 10;

if (n < 0 )
{
  System.out.println("n is negative");
```

```
}
else if (n == 0)
{
  System.out.println("n is zero");
}
else if (n > 0)
{
  System.out.println("n is positive");
}
```

Because n is set to 10 at the start of the code snippet, the output will be that n is positive. This is a simple example, but it illustrates the flow of execution well enough for these purposes.

### Understanding Variable Scope in Statement Blocks

Before moving any further, it's time to throw in a cautionary note about variable scope and statement blocks. A statement block is a number of statements grouped together by being enclosed within two curly braces, {}. Look at the following code snippet:

```
int myVar1 = 100;
System.out.println(myVar1);

if (myVar1 > 0)
{
  int myVar2 = myVar1 * 2;

  System.out.println(myVar1);
  System.out.println(myVar2);
}
System.out.println(myVar2);
```

In this code, you create two integer variables called myVar1 and myVar2, set them to 100 and 200, respectively, and attempt to print them twice. Therefore, you might expect the execution of this code to result in the following:

```
100
100
200
200
```

Actually, attempting to print `myVar2` for the second time, once you're outside the statement block following the `if` statement, will result in a compiler error. This is because `myVar2` is declared *inside* the `if` statement block, so its scope is *local* to that block. Outside of the block, the variable doesn't actually exist, so an error is thrown. For this code to compile and run, you'd need to move the declaration of `myVar2` outside of the `if` block or alternatively remove the last `System.out` line.

You should note, however, that variables declared *outside* of the statement block may be used within the statement block as well, and you're able to access `myVar1` inside and outside of the `if` block.

You'll now put into practice what you've learned about conditional statements. Because of the way tag libraries work and variable scope, you can't simply add a tag after a JSTL `<if>` to provide `else` functionality; you have to turn to a different construct: the JSTL `<choose>...<when>` form.

### *Trying It Out: Working with the JSTL choose...when Construct*

You'll create a simple shopping cart where users enter the number of items they want to buy and then submit their order:

1. First, create a new folder under `webapps` to hold the pages you'll create in this chapter. Call the new directory **Decisions.** Then create a folder called **WEB-INF** within it, and then copy the JSTL `lib` folder inside that.

2. Then create a file called **whenexample.html** in your new directory. This file starts with the standard HTML opening tags:

```
<html>

  <head>
    <title>Chapter 5 Examples</title>
    <style type="text/css">
      .white {
        color: white;
      }
      .heading {
        background-color: #C0C0C0;
      }
    </style>
  </head>

  <body>
```

3. Now you start an HTML form. This is a neat way of getting data from users. When the user clicks the submit button (which you'll come to in a minute), all the data entered on the form can be sent off to a server for processing or sent to another page where it can affect the content of that page. You'll use the latter of these two options, and as the `action` attribute indicates, the second page is called `whenexamplehandler.jsp`:

```
<form method="POST" action="whenexamplehandler.jsp">
```

4. The form itself will be laid out as an HTML table with three columns:

```
 <table border="0" cellpadding="0" cellspacing="0" width="439">
        <tr>
          <td width="157"><b>Shopping Cart</b></td>
          <td width="128"></td>
          <td width="148"></td>
        </tr>
        <tr class="heading">
          <td class="white" width="157">
            Product
          </td>
          <td class="white" width="128">
            ListPrice
          </td>
          <td class="white" width="148">
            Quantity
          </td>
        </tr>
```

5. Each row of the table represents a single item available for purchase:

```
<tr>
  <td width="157">Beginning JSP</td>
  <td width="128">$49.99</td>
```

6. The last column is a textbox where users can enter the quantity they want to order:

```
  <td width="148">
    <input type="text" name="quantity" size="4" />
  </td>
</tr>
```

7. Then you close the table and set up the submit button for when the user has entered all the necessary details. This button uses the `POST` method to pass the form values to the destination given by the `<form>`'s `action` attribute:

```
  </table>
<p>
  <input type="submit" value="Place Order" name="PlaceOrderBtn"/>
</p>
```

8. Now you close the other HTML tags, and you're done with the HTML file:

```
    </form>

  </body>
</html>
```

9. When the user submits the form, the form data entered—which here is just the data in the `quantity` field—is submitted to the `whenexamplehandler.jsp` page. Create a file with this name now, again in the `Decisions` folder. This is quite a short file, and we'll explain it in detail in the "How It Works" section. Here it is in full:

```
<%@ taglib prefix="c" uri="http://java.sun.com/jstl/core_rt" %>
<%@ page info="If Example JSP"%>
<html>

  <head>
    <title>Conditional Statements</title>
  </head>

  <body>
    <b>WHEN Statement Example ( Response ) <br /></b>
    <br />

    <c:choose>
      <c:when test="${param.quantity > 0}" >
        Thank you for your order!!
      </c:when>
      <c:otherwise>
        Sorry, please enter a positive quantity
      </c:otherwise>
    </c:choose>
  </body>
</html>
```

10. Start up Tomcat, and browse to the following URL in your browser: `http://localhost:8080/Decisions/whenexample.html`. Enter a positive number in the Quantity field, as shown in Figure 5-3.

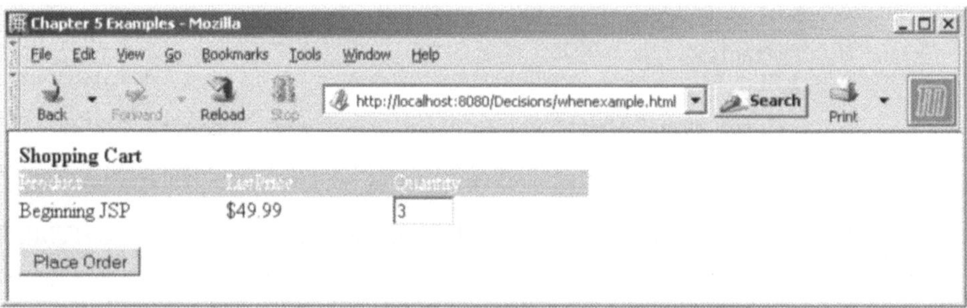

*Figure 5-3. A form for testing the* `choose...when` *loop*

11. Click Place Order, and you should see output as in Figure 5-4.

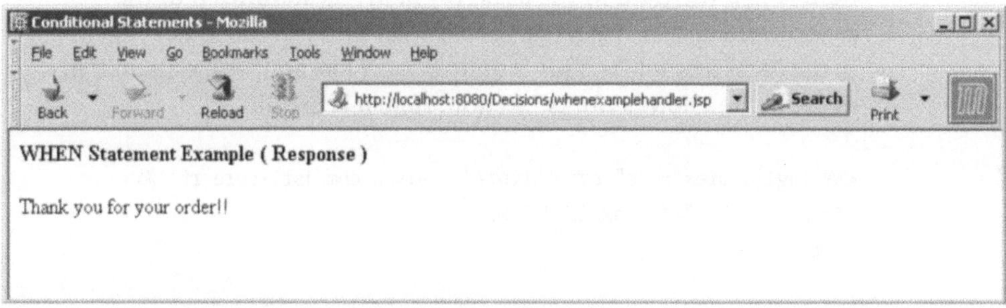

*Figure 5-4. The* `choose...when` *loop responds to your input.*

12. Click your browser's Back button, and try it again, but this time enter **0** in the Quantity field and click Place Order. You should see the message asking you to supply a positive quantity.

*How It Works*

You've already examined the HTML code quite closely, so you'll now concentrate on the second file, `whenexamplehandler.jsp`. This file checks whether `quantity` is greater than zero using the EL inside a JSTL `<when>` tag:

```
<c:when test="${param.quantity > 0}">
```

If this is `true`, what appears before the closing `<when>` tag will be used for the final page, which here is simply the message: *Thank you for your order!!* As you see, the `<c:when ></c:when>` tags act like the `if { }` block in normal Java code.

If, however, the EL condition in the `<when>` tag isn't `true`, then you show the message *Sorry, please enter a positive quantity*:

```
<c:otherwise>
  Sorry, please enter a positive quantity
</c:otherwise>
```

In this case, the `<c:otherwise></c:otherwise>` tags behave like a Java `else` block. Be warned that the relationship between `if...else` and `<c:if>...<c:otherwise>` isn't perfect. Some have likened the JSTL tags to the `switch` statement, which is covered in the "Using the switch Statement" section.

Notice that you could display the quantity of items ordered on this page quite easily by inserting the following EL in `whenexamplehandler.jsp`:

```
<c:when test="${param.quantity > 0}" >
   Thank you for your order of ${param.quantity} items!!
</c:when>
```

The final question in the "Trying It Out: Using the JSTL with Your Pizza Form" section at the end of Chapter 3 touched on the problem of ensuring your users submit meaningful data. In this example, for instance, there's nothing to stop a user from entering letters or other non-numeric characters in the Quantity box. The JSTL will attempt to convert the parameter value to an appropriate type (an integer in this case), but often conversion simply isn't possible, resulting in a screen of user-scaring error messages, as you can see in Figure 5-5.

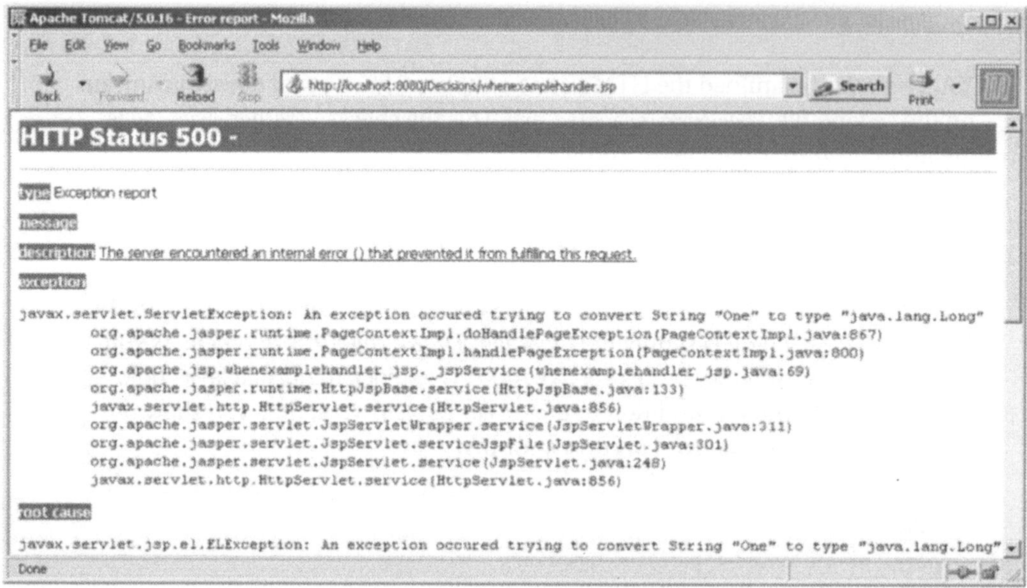


*Figure 5-5. A string has been entered in the form.*

It's important to prevent such unprofessional outcomes in your programs, and you do it by the process of input validation. Validation involves anticipating places where inappropriate input is possible, handling such eventualities by checking the submitted input, and displaying a warning of your own if the input isn't of the correct type. This could involve adding code to the page to perform this task, or you could pass the responsibility off to another component. Chapter 10 introduces Struts, a framework that, among many other things, makes the validation of user input fairly simple.

You can use an `if` statement to gain some simple protection. The final example in Chapter 3 checked that the `title` wasn't `null` but not the `price`. And it didn't check to see that the `price` wasn't a negative number. As a partial solution, you could change the conditional logic to the following:

```
<c:if test="${(param.title != null) && (param.price > 0)}" >
```

Unfortunately, it's still possible that an error could occur should `price` not be a number. The handling of errors (known as *exceptions* in Java) that may occur is an important consideration for any programmer.

## *Nesting if Statements*

You can model this "choice within a choice" in Java by embedding an `if` statement or an `if...else` statement inside another `if` or `if...else` statement. This is known as *nesting* `if` statements and is generally as follows (the nested statements are in bold):

```
if (expression1)
{
  if (expression2)
  {
    Statement Block 1
  }
}
else
{
  if (expression3)
  {
    Statement Block 2
  }
  else
  {
    Statement Block 3
  }
}
```

This ability to nest statements shouldn't be entirely unexpected. Because a statement block is simply one or more lines of Java code, there's no reason why an `if` statement block shouldn't contain further `if` and `if...else` statements.

You'll now see a code snippet to illustrate this point. You'll return to the earlier shipping cost scenario. Here, your customer is allowed free shipping only if more than four items are purchased. If he spends more than $100 on his five or more items, then the customer gets a 5 percent discount as well. However, if he spends more than $2,000 on the five or more items, the customer gets a free television:

```
if ( itemQuantity > 4 )
{
  System.out.println("Free Shipping for You!!");
  if (itemCost > 100)
  {
    System.out.println("5% Discount for You!!");
    if (itemCost > 2000)
    {
```

```
      System.out.println("Free Television for You!!");
    }
  }
}
```

Notice that you have more than one level of nesting here: You can have as many levels as you need, and you can create the same construct with JSTL <choose> tags:

```
<c:choose>
  <c:when test="${itemQuantity > 4}" >
    <c:choose>
      <c:when test="${itemCost > 2000}">
        You've earned a free television, plus a 5% discount and
        free shipping.
      </c:when>
      <c:when test="${itemCost > 100}">
        5% discount on your purchase, in addition to no shipping
        charge.
      </c:when>
      <c:otherwise>
        We will ship your order free of charge.
      </c:otherwise>
    </c:choose>
  </c:when>
</c:choose>
```

## Understanding the Conditional Operator

Java provides a concise way of writing conditional logic with the ?: operator. Because this operator takes three operands, it's known as the *ternary operator*. Most operators take two operands and are thus known as *binary operators*, and there are a few *unary operators* that take just one operand, such as the complement operator.

```
operand1 ? operand2 : operand3
```

operand1 is evaluated, and if it works out to true, then operand2 is returned; otherwise operand3 is returned. Look at the following line:

```
boolean freeShipping = (itemCost > 100) ? true : false;
```

In the previous example, freeShipping will be set to true if itemCost is greater than 100; otherwise it'll be set to false.

Take a look at another example:

```
int x = 20;
int y = (x > 50)? x + 10 : x - 15;
```

Here the integer variable x is initialized to 20. Because (x > 50) evaluates to false, the variable y is assigned the value of the third operand, which has the value x - 15 (which in turn evaluates to 5). Although there's no JSTL equivalent for the ?: operator, it can be useful in Java code elsewhere.

## Using the switch Statement

You've already seen that there's a way to deal with a selection of options using if...else if statements. However, this method can be somewhat untidy. A cleaner alternative is to use the switch statement, the basic syntax of which is as follows:

```
switch (expression)
{
  case <expressionValue 1>
    StatementBlock1;
    break;
  case <expressionValue 2> :
    StatementBlock2;
    break;
  default :
    DefaultStatementBlock;
    break;
}
```

The first thing to note is that there's a single expression to evaluate, which follows the initial switch keyword. The switch keyword is then followed by a sequence of case statements, each of which has an associated *expression value*. At the end of the list of case statements, the default keyword may appear.

This is what happens when a switch statement is encountered:

1. The expression is evaluated, and the result is compared to each case statement's expression value in turn.

2. When a case statement is found where the expression value matches the result of the expression, the statements belonging to that case are executed.

3. If no matching case statement is found, the statements given for the default case are executed.

There are a couple of important things to note about the switch block: First, the expression must return a value of type byte, char, short, or int. Second, if a break statement isn't placed at the end of a particular case statement's code block, all the code for all subsequent case statements will be executed, too. The break statement exits the switch construct, and execution continues from the following statement. This is required because expression values can't contain logical operators, and this behavior allows one block of code to match several case statements. However, it's a pitfall that can often trap the unwary programmer.

> **NOTE** *If you don't include the* break *statement, program flow will fall through to the remaining* case *options and execute all statement blocks until* break *is encountered or the* switch *statement ends.*

The JSTL contains no parallel, but you can create a similar effect using choose...when, as you'll see in the "Trying It Out: Working with the choose...when...when Construct" section. The following example shows a switch statement that displays a list of options according to the value of the fruitChosen variable:

```
switch (fruitChosen)
{
  case 1 :
    System.out.println("Apple");
    System.out.println("Price : $0.40, Color: Green");
    break;
  case 2 :
    System.out.println("Orange");
    System.out.println("Price : $0.45, Color: Orange");
    break;
  default :
    System.out.println("No Fruit Chosen");
    break;
}
```

In the previous code snippet, if fruitChosen is 1, the output produced would be as follows:

```
Apple
Price : $0.40, Color: Green
```

If, however, `fruitChosen` were `5`, it wouldn't match any `case` expression values, so the `default` code would be executed, displaying the message *No Fruit Chosen.*

There's no direct equivalent to the `switch` statement in the JSTL, but you can achieve a similar effect using the `<choose>` tag. In the next example, you'll create a drop-down list that lets the user select a particular fruit and see details about that fruit by clicking a button. You'll use a JSTL `<choose>` tag to select the details for the chosen fruit.

### *Trying It Out: Working with the choose...when...when Construct*

To use the `choose...when...when` construct, follow these steps:

1. You'll create an HTML file to build the initial form displayed to the user. Call this file **whenexample2.html**, and place it in your `Decisions` folder. It starts out identically to your previous HTML file:

```
<html>
  <head>
    <title>Conditional Statements</title>
  </head>
  <body>
```

2. As before, you create an HTML form, containing a table, that will post its data to a JSP:

```
<form method="POST" action="whenexamplehandler2.jsp">
  <table border="0" cellpadding="0" cellspacing="0" width="100%">
    <tr>
      <td><b>View Fruit Details</b></td>
      <td></td>
      <td></td>
    </tr>
    <tr>
      <td colspan="3">
```

3. This time, you create a drop-down list, with the following HTML:

```
<select size="1" name="fruit">
  <option selected value="1">Orange</option>
  <option value="2">Apple</option>
  <option value="3">Pear</option>
</select>
```

4. You need a submit button again, this time labeled *Get Details*:

```
                <input type="submit" value="Get Details"
                       name="GetDetailsBtn" />
              </td>
            </tr>
          </table>
        </form>
      </body>
    </html>
```

5. When the user clicks the Get Details button, they'll be passed to the `whenexamplehandler2.jsp` file. This is fairly short and appears as follows in its entirety:

```
<%@ taglib prefix="c" uri="http://java.sun.com/jstl/core_rt" %>
<html>
  <head>
    <title>Decisions Examples</title>
  </head>
  <body>
    <b>Fruit Details Page</b><br /><br />
    <c:choose>
      <c:when test="${param.fruit eq 1}" >
         Orange<br />
         Price : $0.30, Color: Orange<br />
      </c:when>
      <c:when test="${param.fruit eq 2}" >
         Apple<br />
         Price : $0.35, Color: Red<br />
      </c:when>
       <c:when test="${param.fruit eq 3}" >
         Pear<br />
         Price : $0.50, Color: Brown<br />
      </c:when>
    </c:choose>
  </body>
</html>
```

6. Now browse to `localhost:8080/Decisions/whenexample2.html` in your browser. Select a fruit from the drop-down list, as shown in Figure 5-6.

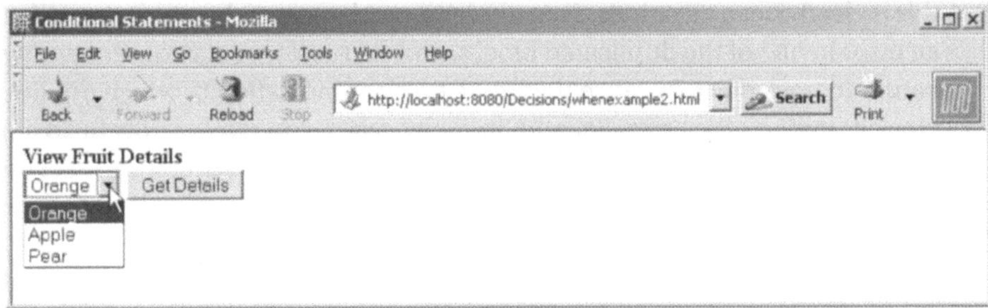


*Figure 5-6. Choose a fruit.*

7. If you choose Apple and click Get Details, you'll see the information shown in Figure 5-7.

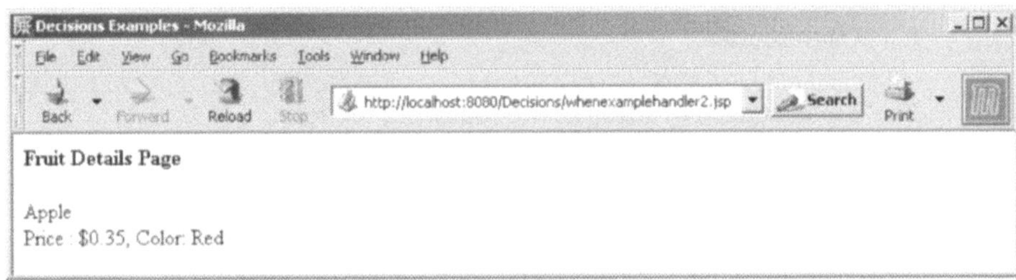


*Figure 5-7. The chosen fruit's details are displayed.*

*How It Works*

The fruit selected in the initial HTML page is stored in a form field called `fruit`, and you use it in the `test` attribute of JSTL `<when>` tags in your JSP page:

```
<c:when test="${param.fruit eq 2}" >
   Apple<br />
   Price : $0.35, Color: Red<br />
</c:when>
```

Notice the JSTL relational operator `eq`, which has the same function as the equals sign. Also note the similarity between the `<c:when>` tag and the `case` statement in Java's `switch` construct.

## Understanding Loops and Iteration

There are many programming situations where you need to execute the same logic repeatedly. Although you could simply write the code several times in sequence, this is clearly not a great idea. First, there's a much greater chance that you'll make an error in one of the duplicated blocks, and that error would consequently be harder to track down because there'd be no clear indication of which duplicated block contained the error. Second, in many cases, you rarely know in advance how many times you need to repeat the same steps. Consequently, just about every programming language has constructs that allow a single block of code to be repeated a given number of times.

Executing the same block of code over and over is known as *iteration*, or *looping*. Java has three types of iterative logic, each represented by one of the following statements:

- `while` statements
- `do...while` statements
- `for` statements

You'll look at each of these in the following sections.

## Using the while Loop

In many situations, you want to repeat a block of code for as long as a given expression remains `true`, and in such cases, you can use the `while` loop. Its syntax is pretty simple:

```
while (expression)
{
  Statement Block
}
```

For example, the following `while` loop will print the authors of each book returned from the database (`rs.next()` moves on to the next record returned from the database):

```
// Now we get the data
ResultSet rs = stmt.executeQuery("SELECT * FROM books");
// We need to iterate over the ResultSet
while (rs.next()) {
  rs.getString("author")
}
```

You have an integer variable, `count`, which you initialize to `1`. The `while` statement itself says that the statement block should be executed over and over until the value of `count` reaches `6`. Each time you loop through the statement block, the value of count is displayed and 1 is added to count, so count will be displayed five times before the while expression returns false.

You'll now move on and look at a variation of the while statement: the do...while statement.

## Using the do...while Loop

Using do...while loops are similar to using while loops, and they repeat a block of code for as long as an expression remains true. The difference is that do...while loops check the value of the expression *after* the code block, not before as in the plain while loop. This really just means that the code block will always execute at least once (even if the condition isn't true when the loop is first encountered).

A pitfall of do...while loops in Java is that a semicolon is required at the end of the while statement, which is something that's frequently forgotten:

```
do
{
  Statement Block
} while (expression);
```

You'll now return to the simplistic while loop that counts up to five. Consider what would happen if you initialize the count variable to 6 instead of 1:

```
int count = 6;
while (count < 6)
{
  System.out.println(count);
  count = count + 1;
}
```

Because the while loop will iterate only while the value of count is less than six, setting the initial value to 6 means that the loop never gets executed.

Now consider what happens if you set up the same counting example using a do...while loop:

```
int count = 6;

do
{
  System.out.println(count);
  count = count + 1;
} while (count < 6);
```

In this case, because the expression isn't checked until the end of the loop, one iteration is allowed to occur, and you can see the value of count displayed, 6.

> **NOTE** *Use the* `while` *loop when you need the condition to be checked before executing the code block, and use* `do...while` *when the code block should execute at least once.*

## *Using the for Statement*

The `for` statement syntax is as follows:

```
for(initialization; termination; increment)
{
  Statement Block
}
```

The `while` and `do...while` constructs let you create general-purpose loops that can be applied to a range of situations. However, in many cases, you want to repeat a block of code a certain number of times and, on each pass through the loop, use the current loop count in some code. Such situations are ideally suited to the `for` loop.

Key to how `for` loops work is a counter variable. You can set this variable to a value on entering the loop, and it'll be increased or decreased by a certain amount at the end of each execution of the code block forming the body of the loop. There's also a test that determines when enough loops have been performed.

This is a simple example of a `for` loop:

```
for (int num = 1; num <= 5; num++)
{
  System.out.println(num);
}
```

The output of this would be as follows:

```
1
2
3
4
5
```

In this case, the loop uses a counter variable called `num`, which is declared and initialized to `1` in the first expression in the brackets following the `for` statement. This expression is the ***initialization expression***, and it's followed by what's called the ***termination expression***. The termination expression gives a condition that must evaluate to `true` for the code in the loop body to be executed (in this case, the loop will continue for as long as `num` is less than or equal to five). The last expression of the `for` syntax is the ***increment expression***, which is executed every time the end of the loop body is reached (and here, increments `num` by one).

The `for` statement is very flexible. The increment expression can be any expression that should be executed at the end of each iteration and need not involve the loop counter at all. The ***initialization expression*** can set the counter to any value you choose, and you can use any numerical type as well as integers. You can, of course, use other variables in any of the three `for` expressions.

As you can see, the `for` loop's initialization expression declares and initializes `num`, but this isn't a requirement; you can just as well use an already existing variable as the counter, and you can even use its existing value by using a "blank" initialization expression:

```
int num = 1;
for (; num <= 5; num++)
```

The JSTL implements for loops using the `<forEach>` tag. Given the concepts of `for` statements just discussed, you should be able to deduce the purpose of most of the attributes shown in the following tag:

```
<%@ taglib prefix="c" uri="http://java.sun.com/jstl/core_rt" %>
<c:forEach begin="3" end="15" step="3" var="index" varStatus="num">

  <c:out value="${index}" />:<c:out value="${num.count}" /><br />

</c:forEach>
```

If you type the previous code into a text file and save it as **forexample.jsp** in your `Decisions` directory, it'll produce the output shown in Figure 5-8 when opened in a browser.

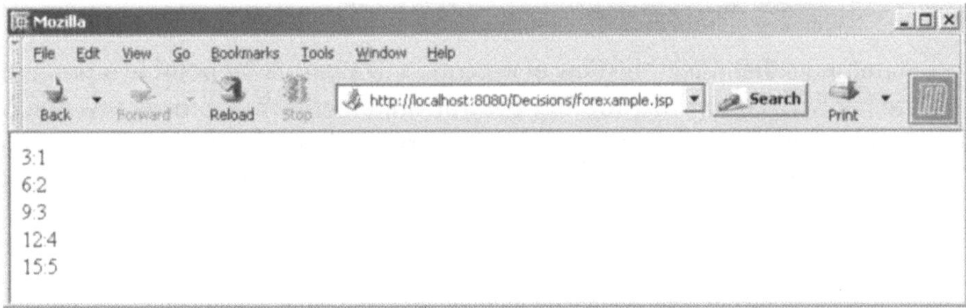


*Figure 5-8. The JSTL's `<forEach>` tag in action*

As you can see, this tag in fact requires two variables to function correctly, and you specify which names to give these using the `var` and `varStatus` attributes. `varStatus` specifies the name to use for the loop counter, and `var` is used internally by the JSTL.

This <forEach> loop mirrors the following Java for loop:

```
for (num = 3; num <= 15; num += 3)
  System.out.println(num);
```

We'll cover other uses of the <forEach> tag later in the "Trying It Out: Using Arrays" section.

### *Iterating Through Arrays*

The for loop is useful when you need to process each element in an array and is often used in conjunction with the length property. This property tells you how many elements the array contains, and therefore you can use it in the termination expression:

```
for(int index = 0; index < thisIsAnArray.length; index++)
```

Note that length will return the declared size of the array, regardless of how many array elements have been initialized. The for loop is particularly suited to arrays because in the loop body, you can use the counter variable to process each element in turn, like so:

```
  System.out.println(moreNumbers[index]);
```

This process is often called *iterating through the array.*

## Introducing Branching Statements

Statements that direct the flow of execution to a particular point in a program are known as *branching* (or *flow control*) statements. You already saw one of these when you looked at the switch construct, where the break statement was needed at the end of case blocks to exit the switch at that point and continue at the line immediately after the switch.

You'll look at this statement in more detail in the following sections, along with two more:

- break
- continue
- return

You'll start with the break statement.

## Using the break Statement

As well as exiting a switch statement, break can terminate any enclosing for, do...while, or while loop. Program control continues at the statement immediately following the enclosing loop.

An example of the break statement in a for loop is as follows:

```
String[] names = {"Matt", "Scott", "Ben", "Laura"};

for (int i=0 ; i < names.length ; i++) {
  if(names[i] == "Ben") {
    System.out.println("Found Ben");
    break;
  }
  System.out.println("Not found Ben");
}
```

In the previous code snippet, if the value of the current array item is equal to "Ben", the break statement is executed. This will result in the termination of the enclosing for statement, so the for loop will never reach Laura in the array. The output of the previous code snippet will therefore be as follows:

Not found Ben

Not found Ben

Found Ben

You should note that a *labeled* break statement is also available. This is useful because it means you can jump to the end of any particular enclosing statement using break and a label. To illustrate this, consider what would happen if you nested the for statement from the previous example inside another for statement:

```
OuterLoop:
for(int counter = 1; counter <= 2; counter++) {
  InnerLoop:
  for(int num = 1; num <= 5; num++) {
    System.out.println(num);
    if (num == 3) {
      break OuterLoop;
    }
  }
} // break directs execution flow to this point
```

Note that the for statements are labeled with OuterLoop and InnerLoop labels, respectively, and that break is also labeled:

```
break OuterLoop;
```

Now when program execution reaches this line, it will jump to the end of the outer for statement, *not* to the end of the inner for statement (as an unlabeled break would) because you specifically stated OuterLoop. The break statement always causes execution to drop to the end of the enclosing code block.

Note that this use of break is generally considered poor programming, and you should use better encapsulation in its place (here, for instance, you could put the InnerLoop in a separate method and replace the break statement with a return). However, sometimes it's valid to "break the rules," so you should be aware of this possible usage.

You'll see that you can label other types of statement in a similar way.

## *Using the continue Statement*

Inside a for, do...while, or while loop, the continue statement will skip to the next iteration of the loop. You can use continue with a label to skip the current iteration of the loop that's referred to by that label.

An example of the continue statement is as follows:

```
String[] orders = {"Done", "Outstanding", "Done", "Outstanding"};

int outstanding = 0;
int done = 0;

for (int i=0 ; i < orders.length ; i++) {
  if(orders[i] == "Outstanding") {
    outstanding++;
    continue;
  }
  done++;
}
System.out.println("No. of outstanding orders: " + outstanding);
System.out.println("No. of completed orders: " + done);
```

When an order is outstanding, the expression in the if statement evaluates to true, the count of outstanding orders is increased, and the continue statement is called. This terminates the current iteration of the for loop at that point, without the count of the completed orders being increased. Therefore, this for statement will show the following:

No. of outstanding orders: 2

No. of completed orders: 2

## *Using the return Statement*

The `return` statement is used within a method, and it returns control back to the code that called the method. That is, on reaching a return statement, the method ends, and the calling code continues from where it left off. If the method should return a value, then the `return` statement *must* include a variable of the required data type. You'll see many examples of this in later chapters.

In the following example, you'll put your newly found knowledge of arrays and JSTL iteration to use in a JSP page.

### *Trying It Out: Using Arrays*

To use an array, follow these steps:

1. This example consists of a single JSP page that allows you to make changes to the `book` table you worked with in Chapter 3. The first thing you need to do then is copy the MySQL Connector/j JAR to the `Decisions` folder's `lib` folder (inside `WEB-INF`).

2. Now you can start writing your JSP page, called `arrayexample.jsp`. You need to include the JSTL and SQL tag libraries:

```
<%@ taglib prefix="c" uri="http://java.sun.com/jstl/core_rt" %>
<%@ taglib prefix="sql" uri="http://java.sun.com/jstl/sql_rt" %>
```

3. Next, you need to provide the connection information for your database:

```
<sql:setDataSource var="datasource"
  driver="com.mysql.jdbc.Driver"
  url="jdbc:mysql://localhost/publish"
  user="publishuser" password="secret" />
```

4. The next section of code is used to update the database when changes have been made. Don't worry about why that appears here just now; we'll explain that once the page is done:

```
<c:if test="${!empty param.title}">
  <c:forEach items="${paramValues.title}" varStatus="i">
    <sql:update dataSource="${datasource}">
      UPDATE book
        SET title = ?,
          price = ?
      WHERE id = ?
```

```
            <sql:param value="${paramValues.title[i.count-1]}" />
            <sql:param value="${paramValues.price[i.count-1]}" />
            <sql:param value="${paramValues.id[i.count-1]}" />
          </sql:update>
        </c:forEach>
      </c:if>
```

5. Now you run a query on the books table, extracting the id, title, and price fields:

```
<sql:query var="books" dataSource="${datasource}">
  SELECT id, title, price FROM book
</sql:query>
```

6. The last thing to create is an HTML form for displaying information from the database:

```
<html>
  <body>
    <form method="post">
      <table border="1">
        <tr>
          <th>id</td><th>title</td><th>price</td>
        </tr>
```

7. You use another JSTL <forEach> to loop through all books that are to be displayed:

```
<c:forEach var="row" items="${books.rows}">
  <input type="hidden" name="id" value="${row.id}" />
  <tr>

    <td>
      <input type="text" name="title" value="${row.title}" size="30" />
    </td>
    <td>
      <input type="text" name="price" value="${row.price}" size="6" />
    </td>
  </tr>
</c:forEach>
```

8. The last row in this table will contain the form's submit button. Because the form doesn't specify an action attribute, this button will post the form information *back to this page itself*:

```
            <tr>
              <td colspan="3" align="center">
                <input type="submit" value="Save Changes" />
              </td>
            </tr>
          </table>
        </form>
      </body>
    </html>
```

9. Open your browser, and go to `http://localhost:8080/Decisions/arrayexample.jsp`. You should see a page that looks something like Figure 5-9.

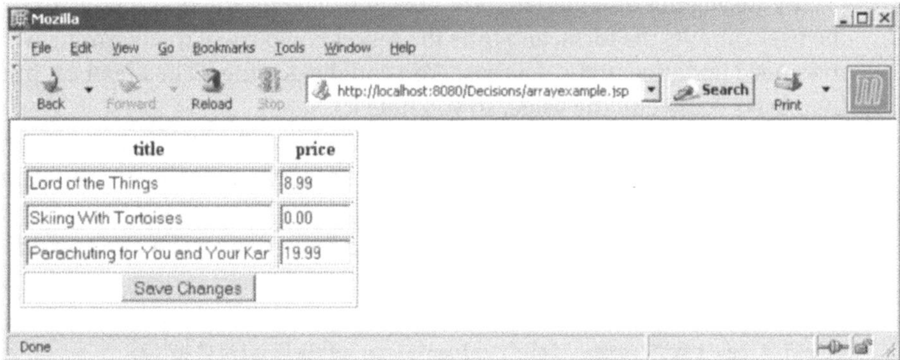


*Figure 5-9. Books to change*

10. Change some values, and click the Save Changes button. You should get a response that looks like Figure 5-10 (depending on the items you chose):

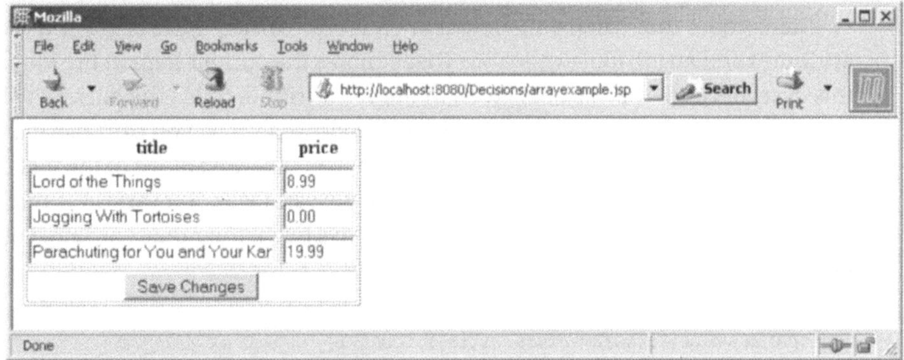


*Figure 5-10. An updated book entry*

### How It Works

In step 4, you added some code inside the following JSTL <if> tag:

```
<c:if test="${!empty param.title}">
```

This tag uses the EL empty operator to see if there's a title parameter for the page that's neither null nor empty. When the page is first accessed from your browser, there won't be any parameters at all, so the <if> block is skipped, and you load up the data from your database and come to the form that will display it on the page. The form has a hidden form field for the row ID of each book:

```
<input type="hidden" name="id" value="${row.id}" />
```

By storing this as a hidden form field, it will be returned to the server when the user submits the form, and thus the server could use it to determine which rows need updating in the database. You could place the ID in a textbox, but then users could edit the value, so you hide it.

Why do you hide the row ID, you may ask? As you'll recall from earlier examples of HTML forms, all values submitted to the server must be contained in one manner of form element or another.

You then create textboxes in the next two rows: one for the title and one for the price:

```
<input type="text" name="title" value="${row.title}" size="30" />
<input type="text" name="price" value="${row.price}" size="6" />
```

When the form is submitted, it posts back to the page itself. In other words, the page is regenerated but this time with the data you submitted available as parameters in the param array. So, now when you get to the first JSTL <if> tag, the test attribute, "${!empty param.title}", will evaluate to true, and you can use the <forEach> tag to iterate over the String array returned by $paramValues.title.

Remember that when you looked at <forEach> earlier, it has begin and end attributes and an attribute called var that denotes the current item in the loop. In this case, because the variable given in the var attribute holds the current value from the loop, which in this case would be the current title, you can't use it as the array index (that must be numerical!). Instead, you take advantage of the fact that the <forEach> tag uses its own status mechanism: varStatus. But varStatus tracks the current iteration starting at one, and as arrays begin their index at zero, you have to do some math:

```
<sql:param value="${paramValues.title[i.count-1]}" />
```

You run through all the parameter values and update the database as necessary using the SQL UPDATE statement. Once the database update is complete, you continue down the page, extract the updated data from the database, and display it in a form just as before.

---

### Why Not Try?

Try these exercises to improve your skills:

- Extend the first example (`whenexample.jsp`) to add a set of conditional statements that grant a 10 percent discount for the first 14 days of each month and an additional 5 percent if the number of items ordered is greater than three. Grant a 25 percent total discount if the total items is greater than ten, regardless of the day of the month. For this example, just add a field for the user to enter the current day of the month, so you can read it as `$param.dayOfMonth`. Of course, a real system would get this information from the server, but you don't need to worry about that here.
- Change the second example (`whenexamplehandler2.jsp`) so that it displays each book name up to and including the one selected. Put another way, if the user selects book 2, print the information for book 1 and book 2.
- Use the JSTL `<forEach>` and `<when>` tags on a JSP page to count from one to 100 by ones, printing every third number (three, six, nine...). Now rewrite it so that it counts by threes. Use the `var` and `varStatus` attributes to verify your output.
- Create an array of first names in "random" order. Use any one of the looping techniques to print the names. Then use `Arrays.sort()` to order the names alphabetically, and print them again.

---

## Summary

This chapter covered the basics of specifying decisions in your code and how you can use these decisions to affect program flow using control statements. There are three key types of control statements:

- **Conditional statements (`if`, `if...else`, and `switch`):** Execution of a block of code is controlled by the result of evaluating an expression.
- **Iterative statements (`for`, `while`, `do...while`):** Repeat the same code block a certain number of times.
- **Branching statements (`break`, `continue`, `return`):** Used to exit a loop, the current loop iteration, or a method, respectively.

The chapter also covered arrays, which are groups of the same data type. They simplify the maintenance and processing of a large amount of variables. The `for` loop (or `<forEach>` tag in a JSP page) is a great tool for processing all the elements of an array in sequence. You looked at two-dimensional arrays and jagged arrays, which are invaluable in many situations. The chapter closed by looking at the `sort` method of the `java.util` package.

The main reason for using arrays and control statements is that they make code simpler, easier to maintain, and more reusable. The next chapter introduces tag libraries, which can simplify JSP scripts still further.

CHAPTER 6

# Reusing Code

**In professional environments,** a formal process typically guides the development of applications. In fact, you can follow dozens—probably hundreds—of different processes, and indeed the topic of managing software development is so rich and complex that we won't even attempt to cover it in this chapter or book.

Most of these design processes, however, share the following overall flow, or, as it's sometimes called, the *development life cycle*:

1. First, you gather all the *requirements* of the software—that is, what it should do.

2. Next, you *design* how the software will fulfill those requirements.

3. Armed with a design, you *develop* the application according to the design—the actual programming.

4. Once the software is created, it's *tested* and debugged.

5. The product is then released, or *deployed.*

6. It then enters the *maintenance* phase during which new bugs are fixed as they're discovered and features are added or changed as the users' requirements change.

Of these phases, which do you suppose is the most time consuming and therefore the most costly? You might be surprised to discover that it's in fact the *maintenance* phase—businesses spend far more maintaining software once it has been deployed than they do actually developing it in the first place.

The lesson here applies to even the smallest of software projects: Develop your applications with an emphasis on making future maintenance as easy as possible because chances are that this is where you'll be spending the majority of your time.

One of the best ways to ease the maintenance burden of any application is to design to *maximize reuse* of code. Therefore, this chapter will show how to reuse JSP code and thus make applications easier to maintain.

As we discuss code reuse, we'll also talk about how to integrate standard Java code into JavaServer Pages (JSP) files. This topic, covered in the last half of this chapter, is in fact very important because it enables you to create Web pages that have the power and extensive features of one of the most popular programming languages on the planet.

So, off you go!

## Introducing Code Reuse

Reusing code *sounds* like a great idea; after all, reusing homework got some of us through school, but that's an entirely different yarn. We've said that designing for reuse makes an application easier to maintain, so you'll now examine why that is.

Imagine that your Web site contains several JSP pages that have a certain element in common, such as the following Hypertext Markup Language (HTML) table of shipping charges:

```
<table border="1">
    <tr>
        <td colspan="2">
            Shipping Rates
        </td>
    </tr>
    <tr>
        <td>
            Small
        </td>
        <td>
            $5.75
        </td>
    </tr>
    <tr>
        <td>
            Large
        </td>
        <td>
            $10.25
        </td>
    </tr>
</table>
```

For the benefit of those who don't speak HTML natively, Figure 6-1 shows what the table actually looks like.

| Shipping Rates | |
|---|---|
| Small | $5.75 |
| Large | $10.25 |

*Figure 6-1. Shipping table*

Now say that one day you need to change this information to add a new shipping category for medium items. If each of the many pages in your Web site contains its own copy of the code, you'd have to go through and change each one in turn, which is tedious at best. And what if you make a mistake on one of the pages or miss one altogether? Ugh.

It'd be so much better if you could simply create this code once and somehow instruct all your pages to insert this single file; you'd be able to change it once, and all your pages would then show the new version straightaway. This gives you a taste of how code reuse can make applications easier to maintain.

## Planning for Reuse

Code reuse makes maintenance easier, but does it let you create applications faster? This might *seem* to be the case, but in reality the answer is more complex. Maximizing code reusability takes planning, and sometimes the extra planning effort, and building the reusable component itself, can take more time than just copying and pasting the same code over and over again.

Reusing code is primarily a mechanism for easing maintenance, not necessarily a mechanism for accelerating development. Sometimes people get confused on this point and sidestep the reusability issue because they think addressing it in their situation would require unnecessary time and effort. Although it often does take longer to design for reuse, it's generally more than worth it in the long run. Poorly designed code not only requires more work to maintain, but it may make improvements too costly, forcing users to put up with unsatisfactory applications or to simply stop using applications into which you've poured a lot of sweat.

> **NOTE** *So planning for reuse can be time consuming, but it's worth it. It requires sitting down and considering what an application needs to accomplish, considering what different JSP pages will be required, and always looking for opportunities to reuse the same chunk of code. There are numerous professional methodologies for doing this, but common sense isn't a bad way to start.*

We should also mention, however, that once you've designed code for reuse on a few projects, you may indeed start to experience dramatic accelerations in new application development as you're able to reuse code from previous projects.

Inevitably, however, while developing an application you'll discover new reuse opportunities you hadn't spotted during the design stage. Often it's worth adjusting the design to cater for such opportunities—a process known as *refactoring*. Many tools in the marketplace make refactoring easier by automating certain aspects of changing the code. Most of these tools aren't geared toward JSP in particular, but many are designed with Java in mind.

## Starting the Web Catalog Application

Just as "a picture is worth a thousand words," a good code example is worth pages of well-worded explanations. So we'll present a small example application that *doesn't* reuse code as well as it could, and then, as you learn ways to reuse code, you'll modify the application appropriately.

### *Trying It Out: Creating a Badly Written JSP Application*

To create an application that doesn't reuse code well, follow these steps:

1. The example application will be a Web catalog comprising two JSP pages powered by the MySQL database program introduced in Chapter 4. The first thing you need to do is create a suitable database. Here's the script to do it:

```
CREATE DATABASE catalog;
 USE catalog;
 CREATE TABLE products (
id INTEGER NOT NULL AUTO_INCREMENT PRIMARY KEY,
name VARCHAR(15),
description VARCHAR(50),
price DECIMAL(7,2));
```

2. Create a user for this database called **catalogDBA**:

```
mysql> GRANT ALL PRIVILEGES ON catalog.*
          -> TO catalogDBA@localhost
          -> IDENTIFIED BY 'secret';
```

3. Now you need to populate the database with some data. Run the following script through MySQL:

```
INSERT INTO products (name, description, price)
     VALUES ("Widget A", "A nice entry-level widget", 5000),
     ("Widget B", "An even better widget", 5625),
     ("Widget C", "This widget is the coolest, and you need it", 6403),
     ("Widget D", "Customers of means will appreciate this widget",
      7500),
     ("Widget E", "This widget will bring you friends and popularity",
      8950),
     ("Widget F", "We distilled happiness and made it into this widget",
      15023),
     ("Widget G", "The widget to make you happier than a March hare",
      35075),
     ("Widget H", "Exclusivity has a price, and it's $750", 75000);
```

4. Now you need a location for the sample application, so create a new folder in Tomcat's `webapps` directory called **GoodDesign**. Inside it, create another folder called **WEB-INF**, and copy the Java Standard Tag Library (JSTL) `lib` folder inside that. Finally, copy the Java Archive (JAR) file for MySQL JDBC support into the `lib` directory as you did in the previous chapter, and you're good to go.

## *Creating the First Page: page1.jsp*

To create the `page1.jsp` page, follow these steps:

1. Create a file called **page1.jsp** in the `GoodDesign` folder. This page will list the cheaper items available from the catalog database. It starts with `taglib` directives for the JSTL core, SQL, and formatting tags:

```
<%@ taglib uri="http://java.sun.com/jstl/core_rt" prefix="c" %>
<%@ taglib uri="http://java.sun.com/jstl/sql_rt" prefix="sql" %>
<%@ taglib uri="http://java.sun.com/jstl/fmt_rt" prefix="fmt" %>
```

2. You now have some setup details to get out of the way, starting with an HTML `<style>` tag:

```
<html>
    <head>
        <title>Apress Catalog</title>
```

```
        <style type="text/css">
            BODY {
                font: 10pt sans-serif;
            }
            DIV.header {
                background: gray;
                color: white;
                padding: 5px 5px 5px 10px;
                font: bold 16pt sans-serif;
            }
            TABLE {
                border-collapse: collapse;
            }
            TH {
                background: black;
                color: white;
                margin: 1px;
            }
            TD {
                border: 1px solid silver;
            }
            .price {
                text-align: center;
            }
        </style>
    </head>
    <body>

        <div class="header">
            Apress Catalog
        </div>
        <p/>
        Welcome to the Apress Catalog.
        <p/>
        We have inexpensive items, shown below, and
        <a href="page2.jsp">expensive items</a>.
        <p/>
```

3. Next, you set up the connection details for your database in a JSTL SQL `<setDataSource>` element. You also create a query that will grab all items cheaper than $100:

```
<sql:setDataSource url="jdbc:mysql://localhost/catalog"
                driver="com.mysql.jdbc.Driver"
                  user="catalogDBA" password="secret"/>

<sql:query var="catalog">
    SELECT * FROM products
    WHERE price < 10000
    ORDER BY price
</sql:query>
```

4. Use an HTML table to display the information pulled from the database:

```
<table width="100%">
    <tr>
        <th>
            Item
        </th>
        <th>
            Description
        </th>
        <th>
            Price
        </th>
    </tr>
```

5. Now that you've set up the table heading, you'll move on to the content. You'll create a new row in the table for each row in the results returned from your query using a JSTL <forEach> element:

```
<c:forEach varStatus="status" var="row"
           items="${catalog.rows}">
    <tr>
        <td>
            ${row.name}
        </td>
        <td>
            ${row.description}
        </td>
        <td class="price">
            <fmt:formatNumber value="${row.price / 100}"
                                  type="currency"/>
        </td>
    </tr>
</c:forEach>
```

6. Close your HTML tags, and the first page is done:

```
        </table>
    </body>
</html>
```

## Creating the Second Page: page2.jsp

To create the page2.jsp page, follow these steps:

1. Your application has a second page that lists items aimed at those customers with less sense than money. Again, you start with some taglib directives and an HTML <style> element:

```
<%@ taglib uri="http://java.sun.com/jstl/core_rt" prefix="c" %>
<%@ taglib uri="http://java.sun.com/jstl/sql_rt" prefix="sql" %>
<%@ taglib uri="http://java.sun.com/jstl/fmt_rt" prefix="fmt" %>
<html>
    <head>
        <title>Apress Catalog</title>
        <style type="text/css">
            BODY {
                font: 10pt sans-serif;
            }
            DIV.header {
                background: gray;
                color: white;
                padding: 5px 5px 5px 10px;
                font: bold 16pt sans-serif;
            }
            TABLE {
                border-collapse: collapse;
            }
            TH {
                background: black;
                color: white;
                margin: 1px;
            }
            TD {
                border: 1px solid silver;
            }
```

```
            .price {
                text-align: center;
            }
        </style>
    </head>
    <body>
        <div class="header">
            Apress Catalog
        </div>
        <p/>
        Welcome to the Apress Catalog.
        <p/>
        We have expensive items, shown below, and
        <a href="page1.jsp">inexpensive items</a>.
        <p/>
```

2. The connection details are the same, but your query is slightly different:

```
<sql:setDataSource url="jdbc:mysql://localhost/catalog"
                driver="com.mysql.jdbc.Driver"
                  user="catalogDBA" password="secret"/>

<sql:query var="catalog">
    SELECT * FROM products
    WHERE price >= 10000
    ORDER BY price
</sql:query>
```

3. You format your query results as a table just as before:

```
        <table width="100%">
            <tr>
                <th>
                    Item
                </th>
                <th>
                    Description
                </th>
                <th>
                    Price
                </th>
```

```
                    </tr>
                    <c:forEach varStatus="status" var="row"
                               items="${catalog.rows}">
                        <tr>
                            <td>
                                ${row.name}
                            </td>
                            <td>
                                ${row.description}
                            </td>
                            <td class="price">
                                <fmt:formatNumber value="${row.price / 100}"
                                                  type="currency"/>
                            </td>
                        </tr>
                    </c:forEach>
                </table>
            </body>
        </html>
```

4. Navigate to `http://localhost:8080/GoodDesign/page1.jsp` in your browser (see Figure 6-2).

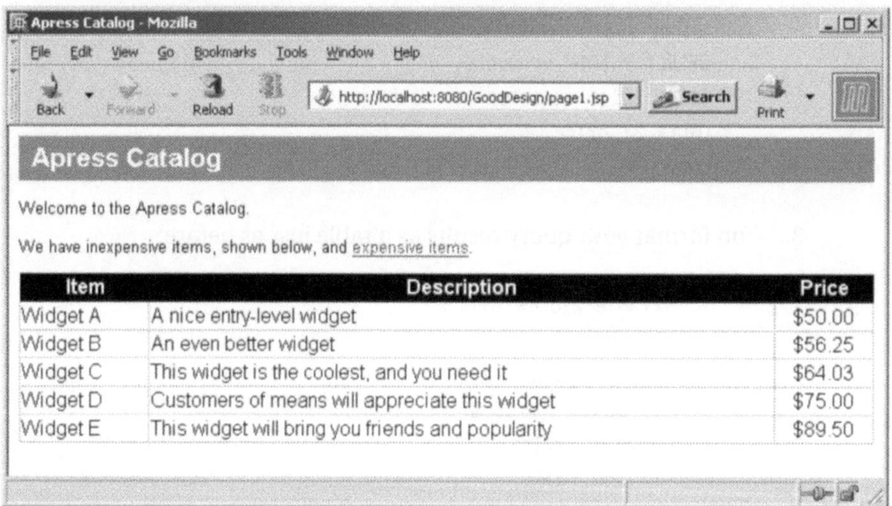


*Figure 6-2. Your first catalog page*

5. Click the expensive items link to see the second page (see Figure 6-3).

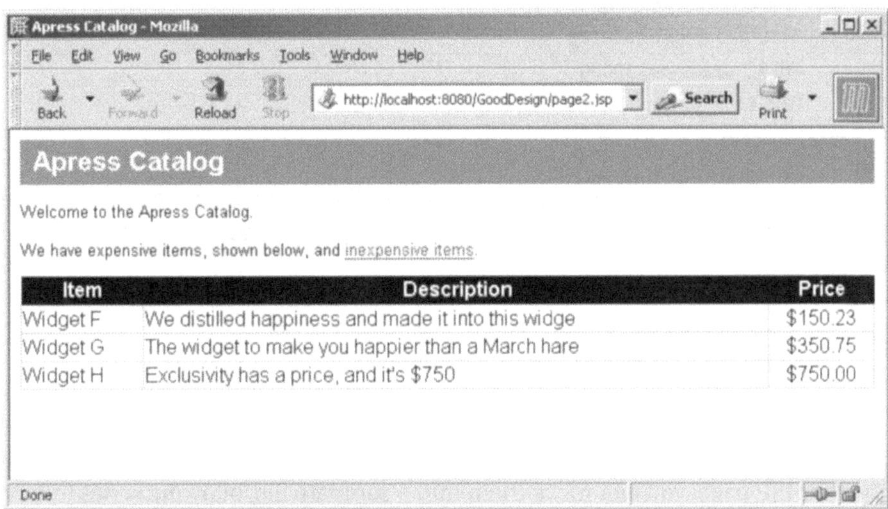


*Figure 6-3. Your second catalog page*

*How It Works*

As you've probably noticed, the two pages are nearly identical. If you have a closer look at the code, you'll see that it's different in only two places. First, the descriptions at the top of each page are different.

This is the description for `page1.jsp`:

```
We have inexpensive items, shown below, and
<a href="page2.jsp">expensive items</a>.
```

This is the description for `page2.jsp`:

```
We have expensive items, shown below, and
<a href="page1.jsp">inexpensive items</a>.
```

Second, the queries you run against the database are different:

This is the query you run for `page1.jsp`:

```
<sql:query var="catalog">
    SELECT * FROM catalog
    WHERE price < 10000
    ORDER BY price
</sql:query>
```

This is the query you run for page2.jsp:

```
<sql:query var="catalog">
    SELECT * FROM catalog
    WHERE price >= 10000
    ORDER BY price
</sql:query>
```

Other than that, the pages are identical. You'll now learn how you can repackage all this duplicated material and make your pages more elegant and reusable at a stroke.

### *Trying It Out: Creating an External Stylesheet*

The <style> element in your files defines the Cascading Style Sheet (CSS) styles that are applied to the Web page. Rather than mix these style definitions in with your JSP page, you can move them into a separate file, allowing styles to be readily shared with other applications. To do this, follow these steps:

1. Create a new folder called **Styles** in the GoodDesign folder, and create a text file there called **style.css**. Place all the CSS rules in it like so:

```
BODY {
    font: 10pt sans-serif;
}
DIV.header {
    background: gray;
    color: white;
    padding: 5px 5px 5px 10px;
    font: bold 16pt sans-serif;
}
TABLE {
    border-collapse: collapse;
}
TH {
    background: black;
    color: white;
    margin: 1px;
}
TD {
    border: 1px solid silver;
}
.price {
    text-align: center;
}
```

2. Now you can replace this information in `page1.jsp` and `page2.jsp` with a `<link>` element for the stylesheet (shown in bold):

```
<html>
    <head>
        <title>Apress Catalog</title>
       <link rel="stylesheet" href="Styles/style.css"
             type="text/css">
    </head>
    <body>
```

3. Open both pages in your browser, and you'll see that the separate stylesheet produces the same display as shown in Figure 6-2 and Figure 6-3. If you make any changes to the stylesheet, or link to an entirely different one, your pages will reflect the changes immediately.

## Understanding Mechanisms for Reuse

JSP has several mechanisms for enabling code reuse, which fall under one of two basic categories:

- **Includes**: These enable the contents of one file or JSP page to be inserted into another JSP page.
- **Custom tags**: These allow developers to create their own JSP tags.

There's considerable overlap in what the two mechanisms can accomplish, and you can often combine the two quite effectively. They're distinguished not by *what* you can do with them but, rather, *how* you can do it.

### *Introducing Includes*

As stated earlier, *includes* are all about taking data from one file and inserting it in another. The two types of includes are as follows:

- Translation-time includes
- Request-time includes

The difference between these two is best understood by reviewing how JSP works. Recall that any JSP tags are translated into HTML when Web browsers request a JSP page. Thus, the following JSP code:

```
My name is ${name}
```

would be *translated* by swapping the JSP Expression Language (EL) for some appropriate HTML, which, depending on the value of `name`, might be something like this:

```
My name is Steve "Dancing Monkey Boy" Ballmer
```

when the page is *requested* by the browser. These two incarnations of a JSP page are the key to the difference between the two types of includes. Translation-time includes will include the content of an external resource, such as another JSP page or an HTML file, *before* the JSP is translated into a servlet. Request-time includes will include the content of another JSP or HTML file *after* the JSP is translated into a servlet.

You'll look at servlets and the process of compiling JSP pages into them in Chapter 9. Until then, you just need to know that translation-time includes are appropriate when the page you're including needs access to all the JSP variables and data in the page that's doing the including. The source code of the included JSP page combines with the source code of the original JSP page, and the two become one big page that's then translated into a servlet.

When the included JSP page *doesn't* need access to internal data of the including JSP page, a request-time include will do just fine.

This doesn't tell the whole story, however. There's another compelling feature of request-time includes: They let you pass settings (called *parameters*) to the included JSP page. This makes it easier to reuse included JSP pages because you can tailor them to the page that's including them.

### Using the Include Directive

You'll now look at how these include thingies work. The first include you'll see is the *include directive*. An include directive is a translation-time include, and it looks like this:

```
<%@ include file="filename.jsp" %>
```

In this case, the file `filename.jsp` located in the same directory as the JSP will be included. You can specify any file path you want, relative to the path of the JSP.

### Using the Include Action

The second include you'll consider is the *include action*. This include is a request-time include. It has this form:

```
<jsp:include page="filename.jsp" />
```

You can pass parameters to JSP pages included with an include action in the following way:

```
<jsp:include page="filename.jsp">
    <jsp:param name="someName" value="someValue" />
</jsp:include>
```

To access the parameter, the included JSP page would use the following syntax:

```
The value for "someName" that you gave me is ${param.someName}.
```

The word `someName` should of course be replaced with your parameter name. You can use both the include directive and the include action anywhere you want to in a JSP page.

### *Trying It Out: Creating a Header and Footer*

To create a header and footer, follow these steps:

1. You'll apply this technique to your sample application and reduce some of that duplicated code. Create a new directory in the `GoodDesign` folder for your new files, and call it **Include**.

2. The code that creates the top of each page is completely identical, so you'll move it into a new file called **header.jspf**. Create this file in the `Include` directory, and enter the following code in it:

```
<div class="header">
    Apress Catalog
</div>
<p/>
Welcome to the Apress Catalog.
<p/>
```

3. The bottom of each page is also identical. Create a file called **footer.jspf** containing the following code in the `Include` folder:

```
<hr/>
&copy; Copyright 2003 Apress Widgets Ltd
```

> **NOTE** *We use the* `.jspf` *extension rather than* `.jsp` *because these files aren't complete JSP files in themselves—they're* JSP fragments. *JSP fragments are intended to be used only within other JSP pages. There's nothing stopping you from using the* `.jsp` *extension, but* `.jspf` *makes their intended use clear.*

4. To use these fragments in your catalog application, you simply need to replace the code they contain with an appropriate include directive. Make a copy of page1.jsp with the name **page1include.jsp**, and change it as shown in bold:

```
<%@ taglib uri="http://java.sun.com/jstl/core_rt" prefix="c" %>
<%@ taglib uri="http://java.sun.com/jstl/sql_rt" prefix="sql" %>
<%@ taglib uri="http://java.sun.com/jstl/fmt_rt" prefix="fmt" %>

<html>
    <head>
        <title>Apress Catalog</title>
       <link rel="stylesheet" href="Styles/style.css"
             type="text/css">
    </head>
    <body>
    <%@ include file="/Include/header.jspf" %>
        We have inexpensive items, shown below, and
        <a href="page2include.jsp">expensive items</a>.
        <p/>
        <sql:setDataSource  url="jdbc:mysql://localhost/catalog"
                           driver="com.mysql.jdbc.Driver"
                             user="catalogDBA" password="secret"/>

        <sql:query var="catalog">
            SELECT * FROM products
            WHERE price < 10000
            ORDER BY price
        </sql:query>

        <table width="100%">
          .
          .
          .
        </table>
    <%@ include file="/Include/footer.jspf" %>
  </body>
</html>
```

5. Similarly, make a copy of page2.jsp called **page2include.jsp**, and change it as follows:

```
<%@ taglib uri="http://java.sun.com/jstl/core_rt" prefix="c" %>
<%@ taglib uri="http://java.sun.com/jstl/sql_rt" prefix="sql" %>
<%@ taglib uri="http://java.sun.com/jstl/fmt_rt" prefix="fmt" %>

<html>
    <head>
        <title>Apress Catalog</title>
       <link rel="stylesheet" href="Styles/style.css"
             type="text/css">
    </head>
    <body>
<%@ include file="/Include/header.jspf" %>
  We have expensive items, shown below, and
        <a href="page1include.jsp">inexpensive items</a>.
        <p/>
        <sql:setDataSource  url="jdbc:mysql://localhost/catalog"
           driver="org.gjt.mm.mysql.Driver"
            user="catalogDBA" password="secret"/>

        <sql:query var="catalog">
            SELECT * FROM products
            WHERE price >= 10000
            ORDER BY price
        </sql:query>

        <table width="100%">
          .
          .
          .
        </table>
    <%@ include file="/Include/footer.jspf" %>
  </body>
</html>
```

6. If you now open the new pages in a browser, you'll see that the headers appear just as they did originally and that the footers now also appear (see Figure 6-4).

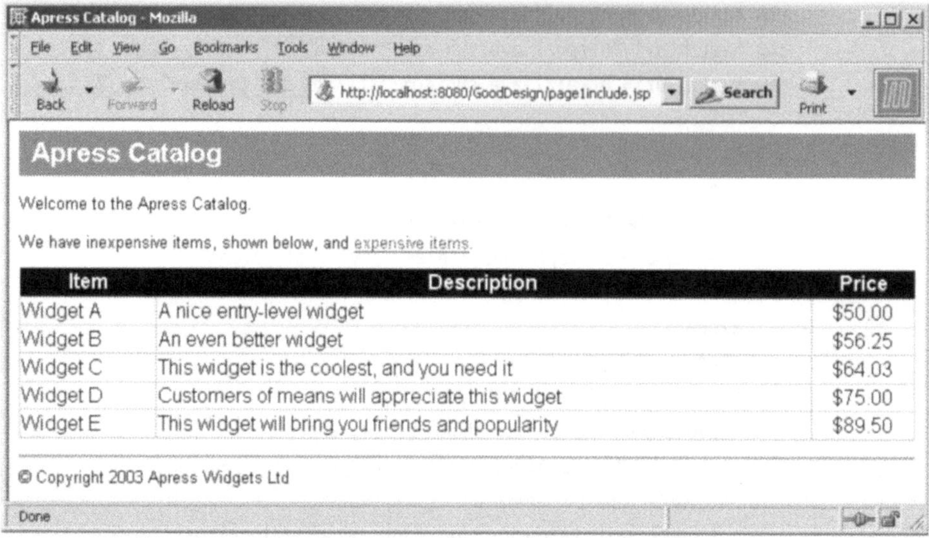


*Figure 6-4. Your first include page*

7. You're already starting to reduce the needlessly repeated code and make your code more maintainable. As a demonstration of the advantages this offers, pretend the powers that be have decided to revamp your site's appearance. Open `footer.jspf`, and change the highlighted lines as shown:

```
<hr/>
<div class="header">&copy; Copyright 2003 Apress Widgets Ltd</div>
```

8. Because it's in the footer, this change will be immediately reflected on all pages that include that header, as you'll see if you open them now (see Figure 6-5).

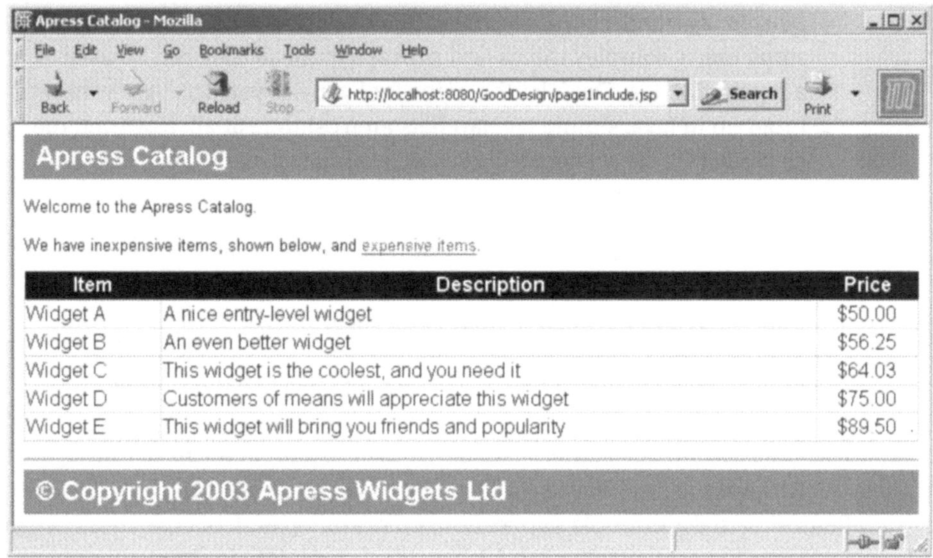


*Figure 6-5. The newly updated footer*

*How It Works*

You extracted the static HTML that creates the top part of pages on your site and placed it in the file `header.jspf`. There was nothing stopping you from including the `taglib` directives in the header, but this isn't generally good practice because not all pages that have the header require all the libraries, and some might require other libraries, so it's best to leave them on the pages where they're used.

It's always a good idea to place related files of a Web application in suitably named directories because it makes them much easier for others to understand. Thus, you placed your header and footer in a new directory called `Include`.

## Introducing Custom Tags

Underneath the banner of custom tags, you'll in fact find three distinct species:

> **Classic tag handlers**: These are the original JSP custom tag mechanism and are rather complex to create. Generally, you wouldn't create your own custom tags of this type; however, you may use them often enough. The JSTL is an example of classic tag handlers.

**Simple tag handlers**: These allow JSP developers who know Java to do some pretty complex things and package them so they can be used as a regular JSP tag. Don't let the name fool you—if you don't know how to program in Java, simple tag handlers aren't simple at all. However, the original JSP custom tag mechanism, introduced many years ago, does indeed make these look very easy to create.

**Tag files**: These are JSP files with certain features that allow them to be included in another JSP file through a tag interface. Think of them as a sort of bridge between includes and custom tags.

In this book, you'll just look at tag files. Tag files are the simplest way to create custom JSP tags. They require no knowledge of Java programming, and they resemble the include action (a request-time include) in terms of functionality.

Perhaps the best way to explain how to use a tag file is to show it in action. Returning to the example application, there's one chunk of code that's begging for reuse: the catalog table itself. It's an ideal candidate for implementation as a tag file.

### *Trying It Out: Creating a Custom Tag*

To create a custom tag, follow these steps:

1. Create a directory for your tag files named **tags** off the `WEB-INF` folder for the `GoodDesign` application. Tag files don't have to be placed in this folder, but it can be easier.

2. Inside the tags folder, create a file called **catalogTable.tag** with the following content:

```
<%@ taglib uri="http://java.sun.com/jstl/fmt_rt" prefix="fmt" %>
<%@ taglib uri="http://java.sun.com/jstl/core_rt" prefix="c" %>
<%@ taglib uri="http://java.sun.com/jstl/sql_rt" prefix="sql" %>
<sql:setDataSource  url="jdbc:mysql://localhost/catalog"
                  driver="com.mysql.jdbc.Driver"
                    user="catalogDBA" password="secret"/>
        <sql:query var="catalog">
            <jsp:doBody/>
        </sql:query>

        <table width="100%">
            <tr>
                <th>
```

```
                Item
            </th>
            <th>
                Description
            </th>
            <th>
                Price
            </th>
        </tr>
        <c:forEach varStatus="status" var="row"
                   items="${catalog.rows}">
            <tr>
                <td>
                    ${row.name}
                </td>
                <td>
                    ${row.description}
                </td>
                <td class="price">
                    <fmt:formatNumber value="${row.price / 100}"
                                      type="currency"/>
                </td>
            </tr>
        </c:forEach>
    </table>
```

This file contains the code that should be executed whenever you use your custom tag. You'll notice that it's pretty much the same code that already creates the table in both pages.

3. Now you need to use your new tag in your application's JSP pages. Make a copy of `page1include.jsp` called **page1tag.jsp**, and do the same for the second page.

4. Because all the functionality is now housed in the `catalogTag` tag you've just created, you can remove all three existing `taglib` directives. However, you need a new one for your own tag:

```
<%@ taglib tagdir="/WEB-INF/tags" prefix="tags" %>
```

Notice that your tag file's `taglib` directive is different from the other three. This difference is because the first three are classic tags and your directive is a simple tag.

5. Now you can use your tag in place of the SQL tags and table that create your catalog. Change page1tag.jsp as follows:

```
<%@ taglib tagdir="/WEB-INF/tags" prefix="tags" %>
        <%@ include file="/Include/header.jspf" %>
        We have inexpensive items, shown below, and
        <a href="page2tag.jsp">expensive items</a>.
        <p/>
        <tags:catalogTable>
            SELECT * FROM products
            WHERE price < 10000
            ORDER BY price
        </tags:catalogTable>
<%@ include file="/Include/footer.jspf" %>
```

6. Change page2tag.jsp similarly:

```
<%@ taglib tagdir="/WEB-INF/tags" prefix="tags" %>


        <%@ include file="/Include/header.jspf" %>
        We have expensive items, shown below, and
        <a href="page1tag.jsp">inexpensive items</a>.
        <p/>
        <tags:catalogTable>
            SELECT * FROM products
            WHERE price >= 10000
            ORDER BY price
        </tags:catalogTable>
<%@ include file="/Include/footer.jspf" %>
```

7. Navigate to http://localhost:8080/GoodDesign/page1tag.jsp in your browser, and you'll see that the output is the same as it was previously.

*How It Works*

Look at how much smaller these files are! You've taken two highly inefficient files (in terms of reuse) and made them much more efficient and maintainable.

You'll now take a closer look at your tag file. First, it starts off with the familiar tag library directives because your tag uses the JSTL. Second, where you previously had SQL statements, you now have a single JSP tag:

```
<jsp:doBody/>
```

This tag will be replaced by whatever appears between the start and end tags of your custom tag when used on a JSP page. Thus, when you use it on your first JSP page like so:

```
<tags:catalogTable>
    SELECT * FROM products
    WHERE price < 10000
    ORDER BY price
</tags:catalogTable>
```

the `<jsp:doBody>` tag will be replaced with the given SQL query.

## Going Beyond JSP

You've spent the first part of this chapter learning how to reuse code using nothing but JSP features. As you've seen, you can do some powerful stuff. But sooner or later, you'll need to tap into a far larger and more flexible resource of features: the Java language itself.

One of the easiest ways to use Java in JSP is through *JavaBeans* in conjunction with the JSP mechanisms you've already seen. JavaBeans are reusable objects created with the Java programming language. However, because you may well have never programmed in Java before, the next part of this chapter concentrates on teaching the basic principles, and then you'll move on to use JavaBeans in JSP.

### What Are Java Objects?

Java is an *object-oriented programming* (OOP) language, which means that coding is all about creating objects that can be used over and over again in either their original form or in new forms created by extending those original forms.

Objects in the programming sense of the word might seem awkward and unnatural at first, but once you come to grips with the concept, they're actually a logical way to think about problems and organize code.

An object in OOP represents some particular "thing," just as it does when you use the word in language. For instance, a newspaper is an object. It has certain properties that make it distinct from any other object—a tree object, a car object, or whatever.

Java defines an object's distinctive properties in what's known as a *class*. A class constitutes a template or a mold that you can then use to create objects of that class; this is known as *instantiating* the class. Each object of a particular class is said to be an *instance* of that class.

A class specifies the variables that are needed to hold necessary information about any instance of that class, and it also specifies code that you can use to manipulate and retrieve that information in the form of *methods*. The information is stored in variables called *attributes*. When you create an object belonging to a certain class, the Java compiler needs to see the definition of the attributes and methods. To make this possible, you have to define each class in its own file with the `.java` extension and a filename that exactly matches the class name. Don't forget that class names and filenames are case-sensitive in Java, so a class called `Bodkin` would have to be defined in a file called `Bodkin.java` if it's to be publicly accessible.

When you call a method to access the attributes of an object, you can pass extra information that may be relevant to that method by enclosing it in parentheses after the method name. Such items of information are called *arguments* or *parameters*. Methods sometimes compute a useful value, and this can be passed back to the code that calls the method (the method is said to *return* a value). Actually, you have already used methods in Chapter 3 when you invoked methods on the `request` object.

One of the great advantages of object orientation is that you can build new class templates on top of existing ones. This is known as *inheritance*. For example, you could make a new class of objects, `Sunday Newspaper`, that "inherits" all of the attributes and methods of `Newspaper` objects but adds new ones of its own, too (such as color comics and additional advertising inserts). You say that the `Sunday Newspaper` class is a *subclass* of `Newspaper`, and `Newspaper` is the *superclass* of `Sunday Newspaper`.

> **NOTE** *This relationship is also often called a* parent-child *relationship. The* `Sunday Newspaper` *(the child) inherits all of the attributes and methods of* `Newspaper` *(the parent). So, children can inherit from parents, but parents don't inherit from children.*

Classes let you separate functionality and associated data into methods and attributes. Classes provide "black box" functionality that you can use without needing any knowledge of how they work. Class *inheritance* enables your code to be more reusable.

## Introducing JavaBeans

*JavaBeans* are Java objects that expose data through *properties* (another name for attributes). For instance, you might have a bean that models a bank account, and such a bean might have account number and balance properties.

Formally, a JavaBean is really nothing more than a Java class that maintains some data (the properties) and follows certain coding conventions. These conventions provide a mechanism for *automated support*; that is, the JSP engine—for example, Tomcat—can inspect the bean and discover what properties it has. This mechanism is called *introspection*.

### Properties

Each item of information that a bean exposes is called a *property*. For an example of public properties, you need look no further than HTML:

```
<p style="font-family: sans-serif; color: blue">
    Did you like that "blue" song that was popular a while back?
</p>
```

In HTML with reference to the `<p>` tag, for example, `style` is an example of a property that can be set against the standard HTML `<p>` tag. You may already be familiar with this type of property.

Like HTML properties, properties in JavaBeans provide a simple approach to being able to pass information to set or retrieve a value to use in your JSP code.

The properties of a JavaBean are publicly exposed using getter and setter methods. These methods follow simple naming conventions, easiest understood by example. If you have a property called `style`, you'd call the getter and setter methods `getStyle()` and `setStyle()`. The method names are simply the capitalized name of the property preceded by either `get` or `set`. This capitalization is required.

To build a JavaBean of your own, all you have to do is write a Java class and obey these rules.

### Building a JavaBean

So what does a JavaBean look like? For this example, you'll define a JavaBean class called `CarBean` that you could use as a component in a car sales Web site. It'll be a component that will model a car and have one property—the make of the car. Here's the code:

```
public class CarBean
{
   private String make = "Ford";

   public CarBean() {}

   public String getMake()
   {
     return make;
   }
```

```
    public void setMake(String make)
    {
      this.make = make;
    }
}
```

There are several things to note here. The first line is where you define the name of the class:

```
public class CarBean
```

Don't worry about the `public` keyword; we'll explain this later. The definition of the contents of the class goes inside the braces following the class name. First, you define a `String` property called `make`, and set its value to `Ford`:

```
private String make = "Ford";
```

Again, ignore the `private` keyword for now.

Second, you set the definition of a special method called the *constructor*:

```
public CarBean() {}
```

A constructor is a special method called when an instance of a new bean is requested, and it always has the same name as the class. You should note that this constructor is empty (there's nothing between the braces), but this is often not the case: You can set properties at instantiation time between these braces.

Moving through the code, you can see that this property has getter and setter methods:

```
public String getMake()
{
  return make;
}
```

The `getMake()` method returns the value of `make`. It doesn't get passed any arguments. The `setMake()` method is, however, passed a `String` argument also called `make`, which sets the `make` property to the same value as the argument:

```
public void setMake(String make)
{
  this.make = make;
}
```

The `void` keyword indicates that this method returns no value. The `this` part is a way of referring to the current `CarBean` object, so `this.make` is simply the `make` property of the current object.

### *Variable Scope*

In the previous section, we ignored the presence of two Java keywords associated with the attributes and methods within the class:

- `public`
- `private`

These keywords refer to the *scope* of an attribute, variable, or method. The scope defines the parts of the code in which the variable or method is recognized, and so you can use that code. The scope of a variable or method depends upon where it's *declared* (defined).

Variables that are defined within a method have *local* scope. This means they can be used only within the confines of the method in which they were declared. However, variables declared as attributes within the class can be used anywhere within the class definition.

But what about when you come to use an object of this class? Which variables declared within the class can you use? The answer to this is that it depends. You can't directly access variables (with local scope) declared within class methods. If an attribute is declared as being `public`, you can access the attribute from outside the class. However, if an attribute is declared as being `private`, you can use it only within the class.

The same is true for the scope of methods in the class. If the method is declared as being `public`, it can be called from outside the class; if it's `private`, it can't be.

You should note that all your attributes in this example are `private`, and all of the getter/setter methods are `public`. There's a good reason for this: It forces you to use these methods to access and modify attribute values. This is much safer than allowing direct access to attributes. For example, using the setter method forces you to provide a value for the attribute that's of the correct data type; otherwise the resetting of the value won't work. In other words, you can make sure that any user who wants to access the data in the bean does so without modifying the data in unpredictable ways. Another advantage is that you can standardize input. For example, a `setState()` method could ensure all abbreviations are capitalized, whether or not they came in that way.

You now understand the code required for a JavaBean, but there's another step to take before you can use it: compilation.

### *Compiling Class Files*

Before you can use a JavaBean, or any class, in an application, you must *compile* it. The process of compilation is converting *source code* into *byte code*. It's this byte code that the Java Virtual Machine (JVM), which runs Java programs, can understand and execute.

Classes are compiled using the *javac* compiler that comes as part of the Java Software Development Kit (SDK) you installed in Chapter 1. You'll see exactly how this is done in the following example.

However, if you want to use a compiled JavaBean in a JSP Web application, the JSP engine—for example, Tomcat—also needs to know where to look for it.

You saw in Chapter 1 that Web applications are stored under the `%CATALINA_HOME%/webapps` directory. If you had a Web application called `cars`, you'd create a directory `cars` in `%CATALINA_HOME%/webapps`.

By default, Tomcat (and any other servlet container) checks for classes in the `/WEB-INF/classes` directory under the Web application directory and any subdirectories of this. So, for your `cars` Web application, Tomcat would look for JavaBeans in the directory `%CATALINA_HOME%/webapps/cars/WEB-INF/classes` and all directories under this. Although it's possible to store your JavaBeans elsewhere, in this chapter you'll store your JavaBeans in this default location.

## Using a JavaBean

You've now defined a JavaBean, and you know that you need to compile it and put in a directory where Tomcat can see it. But that's now the whole story. How do you use it in a JSP page?

Remember how we insisted that the getter and setter methods follow a strict naming convention? In the previous example the need for this convention wasn't clear. Next, we'll introduce *bean tags*, which will allow you to remove the need for scriptlets to call bean methods from the JSP.

JSP provides an approach for utilizing JavaBeans that's based on the concept of tags. These tags are really no more complicated than the standard HTML tags; they have a name, and they take attributes.

Tags are designed to make the page developer's job easier because they allow the designer to use JavaBeans without knowing any Java. The specification provides three tags to support using JavaBeans in your JSP pages:

- `<jsp:useBean>`
- `<jsp:setProperty>`
- `<jsp:getProperty>`

In the following sections, you'll learn about each of these tags and how to use them when working with your JavaBeans.

### *Using the <jsp:useBean> Tag*

The `<jsp:useBean>` tag locates and instantiates a JavaBean. For example:

```
<jsp:useBean id="myCar" class="com.apress.cars.CarBean" />
```

Here, an object of the class `com.apress.cars.CarBean` will be located and created if an instance doesn't already exist. You can refer to this bean later in the page using the value set for the `id` attribute (`myCar`).

Note that for the `<jsp:useBean>` tag you have two ways of closing the tag. You can use the short notation of `/>` shown previously to close the tag. Or, if you want to populate values at instantiation rather than after instantiation, you can use the full `</jsp:useBean>` end tag instead:

```
<jsp:useBean id="myCar" class="com.apress.cars.CarBean" ></jsp:useBean>
```

### *Using the <jsp:setProperty> Tag*

The `<jsp:setProperty>` element sets the value of a property of a bean using the setter method.

If you've instantiated a JavaBean with an `id` of `myCar`, as you did in the previous section, you can use the following tag to set the value of a property of the bean:

```
<jsp:setProperty name="myCar" property="make" value="Ferrari" />
```

Here you're setting the property `make` to the value `Ferrari`. This is where the usefulness of the method naming conventions becomes apparent. This tag takes the bean instance with an `id` of `myCar` and calls the `setMake()` method on it. It passes `Ferrari` to the method as the argument.

### *Using the <jsp:getProperty> Tag*

The `<jsp:getProperty>` element gets a property value using the getter method and returns the property value to the calling JSP page.

As with the `<jsp:setProperty>` tag, you must create or locate a bean with `<jsp:useBean>` before you can use `<jsp:getProperty>`. This is an example of using the tag:

```
<jsp:getProperty name="myCar" property="car" />
```

You get the value of the property `car` from the bean instance `myCar`.

> **NOTE** *Remember to specify the* `<jsp:useBean>` *tag before using either the* `<jsp:setProperty>` *tag or the* `<jsp:getProperty>` *tag; otherwise your JSP page will throw a compile error.*

Now you'll create the `CarBean` class you *described* in the previous section and use it in a JSP page with the bean tags you just reviewed.

### *Trying It Out: Using a JavaBean in JSP*

To use a JavaBean in a JSP page, follow these steps:

1. First, create a folder called **Reuse** for your new application in Tomcat's `webapps` directory. Create a **WEB-INF** subfolder as usual and a folder called **classes** inside it.

   Inside `classes`, create another folder called **com**, one called **apress** inside that, and, finally, one called **cars** inside the new `apress` folder. Don't worry about the directory structure at this point—we'll explain it in a moment.

2. Create a new file in the `cars` directory called **CarBean.java**, and insert the following code:

```
package com.apress.cars;

import java.io.Serializable;

public class CarBean implements Serializable
{
  private String make = "Ford";

  public CarBean() {}

  public String getMake()
  {
    return make;
  }

  public void setMake(String make)
  {
    this.make = make;
  }
}
```

3. Now create a JSP page in the Reuse folder called **carPage.jsp** to demonstrate your bean:

```
<html>
    <head>
        <title>Using a JavaBean</title>
    </head>
    <body>

    <h2>Using a JavaBean</h2>

    <jsp:useBean id="myCar" class="com.apress.cars.CarBean" />

    I have a <jsp:getProperty name="myCar" property="make" /> <br />

    <jsp:setProperty name="myCar" property="make" value="Ferrari" />
    Now I have a <jsp:getProperty name="myCar" property="make" />

    </body>
</html>
```

4. You first need to compile CarBean.java. From a command prompt, change to the classes directory in the Reuse application's WEB-INF folder, and enter the following command:

```
> javac com/apress/cars/CarBean.java
```

   If you get any errors, go over the code and make sure you entered it exactly as it appears here. When compilation is complete, you'll have a file called CarBean.class in the directory.

5. Now start or restart Tomcat, and open http://localhost:8080/Reuse/carPage.jsp in your browser. You should see something like Figure 6-6.

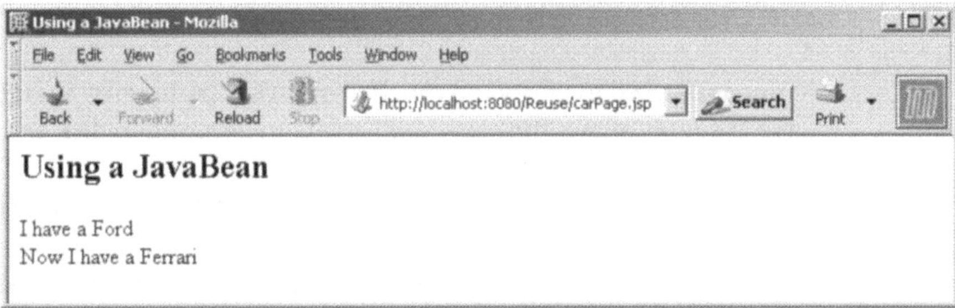


*Figure 6-6. A JSP page using a JavaBean*

*How It Works*

The first line in your JavaBean class is as follows:

```
package com.apress.cars;
```

What is this? Java classes are stored in collections called *packages*. These packages provide an easy way to organize related classes. The names of packages follow a simple structure. You've already come across packages in Chapter 1 when you used the `Date` class. The `Date` class is stored in the `java.util` package.

The name of the package has a direct relation to the directory in which the class is stored under the `classes` folder. For example, because the `Date` class is in the package `java.util`, it'd need to be stored under a `/classes/java/util` directory structure. Similarly, your `CarBean` class is stored under the `classes/com/apress/cars` directory within your `webapps` directory.

> **NOTE** *Classes in the* `java.*` *or* `javax.*` *packages are included automatically using a JAR file. For classes you create in this book, you'll always create a directory structure that corresponds to your package structure under the* `WEB-INF/classes/` *directory. If you're familiar with the* `jar` *utility included with the Java Development Kit (JDK), you could "JAR up" your files—directories and all—and place them under the* `WEB-INF/classes/` *directory. This is an advanced topic, but it's a technique that you'll see commonly used in the Java server-side world.*

Next you have to import a class to use with your class:

```
import java.io.Serializable;
```

This tells the compiler you want to use the `Serializable` class that's in the `java.io` package. Now you declare your class:

```
public class CarBean implements Serializable
```

You don't need to worry too much about what `implements Serializable` means. It simply allows the class and its data to be saved to disk and reloaded by Java programs that use the JavaBean.

You've seen the rest of the class, so you'll now take a look at the JSP code in `carPage.jsp`.

You start off with some simple HTML, defining the title of the page and displaying a heading of *Using a JavaBean*:

```
<html>
  <head>
    <title>Using a JavaBean</title>
  </head>
  <body>

    <h2>Using a JavaBean</h2>
```

Next you issue a `<jsp:useBean>` request to the tag handler, which in turn instantiates the JavaBean:

```
<jsp:useBean id="myCar" class="com.apress.cars.CarBean" />
```

The `<jsp:useBean>` tag provides an `id` for this instance called `myCar`. You can use the `id` to identify the JavaBean in the page. Because each bean instance is given an `id`, you could instantiate many JavaBeans of the same type if you wanted to do so, all with different `id` attributes.

The `<jsp:useBean>` tag also identifies a class that's the location of the compiled code for the JavaBean.

Next you use the `<jsp:getProperty>` and `<jsp:setProperty>` tags to retrieve the initial value of the `make` property for this instance and display it, and then you reset this property to `Ferrari`:

```
I have a <jsp:getProperty name="myCar" property="make" /> <br />

<jsp:setProperty name="myCar" property="make" value="Ferrari" />
```

You finish by displaying this new property value:

```
Now I have a <jsp:getProperty name="myCar" property="make" />
```

### Looking More Closely at JavaBean Methods

Although you've used only getter and setter methods in your bean so far, you should realize that you don't need to have just methods that get and set properties. Methods in your bean could contain any kind of functionality. For example, you might include a method that establishes a database connection, and this method is called from another method in the bean. However, the important thing to remember is that unless you include getter and setter methods, you won't be able to retrieve or set values in the bean using tags.

Another important point that may not be clear to you at the moment is that the properties you get don't have to be bean attributes. Although the bean you created earlier uses accessor methods to retrieve and set attribute values, you can return the value of any variable from a get accessor using a tag, not just object attributes.

For example, say you wanted to calculate the cost of a car after sales tax. You could add two new attributes to your class, which represent the cost before tax (cost) and the tax rate (taxRate):

```
private double cost = 10000.00;
private double taxRate = 17.5;
```

You can also easily add a method that calculates the sales tax:

```
public double getPrice()
{
  double price = (cost + (cost * (taxRate/100)));
  return price;
}
```

Now note that this method follows the standard conventions for a getter method; it returns a value but takes no argument, and it follows the standard naming convention. However, as you'll notice, there's no underlying price attribute in your class. It turns out that you don't necessarily need an underlying attribute—you can generate the attribute on the fly as you've done here. Note that you don't need a setter for the price property. This is because this property is generated from other properties and can't itself be set to any particular value. If you did allow someone to pass you a new value of price via a hypothetical setPrice(double price) method, you'd have no way of determining the cost and taxRate variables from it.

Because the name of the getter method implies that the value returned by the method corresponds to a property called price, you can retrieve this value from a bean instance using a <jsp:getProperty> tag:

```
<jsp:getProperty name="myCar" property="price" />
```

Here the bean instance ID is myCar. You'll now create a new version of your CarBean bean that includes the ability to get the price of the car.

### *Trying It Out: Using Bean Methods*

To use bean methods, follow these steps:

1. Make the highlighted changes to CarBean.java:

```
package com.apress.cars;
import java.io.Serializable;
```

```
public class CarBean implements Serializable
{
  private String make = "Ford";
  private double cost = 10000.00;
  private double taxRate = 17.5;

  public CarBean() {}

  public String getMake()
  {
    return make;
  }

  public void setMake(String make)
  {
    this.make = make;
  }

  public double getPrice()
  {
    double price = (cost + (cost * (taxRate/100)));
    return price;
  }
}
```

2. Open a command prompt, change to the `classes` directory, and run the following command to recompile the JavaBean:

```
> javac com/apress/cars/CarBean.java
```

3. Now create a new JSP page, **carPage2.jsp**, in the `Reuse` folder, and enter the following code in it:

```
<html>
    <head>
        <title>Using a JavaBean</title>
    </head>
    <body>

    <h2>Using a JavaBean</h2>

    <jsp:useBean id="myCar" class="com.apress.cars.CarBean" />

    I have a <jsp:getProperty name="myCar" property="make" /> <br />
```

```
        My car costs $<jsp:getProperty name="myCar" property="price" />

        </body>
    </html>
```

4. Restart Tomcat and open `http://localhost:8080/Reuse/carPage2.jsp` in your browser. You should see something like Figure 6-7.

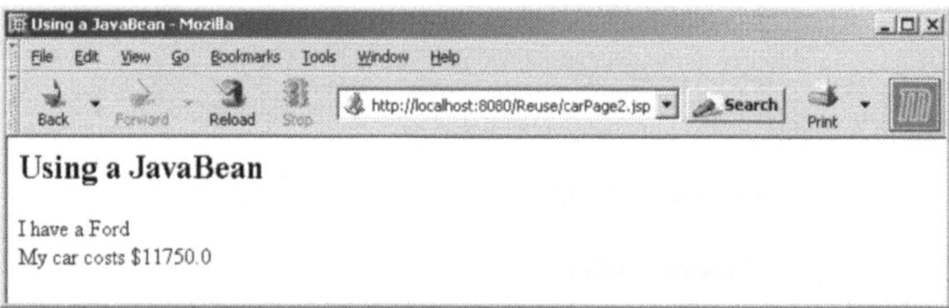


*Figure 6-7. Your JavaBean in use*

*How It Works*

To explain, we'll skip to the new bits you've added. Two new attributes, `cost` and `taxRate`, hold the pretax cost of the car and the sales tax rate:

```
private double cost = 10000.00;
private double taxRate = 17.5;
```

Then you have the method for getting the taxed price of the car:

```
public double getPrice()
{
    double price = (cost + (cost * (taxRate/100)));
    return price;
}
```

Now you'll see how to use the `getPrice()` method in the JSP. As usual, you use the `<jsp:useBean>` tag to create a bean instance, which is given an ID of `myCar`:

```
<jsp:useBean id="myCar" class="com.apress.cars.CarBean" />
```

Then you retrieve the `make` of the car as in the previous example:

```
I have a <jsp:getProperty name="myCar" property="make" /> <br />
```

Finally, you retrieve the post-tax cost of the car, represented by the property `price`, and display it on the Web page:

```
My car costs $<jsp:getProperty name="myCar" property="price" />
```

## A Problem of Currency

So, are you done with this example? Not quite. Take a look at the output of your JSP once again. Do you notice something that doesn't look quite right? Look at the last line:

```
My car costs $11750.0
```

There are quite a few problems with that line. First, in the United States where this example is run, two digits should really be present to the right of the decimal instead of the one zero shown here. But what if you're in continental Europe or Latin America? You might very well use a comma for your decimal point and an entirely different symbol to represent the appropriate currency.

You'll now change this example to display the cost of the car in the proper amount, no matter where you happen to be located.

### *Trying It Out: Formatting Currency*

To format currency, follow these steps:

1. The only file you'll need to change for your example is `carPage2.jsp`. Modify it as highlighted:

```
<%@ taglib uri="http://java.sun.com/jstl/fmt_rt" prefix="fmt" %>
<html>
    <head>
        <title>Using a JavaBean</title>
    </head>
    <body>

    <h2>Using a JavaBean</h2>

    <jsp:useBean id="myCar" class="com.apress.cars.CarBean" />

    I have a <jsp:getProperty name="myCar" property="make" /> <br />

    My car costs <fmt:formatNumber value="${myCar.price}"
                                   type="currency" />

    </body>
</html>
```

2. Navigate to `http://localhost:8080/Reuse/carPage2.jsp` in your browser once again. You should now see a properly formatted currency value customized for your part of the world (see Figure 6-8).

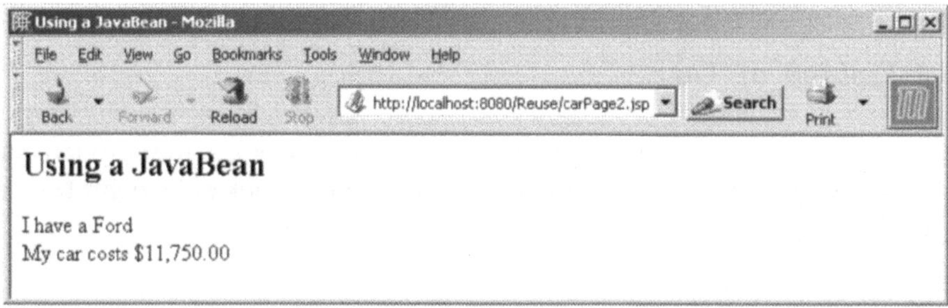


*Figure 6-8. Formatting the price of your car*

*How It Works*

You could have placed logic in `CarBean`'s `getPrice()` method to format your price the way you want it, and indeed, this would have worked fine. However, the JSTL comes with a series of tags designed to format currency, as you've seen earlier in this chapter. Here you leveraged these tags in your JSP instead of making the change in your JavaBean.

However, you can't use the JSTL tag in conjunction with the `<jsp:getProperty>` tag that you used to have because JSP can't use other JSP tags as tag attributes—only text or EL expressions. But not to worry! The `<jsp:useBean>` tag makes JavaBeans available for use with the `<jsp:getProperty>` and `<jsp:setProperty>` tags, as you already know, but it also makes the JavaBean available for use with the JSP EL.

So, to solve your problem, you simply replaced the original line:

```
My car costs $<jsp:getProperty name="myCar" property="price" />
```

with a new line that uses the JSTL and EL in place of the `<jsp:getProperty>` tag:

```
My car costs <fmt:formatNumber value="${myCar.price}"
                               type="currency" />
```

And so you see that you can use either the `<jsp:getProperty>` and `<jsp:setProperty>` tag to access your JavaBeans or the EL. Which you choose is entirely up to you; it's simply a matter of preference. However, to access a JavaBean within tag attributes, you need to use the EL.

## JavaBeans or Enterprise JavaBeans?

Chapter 1 explained that JSP is one part of the Java 2 Enterprise Edition (J2EE) architecture, namely the *presentation tier*. Enterprise JavaBeans (EJBs) are another part of this architecture. EJBs are an advanced topic and beyond the scope of this book. However, as you create bigger and better JSP Web applications, you'll inevitably come across the term.

Our intention here is to warn you not to confuse the JavaBeans you've learned about in this chapter with EJBs. Although they share a similar name, they have very different capabilities, designs, and uses.

JavaBeans are general-purpose components that can be used in a variety of different applications, from very simple to very complex.

EJBs, on the other hand, are components designed for use in complex business applications. They support features commonly used in these types of programs, such as automatically saving and retrieving information to a database, performing many tasks in a single transaction that can be safely aborted if parts of the transaction fail, or communicating other Java components across a network, and so on. Although you could accomplish any one of these EJB features with normal JavaBeans, EJBs make using these complex features easier.

However, EJBs are considerably more complicated to understand, use, and maintain than JavaBeans, and frankly, you'll have your hands full learning JSP technology in this book, so we won't discuss EJBs.

## Summary

This chapter discussed the virtues of code reuse. To summarize the earlier discussion, code reuse makes it easier to maintain your applications after they're developed. Ease of maintenance is important because in the business world, more effort is spent maintaining software than developing it.

After establishing the importance of code reuse, the chapter showed you two mechanisms for reusing code:

- Includes
- Custom tags

You transformed an example program by using these mechanisms.

Furthermore, the chapter introduced you to OOP. The chapter covered the basics of using object methods and showed you how to compile a class and where to store it in a Web application.

Finally, you looked at a specific type of Java class, a JavaBean. You saw how to use these beans to organize your code. You also learned how to use bean tags to instantiate a bean and to set and retrieve data values from the beans. The simplicity of these tags can make your JSP code easier to understand and maintain.

CHAPTER 7

# Performing Time Management

**Because dates and times** are everyday considerations in our lives, it's inevitable that you'll have to deal with them in your applications at some point. In this chapter, you'll learn how to manipulate dates and times in your JavaServer Pages (JSP) pages. You'll start with a look at the date/time classes available in the `java.util` package.

## Introducing the Date Class

The `java.util.Date` class stores a date and time with millisecond precision. To create a `Date` object, you need to use the `Date()` constructor. There are two common ways of using this constructor. The first creates a `Date` instance that holds the current date. For example, the following line will create a `Date` instance called `currentDate`, which holds the current date:

```
Date currentDate = new Date();
```

You may be interested to know that, internally, the `Date` class keeps track of the date by calculating the number of milliseconds that have passed since midnight on January 1, 1970. If you happen to know the number of milliseconds that have passed since that time for any given date, you can use `Date`'s second constructor in this manner:

```
Date myDate = new Date(992710981977);
```

Obviously this isn't particularly user-friendly, but it wasn't designed for human use. You'll come back to this issue in a moment.

### *Retrieving Dates*

Retrieving the date from a `Date` instance is pretty easy. Printing the date in calendar-style format is a matter of just printing the instance itself:

```
System.out.println("Current Date: " + currentDate);
```

The previous line would print *Current Date: Sat Jun 16 18:03:01 GMT+01:00 2004*.

You can also retrieve the number of milliseconds stored in the instance using `getTime()`:

```
System.out.println("Current Date (ms): " + currentDate.getTime());
```

## Comparing Dates

You'll often want to compare two dates to see which one comes first. Because the `java.util.Date` class implements the `Comparable` interface that was covered in the previous section, you can use the `compareTo()` method, as follows, to do this:

```
myDate.compareTo(currentDate);
```

This compares the value of the invoking instance (`myDate` here) to that of the argument passed (`currentDate`). If the values are equal, it returns `0`. If the invoking `Date` is later than the argument `Date` passed, then it returns a positive value. If the invoking `Date` is earlier than the argument, then it returns a negative value. So, assuming that the current date is later than the value in `myDate`, this call should return a negative value.

## Using the Calendar Class

The `Date` class really just performs one function: It represents a given moment in time. Often, however, you want to perform complex calculations involving dates. Consider some of the date-related problems you may want to solve:

- Is January 10, 2030, a Monday?
- How many working days are between now and December 18, 2010?
- Which days of the week will Christmas fall on for the next ten years?

In reality, Java makes working with dates pretty simple. The key is the `java.util.Calendar` class, which is an abstract class (that is, you can't use it directly—you must use one of its subclasses) along with its implementation classes. You can create a `Calendar` instance in the following way:

```
Calendar myTime = Calendar.getInstance();
```

The `Calendar.getInstance()` method figures out what part of the world you're in and creates an appropriate `Calendar` object for you. The `getInstance()` method is static, so you don't need to have an instance of Calendar to use it, as shown in the previous example.

The Calendar class defines a set of constants that makes it easy for you to not only format the date stored in the Calendar instance but also to retrieve specific information from the object such as the month stored, the year stored, and so on. Table 7-1 shows examples of field constants (although there are many others).

*Table 7-1. Field Constants for* Calendar

| Constant | Example Value |
|---|---|
| Calendar.YEAR | 2004 |
| Calendar.MONTH | 5 (0–11, so 5 is June) |
| Calendar.DATE | 16 (1–31) |
| Calendar.HOUR | 6 (1–12) |
| Calendar.MINUTE | 3 (0–59) |
| Calendar.SECOND | 1 (0–59) |
| Calendar.AM_PM | 1 (a.m. is 0, p.m. is 1) |
| Calendar.DAY_OF_WEEK | 7 (1–7, 7 is Saturday) |

These constants are all pretty self-explanatory (DATE is the day of the month), but remember that MONTH goes from 0 to 11, and not from 1 to 12 as you might expect. You can change the values of these constants using get() and set() methods. For example, if myTime is a Calendar instance, you can set the day of the month to the 25th like so:

```
myTime.set(Calendar.DATE, 25);
```

You can see that you must specify the field constant and the new constant value as arguments. If you check the value of Calendar.DATE now using get():

```
System.out.println("Day of the month: " + myTime.get(Calendar.DATE));
```

you'll see the following output: *Day of the month: 25.*

Note that you need to provide the field constant as an argument to get(). If you want, you can retrieve the full date using the getTime() method:

```
System.out.println("Date: " + Calendar.getTime());
```

The output of the previous code would be as follows: *Date: Mon Jun 25 18:03:01 GMT+01:00 2004.*

The `getTime()` method needs no arguments—notice how the day of the week has been automatically changed to match the rest of the date. The full date returned includes the weekday, the local time zone, and the time down to the second. Now, chances are that you're not going to want to display all of this information to a user, and you'll want to be more selective because you have your own standard date format to which you want to adhere. So you'll now look at how Java specifies a date format for objects.

## Formatting Dates

You may have noticed that the standard representation for the date and time varies from country to country. For example, the date format for the United States is as follows:

```
MM/dd/yyyy
```

Here, `MM` is a number from 1 to 12 representing the month, `dd` is the day of the month, and yyyy is the year. For June 16, 2004, this would equate to `06/16/2004`. The United Kingdom date format reverses the order of the month and day:

```
dd/MM/yyyy
```

There are lots more date/time format variations, and Table 7-2 shows some of the most common.

*Table 7-2. Date/Time Formats*

| Format Pattern | Examples |
|---|---|
| `dd-MM-yyyy` | 02-06-2004 |
| `dd MMMM yyyy` | 02 June 2004 |
| `EEE, dd MMMM yyyy` | Sat, 02 June 2004 |
| `HH:mm:ss` | 06:36:33 |
| `hh:mm a` | 06:37 AM |

Notice the use of `EEE` to represent the weekday, `a` to represent a.m./p.m., and `HH`, `mm`, and `ss` to represent hours, minutes, and seconds, respectively.

Java provides a class, `java.text.SimpleDateFormat`, that allows you to format `Date` objects according to user-defined patterns such as these. To do this, you must feed a date format to the `SimpleDateFormat()` constructor, like this:

```
SimpleDateFormat dateFormat = new SimpleDateFormat("EEE, dd MMMM yyyy");
```

In this case you've created a `SimpleDateFormat` object called `dateFormat` that will change the format of a `Date` object to `EEE, dd MMMM yyyy`. So if you have a `Date` object called `currentDate`, you can change it to this new format and print it like so:

```
System.out.println("Date: " + dateFormat.format(currentDate));
```

Notice that you invoked the `format()` method on the `dateFormat` object to actually perform the formatting. The `Date` object you want to format is fed into this method as an argument, and the formatted date is returned as a string.

If you want to format `Calendar` instances, you must first cast the instance into a `Date` instance using the `getTime()` method:

```
String gCalFormatted = dateFormat.format(myTime.getTime());
```

To really understand `Date` objects, you'll now use them in a quick class. Because you've been concentrating on classes in this chapter far more than JSP pages, you'll build a JSP-based example.

### *Trying It Out: Creating Date/Time Classes*

Remember the millennium counters that displayed the days until New Year's Eve 2000? This example does much the same thing—except that the year 2000 has passed us by, so you have the year 3000 to look forward to instead!

The example uses a JavaBean defined in the file `MillenniumCounter.java`. This bean stores the current date and a target date (the new millennium in this case) as attributes and allows you to get, set, and manipulate these dates. Follow these steps:

1. Create a Web application called **Utility**, and create a **WEB-INF** folder and a **classes** subdirectory of `WEB-INF`.

2. Save the following file in the `com\apress\utilities` directory (under the `classes` directory of your `Utility` Web application folder) under the name **MillenniumCounter.java**:

```
package com.apress.utilities;

import java.util.Date;
import java.util.Calendar;

import java.text.SimpleDateFormat;
public class MillenniumCounter
{
```

```
    private SimpleDateFormat dateFormat;
    private Calendar targetDate;

    public MillenniumCounter()
    {
      dateFormat = new SimpleDateFormat("EEE, dd MMMM yyyy");

      targetDate = Calendar.getInstance();
      targetDate.set(targetDate.YEAR, 3000);
      targetDate.set(targetDate.MONTH, 0);
      targetDate.set(targetDate.DATE, 1);
      targetDate.set(targetDate.AM_PM, 0);
      targetDate.set(targetDate.HOUR, 0);
      targetDate.set(targetDate.MINUTE, 0);
      targetDate.set(targetDate.SECOND, 0);
    }

    public String getToday()
    {
      return dateFormat.format(new Date());
    }

    public long getDays()
    {
      Calendar now = Calendar.getInstance();
      if (now.after(targetDate))
        return 0;
      else
      {
        long milliseconds = (targetDate.getTimeInMillis()
                            - now.getTimeInMillis());
        long seconds = milliseconds / 1000;
        long minutes = seconds / 60;
        long hours = minutes / 60;
        long days = hours / 24;

        return days;
      }
    }
  }
```

3. Compile it from the classes directory with this command:

```
> javac com\apress\utilities\MillenniumCounter.java
```

4. Next, you need a JSP page that instantiates the bean and uses it to display how many days there are to go until the new millennium, along with the current date. Save the following file, `MillenniumCounter.jsp`, in the `Utility` folder:

```
<html>
  <head><title>Millennium Counter</title></head>
  <body>

    <jsp:useBean id="counter" scope="page"
                 class="com.apress.utilities.MillenniumCounter"/>

    The current date is ${counter.today}
    <p/>
    Only ${counter.days} days until the new millennium!

  </body>
</html>
```

5. Start Tomcat if it's not already going, and point your browser to the new page at `http://localhost:8080/Utility/MillenniumCounter.jsp`. You should see something like Figure 7-1 (depending on the date, of course):

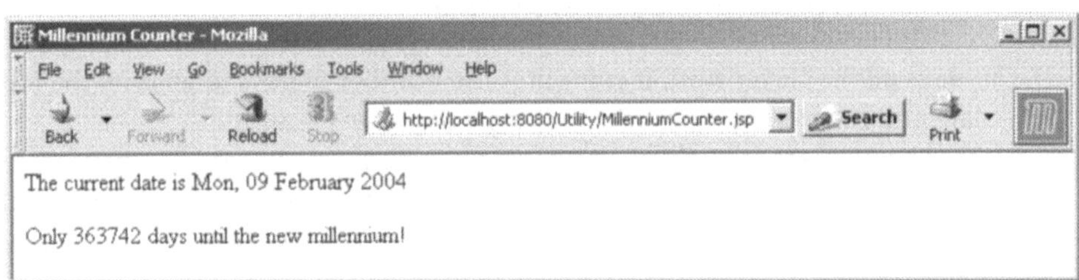


*Figure 7-1. A formatted date in a JSP page*

### *How It Works*

To understand how it works, you'll look first at the bean. You start by stating the package that the bean is in and by importing the utility classes you'll need. The class itself has two attributes: a `SimpleDateFormat` object to hold the date format and a `Calendar` object to hold the target date of the new millennium:

```
private SimpleDateFormat dateFormat;
private Calendar targetDate;
```

Next you initialize your attributes in the constructor. You first initialize the `SimpleDateFormat` object attribute with the format `"EEE, dd MMMM yyyy"`:

```
dateFormat = new SimpleDateFormat("EEE, dd MMMM yyyy");
```

The next attribute to initialize is the target date. You initialize this to the year 3000 by setting all of the field constants of the targetDate instance individually:

```
targetDate = Calendar.getInstance();
targetDate.set(targetDate.YEAR, 3000);
targetDate.set(targetDate.MONTH, 0);
targetDate.set(targetDate.DATE, 1);
targetDate.set(targetDate.AM_PM, 0);
targetDate.set(targetDate.HOUR, 0);
targetDate.set(targetDate.MINUTE, 0);
targetDate.set(targetDate.SECOND, 0);
```

After the constructor you have the getToday() method, which retrieves today's date and returns it in the date format you want:

```
public String getToday()
{
  return dateFormat.format(new Date());
}
```

Note that you could have just returned today's date and used the JSTL to format the date, as you did in previous chapters.

The last method in the bean class, getDays(), is the most interesting because it does all the clever stuff. It computes the number of days to go until the target date and returns this number. You'll now see how it does this.

The first step is to check that the new millennium hasn't already passed you by! You accomplish this by using the after() method of the Calendar class, which returns true if the passed Calendar occurs after the other Calendar:

```
public long getDays()
{
  Calendar now = Calendar.getInstance();
  if (now.after(targetDate))
    return 0;
```

Now, if the present date comes before the year 3000, which is likely, you next calculate the number of milliseconds between the present date and the year 3000:

```
else
{
  long milliseconds = (targetDate.getTimeInMillis()
                           - now.getTimeInMillis());
```

Because humans don't really think in terms of milliseconds, you do some basic math to convert the milliseconds into days:

```
long seconds = milliseconds / 1000;
long minutes = seconds / 60;
long hours = minutes / 60;
long days = hours / 24;
```

Now you just return the value for days, and you're done:

```
  return days;
}
```

Well, you've looked at the bean, so now you'll check out the JSP page. Ignoring the HTML, you start by instantiating a `MillenniumCounter` called `counter`:

```
<jsp:useBean id="counter" scope="page"
             class="com.apress.utilities.MillenniumCounter"/>
```

You then use the JSP EL to access the bean methods. You retrieve and display today's date by accessing the `today` property (via the `getToday()` method):

```
The current date is ${counter.today}
```

Finally, you access the `days` property and display the number of days to go until the new millennium:

```
<p/>
Only ${counter.days} days until the new millennium!
```

And that's it!

## Formatting Dates with the JSTL

As noted before, there's more than one way to do most things in JSP, and formatting dates is no exception. You've seen how to format dates using JavaBeans, so you'll next look at what the JSTL has to offer.

### *Using <fmt:parseDate>*

The first tag you'll learn about is `<fmt:parseDate>`. You can use this tag to read a date into a variable for use on the page. It has nine attributes (see Table 7-3).

*Table 7-3.* `<fmt:parseDate>` *Attributes*

| Attribute | Description | Required? | Default |
|---|---|---|---|
| dateStyle | FULL, LONG, MEDIUM, SHORT, or DEFAULT | No | DEFAULT |
| parseLocale | Locale to use when parsing the date | No | Default locale |
| pattern | Custom parsing pattern used in the same way as the previous date classes | No | None |
| scope | Scope of the variable in which to store the parsed date (only used if var is specified) | No | page |
| timeStyle | FULL, LONG, MEDIUM, SHORT, or DEFAULT | No | DEFAULT |
| timeZone | Time zone of the parsed date | No | Default time zone |
| type | DATE, TIME, or BOTH | No | DATE |
| value | Date value to parse | No | Body of the tag |
| var | Name of the variable in which to store the parsed date (as a java.util.Date) | No | Print to page |

Even though none of the attributes is required, if you omit value, you must provide the tag with a date in its body.

The dateStyle attribute uses the following constants:

- SHORT is numeric, such as 12.18.04.
- MEDIUM is longer, such as Jan 18, 2004.
- LONG is longer, such as January 18, 2004.
- FULL is quite comprehensive, such as Sunday, January 18, 2004 AD.
- DEFAULT is the default for the server's locale (usually the same as MEDIUM).

If the date is to be in a different form than these constants, you must use the pattern attribute to specify the form of the date. This is a very unforgiving tag and will parse date strings only if they're in the exact format specified. Make sure you validate any dates before they get to this tag.

The following example reads a date and places it in a variable for later use:

```
<%@ taglib uri="http://java.sun.com/jstl/fmt_rt" prefix="fmt" %>

<fmt:parseDate var="dateEntered" value="${param.date}"/>

Parsed date: ${dateEntered}
```

This will call the toString() method of the java.util.Date object stored as dateEntered and print the long form of the date (even though it was originally in the default form): *Parsed date: Sun Apr 30 00:00:00 BST 2006.*

To do this with a value that doesn't conform to one of the predefined constants, you'd specify a pattern:

```
<%@ taglib uri="http://java.sun.com/jstl/fmt_rt" prefix="fmt" %>

<fmt:parseDate value="${param.date}" pattern="dd/MM/yy"/>
```

This has the same result as before except that it'll accept date strings only in the form dd/MM/yy and doesn't instantiate a variable for later use; the value of the java.util.Date object is printed to the screen.

## Using <fmt:formatDate>

Although you can use <fmt:parseDate> to read dates into java.util.Date objects, you use <fmt:formatDate> to write formatted dates to the page (or to a String variable). It has eight attributes (see Table 7-4).

*Table 7-4.* <fmt:formatDate> *Attributes*

| **Attribute** | **Description** | **Required** | **Default** |
|---|---|---|---|
| dateStyle | FULL, LONG, MEDIUM, SHORT, or DEFAULT | No | DEFAULT |
| pattern | Custom formatting pattern used in the same way as the previous date classes | No | None |
| scope | Scope of the variable in which to store the formatted date (only used if var is specified) | No | page |
| timeStyle | FULL, LONG, MEDIUM, SHORT, or DEFAULT | No | DEFAULT |
| timeZone | Time zone of the formatted date | No | Default time zone |
| type | DATE, TIME, or BOTH | No | DATE |
| value | java.util.Date object to format | Yes | |
| var | Name of the variable in which to store the formatted date (as a String) | No | Print to page |

The attributes of <fmt:formatDate> are similar to those of <fmt:parseDate>. The main differences are that the value attribute is required and takes a java.util.Date as opposed to a String and that any variable exported is a String, not a java.util.Date. This tag is more forgiving than <fmt:parseDate> and uses the dateStyle and timeStyle attributes to format the input, not to validate it. The following is an example to obtain your default setting:

```
<%@ taglib uri="http://java.sun.com/jstl/fmt_rt" prefix="fmt" %>

<jsp:useBean id="now" class="java.util.Date" />
Default format: <fmt:formatDate value="${now}" dateStyle="DEFAULT"/>
```

The results should be similar to *Default format: Feb 9, 2004.*

As with the date classes you saw earlier, you can use <fmt:formatDate> to format dates using custom patterns:

```
<%@ taglib uri="http://java.sun.com/jstl/fmt_rt" prefix="fmt" %>

<jsp:useBean id="now" class="java.util.Date" />
Custom format: <fmt:formatDate value="${now}" pattern="EEE, dd MMMM yyyy"/>
```

This is the result: *Custom format: Mon, 09 February 2004.*

*Trying It Out: Date Formatting with the JSTL*

In this quick example, you'll build a very simple form to submit a date and a format to use:

1. Create **dateForm.html** in the Utility Web application, and add the following HTML to it. Note the restriction on the format; as noted previously, <fmt:parseDate> is an unforgiving tag and will expect a certain form of input. In a more sophisticated example, you'd check the input and inform readers if they typed in the wrong format (as you did in Chapter 3) or alter the input to the correct format:

```
<html>

  <head><title>A date formatting form</title></head>

  <body>
    <form action="./format.jsp" method="POST">
      <table>
        <tr>
```

```
          <td>Date to format (mm/dd/yyyy): </td>
          <td><input type="text" name="date"/></td>
        </tr>
        <tr>
          <td>Format: </td>
          <td><input type="text" name="format"/></td>
        </tr>
      </table>
      <input type="submit"/>
    </form>
  </body>

</head>
```

2. Create **format.jsp** in the same directory:

```
<%@ taglib uri="http://java.sun.com/jstl/fmt_rt" prefix="fmt" %>

<fmt:parseDate value="${param.date}"
                          var="dateEntered" dateStyle="SHORT"/>

<html>

  <head><title>Formatted date</title></head>

  <body>
    Date entered: ${dateEntered}<br />
    Format: ${param.format}<br />
    <hr />

    Formatted date: <fmt:formatDate value="${dateEntered}"
                                 pattern="${param.format}"/><br />
    Default date: <fmt:formatDate value="${dateEntered}"
                                 dateStyle="DEFAULT"/><br />

  </body>

</html>
```

3. Navigate to `http://localhost:8080/Utility/dateForm.html`, and fill in some values as in Figure 7-2.

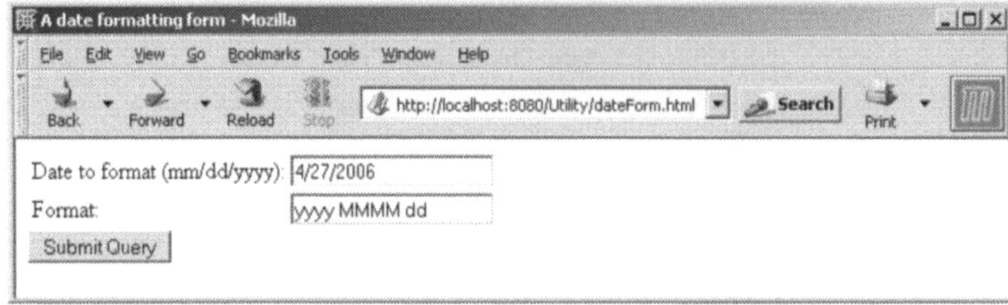

*Figure 7-2. A date-formatting form*

4. Submit the form. You should see something similar to Figure 7-3.

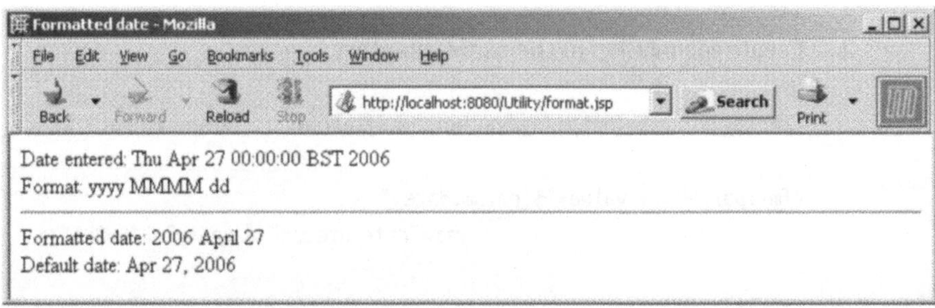

*Figure 7-3. Formatted dates*

### How It Works

The simple form submits to the `format.jsp` page using the `POST` Hypertext Transfer Protocol (HTTP) method. It sends the parameters `date` and `format`:

```
<form action="./format.jsp" method="POST">
  <table>
    <tr>
      <td>Date to format (mm/dd/yyyy): </td>
      <td><input type="text" name="date"/></td>
    </tr>
    <tr>
      <td>Format: </td>
      <td><input type="text" name="format"/></td>
    </tr>
  </table>
  <input type="submit"/>
</form>
```

As noted previously, the parsing tag is very strict and will accept only a predefined format of input date. In this case, you're using `mm/dd/yyyy`.

The formatting functionality isn't much more sophisticated than the form. First, you parse the date string and store it in a variable called dateEntered of type java.util.Date:

```
<fmt:parseDate value="${param.date}" var="dateEntered" dateStyle="SHORT"/>
```

The dateStyle value of SHORT tells the tag to expect input of the type mm/dd/yyyy.

Second, you display the parsed value and the format you're about to use:

```
Date entered: ${dateEntered}<br />
Format: ${param.format}<br />
```

The dateEntered variable is of type java.util.Date, so the first line calls its toString() method to display it in the browser window.

The formatting is the final piece of work the page has to do:

```
Formatted date: <fmt:formatDate value="${dateEntered}"
                                pattern="${param.format}"/><br />
Default date: <fmt:formatDate value="${dateEntered}"
                              dateStyle="DEFAULT"/><br />
```

The first line takes the java.util.Date object and formats it with the String the user submitted with the form. The result is a String that's displayed on the page. The second line is similar to the example you saw in the "<fmt:formatDate>" section and formats the date in the default format for the server.

## Summary

In this chapter you looked at the date manipulation properties of Java and JSP. Flexibility when working with dates is essential when you write Web applications because dates are one of the most common types of data asked for in HTML forms. Whether you're asking for credit card expiry dates or a customer's date of birth, dates appear a lot. However, there are many ways to write dates, and you saw some ways to manipulate dates to make them fit into your application.

Specifically, you dealt with the Java date classes in the java.util package and saw how to retrieve and compare dates. Next you looked at the Calendar class, which allows you to work with all kinds of dates: past, present, and future. You compared this with java.util.Date, which represents a single moment in time. You then learned how to format dates into forms more appropriate for your applications.

You then looked at similar functionality in JSP. Once again you used the JSTL but this time using the <fmt:parseDate> and <fmt:formatDate> tags. These tags allow you to read date strings, store them as java.util.Date objects, and then format them for display in your applications.

CHAPTER 8

# Using JSP and XML Together

**Extensible Markup Language** (XML) has become the de facto standard for data interchange on the Internet these days. It has revolutionized the way the Web works by defining a standard for electronic exchange of information. It has done the same thing for data that Java did for code—it has made it portable.

What is XML, and why is it important? We'll try and answer these and other questions you may have in this chapter, and we'll show how you can use XML in your JavaServer Pages (JSP) applications.

## Introducing XML

Before delving deeper into the guts of XML, you'll examine the acronym XML itself. X, for Extensible, means you can extend the language to meet various requirements. ML, for Markup Language, means it's a language for identifying structures within a document.

XML is extensible because it isn't a fixed language. You can extend it to create your own languages in order to match your particular needs. In a way, XML isn't really a language in itself; rather, it's a standard for defining other languages to fit various computing scenarios, typically in the business or academic spheres.

A markup language is used to add meaning to different parts of a document. Hypertext Markup Language (HTML) is another type of markup language. Its tags give particular meaning to parts of a document. For instance, the `<table>` tag *marks up* a section to represent a table.

To clarify things further, you'll look at some XML documents. The following is a file called `web.xml` used to configure Tomcat:

```
<?xml version="1.0" encoding="ISO-8859-1"?>

<web-app xmlns="http://java.sun.com/xml/ns/j2ee"
     xmlns:xsi="http://www.w3.org/2001/XMLSchema-instance"
     xsi:schemaLocation="http://java.sun.com/xml/ns/j2ee
              http://java.sun.com/xml/ns/j2ee/web-app_2_4.xsd"
     version="2.4">
</web-app>
```

Another XML-like file type you're acquainted with is an HTML file:

```
<html>

  <head><title>A date formatting form</title></head>

  <body>
    <form action="./format.jsp" method="POST">
      <table>
        <tr>
          <td>Date to format (mm/dd/yyyy): </td>
          <td><input type="text" name="date"/></td>
        </tr>
        <tr>
          <td>Format: </td>
          <td><input type="text" name="format"/></td>
        </tr>
      </table>
      <input type="submit"/>
    </form>
  </body>

</html>
```

In many ways, XML is similar to HTML. Both these markup languages use tags to enclose items with particular meaning; these tags are enclosed within angle brackets, as in `<table>`, `<web-app>`, `<html>`, and so on. Also, there will be a corresponding closing tag that has the same name but starts with `</`. These closing tags mark the end of the item referred to by the tag, and in XML, the whole section including the start tag and the end tag is known as an *element.* Note that although many HTML elements don't require a closing tag (such as `<p>` and `<br>`), XML elements must always have a start and an end tag. Both HTML and XML allow elements to be contained, or *nested,* within each other, as you can see from the previous examples (the `<tr>` element is nested within the `<table>` element because it appears after the `<table>` start tag and before the `</table>` end tag). However, XML is much stricter than HTML in this regard because it doesn't allow elements to overlap (that is, if an element's start tag appears after another's start tag, the nested element's end tag must appear before the other's end tag).

There are many other ways in which XML is quite different from HTML. XML isn't limited to a preexisting set of tags, as HTML is, and although HTML is primarily concerned with describing how a document should be laid out in a browser, XML documents are more concerned with describing the data contained in a document, and they're generally quite independent of how that data may be rendered for display.

Both these documents use an XML language, often called an *XML dialect*, to give meaning to the data they contain. The actual markup tags (or XML *elements*) each uses are different, though. For instance, `web.xml` starts with the `<web-app>` element, and the first element in an HTML file is `<html>`.

Methods exist to enforce the dialect so that a document is always understandable. In `web.xml` the `<web-app>` element contains a reference to an XML Schema. An XML Schema is a document that defines what can and can't appear in a dialect and is itself an XML document. Another method for defining a dialect is a Document Type Definition (DTD). These aren't XML documents but rather are written in their own language. You'll see more of these later the "Well-Formed vs. Valid Documents" section.

## Understanding the Structure of XML Data

XML is a vendor-neutral standard, regulated by the World Wide Web Consortium (W3C; `http://www.w3c.org/`). You can find the specification at `http://www.w3c.org/TR/WD-xml`, which contains the formal details of XML syntax. We'll cover the essentials here, starting with a look at a very simple XML document:

```
<?xml version="1.0"?>
<!DOCTYPE Book SYSTEM "book.dtd">
<Book>
  <Author-Name>
    <Last>
      Einstein
    </Last>

    <First>
      Albert
    </First>
  </Author-Name>

  <Book-Name>
    General Relativity
  </Book-Name>

  <Edition Year="1930"/>
  <Bestseller/>
</Book>
```

XML documents are composed of data, enclosed within tags that describe that data. There may also be *processing instructions*, which provide specific details required for an application that will read the XML document, and other elements, such as the `xml` declaration or a DTD declaration as shown here.

Note that the xml declaration starts with <? and ends with ?>, and it doesn't require a closing tag. This notation is also used for processing instructions, but despite the common misconception, the xml declaration isn't strictly speaking a processing instruction. The xml declaration may also specify encoding and standalone attributes, which specify the character encoding used by the document and whether the document depends on any others:

```
<?xml version="1.0" encoding="ISO-8859-1" standalone="yes"?>
```

The DTD declaration, which starts with <! and ends with > and also doesn't require a closing tag, specifies what the name of the first element in the file must be (which here is Book) and also specifies where to find the DTD file that details rules that XML elements in this particular dialect must obey. The SYSTEM part indicates that the DTD can be found at either a relative or an absolute uniform resource locator (URL). If, however, the DTD is officially sanctioned by a standards body, you'd use PUBLIC instead.

Note that DTDs are falling out of favor now, and the more recent XML Schema standard is often preferred because it lets you specify more rigorous rules for an XML dialect. However, DTDs are still used in many companies, partly because of legacy issues and also because DTDs are somewhat easier to create. We'll cover this issue further in the section "Well-Formed vs. Valid Documents."

The actual content of an XML document (that is, the data and XML elements it contains) must obey certain syntax rules as we've hinted at already. We've already mentioned the first element in a document, and this element is known as the *root element*—all other elements must be contained within it. That is to say, all valid XML documents must have one and only one root element. In the XML file shown previously, the root element is <Book>.

All XML elements can contain other XML elements and/or text data as required; such contained elements are known as *child elements* of the containing element. For instance, the previous <Author-Name> element has the child elements <Last> and <First>.

If an element has neither child elements nor text data—that is, if it could be written as so:

```
<Bestseller>
</Bestseller>
```

then you can refer to it using a shorthand form like this:

```
<Bestseller/>
```

Element names can be almost anything you like as long as they start with either a letter or an underscore and don't contain whitespace (such as return characters or spaces). Be aware that XML element names are case-sensitive. As stated previously, all XML elements must have both a start tag and an end tag, unless they use the short form shown previously (`<Bestseller/>`). As we've also said already, XML elements may not overlap. The following is invalid nesting:

```
<Book>
  <Author>
  </Book>
</Author>
```

The following is valid nesting:

```
<Book>
  <Author>
  </Author>
</Book>
```

Because the `<Book>` element is the first to be opened, it should be the last to be closed. In the invalid example, its closing element appears before `</Author>` and is therefore wrong.

XML documents that satisfy these rules are known as *well-formed* documents.

## Attributes

Attributes of an element are listed in the element's start tag and give further meaning to that element. Consider the `<Edition>` element from the example:

```
<Edition Year="1930"/>
```

Its `Year` attribute has the value `1930`. Attributes follow the same rule for names as elements and must have their value between quotes. Only one attribute of the same name may be given for an element.

## Comments

To improve the readability of your XML documents, you can place comments within them using the same syntax as used in HTML files: You place them between `<!--` and `-->` sequences. Well-placed comments can be invaluable when others try to read your XML files (or even when you read them a while after writing them!). As in all programming contexts, prudent use of comments is a very good habit to have. Note that comments don't form part of the actual content of an XML document and may be ignored when the document is read, so you should avoid using code that depends on them.

## Entity References

There are cases when the data in an XML document needs to contain characters that normally have a special purpose, such as the less-than symbol (<) or the apostrophe ('). You can represent these using *entity references*, just as you would in HTML.

An entity reference uses the syntax &entityname; XML has a total of five entity references (see Table 8-1).

*Table 8-1. XML's Entity References*

| Entity Reference | Character | Notes |
|---|---|---|
| < | < | lt stands for *less than.* |
| > | > | gt stands for *greater than.* Only required in attribute values. |
| & | & | The ampersand sign. |
| " | " | Double quotes. |
| ' | ' | A single quote—the apostrophe. |

So, if you had a book with the title *Learn HTML from < to >*, you could describe it by using the following XML element:

```
<Book>
  <Book-Name>
    Learn HTML from &lt; to >
  </Book-Name>
</Book>
```

You don't need to use > for the > character because when this character appears in text data, it's clear that it doesn't mark the end of a tag.

## Character DATA (CDATA) Sections

Entity references let you use characters that normally have a reserved meaning but wouldn't be a great solution if your text data contains many instances of such characters.

The better solution is to place such data inside a character DATA (CDATA) section. These sections begin with the sequence <![CDATA[ and end with ]]>. Text within such sections can contain any characters at all, and their content is preserved as it appears, including any whitespace. Say you had an XML element that contained programming code like so:

```
<Code>
for(int i = 0; i < 10; i++)
{
  if(i < 5) System.err.println("I would rather be fishing.");
  if(i == 5)System.err.println("I would rather be at my PlayStation.");
  if(i > 5) System.err.println("I would rather be at DreamWorld.");
}
</Code>
```

As you can see, this code contains a lot of special characters, and it's formatted in a way you may want to keep. Thus, it'd probably be a good idea to put the whole section in a CDATA section:

```
<Code>
<![CDATA[
for(int i = 0; i < 10; i++)
{
  if(i < 5) System.err.println("I would rather be fishing.");
  if(i == 5)System.err.println("I would rather be at my PlayStation.");
  if(i > 5) System.err.println("I would rather be at DreamWorld.");
}
]]>
</Code>
```

## Well-Formed vs. Valid Documents

As mentioned before, XML documents follow a set of rules that dictates how an XML document must be structured. XML documents that satisfy these rules are said to be *well-formed*. This isn't to be confused with the similar concept of validity. A *valid* XML document conforms to the rules specified in the corresponding DTD or Schema for that dialect. The DTD (or XML Schema) details rules that documents in a particular XML dialect must obey. They specify which elements are defined by that dialect and the attributes that particular elements can have.

Thus, although you can say that the previous example file, `book.xml`, is well-formed because it satisfies the rules of XML, you can't say just by looking at it whether it's valid. To do that, you'd need to see the DTD that it specifies, namely `book.dtd`. Look at that DTD file now:

```
<!ELEMENT Book   (Author-Name+, Book-Name, Edition?, Bestseller?) >
<!ELEMENT Author-Name  (Last, First, Middle?) >
<!ELEMENT Last      (#PCDATA) >
<!ELEMENT First     (#PCDATA) >
<!ELEMENT Book-Name (#PCDATA) >
<!ELEMENT Edition EMPTY>
<!ATTLIST Edition
         Year   CDATA  #REQUIRED>
<!ELEMENT Bestseller EMPTY>
```

The first thing to notice is that all items of a DTD start with `<!` and end with `>`. Items define either elements or attributes.

## Elements

The `<!ELEMENT>` item describes an element that may appear in XML documents that conform to this DTD:

```
<!ELEMENT Book   (Author-Name+, Book-Name, Edition?, Bestseller?) >
```

This line describes an XML element called `Book` and states that the `<Book>` element can have the child elements named in the comma-separated list in parentheses. The order in which these elements are listed in the brackets corresponds to the order that these elements must appear in XML documents. If the order doesn't matter, you can list the elements using just a space rather than a comma to separate them:

```
<!ELEMENT Book   (Author-Name+ Book-Name Edition? Bestseller?) >
```

The + and ? characters indicate how many times the preceding element may occur, according to Table 8-2.

*Table 8-2. XML Symbols*

| Symbol | Meaning |
|---|---|
| , | Strict ordering: Elements must be in the specified order. |
| + | One or more. |
| * | Zero or more. |
| ? | Optional (zero or one). |

So the DTD states that the <Author-Name> element may appear one or more times, the <Edition> element is optional, and so on. If no symbol is present, that element may appear only once, as is the case with the <Book-Name> element.

The <Last> element follows this rule:

```
<!ELEMENT Last       (#PCDATA) >
```

This simply means that this element must contain text data only, as indeed it does in the book.xml file:

```
<Last>
  Einstein
</Last>
```

The final element to look at is this:

```
<!ELEMENT BestSeller EMPTY>
```

EMPTY indicates that the <Bestseller> element must always be empty and not contain any textual data or other nested tags. In other words, it must be either this:

```
<Bestseller/>
```

or this:

```
<Bestseller></Bestseller>
```

### Attributes

The only remaining item in the DTD we haven't discussed is that for the <Edition> element. There are in fact two DTD items that relate to this element:

```
<!ELEMENT Edition EMPTY>
<!ATTLIST Edition
          Year   CDATA  #REQUIRED>
```

These two rules state that the <Edition> element may not contain any text data or child elements and that it has an attribute called Year. This attribute is required, and it's of the type CDATA (character data). Simply omit the #REQUIRED keyword if the attribute isn't required.

An XML element may have multiple attributes, and a DTD can restrict each attribute to one of a given set of values. It can also specify one as a default like this:

```
<!ATTLIST Edition
          Year CDATA #REQUIRED
          Month (Jan | Feb | Mar) 'Jan'>
```

This would add a second attribute to the `<Edition>` element that may have a value of `Jan`, `Feb`, or `Mar`, and the default value is `Jan` if the attribute isn't specified.

### The Problem with DTDs

DTDs have a number of problems:

- The DTD content model is hard to manage. In the DTD application, you've seen how to define a list of subelements with cardinality 1, but allowing them to appear in any particular order is difficult.
- DTDs aren't written in XML. This is a very big disadvantage. You can't use XML applications to read, edit, or build DTDs. If you want to write DTDs from a database or a document, it'd be easier if they could be written in XML.
- DTDs can't validate data types. If you want to restrict an element or an attribute to be a number, a date, or some other specific data type, you can't do that because DTDs can use only the `#PCDATA` and `CDATA` data types.
- DTDs can't validate element contents. You can use an enumeration to validate an attribute value against a list of admitted values, but you can't do the same with attributes. In many situations you'll want to define an element that can only have some specific values; this is very useful when you have to exchange information between different applications using XML.
- You can't use DTDs with namespaces. Namespaces are heavily used to combine two different vocabularies in the same XML document. Because the document can refer to only one external DTD, you can't use a DTD to validate a document that uses multiple namespaces.

That just about wraps it up for DTDs. You'll now look at XML Schemas, which are rapidly gaining ground over DTDs.

## Defining Validity with Schemas

Before delving into the world of XML Schemas, you need to understand the concept of *XML namespaces*.

## XML Namespaces

Namespaces crop up in other areas of programming as well as XML. In general, namespaces serve two basic purposes:

- To group related information under one umbrella
- To avoid name collision between different groups

Namespaces in XML also serve these purposes by associating elements that belong together with a unique identifier. The unique identifier is a uniform resource indicator (URI), and because these can be quite long and unwieldy, a shorthand form is almost always associated with a namespace. Elements that belong to that namespace are then prefixed by the short form, differentiating them from other elements with the same name but belonging to a different namespace. For instance, the XML file has an element called `<Last>` that contains an author's last name. This same element could quite easily be used in another XML dialect, perhaps one that describes the results of a book awards ceremony. This other dialect's `<Last>` element would probably have a quite different meaning, and by having a unique namespace for each dialect, you can quite easily have an XML document that contains both types of element without ambiguity.

You specify the namespace used through the `xmlns` attribute of the root element of an XML document like this:

```
<Book xmlns="http://www.apress.com/bookCatalog"
      xmlns:prize="http://www.apress.com/bookAwards">
```

The unique identifier for these namespaces is given by the value of the `xmlns` attribute in question, and the short prefix for that namespace is the part preceded by the colon (:).

You can see that the first namespace doesn't have any prefix—it's called the *default* namespace, and any elements that don't have a prefix are assumed to belong to it. The second namespace has a prefix of `prize`. The XML document can then contain an element such as this without any ambiguity between the two types of `<Last>` element:

```
<Book-Name>
  <First>
    Joey
  </First>
  <Last>
    Gillespie
  </Last>
```

```
  <prize:Awards>
    <prize:Last/>
  </prize:Awards>
</Book-Name>
```

## XML Schemas

Schemas do the same thing as DTDs, but they overcome many of the shortcomings that DTDs exhibit when applied to XML. Many of their advantages actually stem from the fact that they are themselves written in an XML dialect.

When elements in an XML document must conform to a certain Schema, you specify where a copy of the appropriate Schema can be found using the `schemaLocation` attribute on the document's root element. This attribute is defined by the *schema instance namespace*, which you must therefore declare using an `xmlns` attribute, typically with the prefix `xsi`:

```
<Book
xmlns:xsi="http://www.w3.org/2001/XMLSchema-instance"
    xsi:schemaLocation="Book.xsd">
```

Note the file extension of `.xsd` for the Schema file (which stands for *XML Schema Definition*).

The following is this `Book.xsd` file, equivalent to the DTD you've already seen:

```
<?xml version="1.0"?>
<xs:schema xmlns:xs="http://www.w3.org/2001/XMLSchema">
  <xs:element name="Book">
    <xs:complexType>
      <xs:sequence>
        <xs:element name="Author-Name">
          <xs:complexType>
            <xs:element name="Last" type="xs:string"/>
            <xs:element name="First" type="xs:string"/>
          </xs:complexType>
        </xs:element>
        <xs:element name="Book-Name" type="xs:string"/>
        <xs:element name="Edition">
          <xs:complexType>
            <xs:attribute name="Year" type="xs:string" use="required"/>
          </xs:complexType>
        </xs:element>
```

```
        <xs:element name="Bestseller" />
      </xs:sequence>
    </xs:complexType>
  </xs:element>
</xs:schema>
```

The first thing to spot is the first line of this Schema:

```
<?xml version="1.0"?>
```

This shouldn't be surprising. It is, as we said before, an XML document. After this comes the `<schema>` root element, which defines the `xs` namespace.

### *The Root Element*

The `<schema>` element is the root element of every XML Schema. Notice that its `xmlns` attribute defines the `xs` namespace that qualifies the `<schema>` element itself.

Usually, there are a couple more attributes—namely, `targetNamespace` and `elementFormDefault`. `targetNamespace` specifies the URI to uniquely identify this Schema, and `elementFormDefault` lets you require your elements to always be qualified with the namespace prefix:

```
<xs:schema xmlns:xs="http://www.w3.org/2001/XMLSchema"
           targetNamespace="http://www.apress.com/begjsp2"
           elementFormDefault="qualified">
```

### *Elements*

Elements within a Schema can be either simple or complex.

A *simple element* doesn't contain any nested elements and can't have attributes: It may contain text only between the start and the end tags. This is an example of a simple element from the previous example:

```
<xs:element name="Last" type="xs:string"/>
```

which corresponds to the `Last` tag in the XML:

```
<Last>
  Einstein
</Last>
```

Notice that the type attribute qualifies this element as a string type. This means the value of this element is to be interpreted as plain text. Other possible types include decimal, integer, Boolean, date, and time.

Finally, you can place restrictions on how many times this element may appear by the attributes minOccurs and maxOccurs. If neither is specified, the element can occur only once. maxOccurs="unbounded" allows unlimited occurrences of the element.

## Complex Elements

Complex elements can contain child elements and attributes. This is how you define the <Author-Name> and <Edition> elements:

```
<xs:element name="Author-Name">
  <xs:complexType>
    <xs:element name="Last" type="xs:string"/>
    <xs:element name="First" type="xs:string"/>
  </xs:complexType>
</xs:element>
<xs:element name="Edition">
  <xs:complexType>
    <xs:attribute name="Year" type="xs:string" use="required"/>
  </xs:complexType>
</xs:element>
```

You define child elements for <Author-Name> and an attribute for <Edition> using the Schema <complexType> element. Just as simple elements, attributes can have a default value or a fixed value specified. Any specified default value is automatically given for an attribute when no other value is supplied. If a fixed value is specified, no other value may be specified for that element.

All attributes are optional by default. To explicitly specify whether the attribute is optional, use the use attribute. It can have one of two values, optional or required.

## Restricting the Content

You saw some examples of how to restrict the values contained in your XML documents when you learned how to use the type keyword. With XML Schemas, there are several other ways in which you can restrict content.

### *Restriction on Element Values*

The following example restricts the value of the element <length> to the range from 5 to 10:

```
<xs:element name="length">
 <xs:simpleType>
  <xs:restriction base="xs:integer">
    <xs:minInclusive value="5"/>
    <xs:maxInclusive value="10"/>
  </xs:restriction>
 </xs:simpleType>
</xs:element>
```

### *Restriction on a Set of Values*

In the following example, the <enumeration> element restricts the value of the <language> element to C++, SmallTalk, or Java:

```
<xs:element name="language">
  <xs:simpleType>
   <xs:restriction base="xs:string">
    <xs:enumeration value="C++"/>
    <xs:enumeration value="SmallTalk"/>
    <xs:enumeration value="Java"/>
  </xs:restriction>
 </xs:simpleType>
</xs:element>
```

To limit the content of an XML element to a series of numbers or letters, you use the <pattern> element:

```
<xs:element name="choice">
  <xs:simpleType>
    <xs:restriction base="xs:string">
      <xs:pattern value="[abcd]"/>
    </xs:restriction>
  </xs:simpleType>
</xs:element>
```

In the previous example, the <choice> element can take a value between a and d. You could also do this like so:

```
<xs:pattern value="[a-d]"/>
```

The next example defines an element called <license-key> where the only acceptable value is a sequence of five digits, and each digit must be in the range 0 to 9:

```
<xs:element name="license-key">
  <xs:simpleType>
    <xs:restriction base="xs:integer">
      <xs:pattern value="[0-9][0-9][0-9][0-9][0-9]"/>
    </xs:restriction>
  </xs:simpleType>
</xs:element>
```

The following defines an element called <gender>, which can be either `Male` or `Female`:

```
<xs:element name="gender">
<xs:simpleType>
  <xs:restriction base="xs:string">
    <xs:pattern value="Male|Female"/>
  </xs:restriction>
</xs:simpleType>
</xs:element>
```

There are several other ways of restricting content. However, to cover them all would probably take another book. This concludes the discussion about XML Schemas. You'll next concentrate on how to read and write XML documents. It's time to get your hands dirty by writing some code!

## Reading and Writing XML Documents

To be able to programmatically read and write XML documents, you need an *XML parser*. An XML parser is a program, typically an application programming interface (API) that can read (and write) XML documents. It *parses* the document (breaks it up into its constituent elements) and makes these available to your own programs. To do this, the XML document must generally be well-formed although some parsers can handle XML fragments (these are XML documents that lack a single root element). Validating parsers can tell you if it's valid according to a specified DTD or a Schema.

The following are some popular XML parsers:

- Apache Xerces: `http://xml.apache.org/xerces2-j/index.html`
- IBM's XML4J: `http://alphaworks.ibm.com/tech/xml4j`
- Microsoft's MXSML Parser: `http://msdn.microsoft.com/xml/default.asp`

This book concentrates on the Apache Xerces parser because it's part of the open-source project at Apache and freely available.

Parsers internally use a set of low-level APIs that allow them to interact with the XML documents in question. There are two approaches to parsing XML documents, known as the *push* and *pull* models. An example of a push parser is Simple API for XML (SAX) while the Document Object Model (DOM) uses a pull model.

The push model reads an XML document in sequence, firing events whenever a new part of the document is encountered (such as a start or end tag). You can link these events to your own methods that are then called when that event occurs. This model is quite lightweight and fast, but its main limitation is the sequential access, meaning you can't go back and forth through elements at random.

DOM, on the other hand, reads in the entire XML document at once, creating a model of the document in memory (the DOM tree). This allows you to jump about from element to element as you want, but its main drawback is that loading the whole document can consume a lot of memory and be relatively time consuming, particularly when a document is large.

### *Trying It Out: Downloading, Installing, and Running the Samples for Xerces*

In this section, you'll download, install, and run some of the samples provided with the Xerces parser to illustrate how a parser works and to determine the well-formedness of an XML document. Follow these steps:

1. You can download Xerces from `http://xml.apache.org/xerces2-j/download.cgi`. Download the latest ZIP or TAR file depending on whether you're running Windows or Linux. Look for a file named `Xerces-J-bin.2.6.1.zip` or `Xerces-J-bin.2.6.1.tar.gz`.

2. Unzip the contents of this file into a folder of your choice, such as `C:\java`. The Xerces files will be placed in a subdirectory called `xerces-version_no` (depending on the actual version you downloaded).

3. Add the following paths to your `CLASSPATH` environment variable (as described in Chapter 1) to point to the Xerces Java Archive (JAR) files:

   ```
   ;C:\java\ xerces-2_6_1\xercesImpl.jar;
   C:\ java\ xerces-2_6_1\xercesSamples.jar;
   C:\ java\ xerces-2_6_1\xmlParserAPIs.jar
   ```

   Make sure that you include the first semicolon when adding this to your existing `CLASSPATH` and don't include any spaces. Note that you've included the `xercesSamples.jar` also because you'll run these samples. They aren't required to run the parser itself. Change the semicolons to colons if you're running Linux or Mac OS X.

4. Staying at the command prompt, navigate to the samples directory under the xerces folder and type the following:

```
> cd \java\xerces-2_6_1\samples
> javac ui\TreeView.java
```

5. Now run the compiled class like this:

```
> java ui.TreeView ..\data\personal.xml
```

This should bring up the utility that shows the structure of the XML document in the data folder called personal.xml (see Figure 8-1).

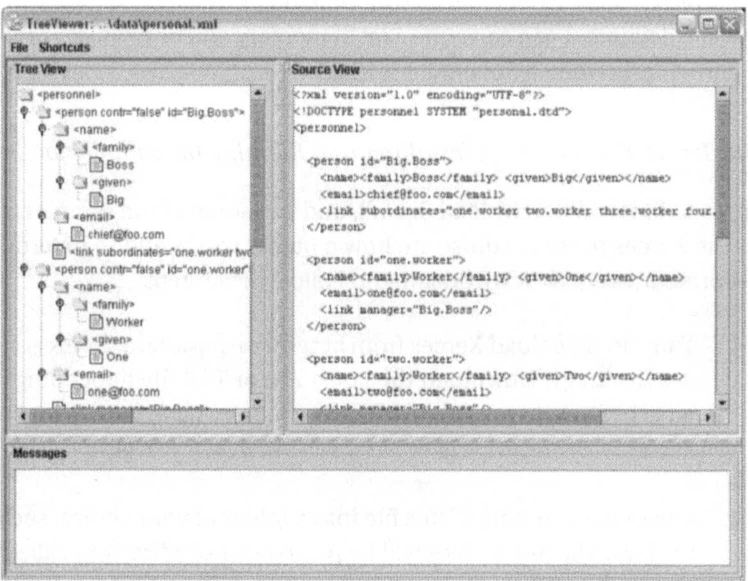


*Figure 8-1. The* personal.xml *structure*

6. Now open this personal.xml in a text editor, and remove the end tag for the first <person> element (the one with id=Big.Boss). Rerun the program by repeating step 5. This time, the screen will show you an error in big red letters, indicating the XML document isn't well-formed (see Figure 8-2).

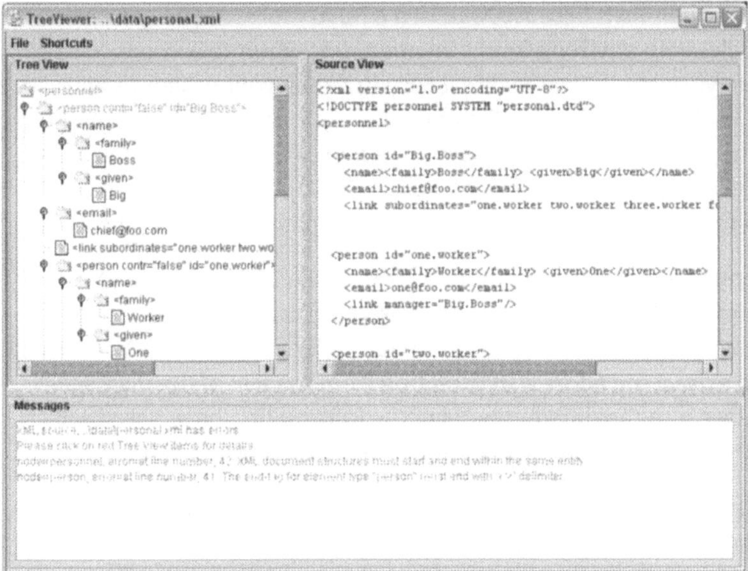


*Figure 8-2. Getting an error*

*How It Works*

This example reads and displays an XML document using a tree structure. The left pane shows the XML elements, and the right shows the actual document, which is basically the source view. The bottom shows messages, such as the error message you got when you removed the closing tag.

You can find the source code for this particular file, `TreeView.java`, in the `samples\ui` folder. A quick look at the source code will show that it uses the DOM as the low-level API for parsing the document (line 127 in the source code).

## XML and JSP

Knowledge of XML is becoming increasingly necessary in all areas of programming, and especially so in the Web application sphere. You've seen XML in use in configuration files such as `web.xml`. Also, XML is finding a place in data sharing, data storing, messaging, and many other areas of application development. Some of the reasons for XML's widespread acceptance include the following:

**Content in plain text**: Because XML isn't a binary format, you can create and edit files with anything from a standard text editor to a visual development environment. That makes it easy to debug your programs and makes it useful for storing small amounts of data. At the other end of the spectrum, an XML front end to a database makes it possible to efficiently store large amounts of XML data as well. So XML provides scalability for anything from small configuration files to a company-wide data repository.

**Data identification**: The markup tags identify the information and break up the data into parts, an e-mail program can process it, a search program can look for messages sent to particular people, and an address book can extract the address information from the rest of the message. In short, because the different parts of the information have been identified, they can be used in different ways by different applications.

**Ease of processing**: As mentioned earlier, regular and consistent notation makes it easier to build a program to process XML data. And because XML is a vendor-neutral standard, you can choose among several XML parsers, any one of which takes the work out of processing XML data.

With these points in mind, you'll now look at some areas where you can apply XML in JSP.

### *Delivering XML Documents with JSP*

So far you've learned a lot about JSP as a technology. You know that JSP pages produce HTML content so they can be displayed in a browser as a regular Web page. However, some devices can't interpret HTML and instead use another markup language called Wireless Markup Language (WML), which makes optimal use of the bandwidth and processing capability available in many mobile phones. Another exciting technology is VoiceXML-based voice services. These voice services let users interact with your applications through speech. One thing common with all these technologies is that the content is authored using XML. WML and VoiceXML are XML documents that conform to a particular Schema. To be able to display this XML in user-friendly output, you need to transform it into either HTML or WML as the case might be. A process known as, unsurprisingly, *transformation* can help you then use the same XML to create multiple forms of output. Transformation is done with the help of another standard XML dialect called Extensible Stylesheet Language (XSL). XSL is similar to Cascading Style Sheets (CSS) and defines styling information for HTML documents; it's also a specification regulated by the W3C. You'll see this in the "Understanding XSL Transformations" section later in the chapter.

If your Web application creates output as XML, you can apply XSL stylesheets to transform these documents into HTML, WML, or any other XML form that the browser in use may require (see Figure 8-3).

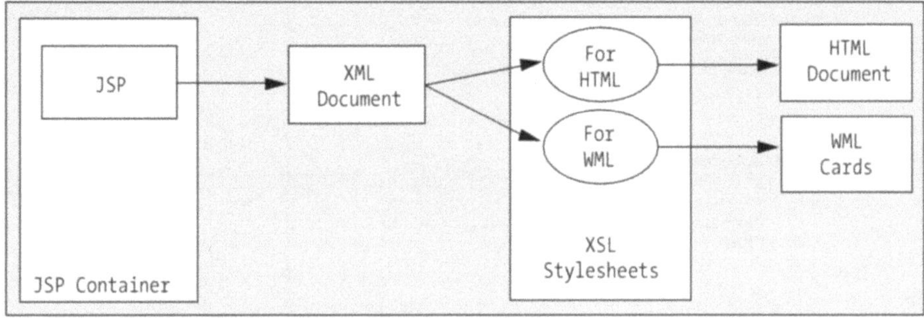


*Figure 8-3. Transformation*

*Trying It Out: Creating XML with JSP*

To create XML with JSP, follow these steps:

1. Create a subdirectory under `%TOMCAT_HOME%/webapps` called **XML.**

2. Create a subdirectory under `XML` called **WEB-INF**.

3. Copy the `lib` directory containing the JSTL JARs from a previous example to the `WEB-INF` directory.

4. Create the following JSP page and save it as **date.jsp** in `%TOMCAT_HOME%/webapps/XML`:

```
<?xml version="1.0"?>
<%@ taglib uri="http://java.sun.com/jstl/fmt_rt" prefix="fmt" %>
<jsp:useBean id="now" class="java.util.Date" />
<date-example>
  <title>Date Example</title>
  <content>
    <heading>Sample JSP XML File</heading>
    <text>The date and time is :
      <fmt:formatDate value="${now}" pattern="dd-MMM-yyyy hh:mm"/>
    </text>
  </content>
</date-example>
```

5. Now restart Tomcat. Visit `http://localhost:8080/XML/date.jsp` in your Web browser. It will produce XML as shown in Figure 8-4. This isn't how it will appear on the screen; you must view the source to see the XML because the browser won't render it.

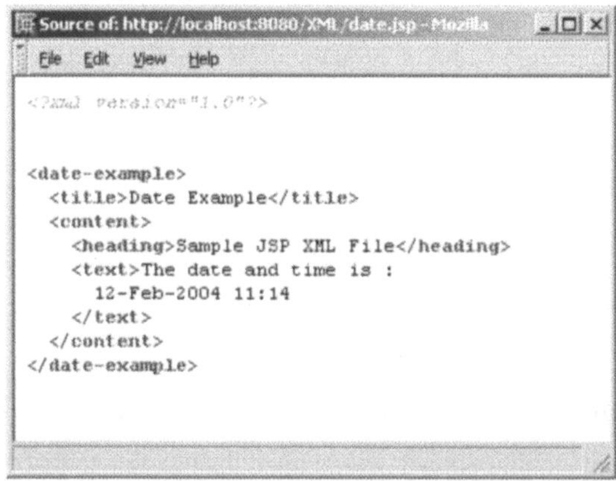


*Figure 8-4. The XML produced by the JSP page*

*How It Works*

As this example shows, creating XML output using JSP is just the same as creating HTML output. The JSP source contains the XML elements that you want to appear in the output, mixed in with the same JSP tags you'd use when creating HTML output. These JSP tags create dynamic content in your XML output just as they do when creating HTML output.

By applying a suitable XSL stylesheet, you can transform XML such as this into HTML or other kinds of documents, including Portable Document Format (PDF), WML, and VoiceXML. In other words, you can create the same output for all your users as XML and, simply by supplying suitable stylesheets, provide a readable display for their browser type.

## JSTL XML Tags

JSTL XML tags provide easy access to XML content. The JSTL XML tags use XPath, another W3C standard, which provides a way to specify and select parts of XML documents.

There are three classes of JSTL XML tags:

- **Core**: Parse, read, and write XML documents.
- **Flow control**: Provide looping and decision capability based on XML content.
- **Transformation**: Provide utilities to transform XML content into other classes of documents.

The XML tags use XPath as a local expression language. XPath expressions are specified in `select` attributes. This means that only values specified for `select` attributes are evaluated using the XPath expression language. All other attributes are evaluated using the rules associated with the global expression language or the EL.

In addition to the standard XPath syntax, the JSTL XPath engine supports the following scopes to access Web application data within an XPath expression:

- `$param`: Request parameter
- `$header`: Header content
- `$cookie`: Cookie identification
- `$initParam`: Context parameters
- `$pageScope`: Any page scope variable
- `$requestScope`: To access request scope variables
- `$sessionScope`: Session scope variable access
- `$applicationScope`: Application scope variable access

These scopes are defined in the same way as their counterparts in the JSTL expression language. For example, `$sessionScope:profile` retrieves the session attribute called `profile`.

You'll now try out a few simple JSTL XML tags.

*Trying It Out: Parsing XML with JSP*

For this example, you'll need the JSTL XML tag library. Follow these steps:

1. Save the following as **parseXML.jsp** in the `XML` folder:

```
<%@ taglib prefix="x"
    uri="http://java.sun.com/jstl/xml_rt" %>

<html>
  <head>
    <title>JSTL XML Support -- Parsing</title>
  </head>
  <body bgcolor="#FFFFFF">
    <h3>Parsing an XML Document using XML tags</h3>
```

```
      <x:parse var="xml">
        <BOOK>
          <AUTHOR>
            <LAST-NAME>
              EINSTEIN
            </LAST-NAME>
          </AUTHOR>
          <BOOK-NAME>
            GENERAL RELATIVITY
          </BOOK-NAME>
        </BOOK>
      </x:parse>

      <!--printing the LAST-NAME element-->
      LAST NAME :
      <x:out select="$xml/BOOK/AUTHOR/LAST-NAME" />
      <br />


      <!--printing the BOOK-NAME element -->
      BOOK NAME :
      <x:out select="$xml/BOOK/BOOK-NAME"/>

      <hr />

    </body>
  </html>
```

2. Visit `http://localhost:8080/XML/parseXML.jsp` in your Web browser. You should see a screen like Figure 8-5.

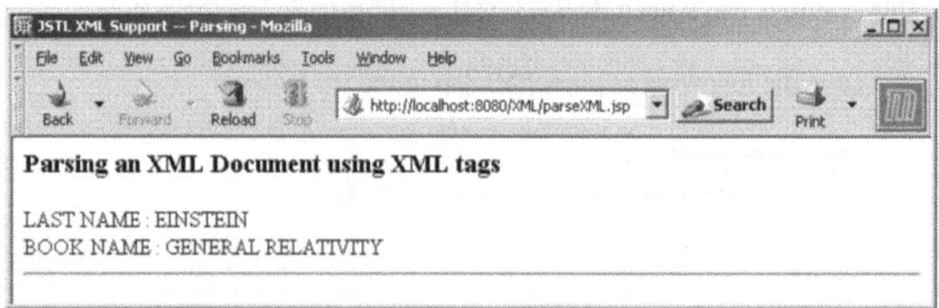


*Figure 8-5. XPath has extracted the required information.*

### *How It Works*

Before the result can be displayed, you need to parse the XML document for which you use the `<x:parse>` tag as shown previously. Generally, you'd specify a URI rather than embedding XML in the JSP page by including an appropriate `uri` attribute on the `<x:parse>` tag:

```
<x:parse uri="/book.xml" var="xml"/>
```

The `var` attribute specifies the variable in which to store the parsed XML. This is then used in the XPath expression.

The root element in the previous XML document is named `<BOOK>`, which contains the two child elements, `<AUTHOR>` and `<BOOK-NAME>`. The element `<AUTHOR>` has another child element called `<LAST-NAME>`. Among these tags, only `<LAST-NAME>` and `<BOOK-NAME>` have content. You retrieve this content using the `<x:out>` tag:

```
<x:out select="$xml/BOOK/AUTHOR/LAST-NAME" />
```

### *Trying It Out: Using XML Flow Control Tags*

In the previous example, you retrieved the required XML elements using XML tags. Now you'll look at another example, which iterates through all the elements in an XML document. This example demonstrates the use of XML flow control tags.

1. Save the following as **iterate.jsp** in the `XML` folder:

```
<%@ taglib prefix="x"
    uri="http://java.sun.com/jstl/xml_rt" %>

<html>
  <head>
    <title>JSTL XML Support -- Flow Control</title>
  </head>
  <body bgcolor="#FFFFFF">
    <h3>Iterating through an XML document</h3>

    <x:parse var="xml">
     <items>
      <item>
       <Fruit Name="Apple">Red Apple</Fruit>
      </item>
```

```
      <item>
       <Vegetable Name="Okra">Fresh Okra</Vegetable>
      </item>
      <item>
       <Beer Name="Dark Island">Fine Beer</Beer>
      </item>
      <item>
       <Beer Name="Kingfisher">Lager Beer</Beer>
      </item>
     </items>
    </x:parse>

    <!--iterate through all the elements -->
    <x:forEach select="$xml/items/item">
      <!--print the current element -->
      ->  <x:out select="." />

      <!--check if the selected element is Beer -->
      <x:if select="./Beer" >
        <!--yes it is beer -->
        * is a Beer
      </x:if>
      <br />
    </x:forEach>

  </body>
</html>
```

2. Visit `http://localhost:8080/XML/iterate.jsp` in your browser (see Figure 8-6).

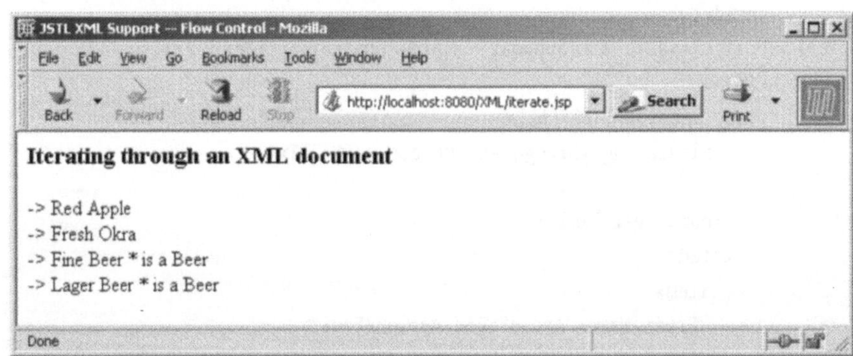


*Figure 8-6. Conditional processing with XML*

*How It Works*

Here you parse an embedded XML element called <items>. You then iterate over all the child elements of <items> and print `* is a Beer` next to any <Beer> elements. You use a <x:forEach> tag to iterate through the document and <x:if> to find out if the element name is Beer:

```
<x:if select="./Beer" >
```

## Understanding XSL Transformations

XSL is an XML dialect that describes rules dictating how a source document can be transformed into a target document. This means that one XML document can be converted into another XML document, an HTML document, or simply plain text. Although these inputs and outputs can be documents, they may also be strings that contain XML content.

The simplest XSL document contains an empty <stylesheet> element:

```
<?xml version="1.0" encoding="iso-8859-1"?>

<xsl:stylesheet version="1.0"
xmlns:xsl="http://www.w3.org/1999/XSL/Transform" />
```

This isn't much use to you because no transformation takes place. Try an example.

*Trying It Out: Transforming XML with XSL*

You'll look at the XSL stylesheet (not to be confused with CSS stylesheets), and then we'll explain it once you've finished the example:

1. Create **book.xsl**, and store it in the XML folder of webapps. This is like your parsing page and contains all of the HTML you'll need. It's simply a template and is similar in concept to the template technique you used in Chapter 6:

```
<?xml version="1.0" encoding="iso-8859-1"?>
<xsl:stylesheet version="1.0"
                xmlns:xsl="http://www.w3.org/1999/XSL/Transform">
  <xsl:output method="html" indent="yes" />
  <xsl:template match="/">
    <html>
      <head>
        <title>JSTL XML Support -- Transforming</title>
      </head>
```

```
      <body bgcolor="#FFFFFF">
        <h3>Transforming an XML Document using XML tags</h3>
        <xsl:apply-templates />
      </body>
    </html>
  </xsl:template>

  <xsl:template match="Author-Name">
    <!--printing the  element-->
    LAST NAME :
    <xsl:apply-templates select="Last"/>
  </xsl:template>

  <xsl:template match="Last">
    <xsl:value-of select="text()" />
    <br />
  </xsl:template>

  <xsl:template match="Book-Name" >
    <!--printing the BOOK-NAME element -->
    BOOK NAME :
    <xsl:value-of select="text()" />

    <hr />
  </xsl:template>
</xsl:stylesheet>
```

2. You'll be using book.xml in this example. When you transform the imported file, the DTD will be checked. You may have to change the following line of code to pass the validation checks:

```
<!DOCTYPE Book SYSTEM "http://localhost:8080/XML/book.dtd">
```

3. Now you need the JSP page that will transform your XML (transformXML.jsp):

```
<%@ taglib prefix="c" uri="http://java.sun.com/jstl/core_rt" %>
<%@ taglib prefix="x" uri="http://java.sun.com/jstl/xml_rt" %>

<c:import url="/book.xml" var="XMLDocument"/>
<c:import url="/book.xsl" var="XSLDocument" />

<x:transform xml="${XMLDocument}" xslt="${XSLDocument}"/>
```

4. Now navigate to `http://localhost:8080/XML/transformXML.jsp`, and you should see the same page as Figure 8-7.

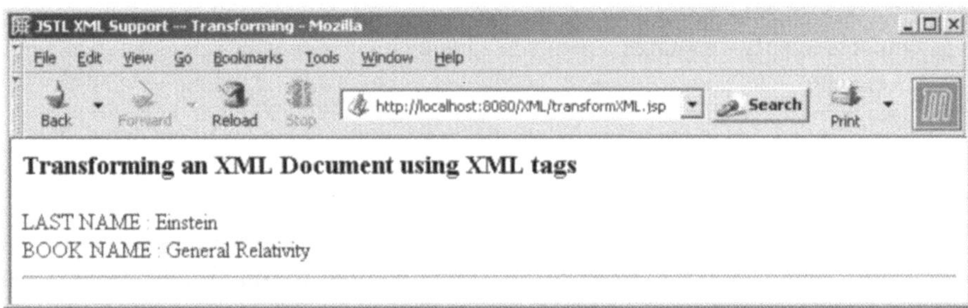


*Figure 8-7. Transforming XML with XSLT*

*How It Works*

You'll look at the XSL stylesheet first.

First you declare the root element, which must always be `<stylesheet>` and is in the `xsl` namespace:

```
<?xml version="1.0" encoding="iso-8859-1"?>
<xsl:stylesheet version="1.0"
                xmlns:xsl="http://www.w3.org/1999/XSL/Transform">
```

`<xsl:output>` specifies the format of the end result, in this case HTML. You want the HTML to be indented so you set `indent` to `"yes"`:

```
<xsl:output method="html" indent="yes" />
```

The first `<xsl:template>` tag is used to match the root element using `"/"`; in this case, it will match `<Book>`. Therefore, this template is always called when processing begins. It's a good idea to place all your main structural elements, such as `<html>` and `<body>`, in this default template:

```
<xsl:template match="/">
  <html>
    <head>
      <title>JSTL XML Support -- Transforming</title>
    </head>
    <body bgcolor="#FFFFFF">
      <h3>Transforming an XML Document using XML tags</h3>
```

You want to place your transformed XML at this point in the HTML document, so you call `<xsl:apply-templates>` to use all the other templates defined in this document:

```
      <xsl:apply-templates />
    </body>
  </html>
</xsl:template>
```

The first specific template matches any `<Author-Name>` elements in the document regardless of their location. If you wanted to match only `<First>` elements that were subelements of `<Author-Name>`, which in turn was a subelement of the root element, you'd use `"/Author-Name/First"`. Note the `"/"` to specify the root element:

```
<xsl:template match="Author-Name">
  <!--printing the Last element-->
  LAST NAME :
```

If there's a match, you want to select the `<Last>` element, so you call the template that will match it:

```
  <xsl:apply-templates select="Last"/>
</xsl:template>
```

The next specific template matches the `<Last>` element:

```
<xsl:template match="Last">
```

The `<xsl:value-of>` tag can obtain the value of many things, such as the text of an element or the value of its attributes. In this case you use XSL's `text()` method to obtain the text of the element:

```
  <xsl:value-of select="text()" />
  <br />
</xsl:template>
```

The final template matches the `<Book-Name>` element and displays its contents:

```
  <xsl:template match="Book-Name" >
    <!--printing the BOOK-NAME element -->
    BOOK NAME :
    <xsl:value-of select="text()" />
    <hr />
  </xsl:template>
</xsl:stylesheet>
```

Once the last template has been called, the processing continues to the end of the default template.

In the JSP page, you import the XML and core tag libraries:

```
<%@ taglib prefix="c" uri="http://java.sun.com/jstl/core_rt" %>
<%@ taglib prefix="x" uri="http://java.sun.com/jstl/xml_rt" %>
```

You're using external XML and XSL files, so you need to use the `<c:import>` tag to get their contents and place the imported strings into variables for use later:

```
<c:import url="/book.xml" var="XMLDocument"/>
<c:import url="/book.xsl" var="XSLDocument" />
```

The transformation is one line of JSP where you take the two strings and apply a transformation. The results are printed to the screen; however, they can also be stored in a variable as is the case with most JSTL tag results:

```
<x:transform xml="${XMLDocument}" xslt="${XSLDocument}"/>
```

This was a very simple example, and it showed the principles of XSL. However, there's so much more to XSL that we just can't cover it properly in this book. Try these other resources:

- `http://www.w3.org/Style/XSL/`
- `http://www.w3schools.com/xsl/`

---

### Why Not Try?

- Write a simple JSP Web application that stores data in XML format using XML tags.

---

## Summary

In this chapter you learned the following:

- XML: its relevance, advantages, and uses
- The difference between validity and well-formedness in the context of XML
- XML parsers
- XSL and XML transformation
- JSP tags to deal with and output XML

You've taken a small tour into the exciting world of XML. This chapter serves only as a very quick introduction, and there's a huge ocean of knowledge out there to be explored.

CHAPTER 9

# Going Behind the Scenes

WHEN WORKING WITH JavaServer Pages (JSP), a certain amount of understanding of what goes on behind the scenes helps you to use the technology effectively and can assist the debugging process when things go wrong.

This chapter focuses on the Java servlet application programming interface (API) and related topics since servlets are the power behind JSP technology. Before any JSP page is run, it's converted into a servlet. The process is as follows:

1. A programmer writes a JSP page and places it in a servlet container.

2. The first time the page is requested, the servlet container converts the JSP into Java source code, creating a servlet that provides the functionality required. The source code is then compiled into a Java class, which the servlet container then loads.

3. The servlet service requests from clients, and the server returns the servlet's responses to the client.

4. If the JSP page is subsequently modified, the server will notice this and re-create the servlet accordingly.

So, servlet technology is an essential part of JSP. This chapter provides an overview of servlets from a programming viewpoint, but you need to finish learning about JSP pages first. In this chapter, you'll look at the following:

- More about Web applications, the `web.xml` file that's used to configure them, and advanced configuration options for JSP pages

- The servlet architecture and how servlets work

- Advanced servlet topics such as session tracking and the servlet context

- Filters, which you use to add request and response functionality to a Web application

If what this chapter covers whets your appetite for more information about servlets, you may want to check out the official home of the servlet API at `http://java.sun.com/products/servlet/`.

## Web Applications and web.xml

A Web application can consist of the following components:

- Servlets
- JSP pages
- JavaBeans and utility classes
- Static documents (Hypertext Markup Language [HTML], images, sounds, and so on)
- Configuration information for the previous elements

As you've seen, a Web application is a structured hierarchy of directories branching out from the root application directory. This physical root directory serves as the Web root for serving files that are part of the application. That is, the physical directory in `webapps`, such as `MyMail`, is accessed by the following uniform resource locator (URL): `http://localhost:8080/MyMail`. This is a mapping, and it tells Tomcat where to look for files requested by browsing users.

The special `WEB-INF` folder within the Web application folder contains the following:

- **The web.xml file**: This is a special configuration file called the *deployment descriptor*. It provides application configuration information for the container.
- **The classes folder**: This folder contains servlets, JavaBeans, and other utility classes, which must be manually compiled into `.class` files.
- **The lib directory**: This contains Java archive (`.jar`) files, the archive format for packaging sets of related Java classes, which provide a convenient way of distributing packages such as the Struts framework that you'll use in the next chapter. All the classes—servlets, JavaBeans, or otherwise—in these `.jar` files will be available to the Web application just the same as regular `.class` files in the `classes` folder.

The deployment descriptor file can contain various types of configuration, deployment, and custom tag library information: It's the glue that holds the Web application together. You've encountered a few of its functions in previous chapters. The following are the most important functions it can provide:

**ServletContext initialization parameters**: You can associate a set of context initialization parameters with a Web application. An application developer can use initialization parameters to convey setup information, such as the name of a system that holds critical data. This data can be included under the tag `<context-param>` in the `web.xml`. It's different from servlet initialization parameters because it defines initialization parameters for the whole application.

**Session configuration**: The `<session-config>` element defines the session parameters for the Web application. For instance, you can define a session timeout for the application.

**Servlet/JSP definitions**: You can define servlet- and JSP-related parameters such as the name of the servlet and its class, the full path, and initialization parameters.

**Servlet/JSP mappings**: Under `<servlet-mapping>` tag, mappings specify URLs that invoke particular servlets.

**Security configuration**: You can configure security constraints for the Web resources concerned with the Web application.

These features will be demonstrated in examples throughout this chapter. For a full description of the elements in the `web.xml` file, refer to Appendix C.

## *web.xml and JSP Pages*

The `web.xml` file starts with these lines:

```
<?xml version="1.0" encoding="ISO-8859-1"?>

<web-app xmlns="http://java.sun.com/xml/ns/j2ee"
  xmlns:xsi="http://www.w3.org/2001/XMLSchema-instance"
  xsi:schemaLocation="http://java.sun.com/xml/ns/j2ee
  http://java.sun.com/xml/ns/j2ee/web-app_2_4.xsd" version="2.4">
```

The first part simply declares that this is an Extensible Markup Language (XML) version 1.0 file, encoded with the ISO-8859-1 (that is, Latin-1) character set. The second part provides schema information for validating the file (that is, to ensure that it meets the requirements of JSP `web.xml` files) as you saw in Chapter 8.

Many configuration options exist in `web.xml`, but only one is directly relevant to JSP pages: `<jsp-config>`.

This configuration element has the following subelements:

- A `<taglib>` element containing tag library information
- A `<jsp-property-group>` element for specifying properties common to a group of JSP pages

## Configuring a Tag Library

So far in this book you've used the `taglib` directive to reference tag libraries by their absolute uniform resource indicator (URI). This is because they're stored in a Java archive (JAR) file and are considered to be stable releases with a constant URI. However, when you're developing tag libraries of your own or have an unpacked version of the tag library, you can specify a URI in `web.xml`.

### *Trying It Out: Configuring a Tag Library*

In this example you'll use the JSP Tag Library (JSTL) Core tags to learn how you can specify a `taglib` URI in `web.xml`. Follow these steps:

1. Create a Web application called **Config**, and create the **WEB-INF\classes** and **WEB-INF\tlds** directories.

2. Expand the `jstl.jar` and `standard.jar` files into the `WEB-INF\classes` directory. To do this from a command prompt, change to `<tomcat_home>/webapps/Config/WEB-INF/classes`. Type **jar xvf jstl.jar**. Type **jar xvf standard.jar**. You should see a set of directories containing class files. This is to simulate the structure of a developmental tag library, which you wouldn't have in a JAR file but you'd have in the expanded structure.

3. The expansion will create a `META-INF` folder in `WEB-INF\classes`. Move the contents of this directory to `WEB-INF\tlds`.

4. Now that you've the required structure, you can use one of the tag libraries. Create **web.xml** in `WEB-INF`, and add the following:

```
<?xml version="1.0" encoding="ISO-8859-1"?>
<web-app xmlns="http://java.sun.com/xml/ns/j2ee"
         xmlns:xsi="http://www.w3.org/2001/XMLSchema-instance"
         xsi:schemaLocation="http://java.sun.com/xml/ns/j2ee
         http://java.sun.com/xml/ns/j2ee/web-app_2_4.xsd"
         version="2.4">

  <jsp-config>
    <taglib>
      <taglib-uri>/jstl/core_rt</taglib-uri>
```

```
        <taglib-location>/WEB-INF/tlds/c-rt.tld</taglib-location>
      </taglib>
    </jsp-config>

</web-app>
```

5. Create **taglib.jsp** in the `Config` folder:

```
<%@ taglib uri="/jstl/core_rt" prefix="c" %>
Value of "name" parameter: <c:out value="${param.name}" />
```

6. Start Tomcat, and navigate to `http://localhost:8080/Config/taglib.jsp?name=JSP`. You should see a page similar to that in Figure 9-1.

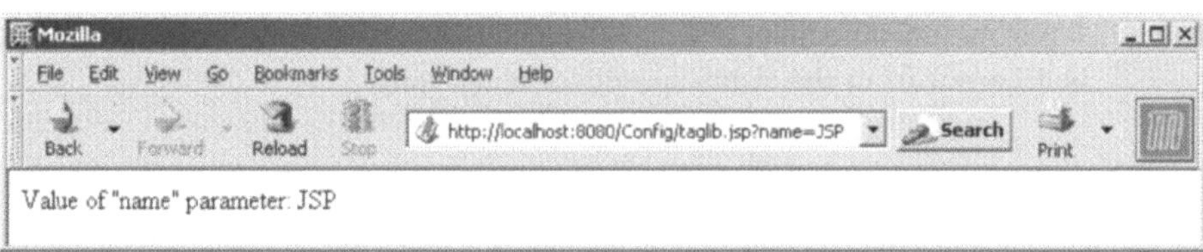


*Figure 9-1. A tag library defined in* `web.xml`

*How It Works*

The crucial configuration is in `web.xml`:

```
<taglib-uri>/jstl/core_rt</taglib-uri>
<taglib-location>/WEB-INF/tlds/c-rt.tld</taglib-location>
```

The `<taglib-uri>` element specifies the URI of the tag library. This can be an absolute URI, such as the URIs you've used throughout the book, or a relative URI, as in this case. Each URI must be unique within each `web.xml`. You then use this URI to refer to this tag library in a JSP page.

The `<taglib-location>` element points to the tag library descriptor (TLD) file for the tag library that you're referencing.

All you need to do now is include this tag library in the JSP page. The only difference when using this tag library is that you must use the URI defined in `web.xml`:

```
<%@ taglib uri="/jstl/core_rt" prefix="c" %>
```

## Configuring a JSP Group

If you have a group of JSP pages that all share common properties, such as they have the same page encoding or they all disallow scripting, you can configure this in `web.xml` using `<jsp-property-group>`. This element has the following subelements:

- `<url-pattern>` specifies which resources should be covered by this set of properties.
- An optional `<el-ignored>` element that should be set `true` or `false`. If `true`, then expression language (EL) terms are ignored.
- An optional `<page-encoding>` element that specifies the page encoding. A translation-time error will occur if a page directive's `pageEncoding` attribute is different from the value specified in `web.xml`.
- An optional `<scripting-invalid>` element that disables scripting on a page.
- An optional `<is-xml>` element that specifies that the pages are XML.
- Zero or more `<include-prelude>` elements that include the specified resource at the beginning of each file in this JSP group.
- Zero or more `<include-coda>` elements that include the specified resource at the end of each file in this JSP group.

So now you can apply some of the principles you've learned in the course of this book to all the JSP pages in an application.

### *Trying It Out: Configuring a JSP Group*

In this example you'll include a header and footer across a series of Web pages, disallow scripting, and enable the EL. Each of these follows the best practices you've seen throughout the book. For this exercise, you'll return to the `GoodDesign` Web application from Chapter 6. Follow these steps:

1. Add the following web.xml file to GoodDesign\WEB-INF:

```
<?xml version="1.0" encoding="ISO-8859-1"?>
<web-app xmlns="http://java.sun.com/xml/ns/j2ee"
        xmlns:xsi="http://www.w3.org/2001/XMLSchema-instance"
        xsi:schemaLocation="http://java.sun.com/xml/ns/j2ee
        http://java.sun.com/xml/ns/j2ee/web-app_2_4.xsd"
        version="2.4">

  <jsp-config>
    <jsp-property-group>
      <url-pattern>*.jsp</url-pattern>
      <el-ignored>false</el-ignored>
      <scripting-invalid>true</scripting-invalid>
      <include-prelude>/Include/header.jspf</include-prelude>
      <include-coda>/Include/footer.jspf</include-coda>
    </jsp-property-group>
  </jsp-config>

</web-app>
```

2. Rename page1tag.jsp to **page1group.jsp** and page2tag.jsp to **page2group.jsp**.

3. Change the following line in page1group.jsp:

```
<a href="page2group.jsp">expensive items</a>.
```

4. Change the following line in page2group.jsp:

```
<a href="page1group.jsp">inexpensive items</a>.
```

5. Remove the following lines from both files:

```
<%@ include file="/Include/header.jspf" %>
<%@ include file="/Include/footer.jspf" %>
```

6. Make sure MySQL is running, and restart Tomcat.

7. Navigate to http://localhost:8080/GoodDesign/page1group.jsp, and you should see the same page as in Figure 9-2.

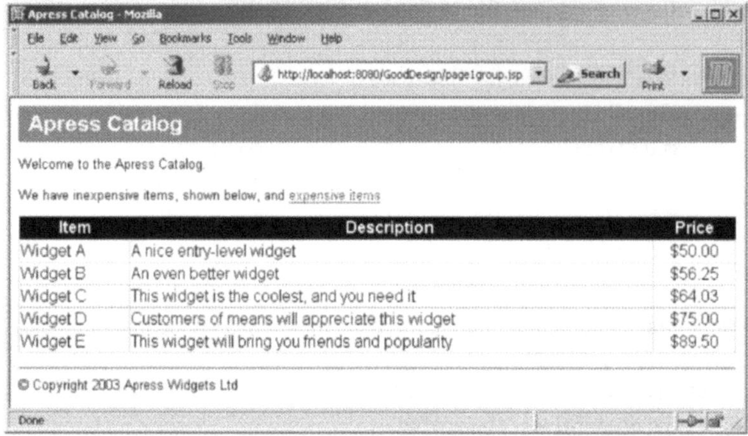


*Figure 9-2. Implicit includes using* `web.xml`

*How It Works*

The `<url-pattern>` element acts like all the other URL pattern elements you've seen in the book so far. This time you've grouped all the JSP pages in the application into the same group:

```
<url-pattern>*.jsp</url-pattern>
```

You then enable EL processing and disable scripting:

```
<el-ignored>false</el-ignored>
<scripting-invalid>true</scripting-invalid>
```

The `isELIgnored` page directive overrides any `web.xml` settings, and a translation error occurs if any scripting is used on a page.

The header and footer are defined as follows:

```
<include-prelude>/Include/header.jspf</include-prelude>
<include-coda>/Include/footer.jspf</include-coda>
```

The resource will be automatically included (as in an `include` directive) at the beginning or end of each JSP page in the group. When there's more than one include-style element in a group, they're included in the order they appear. So, if you had another `<include-coda>` element after the first, it'd be included after the first one, as well.

If you have more than one `<jsp-property-group>` applied to a JSP page, the corresponding include-style elements will be processed in the same order as they appear in `web.xml`. Therefore, if you had another `<jsp-property-group>` element after the original group, any prelude it contains will come after the original group's prelude, and any coda will come after the original group's coda. Note that this isn't how other URL patterns are matched for other configuration elements. For instance, in servlet mappings, only the most specific pattern applies.

## Introducing the Java Servlet Technology

A *servlet* is a Java program that generates dynamic Web content. Servlets are written using the Java servlet API and are managed by a *servlet container* such as Tomcat. As you saw in Chapter 1, Hypertext Transfer Protocol (HTTP) on which the Web is built uses a request-response model where the server receives requests from a browser, processes them, and sends an appropriate response back to the browser (or any other Web client, such as a search engine indexer). The Java servlet API enables you to write Java code to process and respond to client requests. For example, a servlet might be responsible for taking data from an HTML order-entry form and using it to update a company's order database.

As you've seen, servlets run inside a Java-enabled server (a *servlet container*) such as Tomcat, as illustrated in Figure 9-3.

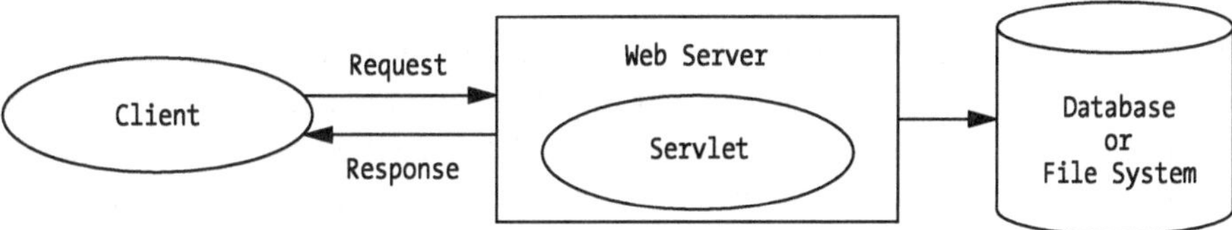


*Figure 9-3. Servlet container architecture*

The servlet container does quite a bit of work. It loads the servlets, routes requests to them, and handles their responses, and it tries its best to make sure that the servlets can keep up with the number of browsers requesting information from them.

### *The Process*

To better understand what happens when a browser sends a request to a servlet, have a closer look at the process:

1. The client sends a request to the container.
2. The container determines which servlet (if any) should receive the request.
3. If the servlet isn't already loaded, the container loads it. Once the servlet is loaded, it typically stays in memory until the container shuts down.

4. The container sends the request to the servlet. The servlet container can send multiple requests to the same servlet at the same time, or it can even load a second copy of a servlet in extreme conditions.

5. The servlet processes the request, builds a response, and passes it to the container.

6. The container sends the response back to the client.

As you can see, the servlet container takes care of the lion's share of this process, relieving you of any requirement to know the complicated details of communicating with Web clients over HTTP and Transmission Control Protocol/Internet Protocol (TCP/IP).

## The Role of Servlets in Web Applications

It's of course fully possible to create complex, exciting Web applications using nothing but JSP. However, many architects prefer to mix servlets and JSP pages when creating Web applications. A common design used in such scenarios works like this: A single servlet acts as a sort of "controller," receiving all requests, performing any necessary tasks, and forwarding the request to a JSP. Manually coded servlets are ideal for the controller component because they can access the Java libraries more easily than a JSP page. They're also much easier to integrate with other, more advanced components, such as Enterprise JavaBeans.

This design is often referred to as the Model-View-Controller (MVC) design pattern (also known as Model 2). Figure 9-4 shows an example of MVC architecture.

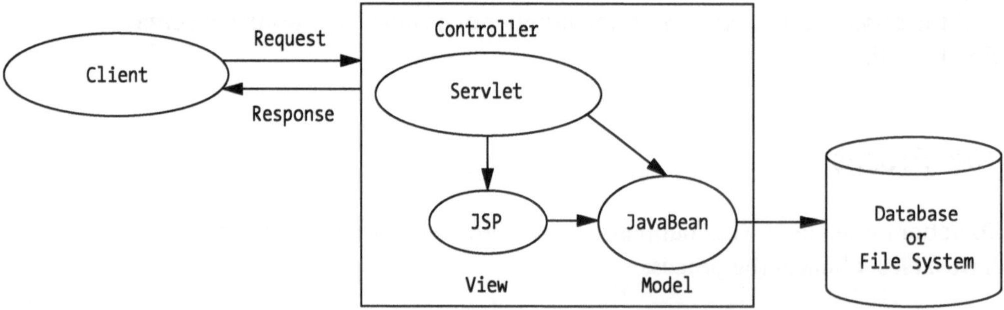


*Figure 9-4. MVC architecture*

The processing is divided into information (the model) and presentation (the view) components, both orchestrated by the controller. The controller servlet processes requests and creates components such as JavaBeans for use by the presentation component (that is, JSP). The controller is also responsible for forwarding individual requests to the appropriate JSP page.

The MVC model makes the Web application structured and modular—hence, it's easier to develop and extend—by dividing the application into three parts:

**Model**: The model represents the core of the application's functionality—what's often referred to as the *business logic*. This core will be shared between all applications, be they Web-based, desktop-based, or whatever. It's quite independent of the view and the controller. JavaBeans can fulfill this function because they can interact with a database or file system in order to maintain the application's data.

**View**: The view presents the data the model represents to the user. The view can access the model's data, but it shouldn't change the data directly; it must pass requests from the user to change the data. In addition, it knows nothing about the controller. The view will be notified when changes to the model (data) occur. If a view is properly separated from the controller and model, a Web interface developer can create the view components without any direct knowledge of what happens in the database or what goes on in the business logic component.

**Controller**: The controller reacts to the user input. It interacts with the model and the view, and it coordinates the flow of data from the model to the view.

Generally speaking, the MVC model is the preferred architecture when creating anything but the simplest of applications. Several reasons for this exist, including the following:

**Flexibility**: Because controllers are responsible for determining which JSP pages to display, you can change the order in which JSP pages are displayed, or even which JSP is displayed, without changing links. You could even decide to use something entirely different from JSP later.

**Reusability**: Because the individual components of the MVC application are separate, you can more easily reuse them. For example, because the model components don't create HTML output, you can use them with a non-Web version of the application. Furthermore, because the view components don't contain any business logic or application data code, you can easily change them to give the application a new look.

**Maintainability**: It's much easier to make modifications and additions to programs when you know where the code is. If code is spread over a bunch of JSP pages, it's hard to know where to look when changing one particular aspect.

In the early days of servlets, most developers who wanted to use the MVC architecture simply created their own. Nowadays, however, you can integrate many third-party MVC architectures with your applications. One of the most popular is Struts, which we'll discuss in the next chapter. Others, however, such as the official Java MVC framework called JavaServer Faces, will be released soon (`http://java.sun.com/j2ee/javaserverfaces`). The site at `http://www.waferproject.org` lists many of these frameworks and has examples for each one.

## The Servlet Architecture

In the following sections, you'll learn how to write a servlet. Servlets are just classes that derive from the abstract class `javax.servlet.http.HttpServlet`. The simplest servlet would be this:

```
import javax.servlet.http.HttpServlet;

public class SimpleServlet extends HttpServlet {}
```

Obviously, this servlet doesn't actually do anything, but it's a legal servlet. We'll now talk about how you can make this servlet *do* something.

As you've already seen, the servlet container accepts a request from a client (such as a Web browser) and forwards it to the servlet, which processes it and sends a response back to the container, which is then forwarded to the client.

The servlet container forwards requests it receives to the servlet by calling the `service()` method on the `HttpServlet` object, passing in two objects: `HttpServletRequest` and `HttpServletResponse`. You can then use the `HttpServletRequest` object to find out details of the request, and various methods on `HttpServletResponse` let you build your response.

The default `service()` method on `HttpServlet` determines the method type of the request and forwards the `HttpServletRequest` and `HttpServletResponse` objects to the appropriate helper method, which for `GET` or `POST` will be either of the following:

- `doGet()` for HTTP `GET` requests
- `doPost()` for HTTP `POST` requests

Thus, instead of overriding the `service()` method, servlet authors can override one of these two methods (or both). These aren't the only two methods, and five similar methods are less commonly used:

- `doHead()` handles HTTP `HEAD` requests. It executes the `doGet()` method but returns only the headers `doGet()` produces.
- `doOptions()` handles HTTP `OPTIONS` requests. This method determines which HTTP methods are directly supported by the servlet and returns that information to the client.
- `doTrace()` handles HTTP `TRACE` requests. It creates a response containing all the headers sent in the `TRACE` request.
- `doPut()` is called for HTTP `PUT` requests.
- `doDelete()` is called for HTTP `DELETE` requests.

Because of these additional methods, it's usually a good idea to not override the `service()` method and instead to override just those methods for the HTTP methods you want to support.

`HttpServlet` has a few extra methods of interest:

- `init()` and `destroy()`, which allow you to initialize resources in your servlet upon startup and, if necessary, release resources when the servlet is taken out of service
- `getServletInfo()`, which the servlet uses to provide information about itself

*Trying It Out: Creating an Example Servlet*

You'll start with a simple example, creating a servlet class that overrides the `doGet()` method to return a simple HTML page to the client when it makes a `GET` request. We'll use this example as a reference when explaining the servlet life cycle. Follow these steps:

1. Start by creating a new Web application folder called **Servlets** in Tomcat's `webapps` directory. Create a subfolder called **WEB-INF**, itself containing a directory called **classes**. Inside `classes`, create the folder structure **com\apress\servlets**.

2. Create a new file called **ExampleServlet.java** in the new `servlets` folder. and save this code in it:

```
package com.apress.servlets;

import java.io.PrintWriter;
import java.io.IOException;
import javax.servlet.ServletException;
```

```
import javax.servlet.http.HttpServlet;
import javax.servlet.http.HttpServletRequest;
import javax.servlet.http.HttpServletResponse;

public class ExampleServlet extends HttpServlet
{

  public void doGet(HttpServletRequest request,
                    HttpServletResponse response)
        throws ServletException, IOException
  {
    response.setContentType("text/html");
    PrintWriter out = response.getWriter();
    out.println("<html><head><title>");
    out.println("Servlet Example");
    out.println("</title></head><body>");
    out.println("<h1>This is an example servlet.</h1>");
    out.println("</body></html>");
    out.close();
  }

  public void doPost(HttpServletRequest request,
                     HttpServletResponse response)
        throws ServletException, IOException
  {
    doGet(request, response);
  }
}
```

3. Now you need to compile your servlet. From the classes directory, enter the following command, all on one line:

```
javac classpath %CATALINA_HOME%\common\lib\servlet-api.jar
     com/apress/servlets/ExampleServlet.java
```

4. You've now got a compiled servlet, but you can't use it yet. Before you can access your servlet, you must tell your servlet container (Tomcat in this case) which requests to forward to your servlet by creating **web.xml** in the WEB-INF directory. This file should contain the following:

```
<?xml version="1.0" encoding="ISO-8859-1"?>
<web-app xmlns="http://java.sun.com/xml/ns/j2ee"
        xmlns:xsi="http://www.w3.org/2001/XMLSchema-instance"
        xsi:schemaLocation="http://java.sun.com/xml/ns/j2ee
```

```
            http://java.sun.com/xml/ns/j2ee/web-app_2_4.xsd"
             version="2.4">
    <servlet>
      <servlet-name>Example</servlet-name>
      <servlet-class>com.apress.servlets.ExampleServlet</servlet-class>
    </servlet>
    <servlet-mapping>
      <servlet-name>Example</servlet-name>
      <url-pattern>*.example</url-pattern>
    </servlet-mapping>
  </web-app>
```

5. Now start Tomcat, and navigate to `http://localhost:8080/Servlets/anything.example`. You should see the servlet's output shown in Figure 9-5.

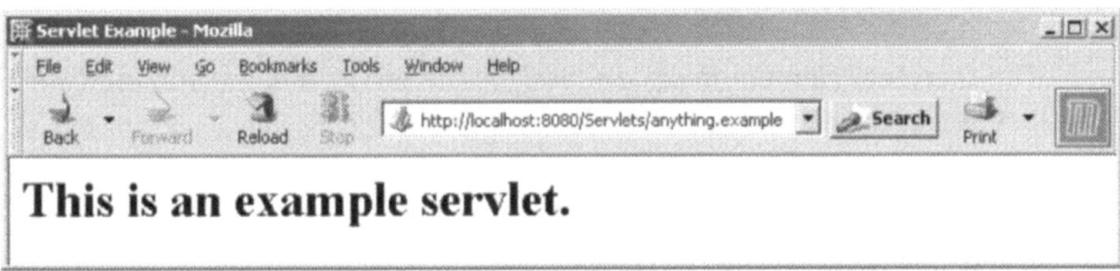


*Figure 9-5. The example servlet*

*How It Works*

The first parts of the code simply import the required resources and set up the class, which extends `HttpServlet`:

```
package com.apress.servlets;

import java.io.PrintWriter;
import java.io.IOException;
import javax.servlet.ServletException;
import javax.servlet.http.HttpServlet;
import javax.servlet.http.HttpServletRequest;
import javax.servlet.http.HttpServletResponse;

public class ExampleServlet extends HttpServlet
```

The `doGet()` method first sets the content type of the response to HTML, which the client uses to render it. The method then creates a `PrintWriter` object called `out`, acquired from the response object:

```
response.setContentType("text/html");
PrintWriter out = response.getWriter();
```

A series of HTML statements are printed to out, and the close() method is called, which flushes and closes the output stream, returning the response to the client.

This class showcases a common strategy when a servlet can treat GET and POST requests exactly the same: routing any POST requests directly to the doGet() method:

```
public void doPost(HttpServletRequest request,
                   HttpServletResponse response)
       throws ServletException, IOException
{
  doGet(request, response);
}
```

The <servlet> element in web.xml assigns the servlet a name and indicates the location of the class that defines it:

```
<servlet>
  <servlet-name>Example</servlet-name>
  <servlet-class>com.apress.servlets.ExampleServlet</servlet-class>
</servlet>
```

You can use this name elsewhere in web.xml to refer to your servlet when providing additional configuration information for it, as when you provide a *mapping* for the servlet. The mapping tells the servlet container to route any request to any URL ending with .example to your servlet:

```
  <servlet-mapping>
    <servlet-name>Example</servlet-name>
    <url-pattern>*.example</url-pattern>
  </servlet-mapping>
</web-app>
```

## The Servlet Life Cycle

The *life cycle* of a servlet is the sequence of events in which a servlet is created, utilized, and finally destroyed. The servlet container manages this for you, creating the servlet object and calling its methods as required. Figure 9-6 illustrates the servlet life cycle in generic terms.

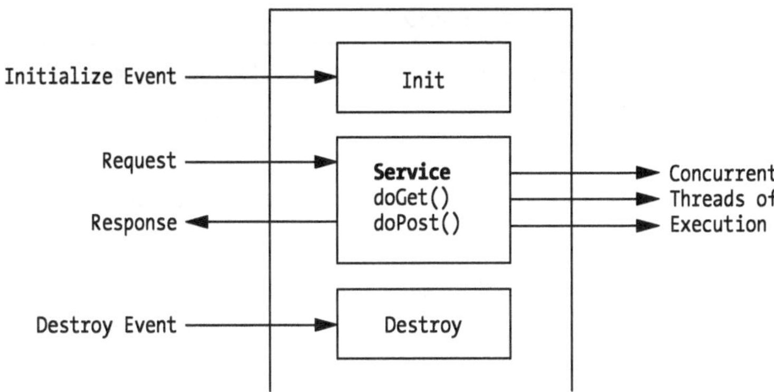


*Figure 9-6. The servlet life cycle*

## Loading, Instantiating, and Initializing

A server loads and instantiates a servlet dynamically when its services are first requested. The servlet's `init()` method should perform any necessary initialization and is called once for each servlet instance before any requests are handled. You only need to override `init()` in your servlet if a specific function needs to be accomplished at initialization. For example, you could use `init()` to load default data.

## Handling Requests

Once the servlet is properly initialized, the container can use it to handle requests. For each request, the servlet's `service()` method is passed an `HttpServletRequest` representing the request and an `HttpServletResponse` object that the servlet can use to create the response for the client.

### The Request Object

The `HttpServletRequest` object allows the servlet to access all the information sent to the servlet container from the client. You have in fact already been introduced to the `HttpServletRequest` object earlier in this book—the implicit JSP `request` object is an example of this same object.

The information `HttpServletRequest` contains includes the URL and query string, the request headers, and in some cases additional information called the *request body*. You have several methods for accessing this information. Because you're already familiar with how to access this information in a JSP page, Table 9-1 compares the JSP method with the Java method.

*Table 9-1. JSP EL Method to Java Method Map*

| Description | JSP Expression Language | HttpServletRequest Method |
|---|---|---|
| Retrieves a request parameter | ${param.myParam} | getParameter("myParam") |
| Retrieves a request header | ${header.headerName} | getHeader("headerName") |
| Retrieves multiple request values | ${paramValues.myParam} | getParameterValues("myParam") |

### The Response Object

A servlet's end product is the HTTP response object encapsulating all the information to be returned to the client, and the HttpServletResponse interface defines methods that servlets use to construct this response.

An HttpServletResponse object provides two ways of returning data to the user: through the Writer object or the ServletOutputStream object, obtained by the getWriter() and getOutputStream() methods, respectively. You should use the first object when the output is text data and the second when the output is binary data (such as an image or a Portable Document Format [PDF] file). Closing the Writer or ServletOutputStream objects with the close() method on either object once the response is created indicates to the server that the response is complete and ready to return to the client.

HttpServletResponse provides a number of other useful methods:

**sendRedirect()**: Redirects the client to a different URL. Here the URL must be an absolute URL. An example of this method is as follows:

```
httpServletResponse.sendRedirect("http://www.amazon.com");
```

**sendError()**: Sends an error message (for example, SC_METHOD_NOT_ALLOWED) to the client using the current error code status; you can also provide an optional descriptive message. An example of this method is as follows:

```
httpServletResponse.sendError(HttpServletResponse.SC_FORBIDDEN);
```

Alternatively, you can also provide an error message:

```
httpServletResponse.sendError(HttpServletResponse.SC_FORBIDDEN,
                              "You don't have access, get lost");
```

You can find the complete list of error codes in the Javadoc documentation for the HttpServletResponse object.

### *Trying It Out: Using the Request and Response Objects*

In this exercise, you'll use some more features of the `request` and `response` objects in the earlier servlet:

1. Make a copy of `ExampleServlet.java` called **DisplayServlet.java**, and modify it with the bold code:

```
package com.apress.servlets;

import java.io.PrintWriter;
import java.io.IOException;
import java.util.Enumeration;
import javax.servlet.ServletException;
import javax.servlet.http.HttpServlet;
import javax.servlet.http.HttpServletRequest;
import javax.servlet.http.HttpServletResponse;

public class DisplayServlet extends HttpServlet
{

  public void doGet(HttpServletRequest request,
                    HttpServletResponse response)
         throws ServletException, IOException
  {
    response.setContentType("text/html");
    PrintWriter out = response.getWriter();
    out.println("<html><head><title>");
    out.println("Servlet Example");
    out.println("</title></head><body>");

    out.println("Query String being processed: <br/>");
    out.println(request.getQueryString());
    out.println("<p>");
    out.println("Request Parameters:<p>");

    Enumeration enumParam = request.getParameterNames();
    while (enumParam.hasMoreElements())
    {
      String paramName = (String) enumParam.nextElement();
      String paramValues[] = request.getParameterValues(paramName);
      if (paramValues != null)
      {
        for (int i = 0; i < paramValues.length; i++)
        {
```

```
                out.print(paramName);
                out.print(" (" + i + "): ");
                out.print(paramValues[i]);
                out.println("<br/>");
            }
        }
    }

    out.println("</body></html>");
    out.close();
  }
}
```

2. Compile the servlet with the following command:

```
javac classpath %CATALINA_HOME%\common\lib\servlet-api.jar
    com/apress/servlets/DisplayServlet.java
```

3. Now you need to change web.xml to use the new servlet like this (note that all <servlet-mapping> elements must come after the <servlet> elements):

```
<?xml version="1.0" encoding="ISO-8859-1"?>
<web-app xmlns="http://java.sun.com/xml/ns/j2ee"
        xmlns:xsi="http://www.w3.org/2001/XMLSchema-instance"
        xsi:schemaLocation="http://java.sun.com/xml/ns/j2ee
        http://java.sun.com/xml/ns/j2ee/web-app_2_4.xsd"
         version="2.4">

  <servlet>
    <servlet-name>Example</servlet-name>
    <servlet-class>com.apress.servlets.ExampleServlet</servlet-class>
  </servlet>

  <servlet>
    <servlet-name>Display</servlet-name>
    <servlet-class>com.apress.servlets.DisplayServlet</servlet-class>
  </servlet>

  <servlet-mapping>
    <servlet-name>Example</servlet-name>
    <url-pattern>*.example</url-pattern>
  </servlet-mapping>
```

```
  <servlet-mapping>
    <servlet-name>Display</servlet-name>
    <url-pattern>*.display</url-pattern>
  </servlet-mapping>
</web-app>
```

4. Restart Tomcat. Then, open your browser, and navigate to a URL something like `http://localhost:8080/Servlets/anything.display?name=Anne&team=Galatasaray`. You should see the request parameters displayed like Figure 9-7.

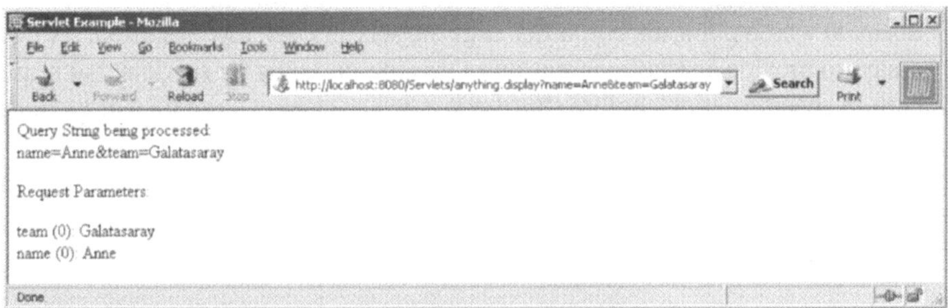


*Figure 9-7. A servlet that displays request parameters*

*How It Works*

This example simply reads the query string parameters and displays them on an HTML page. All the functionality is contained in the class's `doGet()` method. You get the entire query string using the `getQueryString()` method:

```
out.println("Query String being processed: <br/>");
out.println(request.getQueryString());
```

The `HttpServletRequest` object contains all the query string parameters, and you get all their names as an enumeration (a collection of objects) called `enumParam` by calling the `getParameterNames()` method, which returns a collection of parameter names:

```
Enumeration enumParam = request.getParameterNames();
```

An `Enumeration` functions very much like an `Iterator`, by the way, so you can iterate through the contents of `enumParam` using a `while` loop, storing each parameter name in a string called `paramName`:

```
while (enumParam.hasMoreElements())
{
  String paramName = (String) enumParam.nextElement();
```

You can find the value associated with this name by calling getParameterValues():

```
String paramValues[] = request.getParameterValues(paramName);
```

### Unloading

A servlet is typically unloaded from memory once the container is asked to shut down, at which point the container calls the servlet's destroy() method. It's necessary to provide an implementation of this method only for servlets that require certain specific actions before shutdown, such as closing open files or database connections.

## Collaboration Between Servlets

You've seen in earlier chapters how you can get JSP pages to collaborate. This collaboration is possible thanks to a range of separate mechanisms, such as the session and application objects. You can also perform all these tasks with servlets, and that's what you'll look at next.

### Session Tracking

HTTP is by design a *stateless* protocol. This means that Web servers running your applications can't by default remember details of a page showing in any browser from one request to the next. To overcome this when you require your Web applications to maintain data, you must implement a means to store details relevant to each active browser, such as session objects.

Sometimes, it's necessary that a series of requests from a particular client are logically associated with each other through some kind of *session tracking*. Many strategies for this have evolved over time. The Java servlet API takes a tried-and-tested approach: Store objects that pertain to a user on the server in a session object, and then use a cookie stored client-side by the Web browser to specify which session object pertains to which browser. The javax.servlet.http.HttpSession interface allows you to track a user's session fairly simply. This interface is implemented by the same session object that you can so easily use in JSP pages.

Session tracking allows servlets to maintain information about a series of requests from the same user for as long as it's required. To use this mechanism, you need to do the following:

- Obtain the `HttpSession` object from the `HttpServletRequest`.
- Store and retrieve data from the `session` object.
- When you no longer need certain data in the `session` object, remove it. When the entire object is done with, destroy it to conserve server resources by calling `invalidate()`.

The `getSession()` method of the `HttpServletRequest` object returns the session currently associated with the request. If there's no current `session` object, then one is created. You create name/value pairs to store data in the session. The `HttpSession` interface has methods allowing you to store, retrieve, and remove session attributes:

- `setAttribute()`
- `getAttribute()`
- `getAttributeNames()`
- `removeAttribute()`

A *session attribute* is simply an object that has been stored in the session. The `invalidate()` method invalidates the session, which means all the objects in the session are destroyed.

### *Trying It Out: Performing Session Tracking in a Servlet*

In this example, you'll try a servlet that uses session tracking to keep track of how many times it has been accessed by a particular user and to display some details of the current session:

1. Save the following Java code in a file called **SessionTracker.java** in the same folder as before:

```
package com.apress.servlets;

import java.io.PrintWriter;
import java.io.IOException;
import java.util.Date;
import javax.servlet.ServletException;
import javax.servlet.http.HttpServlet;
import javax.servlet.http.HttpServletRequest;
import javax.servlet.http.HttpServletResponse;
import javax.servlet.http.HttpSession;
```

```
public class SessionTracker extends HttpServlet
{
  public void doGet(HttpServletRequest req, HttpServletResponse res)
              throws ServletException, IOException
  {
    res.setContentType("text/html");
    PrintWriter out = res.getWriter();

    HttpSession session = req.getSession(true);

    Integer count = (Integer) session.getAttribute("count");

    if (count == null)
    {
      count = new Integer(1);
    }
    else
    {
      count = new Integer(count.intValue() + 1);
    }

    session.setAttribute("count", count);
    out.println("<html><head><title>SessionSnoop</title></head>");
    out.println("<body><h1>Session Details</h1>");
    out.println("You've visited this page " + count + ((count.intValue()
                == 1) ? " time." : " times.") + "<br/>");
    out.println("<h3>Details of this session:</h3>");
    out.println("Session id: " + session.getId() + "<br/>");
    out.println("New session: " + session.isNew() + "<br/>");
    out.println("Timeout: " + session.getMaxInactiveInterval() +
        "<br/>");
    out.println("Creation time: " + new Date(session.getCreationTime())
                + "<br/>");
    out.println("Last access time: "
                + new Date(session.getLastAccessedTime()) + "<br/>");
    out.println("</body></html>");
  }
}
```

2. Compile the servlet from the classes folder by running the following command:

```
javac classpath %CATALINA_HOME%\common\lib\servlet-api.jar
    com/apress/servlets/SessionTracker.java
```

3. Add the following entry to the `web.xml` file next to the existing `<servlet>` entries:

```
<servlet>
  <servlet-name>SessionTracker</servlet-name>
  <servlet-class>com.apress.servlets.SessionTracker</servlet-class>
</servlet>
```

   and the following entry next to the existing `<servlet-mapping>` entries:

```
  <servlet-mapping>
    <servlet-name>SessionTracker</servlet-name>
    <url-pattern>/Session</url-pattern>
  </servlet-mapping>
```

4. Restart Tomcat, and browse to `http://localhost:8080/Servlets/Session`. You should something similar to Figure 9-8.

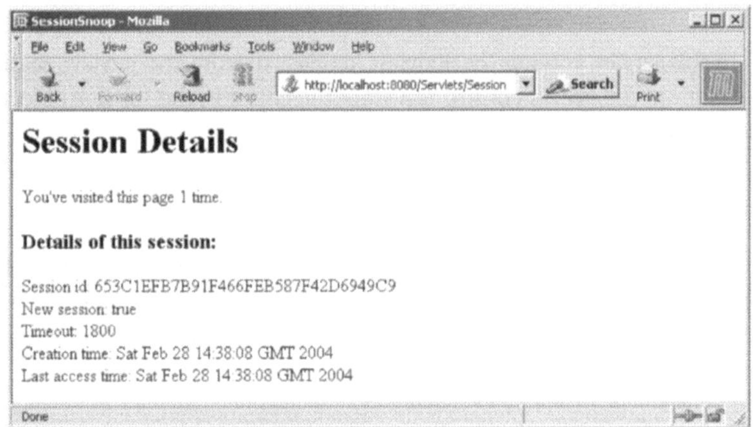


*Figure 9-8. The session servlet*

5. Hit your browser's Reload button several times. You'll notice that the page shows how many times you've visited it, and also it now says *New session: false.*

*How It Works*

First, you set the request content type to HTML, create a `PrintWriter` object, and get the current session (a new one is created if needed):

```
res.setContentType("text/html");
PrintWriter out = res.getWriter();
HttpSession session = req.getSession(true);
```

Every time a page is accessed, you get the count from the session by calling `getAttribute()`, increment it, and store it back in the session. If the `Session` object returns `null`, meaning that no `count` attribute has yet been set, `count` is initialized to one:

```
Integer count = (Integer) session.getAttribute("count");

if (count == null)
{
  count = new Integer(1);
}
else
{
  count = new Integer(count.intValue() + 1);
}
```

In this servlet, you use the `HttpSession` class to store and retrieve session-specific information (the access count). You store the count in the `session` object by calling `setAttribute()`:

```
session.setAttribute("count", count);
```

A session can store only objects, not any primitive data types. Hence, you store objects as type `Integer` rather than as the primitive `int` type. The rest of the servlet creates HTML output showing the number of hits and other standard information stored by the `session` object.

## *The Servlet Context*

The servlet context defines the servlet's view of a Web application. It's a class that implements the `javax.servlet.ServletContext` interface, and a servlet can use it to access all the resources available within the application, to log events, and to store attributes that other servlets with the same context can use. (You encountered the `ServletContext` object earlier in the form of the implicit JSP `application` object.)

For example, so far in this chapter you've placed several servlets in a Web application that's based at `http://localhost:8080/Servlets`; all the resources in the server that are in this application (in other words, that have request paths starting `/Servlets`) share a single, common servlet context.

A servlet can set an object as an attribute into the context by name, just as it can with the `HttpSession`, providing a convenient place to store resources that need to be shared for general use in an application. You can add, retrieve, or remove objects from the context using the following methods of `ServletContext`:

- **void setAttribute(String name, Object attribute)**: Used to store an attribute in a context.
- **Object getAttribute(String name)**: Used to get an attribute from the context.
- **Enumeration getAttributeNames()**: Used to get the names of all the attributes currently stored in the context.
- **void removeAttribute(String name)**: Call this function to remove an attribute from the context.

*Trying It Out: Using Servlet Context Information*

You'll now enhance the previous example to use the servlet context object to keep count of the total number of accesses to a shared resource.

1. Add the following lines to `SessionTracker.java`, and save it in the same place under the name **SessionTracker2.java**:

```
package com.apress.servlets;

import java.io.PrintWriter;
import java.io.IOException;
import java.util.Date;
import javax.servlet.ServletException;
import javax.servlet.http.HttpServlet;
import javax.servlet.http.HttpServletRequest;
import javax.servlet.http.HttpServletResponse;
import javax.servlet.http.HttpSession;

public class SessionTracker2 extends HttpServlet
{
  public void doGet(HttpServletRequest req, HttpServletResponse res)
              throws ServletException, IOException
  {
    res.setContentType("text/html");
    PrintWriter out = res.getWriter();

    HttpSession session = req.getSession(true);
```

```
        Integer totalCount = (Integer) getServletContext()
                                   .getAttribute("com.apress.servlets.total");

        if (totalCount == null)
        {
          totalCount = new Integer(1);
        }
        else
        {
          totalCount = new Integer(totalCount.intValue() + 1);
        }

        Integer count = (Integer) session.getAttribute("count");

        if (count == null)
        {
          count = new Integer(1);
        }
        else
        {
          count = new Integer(count.intValue() + 1);
        }

        session.setAttribute("count", count);
        getServletContext().setAttribute("com.apress.servlets.total",
            totalCount);

        out.println("<html><head><title>SessionSnoop</title></head>");
        out.println("<body><h1>Session Details</h1>");
        out.println("You've visited this page " + count + ((count.intValue()
                    == 1) ? " time." : " times.") + "<br/>");
        out.println("Total number of visits: " + totalCount + "<br/>");
        out.println("<h3>Details of this session:</h3>");
        out.println("Session id: " + session.getId() + "<br/>");
        out.println("New session: " + session.isNew() + "<br/>");
        out.println("Timeout: " + session.getMaxInactiveInterval() +
          "<br/>");

        out.println("Creation time: " + new Date(session.getCreationTime())
                    + "<br/>");
        out.println("Last access time: "
                    + new Date(session.getLastAccessedTime()) + "<br/>");
        out.println("</body></html>");
      }
    }
```

2. Now compile SessionDetails2.java:

```
javac -classpath %CATALINA_HOME%\common\lib\servlet-api.jar
    com/apress/servlets/SessionTracker2.java
```

3. Add the following lines to your web.xml file, next to the other <servlet> entries:

```
<servlet>
  <servlet-name>SessionTracker2</servlet-name>
  <servlet-class>com.apress.servlets.SessionTracker2</servlet-class>
</servlet>
```

and add these lines with the other <servlet-mapping> entries:

```
<servlet-mapping>
  <servlet-name>SessionTracker2</servlet-name>
  <url-pattern>/Session2</url-pattern>
</servlet-mapping>
```

4. Restart Tomcat. For this demo, open two separate copies of your browser and surf to http://localhost:8080/Servlets/Session2 in each one. If you reload a few times in both, you'll get two pages looking something like Figure 9-9.

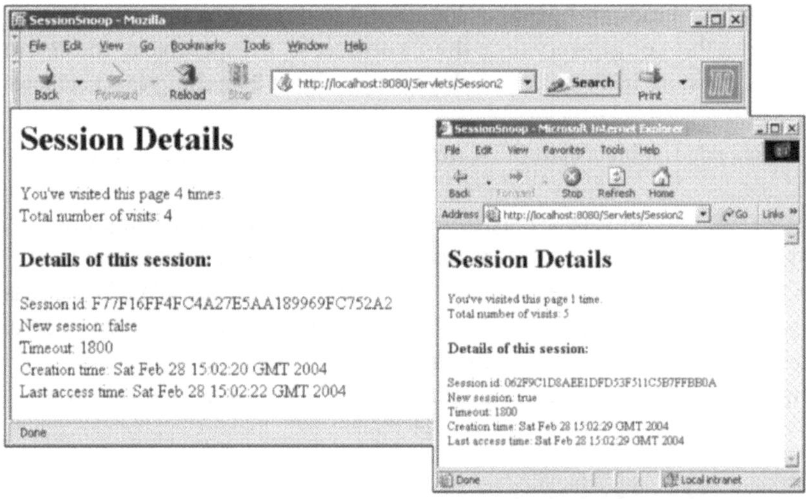


*Figure 9-9. The servlet context keeps track of all the visits to the page.*

*How It Works*

You now have two counters. The first one:

- You've visited this page 28 times.

tracks the number of times the browser has visited the page in a single session. The second counter:

- Total number of visits: 39

tracks the number of times all browsers have visited the page.

To accomplish this, you stored information in the ServletContext object to track the total number of hits:

```
Integer totalCount = (Integer) getServletContext().
    getAttribute("com.apress.servlets.total");

if (totalCount == null) {
  totalCount = new Integer(1);
} else {
  totalCount = new Integer(totalCount.intValue() + 1);
}
```

You access this context by calling the getServletContext() method, and you can get the attribute from the context by calling getAttribute(). You then take this value and increment it by one or initialize it to one if it hasn't yet been set. You increment this count every time there's an access, irrespective of the session status. You then store information in the context object by calling setAttribute():

```
getServletContext().setAttribute("com.apress.servlets.total", totalCount);
```

Any servlet can remove an attribute from the context by calling the removeAttribute() method; therefore, you must take care to ensure that other servlets aren't using the same name for one of their attributes. This is the reason why it's recommended to use scoped names for context attributes, such as com.apress.servlets.total rather than unqualified names such as total. Objects placed in the ServletContext will stay there until the container shuts down.

## Getting Initialization Information

You can pass initialization information such as database connection details to the servlet through a ServletConfig object that's passed to the servlet's init() method. The ServletConfig object obtains this initialization information from `web.xml`. In the following example, you'll get database login information from the `ServletConfig` object.

The `ServletConfig` object contains servlet-specific initialization parameters, so each servlet has its own. The parameters are stored as name/value pairs, and you use the `getInitParameter()` method to access the value of particular named parameters as a string:

```
String paramValue = ServletConfig.getInitParameter("paramName");
```

You can get the names of all of the initialization parameters using the `getInitParameterNames()` method:

```
Enumeration names = ServletConfig.getInitParameterNames();
```

This method returns an enumeration containing all the parameter names. This method is inherited from the `GenericServlet` class (remember that `HttpServlet` extends `GenericServlet`).

The `<context-param>` element in the `web.xml` file associates a set of initialization parameters with a Web application. These are accessed by calling methods on the `ServletContext` object just as you called methods on `ServletConfig` to get servlet parameters:

```
String contextParam = ServletContext.getInitParameter("contextParamName");
```

### *Trying It Out: Getting Initialization Information*

In this example, you'll get initialization information:

1. Create the following servlet in the same place as the other examples, under the name **InitParamServlet.java**. It outputs the database login and port configuration information taken from the `web.xml` file. For demonstration purposes, you'll even output the password, but it isn't normally recommended to display a password in a real application:

   ```
   package com.apress.servlets;

   import javax.servlet.ServletConfig;
   import javax.servlet.ServletContext;
   import javax.servlet.ServletException;
   import javax.servlet.http.HttpServlet;
   import javax.servlet.http.HttpServletRequest;
   import javax.servlet.http.HttpServletResponse;

   import java.io.PrintWriter;
   import java.io.IOException;
   ```

```
public class InitParamServlet extends HttpServlet
{
  public void doGet(HttpServletRequest req, HttpServletResponse res)
              throws IOException, ServletException
  {

    res.setContentType("text/plain");
    PrintWriter out = res.getWriter();

    String url = getInitParameter("URL");

    ServletConfig config = getServletConfig();
    ServletContext context = getServletContext();
    String uid = config.getInitParameter("UID");
    String pwd = config.getInitParameter("PWD");
    String port = context.getInitParameter("some-port");

    out.println("Values retrieved for the init parameters are: ");
    out.println("URL: " + url);
    out.println("UID: " + uid);
    out.println("PWD: " + pwd);
    out.println("some-port: " + port);
  }
}
```

2. Compile the servlet from the same directory as before:

```
javac -classpath %CATALINA_HOME%\common\lib\servlet-api.jar
    com/apress/servlets/InitParamServlet.java
```

3. Open your existing `web.xml` file and add the following bold lines, which provide the initialization information and servlet mapping that your servlet reads:

```
<?xml version="1.0" encoding="ISO-8859-1"?>
<web-app xmlns="http://java.sun.com/xml/ns/j2ee"
  xmlns:xsi="http://www.w3.org/2001/XMLSchema-instance"
  xsi:schemaLocation="http://java.sun.com/xml/ns/j2ee
  http://java.sun.com/xml/ns/j2ee/web-app_2_4.xsd" version="2.4">
  <display-name>A Simple Application</display-name>

  <context-param>
    <param-name>some-port</param-name>
    <param-value>5000</param-value>
  </context-param>
```

```
    <servlet>
      <servlet-name>init</servlet-name>
      <servlet-class>com.apress.servlets.InitParamServlet</servlet-class>
      <init-param>
        <param-name>URL</param-name>
        <param-value>jdbc:mysql://localhost/pizza</param-value>
      </init-param>
      <init-param>
        <param-name>UID</param-name>
        <param-value>matt</param-value>
      </init-param>
      <init-param>
        <param-name>PWD</param-name>
        <param-value>secret</param-value>
      </init-param>
    </servlet>

    <servlet-mapping>
      <servlet-name>init</servlet-name>
      <url-pattern>/init</url-pattern>
    </servlet-mapping>

  </web-app>
```

4. Restart Tomcat, and navigate to `http://localhost:8080/Servlets/init`. You should see something like Figure 9-10.

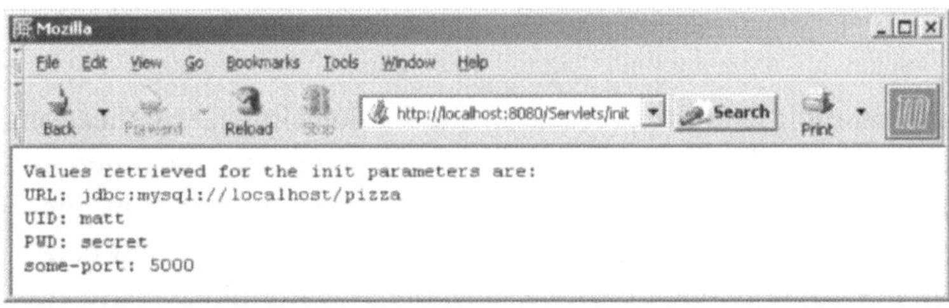


*Figure 9-10. Servlet initialization parameters*

### *How It Works*

You can provide initialization parameters under `<init-param>` tags in `web.xml` for particular servlets. Application-wide parameters are declared using the `<context-param>` element. `web.xml` also contains servlet parameter information.

You can access the parameters declared in the `web.xml` file from inside a servlet in several ways.

The InitParamServlet servlet implements just one method, doGet(). This method first sets the content type to plain text and creates a PrintWriter object:

```
res.setContentType("text/plain");
PrintWriter out = res.getWriter();
```

The init() method, which this servlet inherits from the GenericServlet class, is called when the servlet is created by the Web container. This initialization creates a ServletConfig object, and if no object is specified, methods are called on this object, as when you store the value of the URL attribute in a string called url using getInitParameter():

```
String url = getInitParameter("URL");
```

You can also obtain references to the ServletConfig and ServletContext objects anywhere in your servlet through the following methods:

```
ServletConfig config = getServletConfig();
ServletContext context = getServletContext();
String uid = config.getInitParameter("UID");
String pwd = config.getInitParameter("PWD");
```

You can access parameters declared in the <context-param> element only from the ServletContext object:

```
String port = context.getInitParameter("some-port");
```

## Filters

Often tasks are common to multiple requests and sessions in your applications, and for these you need a *filter*. Filters sit between the client and the underlying Web application, and you use them to examine and modify any requests and responses between the two. You can use filters to quickly prototype new concepts or to add new functionality to your applications—without having to alter the original application.

Filters are Web application components that can be bundled into a Web application archive. However, unlike other Web application components, filters are *chained* to the container's processing pipeline. This means they have access to an incoming request before a servlet does, and they have access to the outgoing response before it's returned to the client.

**NOTE** *A* filter *is a Java class that you can add to a Web application just as you add a servlet.*

You have two distinct ways to look at a filter:

- **The logical view**: The conceptual view of where filters fit within the container architecture
- **The physical view**: How to actually implement, package, and deploy filters

You'll now look at both of these views.

## *The Logical View of a Filter*

A filter can examine and modify the request before it reaches the requested Web resource; it can also examine and modify the response afterward. Figure 9-11 illustrates where filters fit in a container's processing pipeline. A filter intercepts the incoming request before the resource has access to it, and it intercepts the outgoing request before it's returned to the client.

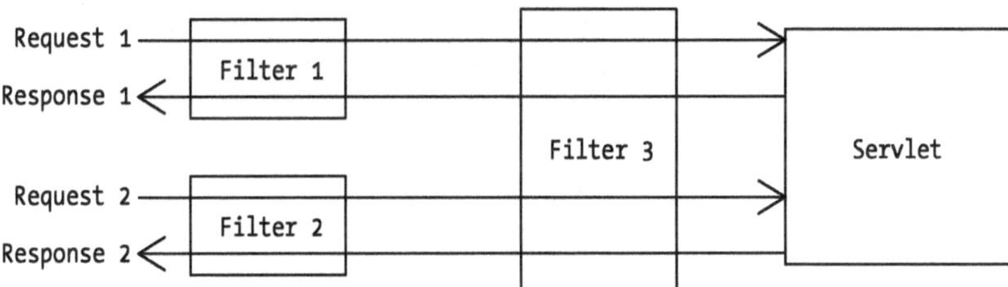


*Figure 9-11. The filter chain*

By combining the processing performed by the filters and the processing performed by the Web resource, you've created a new single unit of processing.

Figure 9-11 also shows how the filters are chained to form a line of processing. Notice how Request 1 and Response 1 pass through Filters 1 and 3 while Request 2 and Response 2 pass through Filters 2 and 3. Therefore, Filter 3 is applied to both requests and both responses.

## The Physical View of a Filter

The physical view of a filter is the view that a Web application deployer or assembler will see. It's the view that a filter developer works with when packaging the filter.

At deployment time, you have the option of associating a filter with a particular Web resource within the Web application.

### The Life Cycle of a Filter

A filter follows a life cycle similar to that of a servlet. A filter has four stages: instantiate, initialize, filter, and destroy.

The container calls the `init()` method of the filter. Immediately after this call, the filter instance must be ready to handle simultaneous requests. Requests come into the filter via a `doFilter()` method, just like requests come into servlets via a `service()` method.

The container will call the filter's `destroy()` method once all outstanding `doFilter()` method calls have been returned. After the `destroy()` method call, the filter is considered inactive. All per-instance cleanup should be implemented in the `destroy()` method, as the underlying Java object may be garbage collected shortly afterward.

Some containers may opt to pool instances of filters for performance reasons, which means that another `init()` method call may come shortly after the `destroy()` call on the *same* instance of a filter. If you're developing filters for containers that pool filter instances, you should be careful when designing your filters.

### The Filter Classes and Interfaces

All filters must implement the `javax.servlet.Filter` interface, which defines three methods: `init()`, `doFilter()`, and `destroy()`.

The container calls the `init()` method to initialize the filter instance:

```
public void init(FilterConfig config) throws ServletException
```

The `FilterConfig` object contains details of the filter and the underlying container. You'll see how you can use this in the following example.

The `doFilter()` method contains the logic of the filter—just as the `service()` method contains the logic of your servlets:

```
public void doFilter(ServletRequest req, ServletResponse res,
                     FilterChain chain) throws IOException, ServletException
```

Remember that a single instance of a filter can be servicing many requests simultaneously. This means that any shared (nonlocal) variables must be accessed via synchronized blocks.

The `FilterChain` argument is vital for proper filter operations. You must call the `doFilter()` method of the `FilterChain` object, unless you want to block further downstream processing (that is, prevent the request from reaching the underlying Web resource associated with the request).

Any code that comes before the call to the `doFilter()` method of `FilterChain` is considered *preprocessing* filter logic. At this stage, the incoming request is available but hasn't yet reached the Web resource.

The code after the call to the `doFilter()` method of `FilterChain` makes up the *postprocessing* filter logic. At this stage, the outgoing response contains the complete response from the Web resource.

> **NOTE** *The call to the* `doFilter()` *method of* `FilterChain` *will invoke the next filter (when chaining) or the underlying Web resource.*

The actual processing by any downstream filters or the underlying Web resources will occur during the call to the `doFilter()` method of `FilterChain`. From the point of view of the filter, the request processing not contained in the filter is folded into the call to the `doFilter()` method of `FilterChain`. This allows you to do something that's typically very difficult to perform in other request-response intercepting mechanisms: you can easily share variables between the preprocessing and the postprocessing logic.

The `destroy()` method will be called by the container before the container destroys the filter instance:

```
public void destroy()
```

*Trying It Out: Creating a Simple Access Filter*

This example filter will deny access to the pizza application if the request comes from a certain IP address, perhaps belonging to a bad customer. Follow these steps:

1. You'll first write the filter. Create a new folder in `WEB-INF\classes` called **filters**. Create **AccessFilter.java**, and add the following code:

   ```
   package filters;

   import javax.servlet.FilterConfig;
   import javax.servlet.ServletRequest;
   ```

```
import javax.servlet.ServletResponse;
import javax.servlet.ServletException;

import java.io.IOException;

public final class AccessFilter implements Filter {

  private FilterConfig filterConfig = null;

  public void init(FilterConfig filterConfig) {
    this.filterConfig = filterConfig;
  }

  public void doFilter(ServletRequest request, ServletResponse response,
                       FilterChain chain)
    throws IOException, ServletException {

    if(request.getRemoteAddr().equals("127.0.0.1")) {
      filterConfig.getServletContext().
        getRequestDispatcher("/denied.jsp").forward(request, response);
    } else {
      chain.doFilter(request, response);
    }
  }

  public void destroy() {
    this.filterConfig = null;
  }
}
```

2. Add the following to the beginning of `web.xml`, after the `<web-app>` element and before any servlet definitions:

```
<filter>
  <filter-name>Access</filter-name>
  <filter-class>filters.AccessFilter</filter-class>
</filter>

<filter-mapping>
  <filter-name>Access</filter-name>
  <url-pattern>/*</url-pattern>
</filter-mapping>
```

3. Create **denied.jsp** in the Pizza folder, and add the following:

```
<html>
  <head><title>Access denied</title></head>
  <body>
    <h1>Access denied</h1>
    <p>
      Sorry, you cannot order any more pizzas. Please pay your bills.
    </p>
  </body>
</html>
```

4. That's all there is to it. Restart Tomcat, and navigate to `http://localhost:8080/Pizza/pizza.jsp`. Because you've denied access to clients from the local machine (127.0.0.1), you should get a page like Figure 9-12.

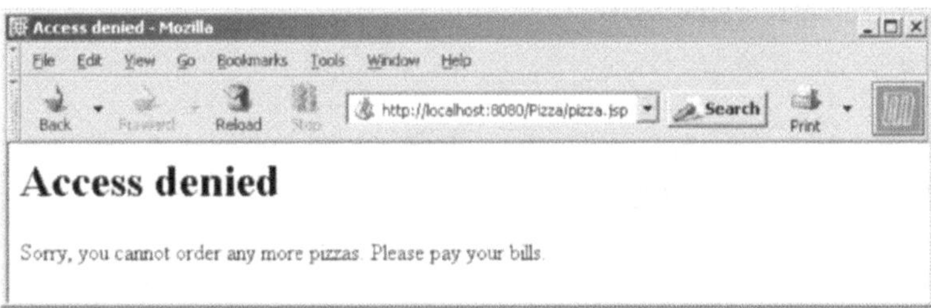


*Figure 9-12. The filter has denied access to the pizza application.*

*How It Works*

The filter is very simple. You start by gaining access to the filter's configuration information, which includes many references to the container's settings:

```
private FilterConfig filterConfig = null;

public void init(FilterConfig filterConfig) {
  this.filterConfig = filterConfig;
}
```

The next stage of the filter's life cycle is request and response processing. The `doFilter()` method will handle all the requests and responses:

```
public void doFilter(ServletRequest request, ServletResponse response,
                     FilterChain chain)
  throws IOException, ServletException {
```

The first part of the method (that is, the part before a call to the FilterChain's doFilter() method) deals with the request. You want to deny access to all users from a certain IP address; in this case you'll use the loopback address to deny users from the local machine. If the IP address matches 127.0.0.1, then you want to forward the request to the denied.jsp page. This is possible because you have access to the underlying container through the FilterConfig object:

```
if(request.getRemoteAddr().equals("127.0.0.1")) {
  filterConfig.getServletContext().
        getRequestDispatcher("/denied.jsp").forward(request, response);
```

If the request isn't from the local machine, you call doFilter() on the FilterConfig object and pass the request down the chain (in this case, to the Web resource as there are no other filters in the chain):

```
} else {
  chain.doFilter(request, response);
}
```

You finish the class with the destroy() method, which removes the current configuration object from memory:

```
public void destroy() {
  this.filterConfig = null;
}
```

Deploying the filter is as simple as deploying a servlet. You give it a name and tell the container the class to use:

```
<filter>
  <filter-name>Access</filter-name>
  <filter-class>filters.AccessFilter</filter-class>
</filter>
```

You then tell the container when to apply the filter using a URL pattern:

```
<filter-mapping>
  <filter-name>Access</filter-name>
  <url-pattern>/*</url-pattern>
</filter-mapping>
```

You can also use a <servlet-name> subelement instead of <url-pattern> to map a filter to a servlet by name.

## Filter Initialization Parameters

The example shows the main points of filters but isn't quite the flexible, plug-and-play module that it should be. Filters should follow the same good practice as other classes, and you should avoid writing them to rely on hard-coded strings. You can avoid this problem by using filter initialization parameters.

### *Trying it Out: Using Filter Initialization Parameters*

You'll convert the access filter to remove any hard-coded strings:

1. Add the bold lines to `AccessFilter.java`:

```
public void doFilter(ServletRequest request, ServletResponse response,
                     FilterChain chain)
    throws IOException, ServletException {

  String ipAddress = filterConfig.getInitParameter("ipAddress");
  String deniedPage = filterConfig.getInitParameter("deniedPage");

  if(request.getRemoteAddr().equals(ipAddress)) {
    filterConfig.getServletContext().
      getRequestDispatcher(deniedPage).forward(request, response);
  } else {
```

2. Add the following bold lines to `web.xml`:

```
<filter>
  <filter-name>Access</filter-name>
  <filter-class>filters.AccessFilter</filter-class>
  <init-param>
    <param-name>ipAddress</param-name>
    <param-value>127.0.0.1</param-value>
  </init-param>
  <init-param>
    <param-name>deniedPage</param-name>
    <param-value>/denied.jsp</param-value>
  </init-param>
</filter>
```

3. Restart Tomcat, and try to access the pizza application. As before, access will be denied.

*How It Works*

The additions to `web.xml` place two initialization parameters called `ipAddress` and `deniedPage` in the `FilterConfig` object:

```
<init-param>
  <param-name>ipAddress</param-name>
  <param-value>127.0.0.1</param-value>
</init-param>
<init-param>
  <param-name>deniedPage</param-name>
  <param-value>/denied.jsp</param-value>
</init-param>
```

You access these initialization parameters with the following lines of code:

```
String ipAddress = filterConfig.getInitParameter("ipAddress");
String deniedPage = filterConfig.getInitParameter("deniedPage");
```

Then use them instead of the hard-coded strings:

```
  if(request.getRemoteAddr().equals(ipAddress)) {
      filterConfig.getServletContext().
        getRequestDispatcher(deniedPage).forward(request, response);
  } else {
```

## Chaining Filters

It's possible to apply multiple filters to a resource. For example, the following filter mappings will apply both the `AccessFilter` and `LogFilter` filters to all the resources in an application:

```
<filter-mapping>
  <filter-name>AccessFilter</filter-name>
  <url-pattern>/*</url-pattern>
</filter-mapping>
<filter-mapping>
  <filter-name>LogFilter</filter-name>
  <url-pattern>/*</url-pattern>
</filter-mapping>
```

The container will construct filter chains based on the order of the filter mappings in `web.xml`. The order of filters within a chain is very important for the proper operation of an application because filter chaining isn't transitive.

> **NOTE** *Applying filter A and then applying filter B isn't necessarily equal to applying filter B and then filter A.*

## Summary

When a Web browser accesses a Web server and makes an HTTP request, the servlet container determines which servlet to invoke based on its configuration settings and calls it with objects representing the request and response. The servlet processes the request, using the request object to obtain information about the request that the browser sent, and sends data back to the client using the response object.

In this chapter, you've learned about the following:

- Features of the servlet technology, how servlets work, and their life cycle
- How JSP pages work behind the scenes: the relevance of servlet technology to JSP developers and that JSP pages are compiled to servlets
- The role of the `web.xml` file in a Web application
- How servlets can collaborate by means of session tracking, the servlet context, and how to forward and include requests when using servlets
- How you can use filters to preprocess requests and postprocess responses

CHAPTER 10

# Implementing the Model 2 Architecture and Using Struts

**THROUGHOUT THIS BOOK,** you've seen how to write JavaServer Pages (JSP) pages, use custom tags, and access relational databases. When putting a certain structure in place for a JSP application, you can use existing *frameworks* that provide a foundation for you to build your applications. Good frameworks encapsulate best practices in Web application architecture and also implement a lot of common functionality that would otherwise have to be reimplemented for each and every Web application.

This chapter concentrates on the Jakarta Struts Framework, which has become something of a standard in the field. It takes care of the architecture and a lot of the basic functionality for a Web application, letting you concentrate on the remaining features that are unique to that application.

In this chapter, you'll learn about the following:

- Naïve—also called Model 1—Web application architecture
- Proper—Model 2 or Model-View-Controller (MVC)—Web application architecture
- How Struts implements Model 2 Web application architecture
- How to install and configure Struts
- Struts architecture and its core classes
- Struts tag libraries, including the Hypertext Markup Language (HTML) and bean libraries
- Dynamic Struts forms that can eliminate Java coding to support HTML forms
- The Struts validator for declarative validation without Java code
- Internationalization of messages, conventions, and validation rules

To demonstrate these features, you'll convert the pizza application from earlier in the book into a Struts pizza application. As the chapter progresses, you'll see how to use each Struts feature in the new application, thus slowly building it up as you go along.

## Architecture of Web Applications

One approach to Web application development is to gather the requirements and quickly chalk out some JSP pages and JavaBeans. Though this approach would probably work to some degree, the end result is unlikely to be maintainable, and it may well be hard to change a certain feature or to introduce new features without breaking other parts of the application. It's also probably not *reusable.* If you need to introduce new functionality, you'd have to repeat a lot of work that you had already done but that's locked up in JSP pages and beans in such a way that you can't use it. By structuring your applications correctly, you can go much further toward achieving the goals of maintainability and reusability.

The first part of this chapter will be dedicated to comparing the naïve approach to Web applications (the Model 1 architecture) to a more sophisticated Model 2 (MVC) one. Having gained some understanding of the issues involved, you'll then look at the way the Struts framework realizes the Model 2 architecture, and you'll discover many of the facilities it has to make Web application development a much more productive and indeed enjoyable experience.

### *JSP Model 1 Architecture*

If you've been following all the examples in this book so far, you'll notice that you've developed JSP pages to present the data to the user. Along the way, you learned that JavaBeans provide a good mechanism to encapsulate some of your functionality into Java classes. You used these JavaBeans directly in your JSP pages via the `<jsp:useBean>` tags. You probably also noticed that most of the JSP pages not only displayed the data to the user, but they were also responsible for controlling the flow of the application. For instance, they contained the logic to display the next page. This control logic was often coded into the JSP pages as scriptlets or, preferably, using JavaBeans or custom tags. Such architecture is known as a *page-centric* architecture, and this particular page-centric architecture is known as the JSP Model 1 architecture. Figure 10-1 shows the JSP Model 1 architecture.

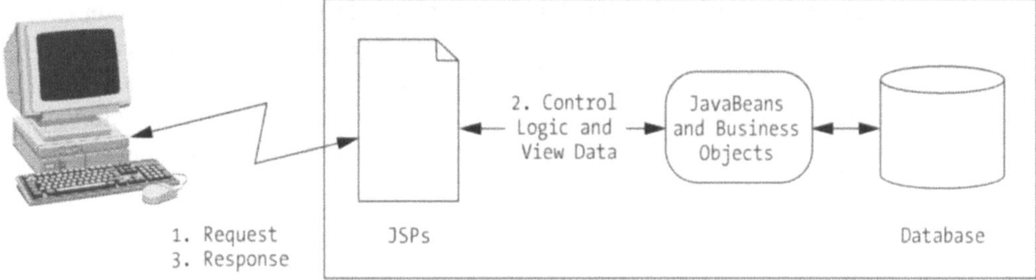


*Figure 10-1. Model 1 architecture*

### Features of the JSP Model 1 Architecture

The main features of Model 1 architecture are as follows:

- You use HTML or JSP files to code the presentation. The JSP files can use JavaBeans or other Java objects to retrieve data if required.
- JSP files are also responsible for all the business and processing logic, such as receiving incoming requests, routing to the correct JSP page, instantiating the correct JSP pages, and so on. This means that the Model 1 architecture is a page-centric design: All the business and processing logic is either present in the JSP page itself or called directly from the JSP page.
- Data access is usually performed using custom tags or through JavaBean calls. Some quick-and-dirty projects use scriptlets in their JSP pages instead.

Therefore, there's a tight coupling between the pages and the logic in Model 1 applications. The flow of the application goes from one JSP page to another using anchor links in JSP pages or the `action` attribute of HTML forms. This is the only kind of application you've seen so far. The pizza application is an example of this.

### Drawbacks of the JSP Model 1 Architecture

The Model 1 architecture has one thing going for it: simplicity. If your project is small, simple, and self-contained, it's the quickest way to get up and running. But the previous example, although by no means large or complicated, already illustrates a number of the disadvantages of Model 1 architecture:

It becomes very hard to change the structure of such Web applications because the pages are *tightly coupled*. They have to be aware of each other. What if you decide that, after updating the quantities in a shopping cart, you want to redirect the user back to the catalog? This could require moving code from the shopping cart page to the catalog page.

Large projects often involve teams of programmers working on different pages, and in the Model 1 scenario, each team would have to have a detailed understanding of the pages on which all of the other teams were working; otherwise, modifying pages could break the flow of the application.

Pages that are linked to from many other pages have to handle those other pages' logic, such as a cart update. In this way, they can accumulate a large amount of code that hasn't got an awful lot to do with the page itself. This reduces their *coherence*, making them harder to understand and to maintain.

Presentation and application control logic are mixed up, making it hard for a Web designer to change the pages without messing up the Java code. And vice versa: it's very hard for a developer to change control logic that may be hidden in lots of HTML markup.

The lack of separation between presentation and logic means that providing multiple presentations carries a very high cost. What if you decide to sell pizzas via Wireless Application Protocol (WAP) or personal digital assistant (PDA) devices? These devices are radically different from Web browsers and require completely different presentation structure and formatting. Your only choice would be to produce a whole new set of pages and duplicate the application logic. You'd have to implement every subsequent change to the logic in more than one place. Soon enough, changes will become very hard to manage, and the implementations will start to diverge.

Of course, the obvious way to get around these problems is to separate out the presentation code from the application control logic. This leads you onto the next architecture, JSP Model 2 architecture.

## JSP Model 2 Architecture

JSP Model 2 architecture, also known as MVC architecture, addresses the problems of the page-centric Model 1 architecture by rigorously separating presentation, control logic, and application state. In the JSP Model 2 architecture, the control flow (or application flow) is embodied in another module called the *controller*, as illustrated in Figure 10-2.

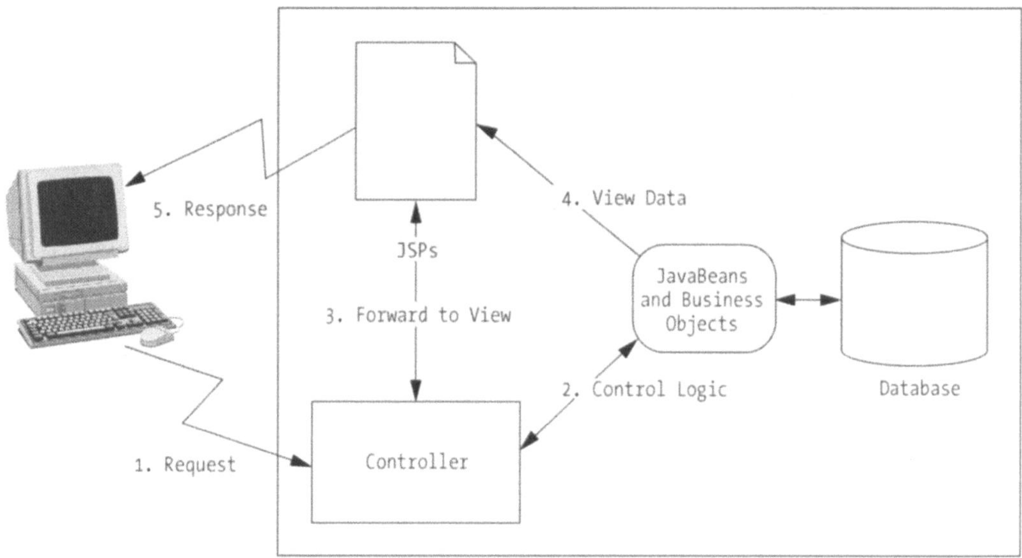


*Figure 10-2. JSP Model 2 architecture*

The controller receives all requests for the application and is responsible for taking the appropriate actions in response to each request. The controller may change some information or initiate some processing by the JavaBeans or other Java objects. Then it will forward the request to the appropriate view, usually a JSP page, which contains the presentation. The view chosen will often depend on the outcome of the processing.

The *model*—represented by the JavaBeans, business objects, and database in Figure 10-2—holds the application state. It usually covers the whole of the business and data layer in the application. In simple applications such as the example shopping cart, it may consist of a number of JavaBeans that model the application state. In more complicated applications, a variety of other Java objects may perform operations for you or provide the interface to the database; these objects may even reside on a different server, as in Enterprise JavaBeans. However, such differences don't concern you here.

**NOTE** *In the pizza application, the processing logic from the processing JSP page must be removed and placed in the model.*

The sole responsibility of the *view*—or JSP pages—is to take the information provided by the controller and the model and present it to the user. It may retrieve data from the model and display it, but it shouldn't change the state of the model or initiate any kind of processing. This is the task of the controller.

> **NOTE** *The presentation in the pizza application won't change because it's in the correct place: the view.*

By introducing a central controlling mechanism, you cleanly separate presentation logic from control flow. As a centralized component, the controller is a great place for implementing other useful features, such as security. You now have three distinct sections within your application:

- The model
- The view
- The controller

Hence, you get the MVC architecture (for more information, go to `http://java.sun.com/blueprints/guidelines/designing_enterprise_applications_2e/`, select the Web Tier, and read section 4.4). Implementing Model 2 architecture is easier than it sounds because many MVC frameworks have been written; the most famous is Jakarta Struts (recall that `http://www.waferproject.org` lists other MVC frameworks).

## The Struts Framework

Jakarta Struts is an open-source Web application framework based on the MVC design pattern. It allows you to fully decouple the business logic, control logic, and presentation of an application, making Web applications more reusable and maintainable. Built on the servlet and JSP application programming interfaces (APIs), it's suited to projects ranging from simple applications to complex enterprise systems. The Struts framework is a part of the Jakarta Project managed by the Apache Software Foundation, and you can download the files from `http://jakarta.apache.org/struts/`. The framework provides the following services:

- A powerful controller servlet, which delegates the application-specific business logic to `Action` classes that you write for a specific application. You configure this controller servlet using an Extensible Markup Language (XML) file.
- A number of JSP tag libraries for JavaBean management, HTML, and JavaScript generation, template handling, and flow control in a JSP page. These libraries are integrated with the controller servlet and automate a lot of common Web application functionality that you'd otherwise have to code by hand.

- A *validator* facility supporting the declaration of validation rules in an XML file. The validator supports both server-side and client-side (JavaScript) validation.

- Excellent *internationalization* support, which allows your application to support any number of languages and to use the language and conventions appropriate to any given user. This doesn't merely include messages but also dates and number formatting, monetary conventions, and validation logic.

- A generic error and exception handling mechanism that fully supports internationalization.

- File upload utilities to allow users to send files to the server using JSP pages.

- A facility to easily set up Java Database Connectivity (JDBC) data sources, including a generic implementation that can turn any ordinary JDBC driver into a `DataSource` with a built-in connection pool.

- Various JavaBean manipulation utilities.

Actually, the last two aren't part of the Struts framework proper but of the Commons code library (`http://jakarta.apache.org/commons/`). However, they ship with Struts, so you don't need to worry about the difference. In the remainder of this chapter, we'll explain how to use many (although not all) of these features.

## Struts Architecture

Struts is a framework supporting the MVC architecture. It comprises a completely general controller implementation supported by classes and tag libraries that implement the model and view aspects. The easiest way to understand where its major components fit inside the MVC architecture is to look at the way they work together to process a Hypertext Transfer Protocol (HTTP) request. Figure 10-3 depicts a high-level overview of Struts' core classes and their interactions.

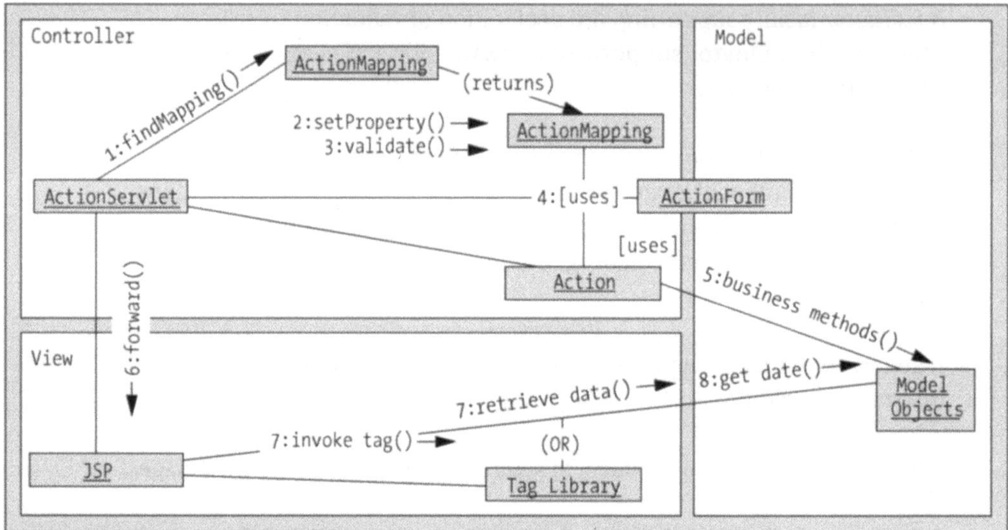


*Figure 10-3. Struts' core classes*

## Struts Classes

You'll now learn about each of the classes in Figure 10-3 in the order in which they're typically invoked. As you'd expect in an MVC framework, every request starts at the Struts controller, the heart of which is the `ActionServlet` class. This servlet is usually mapped to the extension `*.do`. For example, a request for `/process.do` would end up with the `ActionServlet` and tell it that the user has submitted a pizza order:

1. The controller servlet first determines what needs to be done. For every possible action uniform resource locator (URL), such as `/pizza.do`, it determines what needs to happen next. This information is read from Struts configuration files at runtime into instances of the `ActionMapping` class. So the first thing the controller servlet does is call `ActionMappings.findMapping()` to find what the appropriate `ActionMapping` is for the request URL (`/process.do` in this example).

   One of the things you often need to do in Web applications is store field values from an HTML form in a JavaBean. One of the things an action mapping can do is specify an `ActionForm` associated with the action. An `ActionForm` is a form-specific JavaBean that represents the input data from an HTML form. The controller servlet automatically instantiates this bean if necessary and populates it with request parameter values.

Pretend that `/process.do` is invoked by an order page asking the user for a pizza order. The HTML form on this page has a field called `size`. If you supply Struts with an `ActionForm` that has a `size` JavaBean property, it will automatically populate that property with the size entered by the user.

2. `ActionForms` may be part of the application model, or they can be used as a convenient way to move data around.

   Optionally, the controller servlet can ask the `ActionForm` to validate the data that has been submitted by calling `validate()` on the form. If the `ActionForm` indicates that validation fails, the request is forwarded back to the input HTML page with an error message.

   For example, the `ActionForm` could verify that a name has been entered; if it were missing, the request would be forwarded back to the original form with a *Please enter your name* message.

3. The next step is to invoke the `Action` object for the request URL. The `Action` classes provide the application-specific business logic necessary to process the request. You'll generally write one `Action` class for every different action in the application.

   A good `Action` class is small, focused, and easy to understand; it's merely the glue between the controller and the model. Actions aren't a good place to implement complicated business logic. An action will generally call one or more business methods in the model to get the actual work done.

   In the `/process.do` example, the action would initiate the actual order placement.

4. After the action has been completed successfully, the controller forwards the request to the view component. This view is usually a JSP page. The JSP request is forwarded as configured in the Struts configuration file and—you guessed it—contained at runtime in the `ActionMapping` object. These destinations are represented by `ActionForward` objects.

   Struts allows you to set up multiple destinations for a single action, which is useful if an action can have multiple outcomes. For example, writing data to a database could succeed or could fail. You'll probably want to forward to different JSP pages depending on the outcome.

5. The view JSP page can either access the Model directly, using `<jsp:getProperty>` or the Expression Language (EL), or use the *Struts tag libraries* to retrieve data from the model. For example, if you use the tags in the Struts `html` tag library to create HTML forms, the tags will automatically populate the form fields with the values in your `ActionForm`.

In broad terms, this is how Struts handles a request (although there are some details to flesh out that you'll come to in time). First, we'll discuss how to install and configure Struts; second, you'll apply your new knowledge to the shopping cart example.

## Installing and Configuring Struts

The latest source files and binaries for the Struts framework are available from `http://jakarta.apache.org/struts/`. Download the zipped binary distribution of the latest release of Struts 1.1 by following the Binaries link on this page. Linux users should download the `.tar.gz` file from the same location. Once downloaded, extract the contents to your drive. The unpacked folder will contain the following two subdirectories:

- `lib`, which includes the following files:
  - The `struts.jar` file containing the actual Struts code
  - The Commons Java archive (JAR) files and other JARs that Struts requires
  - The tag library descriptors (TLDs) for the Struts custom tags
  - The default validator rules file, `validator-rules.xml`
  - The document type definitions (DTDs) for the configuration files mentioned previously
- `web-apps`, which contains the Web archive (WAR) files for the example applications and Struts documentation

You usually need only the JAR files and the `validator-rules.xml` file from the `lib` directory. The TLDs and DTDs are packaged inside `struts.jar`, where neither Struts nor the JSP engine have any trouble finding them.

## Using Struts in a Web Application

To use the Struts framework in a Web application, you need to perform the following steps:

1. When compiling the Java classes, in particular `Action` classes, the `struts.jar` file must either appear in the `CLASSPATH` environment variable or be specified using the `-classpath` switch on the `javac` command.

2. Applications that use Struts must have a copy of all Struts `.jar` files in their `WEB-INF/lib` folder. The simplest way to do this may be to copy the entire Struts `lib` folder into your application's `WEB-INF` directory.

3. The application's deployment descriptor (`WEB-INF/web.xml`) must declare the Struts `ActionServlet` and map the required requests to the `ActionServlet` as follows:

```
<?xml version="1.0" encoding="ISO-8859-1"?>

<web-app xmlns="http://java.sun.com/xml/ns/j2ee"
         xmlns:xsi="http://www.w3.org/2001/XMLSchema-instance"
         xsi:schemaLocation="http://java.sun.com/xml/ns/j2ee
                                                  web-app_2_4.xsd"
         version="2.4">

  <!-- The Action Servlet -->
  <servlet>
    <servlet-name>action</servlet-name>
    <servlet-class>
      org.apache.struts.action.ActionServlet
    </servlet-class>
    <init-param>
      <param-name>config</param-name>
      <param-value>/WEB-INF/struts-config.xml</param-value>
    </init-param>
    <load-on-startup>1</load-on-startup>
  </servlet>

  <!-- Action Servlet Mapping -->
  <servlet-mapping>
    <servlet-name>action</servlet-name>
    <url-pattern>*.do</url-pattern>
  </servlet-mapping>

</web-app>
```

This excerpt from `web.xml` declares the `ActionServlet` by name and maps request uniform resource indicators (URIs) ending with `.do` to the `ActionServlet`. The (optional) `<load-on-startup>` element must contain a positive integer indicating the priority of this servlet, where lower priorities are loaded before higher ones.

`ActionServlet` takes a host of initialization parameters but all are optional, and in most cases you don't have to worry about them. Refer to the Struts documentation (`http://jakarta.apache.org/struts/userGuide/`) for further details.

4. You'll need to create a Struts configuration file called `struts-config.xml` in the `WEB-INF` directory of your Web application. This file contains the action mapping information, information on the `ActionForm` beans used in your application, global forwards, exception handling, and other information that you might want to set up such as `DataSources` and Struts plug-ins. We'll discuss this configuration file next, and you'll create one for the pizza application.

5. Finally, to support internationalization, Struts heavily uses resource bundles that provide the text for each message used in the application. At the very least, you'll need to create a default message bundle and tell Struts where to find it. We'll discuss resource bundles next.

## Message Resource Bundles and Internationalization

The Struts framework supports internationalization (often abbreviated to i18n—*i* followed by 18 letters and then *n*) and localization. When a Web browser submits an HTTP request, it provides information about the user's locale within the request that Struts uses to adapt responses.

Among other things, internationalization support requires you to no longer just embed messages, labels, and other text inside your JSP pages and Java code. Instead, you have to refer to these messages using *message keys*, and for each locale that you support, you must maintain a *message resources* file that provides the text appropriate for that locale for each message key.

Message resources are normally read from a Java properties file. For example, the contents of your default message resources file—say, `messages.properties`—could be like so:

```
message.1=The first internationalized message.
message.2=The second internationalized message.
```

You can then refer to these messages as `message.1` and `message.2`, respectively. If you want to support the French language, you could add a `messages_fr.properties` file reading the following:

```
message.1=Le premier message internationalisée.
message.2=Le deuxième message internationalisée.
```

The `_fr` appended to the filename tells Java that this file is a French message resource. When the user's locale indicates that French is the preferred language (for instance, if they're in France or French-speaking Canada), the messages will be retrieved from this file. You can even distinguish between different regional variants—for instance, American or British English—by taking the user's country code into account:

```
message.1=The first internationalised message.
message.2=The second internationalised message.
```

If you saved the previous messages as `messages_en_GB.properties` in the same directory as the other files, users favouring British English would see the messages with the word ***internationalized*** sporting an *s* instead of a *z*.

The nice thing is, you need to provide only the messages that are actually ***different*** from the default resource; if a message can't be found in `messages_en_GB.properties`, the region-specific file, Java looks in the language-specific `messages_en.properties` (if it exists) and finally in the default `messages.properties` file. This way, you can maintain these files with the minimum amount of work. All the message resource files for the different languages and countries together are called a ***message resource bundle***. Having a default resource file in American English means that users whose locale isn't specifically supported can at least use the application in its English-language guise.

> **NOTE** *It's usual to save these properties files in the Web application's classpath, that is, in* `WEB-INF/classes`*. They're then referred to as if they were Java classes in a package. For example, the file* `messages.properties` *saved in* `WEB-INF/resources` *is referred to as* `resources.messages` *in code. Note that the* `.properties` *extension is dropped just as the* `.class` *extension is dropped for Java classes.*

Java represents the user's locale with the `java.util.Locale` object. The JSTL uses the locale and resource bundles to output messages and format numbers and dates. Struts, too, uses this locale whenever it needs to display a message so it can do so in the correct language—for example, in the `<html:error>` tag that displays internationalized error messages. The power of Struts is that application developers need not know about the intricacies of these classes to use internationalized and formatted messages.

## Message Resources in the Pizza Application

You'll be using message resources extensively in the pizza application. Save the following in `WEB-INF\classes\resources\messages.properties`:

```
text.pizza.title=Take The Pizza
text.pizza.first.para=Welcome to Take the Pizza Online!
  We're eager to take your order for pizza via our new web form.
text.pizza.second.para= Please fill out the fields below and click on
  "Place Order" when you're done.
text.pizza.your.info=Your Information:
text.pizza.name=Name:
text.pizza.address=Address:
text.pizza.order.type=Order Type:
text.pizza.home.delivery=Home Delivery
text.pizza.take.away=Take Away
text.pizza.additional.toppings=Please Select Any Additional Toppings:
text.pizza.peppers=Peppers
text.pizza.sweetcorn=Sweetcorn
text.pizza.mouse.innards=Mouse Innards
text.pizza.choose.size=Pizza Size:
text.pizza.size=Size:
text.pizza.option.small=Small
text.pizza.option.medium=Medium
text.pizza.option.large=Large
text.pizza.submit=Place Order
text.process.title=Your details
text.process.first.header=Your Details
text.process.name=Name:
text.process.address=Address:
text.process.delivery.type=Delivery type:
text.process.toppings=Toppings:
text.process.size=Pizza size:
text.process.thanks=Thank you for ordering.
```

These are all the strings from the two pizza ordering pages. They've been extracted so that you can support Web pages written in languages other than English. You'll be using another properties file for your database operations called `sql.properties`:

```
sql.apostrophe.replace=\\'
sql.insert.customer=INSERT INTO customer (name, address) VALUES(?, ?)
sql.select.customer=SELECT MAX(customer_id) AS id FROM customer
sql.insert.order=INSERT INTO pizza.order (customer_id, delivery, size)
    VALUES(?, ?, ?)
sql.select.order=SELECT MAX(order_id) AS id FROM pizza.order
sql.insert.topping=INSERT INTO topping (order_id, topping) VALUES(?, ?)
```

Save this in `WEB-INF\classes\resources`. Note that the SQL is prepared statements that will be filled in at runtime by the action.

## The Struts Configuration File

The Struts configuration file configures all components used by the `ActionServlet` to do its work. The root element of the file is `<struts-config>`. It defines the following information, in this order:

**DataSources**: Used to configure connections to external databases in this configuration file. Each data source is defined under a `<data-source>` element, and these elements are in turn grouped together under the element `<data-sources>` in the Struts configuration file.

**ActionForm beans**: Defined within `<form-bean>` element. These elements are grouped together inside the `<form-beans>` element.

**Global exceptions**: A `<global-exceptions>` tag containing zero or more `<exception>` elements. These define the application exceptions that you want Struts to handle and what action should be taken in response to each of them. You can also define these on a per-action basis.

**Global forwards**: You can define global forwards for JSP pages that will be used a lot in your application. Each global forward is defined within a `<forward>` element, and these elements are grouped together under `<global-forwards>`.

**ActionMappings**: An `<action-mappings>` element that can contain zero or more `<action>` elements, each mapping a specific action URL to the `Action` class handling it. These `Action` classes are provided by the application developer. In addition, each `<action>` can have its own private list of exception handlers and forwards.

**Controller configuration**: The `<controller>` element allows a great deal of control over the way the controller servlet operates, including as the debugging level and the automatic capturing of the remote user's `Locale`.

**Message resources**: There can be zero or more <message-resources> elements, each specifying the location of a resource bundle for internationalized messages.

**Struts plug-ins**: Defined using the <plug-in> element. Each plug-in can receive further configuration information from nested <set-property> elements.

The ActionServlet loads the XML configuration file on startup. The name and location of the configuration file can be defined as an initialization parameter to the ActionServlet. If not specified, it defaults to /WEB-INF/struts-config.xml (relative to the Web application root). You can also force the ActionServlet to reload this configuration information programmatically.

You'll now see how to configure the elements of your application by building the struts-config.xml file. You start with the top-level <struts-config> element:

```
<?xml version="1.0" encoding="ISO-8859-1" ?>

<!DOCTYPE struts-config PUBLIC
          "-//Apache Software Foundation//DTD Struts Configuration 1.1//EN"
          "http://jakarta.apache.org/struts/dtds/struts-config_1_1.dtd">
```

You'll now go through the subelements in the order in which they must appear under this element.

## *Configuring JDBC DataSources*

You can define any number of JDBC javax.sql.DataSource objects for the application in the configuration file under the element <data-sources>. Every data source is defined within the <data-sources> element using the <data-source> element. The <data-source> element defines a number of attributes, the most important of which are listed in Table 10-1.

*Table 10-1.* <data-source> *Attributes*

| Element Attribute | Description |
|---|---|
| key | The name used by Action classes for looking up this connection. The default is org.apache.struts.action.DATA_SOURCE (defined in the constant org.apache.struts.Globals.DATA_SOURCE_KEY). |
| type | The name of the actual class that implements the DataSource interface. |

You supply any further configuration information using nested `<set-property>` tags. You can use these tags to set JavaBeans properties on the `DataSource`; they take `property` and `value` attributes to specify the property to set and the value to which to set it.

The default attribute values for `<data-source>` cause it to instantiate a `GenericDataSource` and give it the key. The `GenericDataSource` class wraps an ordinary JDBC `Driver` and turns it into a `DataSource` with a database connection pool. This class has a number of JavaBean properties to configure, the most important of which are listed in Table 10-2.

*Table 10-2.* `<data-source>` *Attributes*

| Element Attribute | Description |
|---|---|
| description | A description of this `DataSource`. |
| driverClass | The fully qualified JDBC `Driver` class used to access the database. |
| url | The JDBC URL used to access the database. |
| user | The username used to log into the database. |
| password | The password used to log into the database. |
| maxCount | The maximum number of connections in the connection pool. |
| readOnly | If `true`, the `Connections` returned by the `DataSource` are read-only; this has performance advantages with some databases. |
| autoCommit | If `true`, the `Connections` returned by the `DataSource` automatically commit the transaction after every SQL statement. |

The following excerpt illustrates how you'll use these attributes to define a `DataSource` for the `pizza` MySQL database:

```
<data-sources>
  <data-source key="pizza">
    <set-property property="driverClass"
                  value="com.mysql.jdbc.Driver" />
    <set-property property="url"
                  value="jdbc:mysql://localhost/pizza" />
  </data-source>
</data-sources>
```

The DataSource will be bound in the application context under the name pizza. You can use it in the JSTL <sql:query>, <sql:update>, and <sql:transaction> tags:

```
<sql:query var="myobject"
           dataSource="${applicationScope.pizza}">
```

You can also retrieve it from within a Struts action using the getDataSource() method:

```
DataSource ds = getDataSource(request, "pizza");
Connection con = ds.getConnection();
```

Now you'll configure a form bean.

## Configuring ActionForm Beans

As noted, the ActionServlet uses ActionForm beans to capture request parameters. These beans have attribute names that correspond to the names of the request parameters. The controller populates the ActionForm for the current action from the request and then passes the instance to the Action class to further process the data.

ActionForm beans are declared globally within the configuration file using <form-bean> elements inside the <form-beans> tag. Table 10-3 lists the important attributes of this element; both name and type attributes are required.

*Table 10-3.* ActionForm *Bean Attributes*

| Attribute | Description |
|---|---|
| name | The name of the form bean in its associated scope (in other words, the name of the request or session attribute that will contain the bean). The Struts ActionMappings can refer to the form bean by name. |
| type | The fully qualified name of the ActionForm class. |

The following example (not from the pizza application) shows how a form bean can be declared:

```
<form-beans>
  <form-bean name="creditCardForm" type="com.apress.shop.CreditCardForm"/>
</form-beans>
```

Here a form bean of type com.apress.shop.CreditCardForm is declared to use the name creditCardForm.

The pizza application uses a very simple form, so you'll use a *dynamic action form* (with validation), which needs `<form-property>` elements nested inside `<form-bean>` to configure them and is of type `DynaValidatorForm`. We'll discuss this next.

## Dynamic Action Forms

Rather than clutter up your source code with additional one-off Java classes that exist just to support a single HTML form, you can use Struts' *dynamic action forms* facility.

This consists of a single class, `org.apache.struts.action.DynaActionForm`, which models an arbitrary JavaBean and allows you to declare what properties it will have in the Struts configuration file.

### Configuring DynamicActionForm Beans

You declare `DynaActionForm` beans in the Struts configuration file using the same `<form-bean>` elements that are used to declare ordinary `ActionForm` beans. The difference is that for a dynamic form, you also specify the form's attributes using nested `<form-property>` tags. This tag takes the attributes listed in Table 10-4.

*Table 10-4.* `<form-property>` *Attributes*

| Element Attribute | Description |
|---|---|
| `name` | The name of the property to define. This attribute is required. |
| `type` | The fully qualified Java class name of the property type. Array types are denoted by appending square brackets ([ ]) to the type name. This attribute is required. |
| `initial` | The initial value for the property. If omitted, primitives will be initialized to zero, and objects will default to `null`. |

The property types supported include the following:

- Primitives (`byte`, `char`, `short`, `int`, `long`, `float`, `double`) and their wrapper classes (`java.lang.Byte`, `java.lang.Character`, and so on)
- Big numbers (`java.lang.BigDecimal` and `java.lang.BigInteger`)
- SQL types (`java.sql.Date`, `java.sql.Time` and `java.sql.TimeStamp`)
- `java.lang.String` and `java.lang.Class`

### *The DynaActionForm Class*

You can't create arbitrary JavaBeans on the fly, and behind the scenes a `DynaActionForm` doesn't work in the same way as a normal `ActionForm` bean. In essence, a dynamic action form is little more than a glorified `Map` mapping property names to their corresponding values. You can even retrieve this underlying `Map`:

```
public Map getMap()
```

This `map` attribute is the easiest way to extract data from dynamic forms using the JSP EL, as demonstrated in the following excerpt from a JSP confirmation page:

```
  .
  .
  .
<tr>
  <td><bean:message key="confirmation.card.number"/></td>
  <td>${creditCardForm.map.cardNumber}</td>
</tr>
<tr>
  <td><bean:message key="confirmation.card.expiry"/></td>
  <td><fmt:formatDate value="${creditCardForm.map.cardExpiry}"/></td>
</tr>
<tr>
  <td><bean:message key="confirmation.card.type"/></td>
  <td>${creditCardForm.map.cardType}</td>
</tr>
  .
  .
  .
```

This snippet displays all three attributes of the credit card form for the user to confirm.

## *The Struts Validator*

One of the most important aims of the Struts framework is to take routine Web application development tasks off your shoulders as much as possible. Form validation must surely count as one of the most routine and mind-numbing tasks there is; perhaps as a consequence, it often ends up being done patchily or in a clumsy, inflexible, difficult way to maintain.

Putting Java validation code in your ActionForm or Action classes is certainly neither clean nor flexible. The validation code ends up being mixed in with other concerns—data representation in the case of ActionForm classes, business logic in the case of Action classes—and Java code is hard to change once a system has been deployed and is in active use. You can also move validation to the browser by incorporating validation JavaScript in your Web pages, but what if the browser doesn't support JavaScript or has it disabled for security reasons? Really, you need to validate user input on the server side regardless of whether you also use JavaScript validation. Needless to say, having both server-side and client-side validation makes the code even harder to write and maintain.

The Struts validator facility provides a way to replace validation Java and JavaScript code with an XML file, which declares your validation constraints. In many cases, no coding is required, and you can generate both server-side and client-side validation from one and the same set of constraints; there's no longer any risk of the two getting out of sync.

### *Configuring Validation Rules*

The Struts validator is a plug-in. For it to work, you need to configure the plug-in in the Struts configuration file (WEB-INF/struts-config.xml) by adding the following entry right before the closing </struts-config> tag:

```
  <plug-in className="org.apache.struts.validator.ValidatorPlugIn">
    <set-property property="pathnames"
         value="/WEB-INF/validator-rules.xml,/WEB-INF/validation.xml"/>
  </plug-in>
</struts-config>
```

This plugs in the validator and tells Struts to read its configuration information from the validator-rules.xml and validation.xml files in the WEB-INF directory.

### *Supported Validator Rules*

The validator-rules.xml file defines the *types* of validation constraints you can apply. It defines the Java classes and methods that implement the server-side validation and contains the JavaScript code that handles the client-side part. It's shipped with a fairly extensive set of rules out of the box; while it's possible to add your own rules, we won't go into this. The rules supported out of the box are as follows:

- The `required` rule indicates that a form field is required and must have a value. If violated, this rule will produce an error with the message key `errors.required`.

- The `minlength` rule enforces a minimum length for the contents of a text field or text area. This rule requires a parameter, `minlength`, specifying a minimum length. Its error message uses the message key `errors.minlength`.

- The `maxlength` rule enforces a maximum length; it requires a `maxlength` parameter, and violations produce a message with the key `errors.maxlength`.

- The `mask` rule checks whether the contents of a text field or text area match the *regular expression* provided in its `mask` parameter. If violated, this rule will produce an error with the message key `errors.invalid`. Regular expressions describe patterns within strings in a very concise machine-readable form.

- The `byte`, `short`, `integer`, `long`, `float` and `double` rules check that the field is a valid value for the given data type. If the rule is violated, the error message will have the keys `errors.byte`, `errors.short`, and so on.

- The `date` rule checks that the field is a valid date; if not, an error message with the key `errors.date` is produced.

- The `range` rule verifies that a number is within the range given by its `min` and `max` parameters; its error key is `errors.range`.

- The `creditCard` rule checks whether the text field is a valid credit card number; this includes verification of the number's built-in checksum. If the number is invalid, a message is displayed corresponding to the key `errors.creditcard`.

- Finally, the `email` rule performs some sanity checks on an e-mail address field. The error message produced has the key `errors.email`.

Between them, these rules will cater to most common validation needs. You'll now see how you can use these rules to put together validation constraints for your forms and actions.

### *Specifying Validation Constraints*

You can specify validation constraints in the `validation.xml` file and any further files you configured the validator plug-in to use. You'll now see an example configuration file such as you'll use for the pizza form:

```
<?xml version="1.0" encoding="ISO-8859-1" ?>

<!DOCTYPE form-validation PUBLIC
          "-//Apache Software Foundation//DTD Commons
            Validator Rules Configuration 1.0//EN"
          "http://jakarta.apache.org/commons/dtds/validator_1_0.dtd">

<!-- This file tells Struts which fields to validate in which forms -->

<form-validation>
  <formset>
```

A validator `<formset>` works much like a file in a message resources bundle and for the same reason: Validation rules may be locale dependent. For instance, a ZIP code or telephone number in the United States differs from one in Britain or France and should be validated differently. The `<formset>` element can take `language` and `country` attributes that identify the locale for the rules contained in the set. The validator will try to find validation rules specific to the country, and failing that, the language. Failing that, it will use the rules defined by the default `<formset>`. Any number of form sets can be inside the file:

```
<form name="pizzaForm">
```

A `<formset>` can contain zero or more `<form>` elements. A `<form>` defines a set of configuration rules for the fields inside the form. In this case, the `<form>` corresponds to the `(Dyna)ActionForm`. As you'll see later, you can also associate a validator `<form>` with the action itself, which is with the `path` attribute of the mapping:

```
<field property="name" depends="required"/>
<field property="address" depends="required"/>
```

The `name` and `address` properties are mapped to a text input. Making these fields depend on the `required` rule is all you need to do here. Note that the text to display next to required fields is specified in a resource bundle with the key `errors.required`:

```
  </form>
</formset>
```

After the `<formset>`, there can be a number of further form sets for other locales:

```
</form-validation>
```

This concludes the walkthrough of the validator configuration file. However, there's much more, so if you're interested, visit `http://jakarta.apache.org/struts/userGuide/building_view.html`.

### *Validator Form Classes*

So how do you actually use the validation rules defined in your `validation.xml` file? Don't worry; once you've written the validator configuration file, things get amazingly simple. Struts has four different classes you can use instead of `ActionForm` (or `DynaActionForm`). All of these classes belong to the package named `org.apache.struts.validator` and provide implementations of the `validate()` method that use the validator configuration file to perform the validation. Other than choosing the right class, there's nothing for you to do.

> **NOTE** *If there's some validation that can't be done using the validator, you can roll your own validator rule (which we won't discuss here; see the validator documentation at* `http://jakarta.apache.org/commons/validator/` *for more information), but it's also perfectly fine to override the* `validate()` *method in your* `ValidatorForm` *subclass and add some code to do the extra validation. Don't forget to call* `super.validate()`*!*

#### *The ValidatorForm Class*

The `ValidatorForm` class is a version of `ActionForm` that performs validation based on the form name; that is, the `name` attribute of the Struts action mapping must correspond to the `name` attribute of the form tag in the validator configuration file. The previous configuration file walkthrough had two examples of this.

Use this class if the validation is related directly to the `ActionForm` object in itself, rather than what you happen to be doing with it.

#### *The ValidatorActionForm Class*

The `ValidatorActionForm` class performs its validation based on the action taken; in other words, the path of the Struts action mapping (see the "Configuring Action Mappings" section) must correspond to the `name` attribute of the form tag in the validator configuration file:

```
<form name="/update">
```

This is most useful if one `ActionForm` object has to be validated in completely different ways, depending on the precise action taken with the information.

### *The DynaValidatorForm and DynaValidatorActionForm Classes*

The `DynaValidatorForm` and `DynaValidatorActionForm` classes are versions of `ValidatorForm` and `ValidatorActionForm`, respectively, that use the dynamic form facility. They work like their nondynamic counterparts, except that you have to define their properties in the `<form-beans>` section of the Struts configuration file.

The excerpt from the configuration file shows the pizza order form declared as a `DynaValidatorForm`:

```
<form-beans>

  <!-- The form beans are all created dynamically -->
  <!-- and validated by Struts -->
  <!-- The validation file is validation.xml -->

  <form-bean        name="pizzaForm"
                     type="org.apache.struts.validator.DynaValidatorForm">
    <form-property name="name" type="java.lang.String"/>
    <form-property name="address" type="java.lang.String"/>
    <form-property name="purchaseType" type="java.lang.String"
                     initial="Home Delivery"/>
    <form-property name="topping" type="java.lang.String[]"/>
    <form-property name="size" type="java.lang.String"/>
  </form-bean>

</form-beans>
```

Here a form bean of type `org.apache.struts.validator.DynaValidatorForm` is declared to use the name `pizzaForm`. After setting up the page forwards, you'll look at how an `ActionMapping` can use this bean. The `purchaseType` property is given an initial value of `Home Delivery` because you need this option to be selected as default.

## *Configuring Global Exceptions*

The next section in the Struts configuration file configures, application-wide, how exceptions thrown in your `Action` classes are handled. These are defined using the `<global-exceptions>` element, which contains an `<exception>` element for each exception that you want Struts to catch and handle. Unhandled exceptions are propagated to the servlet container and handled according to the configuration in `web.xml`. Table 10-5 shows the most frequently used attributes of the `<exception>` element.

*Table 10-5.* `<exception>` *Attributes*

| Element Attribute | Description |
|---|---|
| type | The fully qualified class name of the Exception to catch. |
| path | The resource to forward to if this exception occurs. If no path is given, Struts forwards to the input page of the action that threw the exception. |
| key | The name of the internationalized message to display for this exception. |
| bundle | The ResourceBundle to use to look up the message. |
| scope | Whether the ActionError object used to encapsulate this error should be request-scoped or session-scoped. The default is request. |

Both type and key are required. The following excerpt shows how you handle SQLExceptions in the application:

```
<global-exceptions>
  <exception type="java.sql.SQLException" key="errors.database" />
</global-exceptions>
```

This tells Struts that whenever an action throws a SQLException, it should create an errors.database message and forward the request back to the original page. The error message can then be displayed using the Struts HTML tag library, which we'll discuss in "The HTML Tag Library."

## Configuring Global Forwards

Global forwards help you to avoid hard-coding the page flow of your application by associating a page name with the location of the actual JSP page or other resource. They're defined using the <global-forwards> element, which contains a <forward> element for each global forward. The <forward> element is a convenient way to configure logical names for view resources to which an Action class can forward. You can access these forwards by name using the findForward() method on the ActionMapping. Hardwiring view page names in the Action classes would weaken the separation of responsibilities you're trying to achieve using the MVC architecture; using the logical names provided by <forward> tags gets around this problem.

Table 10-6 lists the most frequently used <forward> attributes.

*Table 10-6.* <forward> *Attributes*

| Element Attribute | Description |
|---|---|
| name | The name of the forward. |
| path | The resource to which to forward. |
| redirect | If true, redirection is used rather than a forward. |

The name and path attributes are required. The following excerpt shows the global forward declaration:

```
<global-forwards>
  <forward   name="pizza" path="/pizzaStruts.jsp" />
  <forward   name="success" path="/processStruts.jsp" redirect="true"/>
</global-forwards>
```

This globally associates the forward name pizza with the /pizzaStruts.jsp page, and it associates the name success with the /processStruts.jsp page. You want to redirect to the success page so that the user doesn't see a .do extension once they've submitted the form.

## Configuring Action Mappings

ActionMapping objects are the heart of the Struts configuration file. They map incoming request URIs to Action classes and associate Action classes with ActionForms. The controller servlet stores these mappings internally. When a request arrives, it examines the request URI, looks up the associated ActionMapping, and ultimately calls the Action class associated with that action mapping. All Action classes use an execute() method to implement the application-specific code. This method returns an instance of the ActionForward class that contains the name of the target resource to which the response has to be forwarded.

ActionMappings are defined using the <action-mappings> element, which may include zero or more <action> elements. The <action> element has a number of attributes and subelements. Table 10-7 describes the attributes defined for the <action> element. You must specify the path attribute and either a type or a forward; all other attributes are optional.

*Table 10-7.* <action> *Attributes*

| Element Attribute | Description |
|---|---|
| path | The request URI path that will invoke this ActionMapping. This path should start with / and not include periods; this also means you should *omit the filename extension* (usually .do). |
| unknown | If the value of this attribute is set to true, this action is used as the default action for request URIs that don't correspond to any action mapping path. |
| type | The fully qualified name of the Action class to which this mapping links. If you specify a type, you can't specify a forward attribute, but you can still supply one or more nested <forward> tags. |
| forward | The resource path to which to forward the request. If you specify a forward attribute, you can't specify an action type to execute or any nested forwards. |
| name | This attribute defines the name of the ActionForm bean associated with this action, as used by the Action class. This is the same name used to define the form bean in a <form-bean> element. |
| attribute | This is the name of the request or session scope attribute under which the ActionForm bean is stored, if different from the name attribute. |
| scope | The value can be either request or session to indicate the scope of the ActionForm bean. The default is request scope. |
| validate | If this attribute is omitted, or its value is set to true, the controller will call the validate() method on the ActionForm bean to perform input validation before the execute() method is called on the action. If validation fails, the request is forwarded to the input form (discussed next). |
| input | Relative path to the input form to which the control must be returned if a bean validation error is encountered or when an exception is thrown that's handled by an <exception> tag without path. |
| parameter | An additional parameter that will be passed to the action. You can use this to supply extra configuration information to your action. |

*Table 10-7.* `<action>` *Attributes (continued)*

| Element Attribute | Description |
|---|---|
| roles | A comma-separated list of user roles. If this is specified, access to this action is restricted to authenticated users with these roles. You can use this as a convenient alternative to setting up security constraints in `web.xml`. |
| prefix | Prefix used to match `request` parameters to bean properties. This is useful if the attributes to be set aren't part of the action form itself, but of a bean contained inside the action form. |
| suffix | Suffix used to match `request` parameters to bean properties. |

The `<action>` element can take a number of nested tags; the most important are as follows:

- Zero or more `<exception>` tags can define exception handling rules specific to the action mapping.
- Zero or more `<forward>` tags can provide the action mapping with additional forward destinations. The `Action` classes can access the forwards by name using the `findForward()` method defined in the `ActionMapping` class; this method takes a `String` representing the name of the forward as an argument and returns an instance of the `ActionForward` class to the `ActionServlet`.

Both of these work in the same way as the global exceptions and forwards discussed previously. If there's any overlap or conflict between the global definitions and the ones local to the `<action>` element, the local definitions take precedence.

This excerpt shows the `<action>` element:

```
<action-mappings>

  <!-- The action mappings -->
  <action     path="/process"
               type="actions.ProcessAction"
               name="pizzaForm"
              scope="session"
              input="pizza">
  </action>

</action-mappings>
```

This mapping matches to a request for /process.do and uses an Action class of the type actions.ProcessAction. A session-scoped form bean with the name pizzaForm is associated with this mapping; the controller will try to match up request parameters with the attributes of pizzaForm and set any values that are appropriate. It will then call the validate() method on pizzaForm. If validation fails, the request is forwarded to the input page, the global forward pizza (which corresponds to pizzaStruts.jsp), together with all the original request information.

If validation succeeds, the execute() method of actions.ProcessAction is called. This action, which you'll write in the "Action Classes" section, will try to forward to the global forward success; this is mapped to the /processStruts.jsp page.

## Configuring the Controller

The configuration file can optionally contain a <controller> element that can tweak the way the controller operates. Table 10-8 describes the attributes you're most likely to use.

*Table 10-8.* <controller> *Attributes*

| Element Attribute | Description |
|---|---|
| debug | Controls the amount of debugging information (indicating such things as the requests being processed by the controller) that should be written to the log file. Higher numbers give more detail. The default is zero, and six is the most serious. |
| inputForward | If set to true, the input attribute of an <action> will specify the name of a local or global forward rather than a resource. |
| locale | If absent, or set to true, the Struts controller will store a Locale object in the session corresponding to the user's locale. |
| maxFileSize | The maximum size of a file upload, for example, "250M" (the default), "100K", or perhaps "7GB" if you expect people to upload whole DVDs at a time. |
| tempdir | Temporary directory used to process file uploads. |
| nocache | Set to true if you'd like the controller to insert headers that attempt to defeat browser and proxy caching. This is necessary if one and the same URL may produce different results depending on the user's session state or external systems (for example, news items being updated every few minutes). |

The following is the `<controller>` element that specifies that the `input` parameter on `<action>` elements use the name of a local or global forward rather than a module-relative path:

```
<controller>
  <set-property property="inputForward" value="true"/>
  <set-property property="debug" value="6"/>
</controller>
```

## Configuring Message Resources

As discussed earlier, the message resource bundles are at the heart of Struts' internationalization support. You can use one or more `<message-resources>` tags to tell Struts where it can find these bundles. Each bundle will be stored as an application-scoped JavaBean. Table 10-9 shows the attributes most often used.

*Table 10-9.* `<message-resources>` *Attributes*

| Element Attribute | Description |
|---|---|
| `key` | The key under which the bundle will be stored in the `ServletContext` and the name by which you can refer to it elsewhere. |
| `parameter` | The name of the bundle to load. Message resource bundles are loaded using the Java class loader, so this can include a package name. |
| `null` | If set to `true`, an unknown message key will return a `null` message. By default, an error message would be returned to help diagnose the problem. |

In many cases, a single bundle is all you need, but you'll be using one for the text in your application, stored as the default:

```
<message-resources parameter="resources.messages"/>
```

and one for all the database operations stored under the key `sql`:

```
<message-resources parameter="resources.sql" key="sql"/>
```

This will cause Struts to load `/WEB-INF/classes/resources/messages.properties` and the other files in the message bundle. The file could also reside inside a `jar` in `/WEB-INF/lib` or somewhere else in the classpath. The first bundle is bound as the default message bundle with the special name `org.apache.struts.action.MESSAGE` (this value is defined in the constant `org.apache.struts.Globals.MESSAGE_KEY`).

### Wrapping Up

With all of the configuration done in the `struts-config.xml` file, you need to close the top-level element:

```
</struts-config>
```

Struts configuration is extremely flexible. For advanced use you can tailor the framework and plug in your own classes, setting their JavaBean properties using nested `<set-property>` tags. Graphical configuration and monitoring tools are supported by optional `<icon-name>`, `<display-name>`, and `<description>` tags that can be nested inside many of the elements described previously. But Struts' power out of the box is more than sufficient for most projects, and the features discussed so far will take you a very long way indeed.

Now that you've thoroughly explored the Struts configuration options, you'll take the  application and turn it into a Struts application. The main change is that you'll use the Struts controller and dynamic `Action` classes. As we discuss the classes, you'll build your application just as you built the configuration.

## Core Struts Components

In the following sections, we'll discuss the relationships between some of the main Struts controller components, namely

- The `ActionServlet` controller, which is at the heart of the Struts framework
- `ActionMapping` objects describing the mapping of a request URI to an action
- `Action` classes, which you write to provide the business logic glue

You'll start by examining the main controller component: `ActionServlet`.

### The ActionServlet Class

The `org.apache.struts.action.ActionServlet` is the main Struts controller component. You've seen that it's usually mapped to the `.do` extension in `web.xml`.

The servlet can take a fair number of configuration parameters in its `<servlet>` declaration. The most important of these is the `config` attribute (see Table 10-10).

*Table 10-10.* `config` *Attribute*

| **Parameter** | **Description** |
|---|---|
| config | The location and name of the configuration file. The default is /WEB-INF/struts-config.xml. |

There are many more attributes, but most of these are either deprecated leftovers from Struts 1.0 or more easily configured using the Struts configuration file.

The ActionServlet class exposes a number of public methods; some of these are mandated by the Servlet interface, the others are either deprecated or important only when you want to extend the Struts framework itself with custom constructs and configuration objects. These are beyond the scope of this book, but you can find more information about them at http://jakarta.apache.org/struts/ and in the documentation that came with the Struts download.

## *The ActionMapping Class*

As you'll see, an instance of the org.apache.struts.action.ActionMapping class representing the action mapping for the request is passed to the execute() method of the Action class. This object encapsulates all the information defined in the <action> element of the configuration file. The ActionMapping class defines getter and setter methods for these attributes.

The most important methods are those used to manipulate the forward list associated with the mapping:

```
public ActionForward findForward(String name)
```

This method returns the ActionForward for the given name; this is an object that encapsulates the destination resource to which to forward. For example, you'll find the following code snippet often at the end of Action classes:

```
return mapping.findForward("success");
```

This finds the local or global forward named success and returns it to the ActionServlet to act upon. Closely related to this is the getInputForward() method:

```
public ActionForward getInputForward()
```

This method returns an ActionForward corresponding to the input attribute of the <action> tag. This can be useful if, after performing some processing in your action, you find that you need to forward the request back to the input form with an error message (although in such cases, throwing an exception and handling it using the <exception> tag might be a more transparent alternative).

Finally, the `findForwards()` method finds all *local* forward names associated with this action:

```
public String[] findForwards()
```

This method doesn't return an exhaustive list of the names recognized by `findForward()` because it disregards any globally defined forwards.

Can you remember that when discussing the <action> tag in the configuration file, there was a `parameter` attribute you could use to pass some extra configuration information into actions? This is the method an action can call to obtain the parameter value:

```
public String getParameter ()
```

## Action Classes

You extend `org.apache.struts.action.Action` to provide classes responsible for processing user requests. When the `ActionServlet` needs a specific type of action for the first time, it instantiates a single object of that class and uses that object to handle *all* requests for that action for the remainder of the application's lifetime.

> **NOTE** *This means all actions you write must be thread safe. The safest thing to do is to use only method-local variables in your* `Action` *classes and never to have any instance variables or static variables in these classes.*

### The ProcessAction Class

The following code is the beginning of the `Action` class. You'll move all the database logic into the action and leave all the presentation in the JSP pages:

```
package actions;

import javax.servlet.http.HttpServletRequest;
import javax.servlet.http.HttpServletResponse;
import javax.servlet.http.HttpSession;

import org.apache.struts.action.Action;
import org.apache.struts.action.ActionForm;
import org.apache.struts.action.ActionForward;
```

```
import org.apache.struts.action.ActionMapping;
import org.apache.struts.validator.DynaValidatorForm;
import org.apache.struts.util.MessageResources;

import java.sql.Connection;
import java.sql.PreparedStatement;
import java.sql.ResultSet;
import java.sql.SQLException;

import javax.sql.DataSource;

public final class ProcessAction extends Action {
```

### *The execute Method*

The most important public method in the `Action` class is `execute()`. You must override this method to implement the business logic you want to execute:

```
public ActionForward execute(ActionMapping mapping,
                             ActionForm form,
                             HttpServletRequest request,
                             HttpServletResponse response)
                        throws SQLException {
```

The first argument is the `ActionMapping` associated with the request. You can use this to find out about the `<action>` attributes, such as `parameter`, and to find the forwards defined for the mapping, as discussed previously. The second argument is the input `ActionForm` defined for the mapping or `null` if no input form has been defined. You'll usually cast this form to the specific type of form expected:

```
DynaValidatorForm dynaForm = (DynaValidatorForm)form;
```

In this case you're using the Struts dynamic form, which is what you specified in the Struts configuration file previously.

The last two arguments are the usual request and response objects. In most cases, it's a good habit not to actually write anything to the response, as that is the responsibility of the view resource to which you're forwarding.

You now get the form entries from your form:

```
String name = (String)
        dynaForm.get("name");
String address = (String)
        dynaForm.get("address");
```

```
String purchaseType = (String)
        dynaForm.get("purchaseType");
String size = (String)
        dynaForm.get("size");
String[] topping = (String[])
        dynaForm.get("topping");
```

It's good practice to avoid hard-coding strings in code, so you'll use a message resource to store the SQL. Here's how you retrieve it (remember you stored it as `sql` by specifying the key in `struts-config.xml`):

```
MessageResources resources = getResources(request, "sql");
```

Databases don't like apostrophes in strings, so you'll need to replace them with a database-specific representation:

```
String apostropheReplace = resources.getMessage("sql.apostrophe.replace");
```

Now you need to replace any apostrophes in the database text strings; otherwise, they will cause errors in the SQL:

```
name = name.replaceAll("'", apostropheReplace);
address = address.replaceAll("'", apostropheReplace);
```

You'll need the session later:

```
HttpSession session = request.getSession();
```

Here's where you get the data source you specified in the configuration file:

```
DataSource dataSource = getDataSource(request, "pizza");
```

Now it's time to start the database operations. First you initialize the connection and the prepared statement:

```
Connection con = null;
PreparedStatement stmt = null;
```

Obtain the connection from the data source:

```
try {
  // Open the connection
  con = dataSource.getConnection();
```

The database logic, last shown in `process.jsp`, is as follows:

1. Start a transaction.
2. Insert the customer's details into the `customer` table.
3. Get the new customer ID from the `customer` table.
4. Insert the order into the `order` table using the customer ID.
5. Get the new order ID from the `order` table.
6. Insert the toppings into the `topping` table using the order ID.
7. Commit the transaction.

You'll now follow this logic in the action.

You start a transaction, as you need to read the last primary key later:

```
con.setAutoCommit(false);
```

The next step is to insert the customer's details into the `customer` table:

```
String sql = resources.getMessage("sql.insert.customer");
// Create the prepared statement
stmt = con.prepareStatement(sql);

// Fill in the name and address parameters
stmt.setString(1, name);
stmt.setString(2, address);

// Now we insert the data
stmt.executeUpdate();
```

Once you've inserted the data, you need the customer's ID:

```
// We need the inserted key
sql = resources.getMessage("sql.select.customer");
stmt = con.prepareStatement(sql);

// This resultset contains the inserted key
// We need to retrieve it in a while loop
ResultSet key = stmt.executeQuery();
```

```
String customer_id = "";

while (key.next()) {
  customer_id = key.getString(1);
}
```

You have the customer's ID, so you can insert the order:

```
// Now insert the order
sql = resources.getMessage("sql.insert.order");

stmt = con.prepareStatement(sql);

stmt.setString(1, customer_id);
stmt.setString(2, purchaseType);
stmt.setString(3, size);

// Now we insert the data
stmt.executeUpdate();
```

You need the order's ID:

```
// We need the inserted key
sql = resources.getMessage("sql.select.order");
stmt = con.prepareStatement(sql);

// This resultset contains the inserted key
// We need to retrieve it in a while loop
key = stmt.executeQuery();

String order_id = "";

while (key.next()) {
  order_id = key.getString(1);
}
```

The final insert adds the toppings:

```
// Insert the topping
sql = resources.getMessage("sql.insert.topping");

stmt = con.prepareStatement(sql);
```

```
// The toppings are in an array, so we need to loop through it
// We insert each one separately
for (int i = 0 ; i < topping.length ; i++) {

  stmt.setString(1, order_id);
  stmt.setString(2, topping[i]);

  // Now we insert the data
  stmt.executeUpdate();
}
```

The last step in the database logic is to commit the transaction:

```
// Commit the transaction and then return to auto-commit mode
con.commit();
con.setAutoCommit(true);
```

If there's an error at any stage, you want to catch it and throw a new `SQLException`. Remember that you set up a global exception handler in `struts-config.xml` to catch `SQLException`s and return to the calling page:

```
} catch (Exception sqle) {
    System.out.println("Error dealing with database");
    System.out.println("Reason: " + sqle.getMessage());
    throw new SQLException(sqle.getMessage());
```

The `finally` block is always called. You'll use this opportunity to close any connections or statements that are open:

```
} finally {
    if(con != null) {
      // Close the Statement and the Connection
      stmt.close();
      con.close();
    }
}
```

As before, you want the user to see the details that they've entered. You'll store them in the session:

```
session.setAttribute("name", name);
session.setAttribute("address", address);
```

```
session.setAttribute("purchaseType", purchaseType);
session.setAttribute("size", size);
session.setAttribute("topping", topping);
```

You've finished with the form, so you'll remove it from memory:

```
if (mapping.getAttribute() != null) {
  if ("request".equals(mapping.getScope())) {
    request.removeAttribute(mapping.getAttribute());
  } else {
    session.removeAttribute(mapping.getAttribute());
  }
}
```

Finally, the execute() method should return an ActionForward object encapsulating the destination to which to forward. Usually, you'll look this object up in the mapping:

```
    return mapping.findForward("success");
  }
}
```

You can create your own ActionForward object if you want, but you should avoid this. These forwards really ought to be set up in the Struts configuration file.

The last thing to note is that the execute() method can throw any type of Exception. These exceptions can be caught and handled using <exception> tags in the Struts configuration file. If you know that your execute() can throw only a few exceptions—for example, SQLException—it's a good idea to make this explicit in your method declaration, as you've done here.

This doesn't make a difference in the behavior or performance of your Action class, but it does make the exceptions that can be thrown very explicit and obvious. As such, it's a valuable piece of documentation that someone else can use to find out which <exception> tags to set up.

> **NOTE** *In the Java language, a subclass is always free to throw fewer exceptions than the parent class or interface declares. This is called the* narrowing down *of the* throws *clause. Throwing more or broader exceptions, on the other hand, is never allowed.*

Phew! We've covered a lot of ground. However, once you've worked your way through this chapter, perhaps by trying out Struts in your own applications and revisiting the class description along the way, you'll gain a good grasp of the most important aspects of the Struts controller framework. You'll now take a look at the tag libraries that support the framework in your JSP view components.

## Introducing the Struts Tag Libraries

A number of tag libraries, which support the development of JSP view components that integrate with the controller, ship with Struts:

- *Bean tags* to manipulate JavaBeans
- *Logic tags* to provide conditionals and looping within a JSP page
- *HTML tags* to support the creation of HTML forms and other HTML elements
- *Nested tags* to ease development when your JSP structure mirrors your object structure
- *Template tags* that provide a simple templating mechanism
- *Tiles tags* to extend the template idea to build a framework for assembling JSP pages from component parts

Entire books have been written on the Struts framework, and it is, unfortunately, far too much to cover in this chapter. In particular, we'll cover only some of the HTML and bean tags.

Looking through the list, it may strike you that there seems to be some overlap with the JSTL and the JSP 2.0 EL. Doesn't the JSTL support all conditional and loop constructs you might need? Doesn't the EL provide very convenient access to bean properties? This is entirely true. The Struts framework was conceived for older platforms that had neither the expression language nor the standard template library. In this chapter, you'll ignore all the tags from the Struts tag library that have been effectively made obsolete and concentrate on what remains.

### *JavaBean Properties in Struts*

Before looking at the tag libraries, you'll first briefly look at the way Struts addresses JavaBean properties. This is important in many of the tags and also determines how the controller matches up request parameters with `ActionForm` properties.

With Struts tags, you usually provide a JavaBean name and the property you want to manipulate, rather than the simple `beanName.propertyName` syntax that the EL uses. The property part supports the following features:

**Simple JavaBean properties**: For example, the `ShoppingCart` class early in this chapter had a simple read-only property `total`, defined by the `getTotal()` method.

**Indexed JavaBean properties**: The `ShoppingCart` class defines an indexed property `item` by defining `getItem(int index)` and `getItem(int index, ShoppingCartItem item)` methods. Note that the JSP EL doesn't support indexed properties defined in this way.

Support for properties that are `Lists`, such as the `books` property in the `ShoppingCart`, is incomplete at the time of writing. `List` properties will work fine with the Struts tags, but the controller will ignore them as request parameters.

**Nested JavaBean properties**: For example, the title of the first book in the cart corresponds to the property `item[0].book.title`. This is quite similar to the EL approach, but the alternative square-bracket syntax (which would be `item[0]['book']['title']`) isn't supported by Struts.

**Mapped properties**: These don't use the Java `Map` interface supported by the EL, but they require that the bean class implement getter and setter methods that take an additional `String` parameter denoting the key. The syntax, too, is a complete departure from the EL-like syntax and uses parentheses around the key (for example, `myProperty(myKey)`).

You can combine all of these features in arbitrary ways. We hope the next version of Struts (or rather, the BeanUtils package used under the hood) will bring full convergence with the JSP EL.

With the preliminaries out of the way, you'll now take a more detailed look at the tag libraries themselves.

## *The Bean Tag Library*

The Struts framework provides a variety of custom tags for handling JavaBeans within JSP pages. The URI for this bean tag library is `http://jakarta.apache.org/struts/tags-bean`. With the enhanced capabilities for expressions and manipulation offered by the JSP EL and the JSTL Core and Formatting tags, however, most of the bean tags have been effectively superseded:

- `<bean:message>` renders an internationalized message string. This is similar to the JSTL `<fmt:message>` tag, but the tight integration with the Struts message resource handling and the replacement string feature make using this tag worthwhile.

- `<bean:define>`, `<bean:page>`, `<bean:cookie>`, `<bean:header>`, and `<bean:parameter>` all define a variable based on some request or page context attribute. You can achieve the same thing using `<c:set>` and the EL, so you won't use these tags.

- `<bean:size>` defines a variable containing the number of elements in a given `Map` or `Collection`.

- `<bean:write>` renders the value of the specified bean property. It's superseded by the JSP EL, `<c:out>`, and the JSTL formatting tags.

- `<bean:include>` includes an external resource, such as `<c:import>`.

- `<bean:resource>` loads a Web application resource and makes it available as a bean.

- `<bean:struts>` exposes a named Struts internal configuration object as a bean.

You'll now learn about the most relevant tags.

### *Message Tag*

We noted earlier that internationalizing your Web application means messages displayed by your Web application are in the preferred language of the user. In effect this means that when the Web application needs to print a message, it refers to a message resource bundle and finds the file containing all of the messages written in the correct language. A Web application may use more than one bundle if the number of messages starts to become unwieldy.

The `<bean:message>` tag allows easy access to any of the resource bundles that have been set up in the Struts configuration file. It allows you to write internationalized messages, labels, prompts, and so on in your JSP page. You can either specify the message key directly or specify a JavaBean name and optionally a property that will yield the key. Table 10-11 describes the most important attributes, which can all take runtime expressions.

*Table 10-11. Common* `<bean:message>` *Attributes*

| Attribute | Description |
|---|---|
| key | The key of the message in the resource file. If you specify the key, you can't specify name or property attributes. |
| name | The name of the JavaBean that contains the message key. If you specify name, you can't specify the key attribute directly. |
| property | The JavaBean property that will be used as the message key. If you specify the JavaBean name but no property, the bean itself will be converted to a string and used as the message key. |
| arg0 | First replacement string value. |
| arg1 | Second replacement string value. |
| arg2 | Third replacement string value. |
| arg3 | Fourth replacement string value. |
| arg4 | Fifth (and last) replacement string value. |
| bundle | The name of the application attribute under which the resources object is stored. If not specified, Globals.MESSAGES_KEY is used (its value is org.apache.struts.action.MESSAGE). When specified, this attribute must match the key specified in <message-resources> in the Struts configuration file. |
| scope | Specify page, request, or application if you want to find the bean specified using name in a specific scope. |

The next example illustrates the use of the <bean:message> tag. Suppose there's a message defined in the resources file as follows:

```
info.myKey=The numbers entered are {0}, {1}, {2}, {3}
```

Further suppose that you use the following message tag:

```
<bean:message key="info.myKey" arg0="5" arg1="6" arg2="7" arg3="8"/>
```

The output written to the JSP page by the message tag would then be *The numbers entered are 5,6,7,8.*

### *The Pizza Application's View*

The view of the pizza application makes extensive use of the `<bean:message>` tag to render the text. Remember that this text is stored in a resource bundle. Here's the start of `pizzaStruts.jsp` with the Struts tag libraries declared:

```
<%@ taglib uri="http://jakarta.apache.org/struts/tags-html" prefix="html" %>
<%@ taglib uri="http://jakarta.apache.org/struts/tags-bean" prefix="bean" %>
<html>
  <head>
```

The title is taken from the resource bundle:

```
  <title><bean:message key="text.pizza.title"/></title>
  <style type="text/css">
    H1 {
      font-size: 12pt;
      font-weight: bold;
    }

    .missing {
      color: red;
    }
  </style>
</head>
```

All other instances of the `<bean:message>` tag are used in the same way: They replace the text of the application with the text from a resource bundle. You'll now look at the HTML tag library before finishing the view.

## *The HTML Tag Library*

The Struts HTML tag library provides a variety of HTML generation tags that are tightly integrated with the Struts controller. Its URI is `http://jakarta.apache.org/struts/tags-html`. There's virtually no overlap with the JSTL and JSP EL here:

- Most of the HTML tags provide HTML form generation support that's tightly integrated with the Struts `ActionForm` concept. For the most part, these tags closely follow their HTML counterparts: `<html:form>`, `<html:text>`, `<html:textarea>`, `<html:password>`, `<html:checkbox>`, `<html:multibox>`, `<html:select>`, `<html:option>`, `<html:options>`, `<html:optionsCollection>`, `<html:radio>`, `<html:file>`, `<html:hidden>`, `<html:button>`, `<html:image>`, `<html:submit>`, `<html:reset>`, and `<html:cancel>`.

- `<html:errors>` and `<html:messages>` render the contents of any errors or messages that have been passed to the view JSP page.
- `<html:javascript>` renders the JavaScript validation code generated by the Struts validator, discussed in "The Struts Validator" earlier.
- `<html:html>`, `<html:frame>`, `<html:base>`, and `<html:img>` all work like the HTML tags of the same name, but they support some extra Struts integration features such the ability to use global forwards instead of resource names.
- `<html:link>` renders an anchor or hyperlink that can refer to Struts' logical forwards; `<html:rewrite>` performs many of the same functions but renders just the URI rather than the entire hyperlink.

Quite a few tags exist, and although we can't possibly discuss them all, we'll go through most of them. Before doing this, though, we'll briefly discuss the way the Struts HTML tags support the many HTML element attributes.

### Standard HTML Element Attributes

The tags that directly correspond to HTML elements, such as `<html:form>`, support all the attributes that their ordinary HTML counterparts could have. These attributes are simply copied straight into the generated HTML. They will not be listed in this section because they're in no way Struts-specific and would only clutter things up. The attributes in question include the JavaScript event hooks, such as `onsubmit` and `onclick`, and attributes such as `style`, `tabindex`, `accesskey`, and `alt`. It should be noted that these attributes are always fully lowercase. HTML may not be case-sensitive, but JSP tags are.

Struts attributes work slightly differently than their HTML counterparts in two cases:

> The Cascading Style Sheet (CSS) attributes `id` and `class` have to be handled differently because these names have a special meaning in JSP tags. The Struts HTML tags use `styleId` and `styleClass` attributes to define them. For example, to incorporate the attribute `class="news"` in the generated HTML element, you'd specify `styleClass="news"` in your Struts HTML tag.
>
> The HTML input field attributes `disabled` and `readonly` don't receive a value, but they make a field disabled or read-only, respectively, merely by their presence. This doesn't fit the JavaBean tag model, so the Struts input field tags have `disabled` and `readonly` attributes that take a Boolean value. In other words, `disabled="false"` will cause the `disabled` attribute to be completely omitted from the generated HTML element.

The standard attributes, such as the additional attributes discussed next, can take runtime expressions in addition to simple string values.

You'll now look at the core of the library; these are the tags that render forms and form controls.

## *Form Construction Tags*

Struts enables you to associate an HTML form with an action mapping and thereby with the `ActionForm` that has been configured as the mapping's input form. The name of the form fields should correspond to properties of the `ActionForm` bean. This can include nested, indexed, and mapped properties in any combination. When the HTML form is rendered, the input fields are populated with the actual values of the bean properties; conversely, when the user submits the HTML form, the bean properties are updated to reflect the values entered into the form.

### *Form Tag*

The `<html:form>` tag renders, you guessed it, an HTML `<form>` element. The main reason to use an `<html:form>` tag over a normal `<form>` is that the Struts tag associates its `action` with a Struts action mapping, and the action mapping in turn dictates which `ActionForm` bean to use to render the contents of the input elements. If the bean specified in the action mapping isn't found, a new bean is created and stored.

The `<form>` tag will generally contain child tags corresponding to the different HTML input fields; these tags are explained later in this section. Table 10-12 describes the attributes for the `<html:form>` tag.

*Table 10-12. Form Tag Attributes*

| Attribute | Description |
|---|---|
| `action` | The action associated with the form, without the `.do` extension. This is specified relative to the Web application root and must match one of the mappings in your Struts configuration file; the mapping should identify the `ActionForm` bean associated with the form. |
| `focus` | The field within the form that should have initial focus. Setting this will generate a small chunk of JavaScript that assigns focus to the named field, which will be ignored by clients that don't support JavaScript or have it disabled. |

As usual, the tag also takes the `method`, `enctype`, `style`, and JavaScript event hook attributes that a normal HTML `<form>` understands.

By way of an example, consider the pizza form:

```
<form action="process.jsp" method="post">
```

The <html:form> equivalent is as follows:

```
<html:form action="/process.do" method="post">
```

There isn't a lot of difference. Behind the scenes, however, the <html:form> tag has inspected the action mapping for its action:

```
<form-bean         name="pizzaForm"
                    type="org.apache.struts.validator.DynaValidatorForm">
<action     path="/process"
             type="actions.ProcessAction"
             name="pizzaForm"
            scope="session"
            input="pizza">
</action>
```

The form knows that its associated ActionForm bean is the pizzaForm; if this form bean doesn't yet exist, it knows it should instantiate it as an object of type org.apache.struts.validator.DynaValidatorForm. The form then makes this information available to its nested input elements, as you'll see in a moment.

You can have any number of <html:form> tags in an HTML page.

### *Text, Hidden, and TextArea Tags*

The <html:text>, <html:hidden>, and <html:textarea> tags must be nested inside an <html:form> tag. They render HTML <input type="text">, <input type="hidden">, and <textarea> elements, respectively. Table 10-13 lists the most important attributes these tags support over and above what their HTML counterparts can take.

*Table 10-13. Text, Hidden, and TextArea Tag Attributes*

| Attribute | Description |
|---|---|
| property | The ActionForm property to which this field corresponds. This will be used as the field name, and the value will default to the form property's value. |
| name | Indicates a JavaBean that should be used in place of the form's normal ActionForm. This is useful if you need to include data from more than one form object in a single HTML form. |
| value | Specified to use a field value other than the ActionForm property value. The value may also be specified in the body of the tag. |
| altKey | Generates an alt attribute by looking up the given message key in the default message resources bundle. Use this for internationalization. |
| titleKey | Generates a title attribute by looking up the given message key in the default message resources bundle. Use this for internationalization. |

The action form property associated with these tags must be a simple scalar—that is, a String, a primitive Java type, or any of their wrapper types (such as int or java.lang.Integer).

So, the pizza form would have the following form:

```
<input type="text" name="name" size="30" value="${sessionScope.name}" />
```

with its <html:text> equivalent:

```
<html:text property="name" size="30"/>
```

The main difference is that you no longer have to specify the value; Struts can figure this out from the property name and the action form associated with the <html:form> tag.

### *Password Tag*

You can use the <html:password> tag for rendering an HTML password control. The difference between a password control and the ordinary text input field is that the password control displays its contents as asterisks. With the exception of redisplay, it supports the same attributes as the <html:text> tag (see Table 10-14).

*Table 10-14. Password Tag Attributes*

| Attribute | Description |
|---|---|
| property | The ActionForm property to which this field corresponds. |
| name | Specified to use a JavaBean other than the form's ActionForm. |
| value | Specified to use a field value other than the ActionForm property value. The value may also be specified in the body of the tag. |
| redisplay | If absent or true, the current value (if any) of the ActionForm property is used as the value for this password field. The browser will show it as a row of asterisks, but the level of security provided is limited—anyone can view the actual password by selecting the browser's View HTML Source option. |
| altKey | Generates an alt attribute by looking up the given message key in the default message resources bundle. Use this for internationalization. |
| titleKey | Generates a title attribute by looking up the given message key in the default message resources bundle. Use this for internationalization. |

In addition to these, the normal HTML attributes for the <input> element are of course also supported.

### *Checkbox and Multibox Tags*

You can use the <html:checkbox> and <html:multibox> tags for rendering checkbox controls. They must be nested within an <html:form> tag and recognize the same set of attributes as the <html:text> tag. The difference between them is the following:

> The <html:checkbox> tag must be associated with a Boolean action form property. You'd typically use this in cases where there were only a few such properties or when the properties were unrelated.
>
> The <html:multibox> tag must be associated with a property returning an array of String values. A multibox is considered "on" when its value (specified either using the value attribute or in the tag body) occurs somewhere in this array. The multibox tag is useful when there are a fair number of related on/off options. Each multibox is associated with the same property but has a different value. Each element in the property's array corresponds to a checkbox that's "on."

An example of the use of <html:checkbox> is as follows:

```
<tr>
  <td><html:checkbox property="married"/></td>
  <td>Check here if you are married</td>
</tr>
```

Here you have a checkbox called married associated with a Boolean action form property. The ActionForm would probably define these methods:

```
public boolean getMarried();
public void setMarried(boolean married);
```

If you've ever set up an account with an online retailer or banks, you've probably been presented with a list of options allowing you to control how your contact details can be used. This would be a good use for the <html:multibox> tag:

```
<tr>
  <td><html:multibox property="doNotContact" value="ourselves"/></td>
  <td>Check if you do not wish to be contacted by us.</td>
<tr>
<tr>
  <td><html:multibox property="doNotContact" value="partners"/></td>
  <td>Check if you do not wish to be contacted by our partners.</td>
</tr>
<tr>
  <td><html:multibox property="doNotContact" value="others"/></td>
  <td>Check if you do not wish your contact details to be forwarded to
      selected third parties.</td>
</tr>
```

All these options are associated with the array-valued bean property doNotContact:

```
public String[] getDoNotContact();
public void setDoNotContact(String[] doNotContact);
```

An example value for this property could be the two-element array {"partners", "others"}. On the HTML page, this would correspond to the second and third checkboxes being ticked. You could achieve the same thing by defining three ordinary Boolean properties and using three checkbox tags, but where the number of options is large, it clutters up your ActionForm with lots of methods.

### Select and Option Tags

You can use the `<html:select>` tag, nested inside an `<html:form>`, for rendering a HTML select control. Table 10-15 lists the important attributes of this tag, above and beyond those of the corresponding HTML element.

*Table 10-15. Select Tag Attributes*

| Attribute | Description |
|---|---|
| property | The ActionForm property to which this field corresponds. This will be used as the field name, and the value will default to the form property's value. |
| name | Specified to use a JavaBean other than the form's ActionForm. |
| multiple | If true, multiple options can be selected. |
| value | Specified to use a field value other than the ActionForm property value. It may also be specified in the body of the tag. The value determines which of the options is currently selected. |
| altKey | Generates an alt attribute by looking up the given message key in the default message resources bundle. Use this for internationalization. |
| titleKey | Generates a title attribute by looking up the given message key in the default message resources bundle. Use this for internationalization. |

The type of ActionForm property associated with this tag depends on the value of the multiple attribute:

- If multiple is false or omitted, the action form property must be a scalar—for example, a String, a primitive Java type, or any of their wrapper types (int or java.lang.Integer). The value of this property corresponds to the selected option.

- If multiple is true, the action form property should be an array of any of the types mentioned previously. Each element of the array is a scalar corresponding to a selected option.

Inside an `<html:select>` tag, you can provide the list of available options using any of the three types of option tag included in the library (or indeed a mixture, if you want).

The simplest is `<html:option>`, which generates a single HTML `<option>` element. Table 10-16 lists its attributes.

*Table 10-16. Option Tag Attributes*

| Attribute | Description |
|---|---|
| value | The value represented by this option. This attribute is required. |
| key | The message key to look up in the message resources bundle. If omitted, you must specify the option text (not a key) in the tag body. |
| bundle | The name of the message bundle to use. Uses the default bundle if omitted. |

An example of the select and option tags would be the following drop-down list for selecting a credit card type:

```
<html:select property="cardType">
  <html:option value="" key="payments.select.please"/>
  <html:option value="MC">MasterCard</html:option>
  <html:option value="VI">Visa</html:option>
  <html:option value="AE">American Express</html:option>
</html:select>
```

This would set the `cardType` property to `MC`, `VI`, or `AE` depending on the type selected. Note that the first option uses a message key to display an internationalized message displaying something such as *Please Select in the local language*, and the others use hardwired credit card brand names.

### *The optionsCollection Tag*

Often, you don't have a limited set of hardwired options as shown previously but a long list of possible options or perhaps a list that's populated from the data in a database table. One way to handle this would be to loop over the list of options with the `<c:forEach>` tag and extract the label and value from each. Struts provides a convenient way to achieve the same thing using the `<html:optionsCollection>` tag. Table 10-17 describes its attributes.

*Table 10-17.* `<html:optionsCollection>` *Attributes*

| Attribute | Description |
|---|---|
| name | The name of the JavaBean that provides you with the options. If omitted, the tag will use the `ActionForm` associated with the current `<html:form>`. |
| property | The property of the JavaBean indicated by `name` (or the current `ActionForm`, if omitted) that will return the collection of option beans. |
| value | The option bean property that will return the value. Defaults to `value`. |

*Table 10-17.* `<html:optionsCollection>` *Attributes (continued)*

| Attribute | Description |
|---|---|
| `label` | The option bean property that will return the label. Defaults to `label`. If there's no difference between your labels and your values, it's perfectly valid to use a single property name for both `value` and `label`. |
| `filter` | If `true` or omitted, characters such as < that might mess up the generated HTML are filtered out. |

Supposing the `ActionForm` provides a `getSupportedCardTypes()` method returning an array of `CardType` objects:

```
public class CardType
{
  .
  .
  .
  public String getLabel() { return label; }
  public String getValue() { return value; }
}
```

Then you could amend the previous example to read simply as follows:

```
<html:select property="cardType">
  <html:option value="" key="payment.select.please"/>
  <html:optionsCollection property="supportedCardTypes"/>
</html:select>
```

There's another, older `<html:options>` tag to generate a list of options. You can use this tag in a large number of ways, and it can be quite confusing. In most cases, the `<html:optionsCollection>` tag will do the job just fine and is much clearer.

### *Radio Tag*

You can use the `<html:radio>` tag nested within an `<html:form>` tag for rendering one or more HTML radio button controls. Table 10-18 explains the attributes of this tag.

*Table 10-18. Radio Tag Attributes*

| Attribute | Description |
|---|---|
| property | The ActionForm property to which this field corresponds. |
| name | Specified to use a JavaBean other than the form's ActionForm. |
| value | The value to which this radio button selection corresponds. This attribute is required. |
| idName | Name of a bean that will provide you with the value of the radio tag. If an idName is provided, then value isn't interpreted as the value itself, but as the property of the bean that returns the value. This attribute is most often used when iterating over a collection of possible values. |
| altKey | Generates an alt attribute by looking up the given message key in the default message resources bundle. Use this for internationalization. |
| titleKey | Generates a title attribute by looking up the given message key in the default message resources bundle. Use this for internationalization. |

For example, if the supportedCardTypes property of cardForm returns an array of CardType objects, each with value and label attributes, a radio group for selection between the credit card types could be rendered with the following code snippet:

```
<c:forEach items="${cardForm.supportedCardTypes}" var="type">
  <html:radio property="cardType" idName="type" value="value"/>
  ${type.label}<br/>
</c:forEach>
```

This is how the drop-down box from the previous example could be rendered as a radio group. The generated HTML would look something like the following:

```
  <input type="radio" name="cardType" value="VI"/>
  Visa<br/>

  <input type="radio" name="cardType" value="MC"/>
  Mastercard<br/>

  <input type="radio" name="cardType" value="AI"/>
  American Express<br/>
```

### Button Tags

The Struts HTML tag library supports four button tags:

- `<html:submit>` renders a submit button that will submit the enclosing form to the server.
- `<html:cancel>` renders a cancel button. This is actually no more than a submit button with a special name. The Struts controller recognizes this name and bypasses its form validation code. The action is invoked as normal and will have to call `isCancelled()` to find out whether the form has been cancelled.
- `<html:reset>` renders a reset button that will reset all form fields to their initial values.
- `<html:button>` renders an HTML push button control without default behavior, so you need to add JavaScript to the `onclick` attribute to actually make it do something useful.

These tags must be nested inside an `<html:form>` tag and include the following attributes above and beyond those of their normal HTML counterparts (see Table 10-19).

*Table 10-19. Button Tag Attributes*

| Attribute | Description |
| --- | --- |
| `property` | Name of the request parameter that will be submitted for the button. Don't specify this for a cancel button! |
| `name` | Specified to use a JavaBean other than the form's `ActionForm`. |
| `value` | The value of the button label. This may also be specified in the body of the tag. The value is also submitted as part of the request. |
| `altKey` | Generates an `alt` attribute by looking up the given message key in the default message resources bundle. Use this for internationalization. |
| `titleKey` | Generates a `title` attribute by looking up the given message key in the default message resources bundle. Use this for internationalization. |

For example, the following code would render a submit and a cancel button for a payment form, complete with an internationalized button label rendered using the `<bean:message>` tag:

```
<html:submit><bean:message key="payment.button.submit"/></html:submit>
<html:cancel><bean:message key="payment.button.cancel"/></html:cancel>
```

### *Message Retrieval Tags*

The HTML tag library contains a tag that allows you to render error messages in HTML easily and quickly.

The `<html:errors>` tag retrieves one or more errors and displays them. To help you with the HTML layout of these messages, this tag also allows you to include four special keys in your message resources that will be included at specific points in the list:

- `errors.header`, if defined, will be printed before the first error message.
- `errors.footer`, if defined, will be printed after the last error message. If there are no messages, neither header nor footer will be printed.
- `errors.prefix`, if defined, will be printed before every error message.
- `errors.suffix`, if defined, will be printed after every error message.

You can also use the tag to display errors from keys stored in simple `String` objects and `String` arrays. Table 10-20 describes the most important attributes supported by the tag.

*Table 10-20. Errors Tag Attributes*

| **Attribute** | **Description** |
|---|---|
| `property` | Name of the property for which error messages should be displayed. This filter functionality allows you to print error messages right next to the relevant form field. If this attribute is omitted, all messages are displayed regardless of the property to which they belong. |
| `name` | The name under which the errors object is stored. You won't usually specify this because it's normally stored under `Globals.ERROR_KEY` (`org.apache.struts.action.ERROR`), which is the default value of this attribute. |
| `bundle` | The name of the application attribute under which the resources object is stored. If not specified, `Globals.MESSAGES_KEY` is used (its value is `org.apache.struts.action.MESSAGE`). When specified, this attribute must match the key specified in `<message-resources>` in the Struts configuration file. |

When all messages are being displayed (that is, there's no property attribute), the messages are displayed by property, with the properties in the order in which they were first added. Within a property, the associated messages are displayed in the order in which they were added.

For example, the default message resource contains the following messages (add them to the existing file):

```
errors.header=<font color="red">
errors.footer=</font>
errors.required=* Required field
errors.database=There was a database error. Please phone you on 555-1234.
```

errors.header and errors.footer ensure that all error messages are printed in a red font. The errors.required message will be printed next to any form fields that fail a validation, as you'll see in the next section (recall that this is a standard key defined by Struts for this purpose). errors.database is a custom key you'll use to inform the user if there was an error in the database.

Once you buy into the Struts way of doing things, you can accomplish a lot with very little code indeed.

## Finishing the View

Now that you've seen the HTML tags, you'll finish the view. The first <html:errors> tag displays any errors.database errors, which in this case occur only if a SQLException is thrown in an action and control is returned to this page. The errors.database key was set in messages.properties:

```
  <body>
    <html:errors property="errors.database"/>
```

The form now sends its data to the process.do URL, which is mapped to the controller servlet in web.xml. Therefore, when the user submits this form, it goes to the controller and then the appropriate action as specified in struts-config.xml:

```
<html:form action="/process.do" method="post">
```

All the text is now stored in a resource bundle:

```
<p>
<bean:message key="text.pizza.first.para"/>
</p>
<p>
<bean:message key="text.pizza.second.para"/>
</p>
```

```
<h1><bean:message key="text.pizza.your.info"/></h1>
<table>
  <tr>
    <td>
      <bean:message key="text.pizza.name"/>
    </td>
    <td>
```

The text inputs are now <html:text> tags. Each element to which you attached a validation rule has an associated <html:errors> tag. When the Struts validator finds a validation error, control is passed back to this page in the same way as with the SQLException previously:

```
    <html:text property="name" size="30"/>
    <html:errors property="name"/>
  </td>
</tr>
<tr>
  <td>
    <bean:message key="text.pizza.address"/>
  </td>
  <td>
```

The address text area is now an <html:textarea> tag, with associated <html:errors>:

```
      <html:textarea rows="4" cols="40" property="address"/>
      <html:errors property="address"/>
    </td>
  </tr>
</table>

<h1><bean:message key="text.pizza.order.type"/></h1>
<table>
  <tr>
    <td>
```

The radio buttons are now <html:radio> tags. Recall that Home Delivery is selected as the default by setting the value in struts-config.xml. You haven't associated any <html:errors> tags with these fields because they're not validated:

```
          <html:radio property="purchaseType" value="Home Delivery" />
        </td>
        <td>
          <bean:message key="text.pizza.home.delivery"/>
        </td>
      </tr>
      <tr>
        <td>
          <html:radio property="purchaseType" value="Take Away"/>
        </td>
        <td>
          <bean:message key="text.pizza.take.away"/>
        </td>
      </tr>
    </table>

    <h1><bean:message key="text.pizza.additional.toppings"/></h1>
    <table>
      <tr>
        <td>
```

The toppings checkboxes are `<html:multibox>` tags:

```
          <html:multibox property="topping" value="Peppers"/>
        </td>
        <td>
          <bean:message key="text.pizza.peppers"/>
        </td>
      </tr>
      <tr>
        <td>
           <html:multibox property="topping" value="Sweetcorn"/>
        </td>
        <td>
          <bean:message key="text.pizza.sweetcorn"/>
        </td>
      </tr>
      <tr>
        <td>
          <html:multibox property="topping" value="Mouse innards"/>
        </td>
        <td>
          <bean:message key="text.pizza.mouse.innards"/>
        </td>
```

```
  </tr>
</table>
<h1><bean:message key="text.pizza.choose.size"/></h1>
<table>
  <tr>
    <td>
      <bean:message key="text.pizza.size"/>
    </td>
    <td>
```

You use the <html:select> element to render the select box. The value attribute specifies which <option> to select as the default. The <html:option> tags render the <option> elements. You've placed the text shown to the user in a resource bundle. Though the value is in English, it won't affect users who are viewing the page in other languages:

```
      <html:select property="size" value="Medium">
        <html:option key="text.pizza.option.small" value="Small"/>
        <html:option key="text.pizza.option.medium" value="Medium"/>
        <html:option key="text.pizza.option.large" value="Large"/>
      </html:select>
    </td>
  </tr>
</table>
```

The final control is <html:submit>. You've also stored the label for this tag in a resource bundle:

```
      <html:submit><bean:message key="text.pizza.submit"/></html:submit>
    </html:form>
  </body>
</html>
```

The processing page isn't really a processing page any more. You've removed all the logic and placed it in the action. This means that processStruts.jsp simply shows the user what they've entered:

```
<%@ taglib uri="http://jakarta.apache.org/struts/tags-bean" prefix="bean" %>
<html>
  <head>
    <title><bean:message key="text.process.title"/></title>
    <style type="text/css">
      H1 {
        font-size: 12pt;
```

```
            font-weight: bold;
          }
        </style>
      </head>

      <body>
        <h1><bean:message key="text.process.first.header"/></h1>

        <table>
          <tr>
            <td><bean:message key="text.process.name"/></td>
            <td>${sessionScope.name}</td>
          </tr>
          <tr>
            <td><bean:message key="text.process.address"/></td>
            <td>${sessionScope.address}</td>
          </tr>
          <tr>
            <td><bean:message key="text.process.delivery.type"/></td>
            <td>${sessionScope.purchaseType}</td>
          </tr>
          <tr>
            <td><bean:message key="text.process.toppings"/></td>
            <td>${sessionScope.topping[0]}</td>
          </tr>
          <tr>
            <td></td>
            <td>${sessionScope.topping[1]}</td>
          </tr>
          <tr>
            <td></td>
            <td>${sessionScope.topping[2]}</td>
          </tr>
          <tr>
            <td><bean:message key="text.process.size"/></td>
            <td>${sessionScope.size}</td>
          </tr>
        </table>

        <p><bean:message key="text.process.thanks"/></p>

      </body>
    </html>
```

So, you've taken the old, has-been application and turned it into a shiny new MVC application. All the processing logic is in the model (`ProcessAction`), and all the presentation is in the view (`pizzaStruts.jsp` and `processStruts.jsp`). The controller is the glue that holds them together.

## Summary

In this chapter, you examined how you can optimize the architecture of a JSP application. In particular, you learned how you can use the Jakarta Struts framework to efficiently write applications that are maintainable, reusable, and flexible. Throughout the chapter, you went through the pizza application to try the techniques. These were the most important issues covered:

- JSP Model 1 architecture, where the JSP pages contain both the presentation logic and the application logic, and its impact on the key success factors of maintainability, reusability, and the way developers with different skill sets can work on the same problem

- JSP Model 2 or MVC architecture, which uses a controller to overcome the drawbacks of the JSP Model 1 architecture; how it facilitates the cooperation of developers with different skill sets; and how it promotes maintainability and reusability

- The reasons for using third-party Web application frameworks

- The Model 2 (MVC) architecture as implemented by Struts, including the operation of the core `ActionServlet`, `ActionMapping`, `ActionForm`, and `Action` components

- Struts configuration and deployment in an application

- Important tags from the Struts bean and HTML tag libraries

- Dynamic action forms that can help you eliminate some of your Java `ActionForm` classes

- Declarative validation using the validator

There's a lot more to Struts than you saw in this chapter, so you may want to visit the Web site or read a book such as *Pro Jakarta Struts*, Second Edition (Apress, 2004) to find out more.

APPENDIX A

# JSP Syntax Reference

**This appendix describes** the syntax for JavaServer Pages (JSP) 2.0. Our intention is to provide you with a reference that's complete and useful but more compact than the specification. (The JSP 2.0 specification weighs in at 478 pages!)

> **NOTE** *JSP specifications from version 2.0 on are available by visiting* `http://java.sun.com/products/jsp/`.

This appendix looks in turn at the following:

- **Various preliminary details**: The notation we use, how you specify uniform resource locators (URLs) in JSP code, and the various types of commenting you can use.
- **The JSP directives**: The `page`, `taglib`, and `include` directives.
- **JSP scripting elements**: Declarations, scriptlets, and expressions.
- **JSP standard actions**: The `<jsp:useBean>`, `<jsp:setProperty>`, `<jsp:getProperty>`, `<jsp:include>`, and `<jsp:forward>` actions.
- **Tag libraries**: A brief review of the syntax for using tag libraries.
- **Implicit objects**: The implicit objects that are available within a JSP page such as `request`, `response`, `session`, and `application`. Appendix B covers these in more detail.
- **Attributes**: Various predefined request and application attributes that you may find useful.

## Preliminaries

Before getting stuck in the details, the following sections make a few miscellaneous observations.

### Notation

This appendix uses the following notation:

- *Italics* show what you'll have to specify.
- **Bold** shows the default value of an attribute. Attributes with default values are optional if you're using the default; sometimes, where the default value is a little complicated, we use **default** to indicate that the default is described in the following text.
- When an attribute has a set of possible values, those are delimited by |:

```
import="package.class, package.*, ..."
session="true|false"
```

### URL Specifications

URLs specified within JSP tags can be of two sorts:

- *Context-relative* paths start with /; the base URL is provided by the Web application to which the JSP page belongs. For example, in a Web application hosted at `http://localhost:8080/begjsp-appendixA/`, the URL `/pageurl.jsp` would be equivalent to `http://localhost:8080/begjsp-appendixA/pageurl.jsp`.
- *Page-relative* paths are relative to the JSP page in which they occur. Unlike context-relative paths, page-relative paths don't start with /; for instance, a page application hosted at `http://localhost:8080/begjsp-appendixA/morespecs/urlspec.jsp` might give a page as `subfolder/urlspec.jsp`, which would be equivalent to `http://localhost:8080/begjsp-appendixA/morespecs/subfolder/urlspec.jsp`.

### *Comments*

Two sorts of comments are allowed in JSP code: JSP and HTML comments:

```
<!-- HTML comments remain in the final client page.
     They can contain JSP expressions, which will be processed by the JSP
     container.
-->

<%-- JSP comments are hidden from the final client page --%>
```

Remember too that within scriptlets (inside `<% %>`), you can use standard Java comments:

```
<%
  /* This Java comment starts with a slash asterisk, and continues
     until we come to a closing asterisk slash
  */

  // Comments starting with a double slash continue to the end of the line
%>
```

## Directives

*Directives* are instructions to the JSP container regarding setting page properties, importing tag libraries, and including content within a JSP; because directives are instructions rather than in-out processes, they can't produce any output via the `out` stream.

### *The page Directive*

The `page` directive specifies attributes for the page; all the attributes are optional, and the essential ones have default values, shown in bold:

```
<%@ page language="java"
         extends="package.class"
         import="package.class, package.*, ..."
         session="true|false"
         buffer="none|default|sizekb"
         autoFlush="true|false"
         isThreadSafe="true|false"
         info="Sample JSP to show tags"
```

```
        isErrorPage="true|false"
        errorPage="ErrorPage.jsp"
        contentType="TYPE|
                     TYPE; charset=CHARSET|
                     text/html; charset=ISO-8859-1"
        pageEncoding="default"
        isELIgnored="true|false"
%>
```

Bear the following in mind when using this directive:

- The default buffer size is defined to be *at least* 8 kilobytes (KB).
- The errorPage attribute contains the relative URL for the error page to which this page should go if there's an unhandled error on this page.
- The specified error page file must declare isErrorPage="true" to have access to the Exception object.
- The contentType attribute sets the MIME type and the character set for the response. The default value is "text/html" for standard JSP pages and "text/xml" when implementing JSP documents in Extensible Markup Language (XML) format.
- The pageEncoding attribute defines the character encoding for the JSP page. The default is that specified in the contentType attribute or "ISO-8859-1" if none was specified there.

This is an example of the code that may be used for an error page:

```
<%@ page language="java"
        isErrorPage="true" %>

<html>
  <body>
    <!-- This displays the fully-qualified name of the exception
        and its message-->
    <%= exception.toString() %>
    <br>

    <!-- This displays the exception's descriptive message -->
    <%= exception.getMessage() %>
  </body>
</html>
```

The page will print the error message received.

This directive can also switch on support for scripting and EL in the JSP document, using the `isELIgnored` attribute, which sets Expression Language (EL) support. Settings in `web.xml` may influence the behavior of this attribute. For this attribute, a value of `true` enables support, and `false` disables it. The default value is `true`.

## The taglib Directive

A *tag library* is a collection of tags used to extend a JSP container functional model. The `taglib` directive defines a tag library namespace for the page, mapping the uniform resource indicator (URI) of the tag library descriptor to a prefix that can be used to reference tags from the library on this page.

```
<%@ taglib ( uri="tagLibraryURI" | tagdir="tagDir" ) prefix="tagPrefix" %>

.
.
.

<tagPrefix:tagName attributeName="attributeValue" >
  JSP content
</tagPrefix:tagName>

<tagPrefix:tagName attributeName="attributeValue" />
```

You can assume that the tag library descriptor (TLD) defines a `tagName` element.

`tagdir` indicates this prefix is for identifying tag extensions installed in the `/WEB-INF/tags/` directory or a subdirectory. If a `TLD` is present in the specified directory, it's used. Otherwise, an implicit tag library descriptor, generated by the container, is used. A translation error must occur if the value doesn't start with `/WEB-INF/tags/`. A translation error must occur if the value doesn't point to a directory that exists. A translation error must occur if used in conjunction with the `uri` attribute.

## The tag Directive

You can use most JSP directives in simple tag handler code files. Note that the `page` directive itself isn't used; instead, you use the `tag` directive, which may only be used in tag files. Here's the syntax:

```
<%@ tag tag_directive_attr_list %>

tag_directive_attr_list ::=
  { display-name="display-name" }
  { body-content="scriptless|tagdependent|empty" }
  { dynamic-attributes="name" }
  { small-icon="small-icon" }
  { large-icon="large-icon" }
  { description="description" }
  { example="example" }
  { language="scriptingLanguage" }
  { import="importList" }
  { pageEncoding="peinfo" }
  { isELIgnored="true|false" }
```

This is an example tag directive:

```
<%@ tag name="msg"
  display-name="Message"
  body-content="scriptless"
  dynamic-attributes="user"
  small-icon="/WEB-INF/small-icon.jpg"
  large-icon="/WEB-INF/large-icon.jpg"
  description="Simple usage of a tag directive"
%>
```

## The include Directive

There are two include tags: the include directive and the jsp:include action.

The include directive includes a static file at translation time, adding any JSP in that file to this page for run-time processing:

```
<%@ include file="header.html" %>
```

See also the jsp:include action.

## The attribute Directive

The attribute directive is analogous to the <attribute> element in the TLD and allows you to declare custom action attributes. This is the syntax:

```
<%@ attribute attribute_directive_attr_list %>

attribute_directive_attr_list ::=
  name="attribute-name"
  { required="true|false" }
  { fragment="true|false" }
  { rtexprvalue="true|false" }
  { type="type" }
  { description="description" }
```

### *The variable Directive*

The `variable` directive is analogous to the `<variable>` element in the TLD and allows you to define a variable exposed by the tag handler. This is the syntax:

```
<%@ variable variable_directive_attr_list %>

variable_directive_attr_list ::=
  ( name-given="output-name" |
    ( name-from-attribute="attr-name" alias="local-name"))
  { variable-class="output-type" }
  { declare="true|false" }
  { scope="AT_BEGIN|AT_END|NESTED" }
  { description="description" }
```

## Scripting Elements

You use scripting elements to include snippets of Java code within a JSP: to declare variables and methods, to execute arbitrary Java code, and to display the result of Java expressions.

### *Declarations*

The following syntax allows you to declare variables and methods for the page. These are placed in the generated servlet *outside* the `_jspService()` method; in other words, variables declared here will be instance variables of the servlet. Declarations don't produce any output.

This is an example of declaring a variable:

```
<%! String  message; %>
```

The following code declares a variable and initializes it:

```
<%! String message = "variable declarared"; %>
```

You can define a method for use on the global page like so:

```
<%! public String showMessage() { return message; } %>
```

Declaration tags are mainly used in conjunction with scriptlets.

## Scriptlets

Scriptlets enclose Java code (on however many lines) that's evaluated *within* the generated servlet's _jspService() method to generate dynamic content:

```
<%
  // Java code
%>
```

Take care when using adjacent scriptlet blocks; this code:

```
<% if(user.isLoggedIn) { %>
     <p>Hi!</p>
<% } %>
<% else { %>
     <p>Please log in first...</p>
<% } %>
```

isn't legal because you've broken the else block into two scriptlets.

## Expressions

Expressions return a value from the scripting code as a String to the page:

```
<p>Hello there,
<%= userName %>
Good to see you.</p>
```

## Standard Actions

The standard actions provide various facilities for manipulating JavaBeans components, including and forwarding control to other resources at request time and generating HTML to use the Java plug-in.

### `<jsp:useBean>`

The `<jsp:useBean>` tag checks for an instance of a bean of the given `class` and `scope`. If a bean of the specified class exists, it references it with the `id`; otherwise it instantiates it. The bean is available within its `scope` with its `id` attribute:

```
<jsp:useBean id="aBeanName"
             scope="page|request|session|application"
             typeSpecification
/>
```

You can include code between the `<jsp:useBean>` tags, as shown in the second example; this code will be run only if the `<jsp:useBean>` tag successfully instantiated the bean:

```
<jsp:useBean id="anotherBeanName"
             scope="page|request|session|application"
             typeSpecification
>
  <jsp.setProperty name="anotherBeanName"
                   property="*|propertyName" />
</jsp:useBean>
```

There's a lot of flexibility in specifying the type of the bean (indicated by *typeSpecification* previously). You can use the following:

- class="*package.class*"
- type="*typeName*"
- class="*package.class*" type="*typeName*" (and with terms reversed)
- beanName="*beanName*" type="*typeName*" (and with terms reversed)

where the following is true:

- typeName is the class of the scripting variable defined by the id attribute, that is, the class that the bean instance is cast to (whether the class, a parent class, or an interface the class implements).
- beanName is the name of the bean, as used in the instantiate() method of the java.beans.Beans class.

## <jsp:setProperty>

The <jsp:setProperty> tag used previously sets the property of the bean referenced by name using the value:

```
<jsp.setProperty name="anotherBeanName"
                 propertyExpression
/>
```

The *propertyExpression* can be any of the following:

- property="*"
- property="*propertyName*"
- property="*propertyName*" param="*parameterName*"
- property="*propertyName*" value="*propertyValue*"

where the following is true:

- The * setting tells the tag to iterate through the request parameters for the page, setting any values for properties in the bean whose names match parameter names.
- The param attribute specifies the parameter name to use in setting this property.
- The value attribute can be any run-time expression as long as it evaluates to a String.
- Omitting value and param attributes for a property assumes that the bean property and request parameter name match.
- The value attribute String can be automatically cast to boolean, byte, char, double, int, float, long, and their class equivalents. Other casts will have to be handled explicitly in the bean's set*PropertyName*() method.

## *<jsp:getProperty>*

The final bean-handling action is `<jsp:getProperty>`, which gets the named property and outputs its value for inclusion in the page as a `String`:

```
<jsp:getProperty name="anotherBeanName" property="propertyName" />
```

## *<jsp:param>*

The `<jsp:param>` action is used within the body of `<jsp:forward>`, `<jsp:include>`, and `<jsp:plugin>` to supply extra name/value parameter pairs to the included or forwarded page. It has the following syntax:

```
<jsp:param name="parameterName" value="parameterValue" />
```

## *<jsp:forward>*

To forward the client request to a static resource, whether it's an HTML file, a JSP page, or a servlet class in the same context as the page, use the following syntax:

```
<jsp:forward page="relativeURL" />
```

or this syntax:

```
<jsp:forward page="relativeURL" >
  <jsp:param name="parameterName" value="parameterValue" />
</jsp:forward>
```

where the following is true:

- The `page` attribute for `<jsp:forward>` can be a run-time expression.
- The `value` attribute for `<jsp:param>` can be a run-time expression.

## <jsp:include>

The <jsp:include> action includes a static or dynamically referenced file at run time:

```
<jsp:include page="relativeURL" flush="true|false" />
```

or the following:

```
<jsp:include page="relativeURL"
             flush="true|false" >
  <jsp:param name="parameterName" value="parameterValue"/>
</jsp:include>
```

where the following is true:

- The page attribute can be the result of some run-time expression.
- The optional flush attribute determines whether the output buffer will be flushed before including the specified resource. The default value is "false". (Note that in JSP 1.1 this attribute was mandatory, and the only permissible value was "true".)
- The jsp:param tag allows parameters to be appended to the original request, and if the parameter name already exists, the new parameter value takes precedence in a comma-delimited list.

## <jsp:plugin>

The <jsp:plugin> action enables the JSP to include a bean or an applet in the client page. It has the following syntax:

```
<jsp:plugin type="bean|applet"
            code="class"
            codebase="classDirectory"
            name="instanceName"
            archive="archiveURI"
            align="bottom|top|middle|left|right"
            height="inPixels"
            width="inPixels"
            hspace="leftRightPixels"
```

```
            vspace="topBottomPixels"
            title="title"
            jreversion="1.2|number"
            nspluginurl="pluginURL"
            iepluginurl="pluginURL"
            mayscript="true|false">
  <jsp:params>
    <jsp:param name="parameterName" value="parameterValue">
  </jsp:params>
  <jsp:fallback>Problem with plugin</jsp:fallback>
</jsp:plugin>
```

Most of these attributes are direct from the HTML specification (`http://www.w3.org/TR/html4/`); the exceptions are `type`, `jreversion`, `nspluginurl`, and `iepluginurl`:

- The `name`, `archive`, `align`, `height`, `width`, `hspace`, `vspace`, `jreversion`, `nspluginurl`, and `iepluginurl` attributes are optional.
- The `<jsp:param>` tag's `value` attribute can take a run-time expression.
- The `jreversion` is the Java Runtime Environment specification version that the component requires.
- `nspluginurl` and `iepluginurl` are the URLs where the Java plug-in can be downloaded for Netscape Navigator and Internet Explorer.

`jsp:fallback` can occur only as a direct child of the `<jsp:plugin>` element. Using the `jsp:fallback` element in any other context will result in a translation-time error. The `<jsp:fallback>` element indicates the content to be used by the client browser if the plug-in can't be started.

## <jsp:element>

The `<jsp:element>` action dynamically defines the value of the tag of an XML element. This action can be used in JSP pages, tag files, and JSP documents.

This action can have the `<jsp:attribute>` and `<jsp:body>` actions as its body. They're optional:

```
<jsp:element name="name">
  jsp:attribute*
  jsp:body?
```

```
</jsp:element>
```

## <jsp:attribute>

The <jsp:attribute> action has two uses: The page author can define an action's attribute in the body of an XML element instead of in the attribute of the opening tag. It also allows the page author to specify the attributes of the element when used inside a <jsp:element> action (see the previous section). This action may only appear as a subelement of standard and custom actions:

```
<jsp:element name="name">
  <jsp:attribute name="firstname">Matthew</jsp:attribute>
  <jsp:attribute name="lastname">Moodie</jsp:attribute>
</jsp:element>
```

If one or more of these actions are used, the body of the tag can be specified only with a <jsp:body> action. If this is omitted, then the body of the tag is empty.

## <jsp:body>

The body of an action is normally defined as the body of the tag. Then you can also define the body of an action using the <jsp:body> standard action. This is required if one or more <jsp:attribute> elements appear in the body of the tag.

## <jsp:invoke>

The <jsp:invoke> standard action can be used only in tag files. It takes the name of a fragment and invokes the fragment, sending the output of the result to the JspWriter or to a scoped attribute. If the fragment identified by the given name is null, <jsp:invoke> will behave as though it was passed a fragment that produces no output:

```
<jsp:invoke fragment="name"
            var="var_name"
            varReader="reader"
            scope="page">
```

fragment is the name used to identify this fragment during this tag invocation. var is the name of a scoped attribute in which to store the result of the fragment invocation, as a java.lang.String object. varReader is the name of a scoped attribute in which to store the result of the fragment invocation, as a java.io.Reader object. scope acts as other scope attributes.

## <jsp:doBody>

The <jsp:doBody> action behaves like <jsp:invoke> except that it operates on the body of the tag instead of on a specific fragment passed as an attribute. Because it always operates on the body of the tag, there's no name attribute for this standard action, though its other attributes are identical to <jsp:invoke>.

## <jsp:text>

You can use the <jsp:text> action to enclose template data in a JSP page, a JSP document, or a tag file. It has no attributes and can appear anywhere that template data can.

## <jsp:output>

You can use <jsp:output> only in JSP documents and in tag files in XML syntax. It's used to modify properties of the output of a JSP document or a tag file. In JSP 2.0 there are four properties that can be specified, all of which affect the output of the XML prolog:

```
<jsp:output ( omit-xml-declaration="yes|no|true|false" )
              { doctypeDecl } />

doctypeDecl ::= ( doctype-root-element="rootElement"
  doctype-public="PubidLiteral"
  doctype-system="SystemLiteral" ) |
    ( doctype-root-element="rootElement"
  doctype-system="SystemLiteral" )
```

## <jsp:root>

<jsp:root> can appear only as the root element in a JSP document or in a tag file in XML syntax. However, they don't need a <jsp:root> element as their root element; there are two reasons for using <jsp:root>: indicating XML content and accommodating the generation of content that isn't a single XML document.

This element has a mandatory version attribute indicating which version of JSP the page is using. It can have any number of xmlns attributes:

```
<jsp:root xmlns:jsp="http://java.sun.com/JSP/Page" version="2.0">
  body
```

```
</jsp:root>
```

## *<jsp:declaration>*

You use `<jsp:declaration>` to declare scripting language constructs that are available to all other scripting elements. It has no attributes, and its body is the declaration itself:

```
<jsp:declaration> Date now = new Date(); </jsp:declaration>
```

## *<jsp:scriptlet>*

`<jsp:scriptlet>` has no attributes, and its body is the scriptlet. It's used on XML JSP pages to include scriptlets:

```
<jsp:scriptlet> out.print("Hello, world"); </jsp:scriptlet>
```

## *<jsp:expression>*

`<jsp:expression>` has no attributes, and its body is the expression:

```
<jsp:expression> session.getAttribute("user"); </jsp:expression>
```

# Tag Libraries

The syntax for using tag libraries is similar to that for the standard actions except of course that the tag names and attributes are defined in the tag library itself rather than by the JSP standard. Each tag library is associated with a *prefix* by using the `taglib` directive to map the prefix to a URI identifying the tag library. For example, using the Jakarta Taglibs project's `request` tag library (`http://jakarta.apache.org/taglibs/doc/request-doc/intro.html`) looks like this:

```
<%@ taglib uri="http://jakarta.apache.org/taglibs/request-1.0" prefix="req"
%>
```

Within the JSP, you can then use tags from the library by using the prefix defined in the `taglib` directive and the tag's name. For example:

```
<req:attributes id="loop">
  Name: <jsp:getProperty name="loop" property="name"/>
  Value: <jsp:getProperty name="loop" property="value"/>
</req:attributes>
```

You can set up the mapping between a particular URI (as used in the `taglib` directive) and the tag library descriptor in one of two ways. In JSP, it's possible to package tag libraries so that the mapping is automatic, based on settings contained in the tag library descriptor file. Alternatively, you can make an entry in the `web.xml` file to map a URI to a tag library descriptor file:

```
<taglib>
  <taglib-uri>http://jakarta.apache.org/taglibs/request-1.0</taglib-uri>
  <taglib-location>/WEB-INF/request.tld</taglib-location>
</taglib>
```

## Implicit Objects

JSP defines a number of implicit objects that JSP scripting elements can use:

- `request`, of type `javax.servlet.http.HttpServletRequest`
- `response`, of type `javax.servlet.http.HttpServletResponse`
- `out`, of type `javax.servlet.jsp.JspWriter`
- `session`, of type `javax.servlet.http.HttpSession`
- `application`, of type `javax.servlet.ServletContext`
- `exception`, of type `java.lang.Throwable`
- `config`, of type `javax.servlet.ServletConfig`
- page, a reference to the implementing servlet class for the JSP
- `pageContext`, of type `javax.servlet.jsp.PageContext`

Appendix B gives details of these objects and the methods that each makes available. The JSP and servlet specifications define many more classes and interfaces; to find out more about them, you should consult the online documentation as described in Appendix D.

APPENDIX B

# JSP Implicit Objects

**The JavaServer Pages (JSP) technology** defines a number of implicit objects that scripting elements can use. This appendix gives details of these objects and the methods that each of them exposes. The JSP and servlet specifications define many more classes and interfaces; to find out more about them, you should consult the online documentation as described in Appendix D.

> **NOTE** *This appendix lists* all *the methods available for each object (except those defined in* `java.lang.Object`*), irrespective of which class or interface defines the methods.*

The implicit objects are as follows:

- `request`
- `response`
- `out`
- `session`
- `application`
- `exception`
- `config`
- `page`
- `pageContext`

## The request Object

The request object is an instance of a class that implements the javax.servlet.http.HttpServletRequest interface. It represents the request made by the client and makes the following methods available.

getAttribute() returns the value of the specified request attribute name. The return value is an Object or subclass if the attribute is available to the invoking ServletRequest object or null if the attribute isn't available:

```
public Object getAttribute(String name)
```

getAttributeNames() returns an Enumeration containing the attribute names available to the invoking ServletRequest object:

```
public java.util.Enumeration getAttributeNames()
```

getAuthType() returns the name of the authentication scheme used in the request or null if no authentication scheme was used. It returns one of the constants BASIC_AUTH, FORM_AUTH, CLIENT_CERT_AUTH, or DIGEST_AUTH, or it returns null if the request wasn't authenticated:

```
public String getAuthType()
```

getCharacterEncoding() returns a String object containing the character encoding used in the body of the request or null if there's no encoding:

```
public String getCharacterEncoding()
```

getContentLength() returns the length of the body of the request in bytes or -1 if the length isn't known:

```
public int getContentLength()
```

getContentType() returns a String object containing the Multipurpose Internet Mail Extensions (MIME) type ("text/plain", "text/html", "image/gif", etc.) of the body of the request or null if the type isn't known:

```
public String getContentType()
```

getContextPath() returns the part of the request uniform resource indicator (URI) that indicates the context path of the request. The context path is the first part of the URI and always begins with the / character. For servlets running in the root context, this method returns an empty String. For example, if there's an incoming request from request http://localhost/guide/suburbs/index.jsp, then getContextPath() would return "/guide":

```
public String getContextPath()
```

getCookies() returns an array containing any Cookie objects sent with the request or null if no cookies were sent:

```
public Cookie[] getCookies()
```

getDateHeader() returns a long value that represents the date specified in the named header and is the number of milliseconds since January 1, 1970, Greenwich mean time (GMT). This method is used with a header that contains a date, and it returns -1 if the request doesn't contain the specified header:

```
public long getDateHeader(String name)
```

getHeader() returns the value of the specified header expressed as a String object or null if the request doesn't contain the specified header:

```
public String getHeader(String name)
```

The following is an example Hypertext Transfer Protocol (HTTP) request:

```
GET /search?index=servlets+jsp HTTP/1.1
Accept: image/gif, image/jpg, */*
Accept-Encoding: gzip
Connection: Keep-Alive
Cookie: userID=id66589
Host: www.mycompany.com
Referer: http://www.mycompany.com/getproducts.html
User-Agent: Mozilla/4.6 [en] (WinXP; U)
```

For example, if the usage is getRequest("Connection"), it'd return "Keep-Alive".

getHeaderNames() returns an Enumeration containing all of the header names used by the request:

```
public java.util.Enumeration getHeaderNames()
```

getHeaders() returns an Enumeration containing all of the values associated with the specified header name. The method returns an empty enumeration if the request doesn't contain the specified header:

```
public java.util.Enumeration getHeaders(String name)
```

getInputStream() returns a ServletInputStream object that can be used to read the body of the request as binary data:

```
public ServletInputStream getInputStream()
        throws java.io.IOException
```

`getIntHeader()` returns the value of the specified header as an `int`. It returns `-1` if the request doesn't contain the specified header, and it throws a `NumberFormatException` if the header value can't be converted to an `int`. This method was made for convenience when the header type is known to be an integer; this way it can be absorbed by the code without any conversion:

```
public int getIntHeader(String name)
```

`getLocalAddr()` returns the Internet Protocol (IP) address of the server where the request was received:

```
public String getLocalAddr()
```

`getLocale()` returns the preferred locale of the client that made the request:

```
public java.util.Locale getLocale()
```

`getLocales()` returns an `Enumeration` containing, in descending order of preference, the locales that are acceptable to the client machine:

```
public java.util.Enumeration getLocales()
```

`getLocalName()` returns the hostname of the server where the request was received:

```
public String getLocalName()
```

`getLocalPort()` returns the port on the server where the request was received:

```
public int getLocalPort()
```

`getMethod()` returns the name of the HTTP method used to make the request. Typical return values are `"GET"`, `"POST"`, or `"PUT"`:

```
public String getMethod()
```

`getParameter()` returns a `String` object containing the value of the specified parameter or `null` if the parameter doesn't exist:

```
public String getParameter(String name)
```

getParameterMap() returns a Map containing the request parameters:

```
public java.util.Map getParameterMap()
```

getParameterNames() returns a Enumeration containing the parameters contained within the invoking ServletRequest object:

```
public java.util.Enumeration getParameterNames()
```

getParameterValues() is used when a parameter may have more than one value associated with it. The method returns a String array containing the values of the specified parameter or null if the parameter doesn't exist:

```
public String[] getParameterValues(String name)
```

getPathInfo() returns any additional path information contained in the request uniform resource locator (URL). This extra information will be after the servlet path and before the query string. It returns null if there's no additional path information. For example, in the incoming request from http://localhost/innersuburbs/, getPathInfo() would return "/innersuburbs":

```
public String getPathInfo()
```

getPathTranslated() returns the same information as the getPathInfo() method, but translated into a real path:

```
public String getPathTranslated()
```

getProtocol() returns the name and version of the protocol used by the request. A typical return String would be "HTTP/1.1":

```
public String getProtocol()
```

getQueryString() returns the query string that was contained in the request URL without any decoding from the container or null if there was no query string:

```
public String getQueryString()
```

getReader() returns a BufferedReader object that can be used to read the body of the request as character data:

```
public java.io.BufferedReader getReader()
        throws java.io.IOException
```

getRemoteAddr() returns a String object containing the IP address of the client machine that made the request:

```
public String getRemoteAddr()
```

getRemoteHost() returns a String object containing the name of the client machine or the IP address if the name can't be determined:

```
public String getRemoteHost()
```

getRemotePort() returns the port number of the client or last proxy that sent the request:

```
public int getRemotePort()
```

getRemoteUser() returns the login of the user making the request or null if the user hasn't been authenticated:

```
public String getRemoteUser()
```

getRequestDispatcher() returns a RequestDispatcher object that acts as a wrapper around the resource located at the specified path. The path must begin with / and can be a relative path:

```
public RequestDispatcher getRequestDispatcher(String path)
```

getRequestedSessionId() returns the session ID that was specified by the client or null if the request didn't specify an ID:

```
public String getRequestedSessionId()
```

getRequestURI() returns a subsection of the request URL, from the protocol name to the start of the query string (the query string isn't included):

```
public String getRequestURI()
```

getRequestURL() reconstructs the URL used to make the request including the protocol, server name, port number, and path, but excluding the query string:

```
public StringBuffer getRequestURL()
```

getScheme() returns the scheme ("http", "https", "ftp", and so on) used to make the request:

```
public String getScheme()
```

getServerName() returns a String object containing the name of the server that received the request:

```
public String getServerName()
```

getServerPort() returns the port number that received the request:

```
public int getServerPort()
```

getServletPath() returns the part of the request URL that was used to call the servlet, without any additional information or the query string:

```
public String getServletPath()
```

getSession() returns the HttpSession object associated with the request. By default, if the request doesn't currently have a session, calling this method will create one. Setting the boolean parameter create to false overrides this:

```
public HttpSession getSession(boolean create)
public HttpSession getSession()
```

getUserPrincipal() returns a java.security.Principal object containing the name of the current authenticated user. If the user hasn't been authenticated, the method returns null:

```
public java.security.Principal getUserPrincipal()
```

isRequestedSessionIdFromCookie() returns true if the session ID came in from a cookie:

```
public boolean isRequestedSessionIdFromCookie()
```

isRequestedSessionIdFromURL() returns true if the session ID came in as part of the request URL:

```
public boolean isRequestedSessionIdFromURL()
```

isRequestedSessionIdValid() returns true if the session ID requested by the client is still valid:

```
public boolean isRequestedSessionIdValid()
```

isSecure() returns true if the request was made using a secure channel, for example, HTTPS:

```
public boolean isSecure()
```

isUserInRole() returns true if the authenticated user has the specified logical role or false if the user isn't authenticated:

```
public boolean isUserInRole(String role)
```

removeAttribute() makes the specified attribute unavailable to the invoking ServletRequest object. Subsequent calls to the getAttribute() method for this attribute will return null:

```
public void removeAttribute(String name)
```

setAttribute() binds a value to a specified attribute name. Note that attributes will be reset after the request is handled:

```
public void setAttribute(String name,
                         Object o)
```

setCharacterEncoding() overrides the character encoding used in the body of this request:

```
public void setCharacterEncoding(String env)
    throws java.io.UnsupportedEncodingException
```

The following String constants are used to identify the different types of authentication that may have been used to protect the servlet. They have the values BASIC, FORM, CLIENT_CERT, and DIGEST, respectively:

```
public static final String BASIC_AUTH
public static final String FORM_AUTH
public static final String CLIENT_CERT_AUTH
public static final String DIGEST_AUTH
```

These methods are deprecated and shouldn't be used in new code—they exist for compatibility with existing code:

```
public String getRealPath(String path)
public boolean isRequestedSessionIdFromUrl()
```

Use ServletContext.getRealPath(java.lang.String) instead of getRealPath(String path), and use ServletContext.isRequestedSessionIdFromURL() instead of isRequestedSessionIdFromUrl().

## The response Object

The response object is an instance of a class that implements the javax.servlet.http.HttpServletResponse interface. It represents the response to be made to the client, and it makes the following methods available.

addCookie() adds the specified cookie to the response (you can add more than one cookie):

```
public void addCookie(Cookie cookie)
```

addDateHeader() adds a response header containing the specified header name and the number of milliseconds since January 1, 1970, GMT. You can use this method to assign multiple values to a given header name:

```
public void addDateHeader(String name,
                          long date)
```

addHeader() adds a response header with the specified name and value. You can use this method to assign multiple values to a given header name:

```
public void addHeader(String name,
                      String value)
```

addIntHeader() adds a response header with the specified name and int value. This method can assign multiple values to a given header name:

```
public void addIntHeader(String name,
                         int value)
```

containsHeader() returns true if the response header includes the specified header name. You can use this method before calling one of the set() methods to determine if the header value has already been set:

```
public boolean containsHeader(String name)
```

encodeRedirectURL() encodes the specified URL or returns it unchanged if encoding isn't required. This method is used to process a URL before sending it to the sendRedirect() method:

```
public String encodeRedirectURL(String url)
```

encodeURL() encodes the specified URL by including the session ID or returns it unchanged if encoding isn't needed. All URLs generated by a servlet should be processed through this method to ensure compatibility with browsers that don't support cookies:

```
public String encodeURL(String url)
```

flushBuffer() causes any content stored in the buffer to be written to the client. Calling this method will also commit the response, meaning that the status code and headers will be written:

```
public void flushBuffer()
        throws java.io.IOException
```

getBufferSize() returns the buffer size used for the response or 0 if no buffering is used:

```
public int getBufferSize()
```

getCharacterEncoding() returns a String object containing the character encoding used in the body of the response. The default is "ISO-8859-1", which corresponds to Latin-1:

```
public String getCharacterEncoding()
```

getContentType() returns the MIME type of this response. The content type must have been set using setContentType() for this method to return a value; if no content type has been specified, this method returns null. If character encoding has been specified, the charset parameter is included in the return value. If no character encoding has been specified, the charset parameter is omitted:

```
public String getContentType()
```

getLocale() returns the locale that has been assigned to the response. By default, this will be the default locale for the server:

```
public java.util.Locale getLocale()
```

getOutputStream() returns an object ServletOutputStream object that can be used to write the response as binary data:

```
public ServletOutputStream getOutputStream()
        throws java.io.IOException
```

getWriter() returns a PrintWriter object that can be used to write the response as character data:

```
public java.io.PrintWriter getWriter()
        throws java.io.IOException
```

isCommitted() returns true if the response has been committed, meaning that the status code and headers have been written:

```
public boolean isCommitted()
```

reset() clears the status code and headers and any data that exists in the buffer. If the response has already been committed, calling this method will cause an exception to be thrown:

```
public void reset()
        throws java.lang.IllegalStateException
```

resetBuffer() clears the content of the response buffer without clearing the headers or status code. It will throw an IllegalStateException if the response has been committed:

```
public void resetBuffer()
```

sendError() sends an error response back to the client machine using the specified error status code. You can also provide a descriptive message. This method must be called before the response is committed (in other words, before the status code and headers have been written):

```
public void sendError(int sc,
                      String msg)
        throws java.io.IOException
public void sendError(int sc)
        throws java.io.IOException
```

sendRedirect() redirects the client machine to the specified URL. This method must be called before the response is committed (in other words, before sending it to the client):

```
public void sendRedirect(String location)
        throws java.io.IOException
```

`setBufferSize()` requests a buffer size to be used for the response. The actual buffer size will be at least this large:

```
public void setBufferSize(int size)
```

`setCharacterEncoding()` sets the MIME charset of the response. It overrides any previous charset setting, no matter how it was applied:

```
public void setCharacterEncoding(String charset)
```

`setContentLength()` sets the length of response body:

```
public void setContentLength(int len)
```

`setContentType()` sets the content type of the response sent to the server. The `String` argument specifies a MIME type and may also include the type of character encoding, for example, `"text/plain; charset=ISO-8859-1"`:

```
public void setContentType(String type)
```

`setDateHeader()` sets the time value of a response header for the specified header name. The time is the number of milliseconds since January 1, 1970, GMT. If the time value for the specified header has been previously set, the value passed to this method will override it:

```
public void setDateHeader(String name,
                          long date)
```

`setHeader()` sets a response header with the specified `name` and `value`. If the value for the specified header has been previously set, the value passed to this method will override it:

```
public void setHeader(String name,
                      String value)
```

`setIntHeader()` sets a response header with the specified name and `int` value. If the `int` value for the specified header has been previously set, the value passed to this method will override it:

```
public void setIntHeader(String name,
                         int value)
```

`setLocale()` specifies the locale that will be used for the response:

```
public void setLocale(java.util.Locale loc)
```

`setStatus()` sets the status code and should be one of `SC_ACCEPTED`, `SC_OK`, `SC_CONTINUE`, `SC_PARTIAL_CONTENT`, `SC_CREATED`, `SC_SWITCHING_PROTOCOLS`, or `SC_NO_CONTENT`:

```
public void setStatus(int sc)
```

The following constants represent the status codes defined in the HTTP specification (visit `http://www.w3.org/TR/html401/` for more information):

```
public static final int SC_CONTINUE
public static final int SC_SWITCHING_PROTOCOLS
public static final int SC_OK
public static final int SC_CREATED

public static final int SC_FOUND
public static final int SC_ACCEPTED
public static final int SC_NON_AUTHORITATIVE_INFORMATION
public static final int SC_NO_CONTENT
public static final int SC_RESET_CONTENT
public static final int SC_PARTIAL_CONTENT
public static final int SC_MULTIPLE_CHOICES
public static final int SC_MOVED_PERMANENTLY
public static final int SC_MOVED_TEMPORARILY
public static final int SC_SEE_OTHER
public static final int SC_NOT_MODIFIED

public static final int SC_USE_PROXY
public static final int SC_BAD_REQUEST
public static final int SC_UNAUTHORIZED
public static final int SC_PAYMENT_REQUIRED
public static final int SC_FORBIDDEN
public static final int SC_NOT_FOUND
public static final int SC_METHOD_NOT_ALLOWED
public static final int SC_NOT_ACCEPTABLE
public static final int SC_PROXY_AUTHENTICATION_REQUIRED
public static final int SC_REQUEST_TIMEOUT
public static final int SC_CONFLICT
public static final int SC_GONE
public static final int SC_LENGTH_REQUIRED
public static final int SC_PRECONDITION_FAILED
public static final int SC_REQUEST_ENTITY_TOO_LARGE
public static final int SC_REQUEST_URI_TOO_LONG
public static final int SC_UNSUPPORTED_MEDIA_TYPE
public static final int SC_REQUESTED_RANGE_NOT_SATISFIABLE
public static final int SC_EXPECTATION_FAILED
```

```
public static final int SC_INTERNAL_SERVER_ERROR
public static final int SC_NOT_IMPLEMENTED
public static final int SC_BAD_GATEWAY
public static final int SC_SERVICE_UNAVAILABLE
public static final int SC_GATEWAY_TIMEOUT
public static final int SC_HTTP_VERSION_NOT_SUPPORTED
public static final int SC_TEMPORARY_REDIRECT
```

These methods are deprecated and shouldn't be used in new code—they exist for compatibility with existing code:

```
public String encodeUrl(String url)
public String encodeRedirectUrl(String url)
public void setStatus(int sc,
                      String sm)
```

## The out Object

The `out` object is an instance of the `javax.servlet.jsp.JspWriter` class. It's used to create the content returned to the client and has the following useful methods available.

`clear()` clears the contents of the buffer; it throws an exception if some data has already been written to the output stream:

```
public abstract void clear()
        throws java.io.IOException
```

`clearBuffer()` clears the contents of the buffer but doesn't throw an exception if some data has already been written to the output stream:

```
public abstract void clearBuffer()
        throws java.io.IOException
```

`close()` flushes and then closes the output stream:

```
public abstract void close()
        throws java.io.IOException
```

`flush()` flushes the output buffer and sends any bytes contained in the buffer to their intended destination. `flush()` will flush all the buffers in a chain of `Writers` and `OutputStreams`:

```
public abstract void flush()
        throws java.io.IOException
```

`getBufferSize()` returns the size in bytes of the output buffer:

```
public int getBufferSize()
```

`getRemaining()` returns the number of bytes still contained in the buffer. It will return `0` if it's unbuffered:

```
public abstract int getRemaining()
```

`isAutoFlush()` returns `true` if the buffer flushes automatically when an overflow condition occurs:

```
public boolean isAutoFlush()
```

`newLine()` writes a new line character to the output stream:

```
public abstract void newLine()
        throws java.io.IOException
```

`print()` prints the specified primitive data type, `Object`, or `String` to the client:

```
public abstract void print(boolean b)
        throws java.io.IOException
public abstract void print(char c)
        throws java.io.IOException
public abstract void print(int i)
        throws java.io.IOException
public abstract void print(long l)
        throws java.io.IOException
public abstract void print(float f)
        throws java.io.IOException
public abstract void print(double d)
        throws java.io.IOException
public abstract void print(char[] s)
        throws java.io.IOException
public abstract void print(String s)
        throws java.io.IOException
public abstract void print(Object obj)
        throws java.io.IOException
```

Here's an example:

```
<%
  try
  {
    boolean b = false;
    out.print(b);

  }
  catch(java.io.IOException ioe)
  {
    //Catch error.
  }
%>
```

The previous will print *false* in the browser window.

`println()` prints the specified primitive data type, `Object`, or `String` to the client, followed by a new line character at the end. The no-argument version simply writes a new line character:

```
public abstract void println()
        throws java.io.IOException
public abstract void println(boolean x)
        throws java.io.IOException
public abstract void println(char x)
        throws java.io.IOException
public abstract void println(int x)
        throws java.io.IOException
public abstract void println(long x)
        throws java.io.IOException
public abstract void println(float x)
        throws java.io.IOException
public abstract void println(double x)
        throws java.io.IOException
public abstract void println(char[] x)
        throws java.io.IOException
public abstract void println(String x)
        throws java.io.IOException
public abstract void println(Object x)
        throws java.io.IOException
```

For example:

```
<%
  try
  {
```

```
    out.println("<html><title>Page Title</title></html>");
  }
  catch(java.io.IOException ioe)
  {
    //Catch error.
  }
%>
```

## The session Object

The `session` object is an instance of a class that implements the `javax.servlet.http.HttpSession` interface. You can use it to store session state for a user, and it makes the following methods available.

`getAttribute()` returns the `Object` bound to the specified `name` in this session or `null` if it doesn't exist:

```
public Object getAttribute(String name)
```

`getAttributeNames()` returns an `Enumeration` of `String` objects containing the names of all the objects bound to this session:

```
public java.util.Enumeration getAttributeNames()
```

`getCreationTime()` returns the time when the session was created in milliseconds since midnight January 1, 2003, GMT:

```
public long getCreationTime()
```

`getId()` returns a `String` object containing a unique identifier for this session:

```
public String getId()
```

`getLastAccessedTime()` returns the last time a client request associated with the session was sent. The return value is the number of milliseconds since midnight January 1, 1970, GMT:

```
public long getLastAccessedTime()
```

`getMaxInactiveInterval()` returns the number of seconds the server will wait between client requests before the session is invalidated. A negative return value indicates that the session will never time out:

```
public int getMaxInactiveInterval()
```

getServletContext() returns the ServletContext of this session:

```
public ServletContext getServletContext()
```

invalidate() invalidates the session and unbinds any objects bound to it:

```
public void invalidate()
```

isNew() returns true if the server has created a session that hasn't yet been accessed by a client:

```
public boolean isNew()
```

removeAttribute() removes the Object bound to the specified name from this session:

```
public void removeAttribute(String name)
```

setAttribute() binds an Object to the specified attribute name in this session. If the attribute name already exists, the Object passed to this method will replace the previous Object:

```
public void setAttribute(String name,
                         Object value)
```

setMaxInactiveInterval() specifies the number of seconds the server will wait between client requests before the session is invalidated. If a negative value is passed to this method, the session will never time out:

```
public void setMaxInactiveInterval(int interval)
```

These methods are deprecated and shouldn't be used in new code—they exist for compatibility with existing code:

```
public HttpSessionContext getSessionContext()
public Object getValue(String name)
public String[] getValueNames()
public void putValue(String name,
                     Object value)
public void removeValue(String name)
```

## The application Object

The `application` object is an instance of a class that implements the `javax.servlet.ServletContext` interface, and it allows the page to obtain and to set data information about the Web application in which it's running. It makes available the following methods.

`getAttribute()` returns the value of the specified attribute name. The return value is an `Object` or subclass if the attribute is available to the invoking `ServletContext` object or `null` if the attribute isn't available:

```
public Object getAttribute(String name)
```

`getAttributeNames()` returns an `Enumeration` containing the attribute names available to the invoking `ServletContext` object:

```
public java.util.Enumeration getAttributeNames()
```

`getContext()` returns the `ServletContext` object for the resource at the specified path on the server. The path argument is an absolute URL beginning with /:

```
public ServletContext getContext(String uripath)
```

`getInitParameter()` returns a `String` object containing the value of the specified initialization parameter or `null` if the parameter doesn't exist:

```
public String getInitParameter(String name)
```

`getInitParameterNames()` returns a `Enumeration` containing the initialization parameters associated with the invoking `ServletContext` object:

```
public java.util.Enumeration getInitParameterNames()
```

`getMajorVersion()` returns the major version of the Java servlet API that the server supports. For servers supporting version 2.3 of the servlet specification, this method will return `2`:

```
public int getMajorVersion()
```

`getMimeType()` returns the MIME type of the specified file or `null` if the MIME type can't be ascertained. Typical return values will be `"text/plain"`, `"text/html"`, and `"image/jpg"`:

```
public String getMimeType(String file)
```

getMinorVersion() returns the minor version of the Java servlet API that the server supports. For servers supporting version 2.3 of the servlet specification, this method will return 3:

```
public int getMinorVersion()
```

getNamedDispatcher() returns a RequestDispatcher object that will be wrapped around the named servlet:

```
public RequestDispatcher getNamedDispatcher(String name)
```

getRealPath() returns a String object containing the real path, in a form appropriate to the platform on which the servlet is running, corresponding to the given virtual path. An example of a virtual path might be "/blah.html":

```
public String getRealPath(String path)
```

getRequestDispatcher() returns a RequestDispatcher object that acts as a wrapper around the resource located at the specified path. The path must begin with / and is interpreted relative to the current context root:

```
public RequestDispatcher getRequestDispatcher(String path)
```

getResource() returns a URL object that's mapped to the specified path or null if there's no resource mapped to the path. The path must begin with / and is interpreted relative to the current context root:

```
public java.net.URL getResource(String path)
        throws java.net.MalformedURLException
```

getResourceAsStream() returns the resource at the specified path as an InputStream object:

```
public java.io.InputStream getResourceAsStream(String path)
```

getResourcePaths() returns all the paths to resources held in the Web application as String objects beginning with a /:

```
public java.util.Set getResourcePaths()
```

getServerInfo() returns a String object containing information about the server on which the servlet is running. At a minimum, the String will contain the servlet container name and version number:

```
public String getServerInfo()
```

The following will display *Apache Tomcat/5.0.16* for Tomcat 5.0.16:

```
<% out.print(application.getServerInfo()); %>
```

`getServletContextName()` returns the name of the Web application, as specified in the `<display-name>` element in `web.xml`:

```
public String getServletContextName()
```

`log()` is used to write a message to the servlet engine's log file. The second version writes both an explanatory message and a stack trace for the specified `Throwable` exception to the log file:

```
public void log(String msg)
public void log(String message,
                Throwable throwable)
```

`removeAttribute()` makes the specified attribute unavailable to the invoking `ServletContext` object. Subsequent calls to the `getAttribute()` method for this attribute will return `null`:

```
public void removeAttribute(String name)
```

`setAttribute()` binds a value to a specified attribute name:

```
public void setAttribute(String name,
                         Object object)
```

These methods are deprecated and shouldn't be used in new code—they exist for compatibility with existing code:

```
public Servlet getServlet(String name)
      throws ServletException
public java.util.Enumeration getServletNames()
public java.util.Enumeration getServlets()

public void log(Exception exception,
                String msg)
```

## The exception Object

The `exception` object is an instance of the `java.lang.Throwable` class. It's available in error pages only, and it represents the exception that occurred that caused control to pass to the error page. Its most useful methods are as follows.

`getLocalizedMessage()` returns a localized description of this `Throwable` object. In many cases, this will return the same result as `getMessage()`:

```
public String getLocalizedMessage()
```

`getMessage()` returns the error message string of this `Throwable` object:

```
public String getMessage()
```

`printStackTrace()` prints information about this `Throwable` object, along with a listing of the method calls that led to the error condition arising. The output can be directed to the standard error stream or to a specified `PrintStream` or `PrintWriter` object:

```
public void printStackTrace()
public void printStackTrace(PrintStream ps)
public void printStackTrace(PrintWriter pw)
```

`toString()` returns a short description of this `Throwable` object:

```
public String toString()
```

If an error message was supplied when the object was created, the result is the `Throwable` class's name, followed by a colon and a space, followed by that message. For example, the following:

```
<%
  try
  {
    throw new Exception("Here's my Exception");
  }
  catch(Exception e)
  {
    out.print(e.toString());
  }
%>
```

outputs the following: *java.lang.Exception: Here's my Exception.*

## The config Object

The config object is an instance of the javax.servlet.ServletConfig interface. You can use it to make initialization parameters available, and it has the following methods.

getInitParameter() returns the value of the specified initialization parameter or null if the parameter doesn't exist:

```
public String getInitParameter(String name)
```

getInitParameterNames() returns an Enumeration of String objects containing the names of all of the servlet's initialization parameters:

```
public java.util.Enumeration getInitParameterNames()
```

getServletContext() returns the ServletContext object associated with the invoking servlet. A ServletContext object contains information about the environment in which the servlet is running:

```
public ServletContext getServletContext()
```

getServletName() returns the name of the servlet. If the servlet is unnamed, the method will return the servlet's class name:

```
public String getServletName()
```

## The page Object

The page object is a reference to the servlet object that implements this JSP page. JSP page authors don't often use this object because it's very expensive memory-wise.

## The pageContext Object

The pageContext object is an instance of the javax.servlet.jsp.PageContext class and is used by the container-generated servlet code for your JSP page to access the various scopes available within the JSP page. JSP page authors don't often use this object because they were intended to be generated by the container, but it's important when writing tag libraries:

```
<%
HttpSession thisSession = pageContext.getSession();
%>
```

APPENDIX C

# XML Configuration Files

**This appendix documents** in detail the three most commonly used Extensible Markup Language (XML) configuration files in JavaServer Pages (JSP) applications:

**The Web application deployment descriptor file (web.xml)**: This is a configuration file used by servlet containers that meet the Java 2 Enterprise Edition (J2EE) specification, such as Apache Tomcat. The servlet container reads this file on startup. This file is placed in the `WEB-INF` folder of your Web application.

**Tag library descriptor (`.tld`) files**: This is a descriptor file for a tag library. This file describes the tag library implementation contained in a Java Archive (JAR) file to the servlet container. This file too is generally stored in the `WEB-INF` folder of your Web application.

**The Struts configuration file (struts-config.xml)**: This file configures Web applications based on the Struts framework, discussed in Chapter 10. The Struts framework is an open-source Model-View-Controller (MVC) implementation using JSP servlet technology.

## Common Elements of web.xml

The `<description>`, `<display-name>`, and `<icon>` elements can occur in several places as subelements of other elements within `web.xml`.

### *<description>*

The `<description>` element appears in a number of places within the `web.xml` file to provide a description of its parent element.

### *<display-name>*

The `<display-name>` element contains a short name for its parent element and is displayed by graphical user interface (GUI) tools.

### <icon>

The <icon> element references icons that will be used by a GUI tool to represent its parent element. It contains the following:

- An optional <small-icon> element containing the location within the application of a 16×16 pixel icon
- An optional <large-icon> element containing the location within the application of a 32×32 pixel icon

## <web-app>: Root Element

The <web-app> element is the root element of the web.xml file. This means that every web.xml file must contain one and only one such element, and all other elements must be contained within it. It contains the following:

- An optional <icon> element
- An optional <display-name> element
- An optional <description> element
- An optional <distributable> element
- Zero or more <context-param> elements
- Zero or more <filter> elements
- Zero or more <filter-mapping> elements
- Zero or more <listener> elements
- Zero or more <servlet> elements
- Zero or more <servlet-mapping> elements
- An optional <session-config> element
- Zero or more <mime-mapping> elements

- An optional <welcome-file-list> element
- Zero or more <error-page> elements
- Zero or more <jsp-config> elements
- Zero or more <resource-env-ref> elements
- Zero or more <resource-ref> elements
- Zero or more <security-constraint> elements
- An optional <login-config> element
- Zero or more <security-role> elements
- Zero or more <env-entry> elements
- Zero or more <ejb-ref> elements
- Zero or more <ejb-local-ref> elements
- Zero or more <service-ref> elements
- Zero or more <message-destination-ref> elements
- Zero or more <message-destination> elements
- Zero or more <local-encoding-mapping-list> elements

## Child Elements of <web-app>

The following sections cover the permissible child elements that <web-app> may have (other than those already described).

### <distributable>

The <distributable> element, if present, declares that this Web application can be deployed in a distributed servlet container or servlet container executing across multiple Java virtual machines (JVMs) running either on the same host or on different hosts.

## *<context-param>*

The `<context-param>` element declares a context initialization parameter. It contains the following:

- A `<param-name>` element containing the parameter's name
- A `<param-value>` element containing the parameter's value
- An optional `<description>` element (see earlier description)

## *<filter>*

The `<filter>` element declares a filter. A *filter* is a Java class that preprocesses the request data received from clients. This preprocessing may include decryption, formatting, or other processes. This element contains the following:

- An optional `<icon>` element
- A `<filter-name>` element containing the filter's name
- An optional `<display-name>` element
- An optional `<description>` element
- A `<filter-class>` element containing the filter's class name
- Zero or more `<init-param>` elements containing initialization parameters for the filter

Each `<init-param>` element contains the following:

- A `<param-name>` element containing the parameter name
- A `<param-value>` element containing the parameter value
- An optional `<description>` element

## *<filter-mapping>*

You use the `<filter-mapping>` element to map a filter to a servlet or a set of uniform resource locators (URLs). It contains the following:

- A <filter-name> element containing the name of a filter declared by a <filter> element
- Either a <url-pattern> element containing a URL pattern to match or a <servlet-name> element containing the name of a servlet declared by a <servlet> element
- Zero to four <dispatcher> elements

The <dispatcher> elements can have one of the following values: FORWARD, REQUEST, INCLUDE, and ERROR. FORWARD applies the filter to RequestDispatcher.forward() calls. REQUEST applies the filter to ordinary client calls to the path or servlet. INCLUDE applies the filter to RequestDispatcher.include() calls. ERROR applies the filter to the error page mechanism. If the <dispatcher> element is omitted, the default value is REQUEST.

## <listener>

You can use the <listener> element to declare an application listener. It contains the following:

- A <listener-class> element containing the listener's class name
- <description>, <display-name>, and <icon> elements

## <servlet>

The <servlet> element declares a servlet. It contains the following:

- An optional <icon> element.
- A <servlet-name> element containing the servlet's name.
- An optional <display-name> element.
- An optional <description> element.
- Either a <servlet-class> element containing the listener's class name or a <jsp-file> element containing the location within the Web application of a JSP file.
- <init-param> elements.

- An optional <load-on-startup> element indicating that the servlet should be loaded when the Web application starts up and containing an optional positive integer value indicating the order in which servlets should be started. If a <jsp-file> was specified, then the JSP should be precompiled and loaded.

- <security-role-ref> elements.

- An optional <run-as> element that specifies the identity under which the servlet should run.

Each <init-param> element contains the following:

- A <param-name> element containing the parameter name

- A <param-value> element containing the parameter value

- An optional <description> element

A <security-role-ref> element maps a role name called from within the servlet and the name of a security role defined for the Web application. It contains the following:

- An optional <description> element

- A <role-name> element containing the role name used within the servlet

- An optional <role-link> element containing the name of a role defined in a <security-role> element

### *<servlet-mapping>*

The <servlet-mapping> element maps a servlet to a URL pattern. It contains the following:

- A <servlet-name> element containing the name of a servlet declared by a <servlet> element

- A <url-pattern> element containing a URL pattern to match

### *<session-config>*

The `<session-config>` element configures the session tracking for the Web application. It contains the following:

- An optional `<session-timeout>` element containing the default session timeout for this Web application, which must be a whole number of minutes. The default behavior of the container without this attribute is to never time out.

### *<mime-mapping>*

The `<mime-mapping>` element maps a filename extension to a Multipurpose Internet Mail Extensions (MIME) type. It contains the following:

- An `<extension>` element containing a filename extension
- A `<mime-type>` element containing a defined MIME type

### *<welcome-file-list>*

The `<welcome-file-list>` element defines an ordered list of welcome files. It contains the following:

- One or more `<welcome-file>` elements containing a filename to use as a welcome file

### *<error-page>*

The `<error-page>` element maps an error code or exception type to a resource (*error page*) to use if that error condition arises. It contains the following:

- Either an `<error-code>` element containing an HTTP error code or an `<exception-type>` element containing the class name of a Java exception type
- A `<location>` element containing the location of the error page resource within the Web application

## <jsp-config>

The <jsp-config> element declares JSP configuration options. It contains the following:

- A <taglib> element containing tag library information
- A <jsp-property-group> element for specifying properties common to a group of JSPs

The <taglib> element contains the following subelements:

- A <taglib-uri> element containing a uniform resource indicator (URI) to identify the tag library
- A <taglib-location> element containing the location within the Web application of the tag library descriptor file (.tld file)

The <jsp-property-group> element has the following subelements:

- A <url-pattern> element specifying which resources should be covered by this set of properties.
- An optional <el-ignored> element that should be set to true or false. If true, then Expression Language (EL) terms are ignored.
- An optional <page-encoding> element that specifies the page encoding. A translation-time error will occur if a page directive's pageEncoding attribute is different from the value specified in web.xml.
- An optional <scripting-invalid> element that disables scripting on a page.
- An optional <is-xml> element that specifies that the pages are XML.
- Zero or more <include-prelude> elements that include the specified resource at the beginning of each file in this JSP group.
- Zero or more <include-coda> elements that include the specified resource at the end of each file in this JSP group.

## *<resource-env-ref>*

The `<resource-env-ref>` element declares that the Web application references an administered object such as a Java Message Service (JMS) resource destination. It contains the following:

- An optional `<description>` element.
- A `<resource-env-ref-name>` element containing the name of the resource environment.
- A `<resource-env-ref-type>` element containing the type of the resource environment reference. J2EE Web containers are required to support `javax.jms.Topic` and `javax.jms.Queue`

## *<resource-ref>*

The `<resource-ref>` element declares that the Web application references an external resource such as a data source reference. It contains the following:

- An optional `<description>` element.
- A `<res-ref-name>` element containing the name of the resource factory reference.
- A `<res-type>` element specifying the type of the data source.
- A `<res-auth>` element indicating whether the application code signs on to the resource programmatically or whether the container should sign on based on information supplied by the application deployer. Contents must be either `Application` or `Container`.
- An optional `<res-sharing-scope>` element specifying whether connections can be shared. Contents must be either `Shareable` (the default) or `Unshareable`.

## *<security-constraint>*

The `<security-constraint>` element applies security constraints to one or more collections of Web resources. It contains the following:

- An optional `<display-name>` element
- One or more `<web-resource-collection>` elements
- An optional `<auth-constraint>` element
- An optional `<user-data-constraint>` element

A `<web-resource-collection>` element identifies a set of resources within the application; it can be qualified by specifying particular Hypertext Transfer Protocol (HTTP) method(s) such as `GET` or `POST`. (By default, the security constraint applies to all HTTP methods.) It contains the following:

- A `<web-resource-name>` element containing the name of the Web resource collection
- An optional `<description>` element
- One or more `<url-pattern>` elements, each containing a URL pattern to match
- Zero or more `<http-method>` elements, each containing the name of an HTTP method

An `<auth-constraint>` element indicates that certain user roles should be permitted to access these Web resources. It contains the following:

- An optional `<description>` element
- Zero or more `<role-name>` elements each containing a role referenced in a `<security-role-ref>` element or the special name * that indicates all roles in this application

A `<user-data-constraint>` element indicates how data transmitted between the client and the application should be protected. It contains the following:

- An optional `<description>` element
- A `<transport-guarantee>` element, which can have one of the three values in Table C-1

*Table C-1.* `<transport-guarantee>` *Values*

| Value | Description |
|---|---|
| NONE | No transport guarantee is required. |
| INTEGRAL | The data must not be changed in transit. |
| CONFIDENTIAL | Others may not view the data en route. |

## *<login-config>*

The `<login-config>` element configures the authentication mechanism for this application. It contains the following:

- An optional `<auth-method>` element specifying the authentication mechanism. It must contain the text `BASIC`, `DIGEST`, `FORM`, or `CLIENT-CERT`.
- An optional `<realm-name>` element specifying the realm name for HTTP basic authorization.
- An optional `<form-login-config>` element to configure form-based authentication. It contains a `<form-login-page>` element specifying the login page and a `<form-error-page>` element specifying the error page used if login is unsuccessful.

## *<security-role>*

The `<security-role>` element declares a security role used in the Web application's security-constraints. It contains the following:

- An optional `<description>` element
- A `<role-name>` element containing the name of the role

## *<env-entry>*

The `<env-entry>` element declares an application's environment entry. It contains the following:

- An optional `<description>` element.
- An `<env-entry-name>` element containing the environment entry's name.

- An optional <env-entry-value> element containing the environment entry's value.
- An <env-entry-type> element containing the environment entry value's Java type. Legal values are java.lang.Boolean, java.lang.String, java.lang.Integer, java.lang.Double, and java.lang.Float.

## *<ejb-ref>*

The <ejb-ref> element declares a reference to an Enterprise JavaBean (EJB). It contains the following:

- An optional <description> element
- An <ejb-ref-name> element containing the Java Naming and Directory Interface (JNDI) name of the EJB
- An <ejb-ref-type> element containing the expected type of the EJB, either Entity or Session
- A <home> element containing the type (the name of the class) of the EJB's home interface
- A <remote> element containing the type of the EJB's remote interface
- An optional <ejb-link> element specifying that this EJB reference is linked to the named EJB in the encompassing J2EE application.

## *<ejb-local-ref>*

You use <ejb-local-ref> to declare a reference to an EJB's local home. The declaration consists of the following:

- An optional <description> element
- An <ejb-ref-name> element containing the JNDI name of the EJB
- An <ejb-ref-type> element containing the expected type of the EJB, either Entity or Session
- A <local-home> element used to specify the local home interface of the EJB

- A `<local>` element used to specify the local interface of the EJB
- An optional `<ejb-link>` element used to specify the referenced EJB

### <service-ref>

`<service-ref>` declares reference to a Web service. It contains the following:

- A `<service-ref-name>` element used to specify the name of the Web service. This should begin with `/service/`.
- A `<service-interface>` element used to define the fully qualified class name of the interface on which the client depends.
- An optional `<wsdl-file>` element used to specify the path to a Web Service Description Language (WSDL) file.
- An optional `<jaxrpc-mapping-file>` element containing the name of a file that describes the Java API for XML-Based RPC (JAX-RPC) mapping between the Java interfaces used by the application and the WSDL description in the `<wsdl-file>` element.
- An optional `<service-qname>` used to specify the WSDL service element.
- Zero or more `<port-component-ref>` elements declaring a client dependency on the container.
- Zero or more `<handler>` elements declaring the handler for a port component.

### <message-destination>

`<message-destination>` declares a message destination. It contains the following:

- A `<message-destination-name>` element used to specify the name of a message destination

### <message-destination-ref>

`<message-destination-ref>` contains a declaration of a message destination. It contains the following:

- A <message-destination-ref-name> element that specifies the JDNI name of a message destination
- A <message-destination-type> element specifying the type of the destination.
- A <message-destination-usage> element specifying the use of the message destination
- An optional <message-destination-link> element that links a destination to a message reference or message EJB

### *<locale-encoding-mapping-list>*

<locale-encoding-mapping-list> contains mappings between the locale and the encoding. It contains the following:

- One or more <locale-encoding-mapping> elements used to specify a single mapping

  <locale-encoding-mapping> contains the following subelements:

- A <locale> element used to specify the locale
- An <encoding> element used to specify the encoding

## Common Elements of the Tag Library Descriptor

The <description>, <display-name>, and <icon> elements can occur in several places in a Tag Library Descriptor (TLD) file, and they have the same meanings described for web.xml.

### *<taglib>: Root Element*

The <taglib> element is the root element of a .tld file. It contains the following:

- A <tlib-version> element
- A <short-name> element
- An optional <uri> element

- An optional `<display-name>` element
- An optional `icon>` element
- An optional `<description>` element
- An optional `<validator>` element
- Zero or more `<listener>` elements
- Zero or more `<tag>` elements
- Zero or more `<tag-file>` elements that specify tag files in this library
- Zero or more `<function>` elements that specify an EL function
- Zero or more `<taglib-extension>` elements that provide information about this taglib, mainly for use by tools

## *Child Elements of <taglib>*

The permissible subelements of `<taglib>` are as follows.

### *<tlib-version>*

The `<tlib-version>` element contains the version number of the tag library.

### *<jsp-version>*

The `<jsp-version>` element contains the JSP version that the tag library requires (`1.2` by default).

### *<short-name>*

The `<short-name>` element contains a short name for the tag library.

### *<uri>*

The `<uri>` element contains a URI uniquely identifying the tag library.

### *<validator>*

The <validator> element defines a validator to check that a JSP page uses the tag library correctly. It contains the following:

- A <validator-class> element containing the name of the TagLibraryValidator class
- Zero or more <init-param> elements

An <init-param> element defines initialization parameters for the validator and contains the following:

- A <param-name> element containing the parameter name
- A <param-value> element containing the parameter value
- An optional <description> element

### *<listener>*

The <listener> element defines an event listener for the Web application using the tag library. It contains the following:

- A <listener-class> element containing the name of the listener class
- <description>, <display-name>, and <icon> elements

### *<tag>*

The <tag> element defines a tag. It contains the following:

- A <name> element containing the tag's name.
- A <tag-class> element containing the name of the tag handler class.
- An optional <tei-class> element containing the name of the TagExtraInfo class for the tag.
- An optional <body-content> element describing the body content of the tag: either tagdependent, JSP, or empty.

- An optional `<display-name>` element.
- An optional `< icon>` element.
- An optional `<description>` element.
- Zero or more `<variable>` elements.
- Zero or more `<attribute>` elements.
- An optional `<dynamic-attributes>` element specifying whether this tag supports additional attributes with dynamic names. If `true`, the `<tag-class>` must implement the `javax.servlet.jsp.tagext.DynamicAttributes` interface; it defaults to `false`.
- An optional `<example>` element that shows an example of this tag in use.
- Zero or more `<tag-extension>` elements that provide information about this tag, mainly for use by tools.

A `<variable>` element declares that this tag defines a scripting variable. It contains the following:

- An optional `<description>` element.
- Either a `<name-given>` element containing the name of the scripting variable or a `<name-from-attribute>` element containing the name of the tag attribute that will give the scripting variable's name at runtime.
- An optional `<variable-class>` element containing the class name of the scripting variable. The default is `java.lang.String`.
- An optional `<declare>` element whose contents indicate whether the scripting variable is to be defined; the default is `true`.
- An optional `<scope>` element whose contents indicate the scope of the scripting variable. Possible values are `NESTED` (the default), `AT_BEGIN`, or `AT_END`.

An `<attribute>` element defines an attribute of the tag. It contains the following:

- An optional `<description>` element.
- A `<name>` element containing the name of the attribute.

- An optional `<required>` element whose contents indicate whether the attribute is required or optional. Legal values are `true`, `false` (the default), yes, and `no`.
- An optional `<rtexprvalue>` element whose contents indicate whether the attribute value can be a run-time expression scriptlet rather than a static value. Legal values are `true`, `false` (the default), yes, and `no`.
- An optional `<type>` element containing the type of the attribute's value. (For static values, this is always `java.lang.String`.) This element can occur only with `<rtexprvalue>`.
- An optional `<fragment>` element specifying whether this attribute is a fragment. It can't be used with either `<rtexprvalue>` or `<type>`.

## *<tag-file>*

`<tag-file>` defines an action in this tag library implemented as a `.tag` file. It contains the following:

- A `<name>` element uniquely identifying the action name.
- A `<path>` element specifying where to find the `.tag` file. This must begin with `/META-INF/tags` if the file is in a JAR. Otherwise it must begin with `/WEB-INF/tags/`.
- An optional `<example>` element showing an example of the tag in use.
- Zero or more `<tag-extension>` elements that provide information about this tag, mainly for use by tools.

## *<function>*

You use `<function>` to provide information on each function in the tag library that's to be exposed to the EL. It contains the following:

- A `<name>` element uniquely identifying this function
- A `<function-class>` element specifying the Java class that defines this function
- A `<function-signature>` element specifying the Java language signature of this function

- An optional `<example>` element showing an example of the tag in use
- Zero or more `<function-extension>` elements that provide information about this tag, mainly for use by tools

### <taglib-extension>

`<taglib-extension>` provides information about this taglib, mainly for use by tools. They must not affect the behavior of a container.

## Common Elements of the Struts Config File

Note that within the Struts configuration file the ordering of elements is significant. You should additionally note the following:

- All URL paths are context-relative; in other words, they must start with a / and are relative to the root of the Web application.
- In addition to the attributes listed next, all elements in the Struts configuration file have an implied `id` attribute.

The `<set-property>`, `<description>`, `<display-name>`, `<icon>`, `<large-icon>`, and `<small-icon>` elements can occur in several places within the Struts configuration file, so we'll describe them only once.

### <set-property>

You use the `<set-property>` element to configure JavaBeans components by specifying a property name and value. It has no content but has the following attributes:

- `property` specifies the name of the bean property to be set.
- `value` specifies the new property value in a string representation.

### <description>

The `<description>` element contains a description of the parent element.

### *<display-name>*

The `<display-name>` element contains a short name for its parent element for GUI tools to display.

### *<icon>*

The `<icon>` element references icons that will be used by a GUI tool to represent its parent element. It contains the following:

- An optional `<small-icon>` element containing the location, relative to the file, of a 16×16 pixel icon
- An optional `<large-icon>` element containing the location, relative to the file, of a 32×32 pixel icon

## *<struts-config>: Root Element*

The `<struts-config>` element is the root element of the Struts configuration file. It contains the following:

- An optional `<data-sources>` element
- An optional `<form-beans>` element
- An optional `<global-forwards>` element
- An optional `<global-exceptions>` element
- An optional `<action-mappings>` element
- An optional `<controller>` element
- An optional `<message-resources>` element
- An optional `<plug-in>` element

## *<data-sources> and <data-source>*

The `<data-sources>` element describes a set of `DataSource` objects. You configure the individual `DataSource` objects through nested `<data-source>` elements.

Each <data-source> element describes a DataSource object that will be instantiated, configured, and made available as a servlet context attribute. Any object can be specified as long as it implements javax.sql.DataSource and can be configured entirely from JavaBean properties. The following attributes are required:

- className is the configuration bean for this DataSource object. If specified, the object must be a subclass of the default configuration bean.
- key is the servlet context attribute key under which this data source will be stored.
- type is a fully qualified Java class name for this DataSource object. The class must implement javax.sql.DataSource, and the object must be configurable entirely from JavaBean properties.

Several additional attributes are now deprecated (that is, no longer recommended) because they applied only to the default DataSource class.

<data-source> has an optional <set-property> subelement.

## *<global-exceptions> and <exception>*

The <global-exceptions> element describes a set of exceptions that might be thrown by an Action object. You configure the handling of individual exception types through child <exception> elements. An <action> element may override a global exception handler by registering a local exception handler for the same exception type.

The <exception> element registers an ExceptionHandler for an exception type. The following are the important attributes:

- className is the configuration bean for this ExceptionHandler object. If specified, className must be a subclass of the default configuration bean org.apache.struts.config.ExceptionConfig.
- handler is the fully qualified Java class name for this exception handler (org.apache.struts.action.ExceptionHandler).
- key is the key to use with this handler's message resource bundle that will retrieve the error message template for this exception.
- path is the module-relative URI to the resource that will complete the request/response if this exception occurs.
- scope is the context (request or session) to access the ActionError object (org.apache.struts.action.ActionError) for this exception.

- type is the fully qualified Java class name of the exception type to register with this handler.

- bundle is the resource bundle to use with this exception. The default is Globals.MESSAGES_KEY.

## <form-beans> and <form-bean>

The <form-beans> element describes the set of form bean descriptors for this application module. An attribute called type is defined for this element, but this attribute is deprecated in Struts 1.0.

This element has <form-bean> child elements that each define a form bean that will be configured to handle form submissions. It may have the following attributes:

- className allows you to override the default class Struts uses to represent a form bean internally.

- name specifies a unique identifier for this form bean, which will be used to reference it in <action> elements. (This is required.)

- type specifies the name of the form bean class to be used; it must extend org.apache.struts.action.ActionForm. (This is required.)

## <global-forwards> and <forward>

The <global-forwards> element contains zero or more <forward> child elements, specifying named forwards that will be available to all Struts actions (unless overridden within an <action> element). It also has a type attribute, but this is again deprecated in Struts 1.0.

The <forward> element maps a logical name to a Web resource and has the following attributes:

- className allows you to override the default class Struts uses to represent a forward internally. You won't commonly use this attribute.

- name specifies a unique identifier for this forward, which will be used to reference it within your application. (This is required.)

- path specifies the location of the Web resource. (This is required.)

- `redirect` allows you to specify whether control should be redirected to this resource (value `true`), rather than forwarding to it (`false`). The default is `false`.

- `contextrelative` is set to `true` if, in a modular application, the path attribute starts with a slash (/) and should be considered relative to the entire Web application rather than the module.

## *<action-mappings> and <action>*

The `<action-mappings>` element contains zero or more `<action>` elements, which map request URLs to `Action` classes. It also has a `type` attribute, which represents a fully qualified Java class to use when instantiating `ActionMapping` objects.

Each `<action>` element maps a request path to an `Action` class. Its attributes are listed next; exactly one of `forward`, `include`, or `type` must be specified:

- `type` specifies the class name of the action class (which must extend `org.apache.struts.action.Action`) to be used to process requests for this mapping if the `forward` or `include` attribute isn't included.

- `forward` specifies the path of the servlet or JSP that will process this request, instead of instantiating and calling the `Action` class specified by `type`.

- `include` specifies the path of the servlet or JSP that will process this request, instead of instantiating and calling the `Action` class specified by `type`.

The remaining `<action>` attributes are as follows:

- `path` (which is required) defines the path of the submitted request that will be processed by this action, starting with a / character. If Struts was used with an extension-based `<servlet-mapping>` element, then the filename extension should be omitted here.

- `name` specifies the name of the form bean (if any) associated with the action.

- `attribute` specifies the name of the request-scope or session-scope attribute under which the form bean is accessed if it's something other than the bean's specified `name`. It's optional if `name` is specified but otherwise isn't allowed.

- `scope` specifies the scope (`request` or `session`) in which the form bean is located, if any. It's optional if `name` is specified but otherwise isn't allowed.

- `input` specifies the path of the input form to which control should be returned if a validation error is encountered. It's required if `name` is specified and the input bean returns validation errors, is optional if `name` is specified and the input bean doesn't return validation errors, and isn't allowed if `name` isn't specified.
- `parameter` specifies configuration information for the action.
- `prefix` specifies a prefix used to match request parameter names to form bean properties, if any. It's optional if `name` is specified but otherwise isn't allowed.
- `suffix` specifies a suffix used to match request parameter names to form bean properties names, if any. It's optional if `name` is specified but otherwise isn't allowed.
- `unknown` specifies whether this action should be configured to handle all requests not handled by another action.
- `validate` specifies whether the form bean's `validate()` method should be called prior to calling the action.
- `className` allows you to override the default class Struts uses to represent an action mapping internally. You won't commonly use this attribute.
- `roles` is a comma-delimited list of roles that are allowed to access this `ActionMapping`.

## <controller>

The `<controller>` element describes the controller bean that encapsulates an application module's run-time configuration. The following attributes are defined:

- `bufferSize` is the size of the input buffer used when processing file uploads.
- `className` is the fully qualified Java class name of the `ControllerConfig` subclass for this controller object. If specified, the object must be a subclass of `org.apache.struts.config.ControllerConfig`.
- `contentType` is the default content type (and optional character encoding) to be set on each response. It may be overridden by the action, JSP page, or other resource to which the request is forwarded.

- `forwardPattern` is the replacement pattern defining how the path attribute of a `<forward>` element is mapped to a context-relative URL when it starts with a slash (and when the `contextRelative` property is `false`).

> **NOTE** `forwardPattern` *may consist of any combination of the following:* `"$M"`, *which means it's replaced by the module prefix of this module;* `"$P"`, *which means it's replaced by the path attribute of the selected* `<forward>` *element; and* `"$$"`, *which causes a literal dollar sign to be rendered. If not specified, the default* `forwardPattern` *is* `"$M$P"`, *which is consistent with the previous behavior of forwards.*

- `inputForward` should be set to `true` for the input attribute of `<action>` elements to be the name of a local or global `ActionForward`, which will then be used to calculate the final URL. Set this to `false` (the default) to treat the input parameter of `<action>` elements as a module-relative path to the resource to be used as the input form.

- `locale` should be set to `true` for a `Locale` object to be stored in the user's session if not already present.

- `maxFileSize` is the maximum size (in bytes) of a file to be accepted as a file upload. This can be expressed as a number followed by a `"K"`, `"M"`, or `"G"`, which are interpreted to mean kilobytes, megabytes, and gigabytes, respectively.

- `memFileSize` is the maximum size (in bytes) of a file whose contents will be retained in memory after uploading. Files larger than this threshold will be written to some alternative storage medium, typically a hard disk. This can be expressed as a number followed by a `"K"`, `"M"`, or `"G"`, which are interpreted to mean kilobytes, megabytes, and gigabytes, respectively.

- `multipartClass` is the fully qualified Java class name of the multipart request handler class to be used with this module.

- `nocache` should be set to `true` if you want the controller to add HTTP headers for avoiding caching to every response from this module.

- `pagePattern` is the replacement pattern defining how the page attribute of custom tags are mapped to a context-relative URL of the corresponding resource.

> **NOTE** pagePattern *may consist of any combination of the following:* "$M", *which means it's replaced by the module prefix of this module;* "$P", *which means it's replaced by the value of the* page *attribute; and* "$$", *which causes a literal dollar sign to be rendered. If not specified, the default* forwardPattern *is* "$M$P", *which is consistent with previous behavior of URL evaluation for page attributes.*

- processorClass is the fully qualified Java class name of the RequestProcessor subclass to be used with this module.
- tempDir is the temporary working directory to use when processing file uploads.

## *<message-resources>*

<message-resources> describes a MessageResources object with message templates for this module. The following attributes are defined:

- className is the configuration bean for this message resources object. If specified, the object must be a subclass of org.apache.struts.config.MessageResourcesConfig.
- factory is the fully qualified Java class name of the MessageResourcesFactory subclass to use for this message resources object.
- key is the servlet context attribute under which this message resources bundle will be stored. The default attribute is Globals.MESSAGES_KEY. The application module prefix (if any) is appended to the key (${key}${prefix}).
- null should be set to true for the message resources to return a null string for unknown message keys or false to return a message with the bad key value.
- parameter is the configuration parameter to be passed to the createResources() method of the factory object.

## *<plug-in>*

<plug-in> specifies the fully qualified Java class name of an application plug-in module that receives notification of application startup and shutdown. An instance of the specified class is created for each element, and it can be configured with nested <set-property> elements. The following attribute is supported:

- <className> is the fully qualified class name of the plug-in object.

APPENDIX D

# Getting More Information

**THIS APPENDIX SHOWS** you where you can find more information about JavaServer Pages (JSP) and Java.

## Java Development Kit Documentation

You should definitely download and install the Java Development Kit (JDK) documentation; it provides a huge amount of information about the Java platform itself, such as the following:

- Instructions for using the Java command-line tools (`javac`, `java`, and so on).
- Guides to Java features such as input/output (I/O), networking, `.jar` files, and so on.
- Most important, documentation on the various classes that make up the Java platform. These are commonly known as *Javadocs* because they're generated by a tool known as `javadoc`.

You can download the documentation from `http://java.sun.com/j2se/1.4.2/docs/index.html`. If you're using Windows, the file comes in the form of a `.zip` file, which you should unzip into your JDK directory (for example, into `C:\jdk1.4.2`); alternatively, packages in `.rpm` and `.gzip` format are also available for Linux users. Once this is done, you can browse to the `index.html` file to start reading—typically this means pointing your Web browser to `C:\jdk1.4.2\docs\index.html`, as shown in Figure D-1.

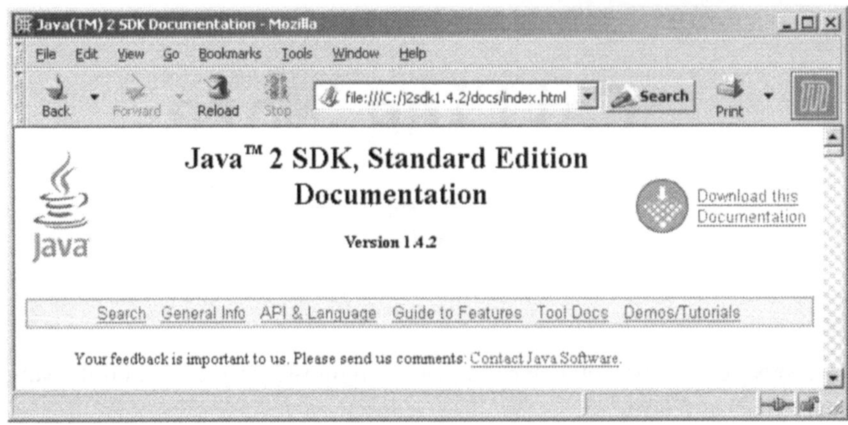


*Figure D-1. Java 2 Standard Edition (J2SE) 1.4.2 documentation*

As you'll see if you scroll down this page, there's a lot of information; it's well worth spending some time exploring what's available. We'll focus on one particular part of the documentation, the application programming interface (API) guide. If you scroll down to the API & Language Documentation section, you'll find the Java 2 Platform API Specification link. Clicking this link takes you to a page like the one shown in Figure D-2.

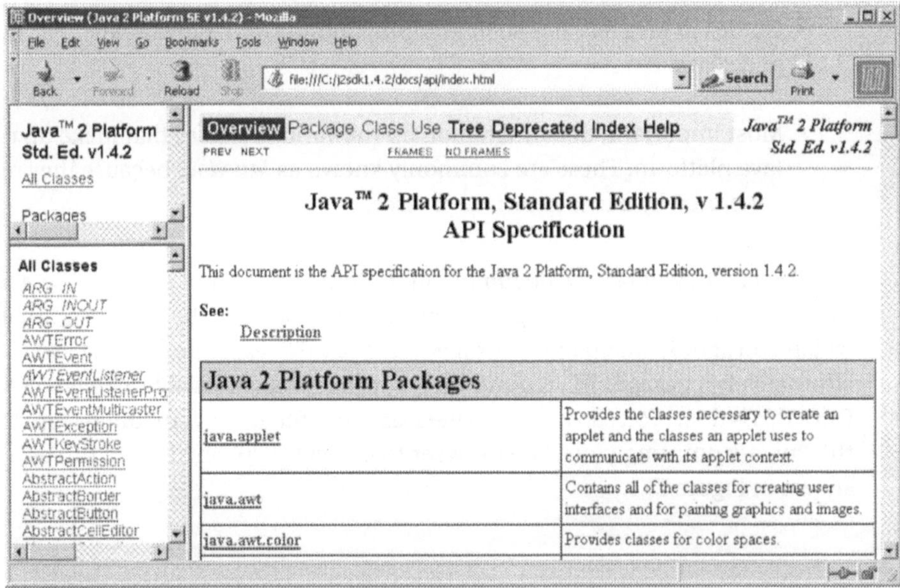


*Figure D-2. J2SE 1.4.2 API documentation*

You'll see a lot of information here because there are a lot of classes and interfaces in the Java platform; in fact, more than 1,800 classes and interfaces are listed! Fortunately, they're all nicely categorized into packages, which makes it easier to find what you're looking for.

You'll see that Figure D-2 is divided into three areas. The main area, on the right, initially contains a descriptive list of packages; on the top left there's a quick summary of packages, and on the bottom left there's a complete list of classes and interfaces.

If you click a package's name in the list at the top left, the bottom-left frame is replaced with a list of the classes and interfaces in that package only. Clicking a package's name in the main part of the screen replaces that frame with a descriptive overview of that package only.

So, say you're interested in the `java.io.File` class. In the top-left frame, scroll down to `java.io`, and click that link. The bottom-left frame now contains a list of the contents of that package only; to get to the overview of that package, click the text *java.io* at the top of the bottom-left frame, as shown in Figure D-3.

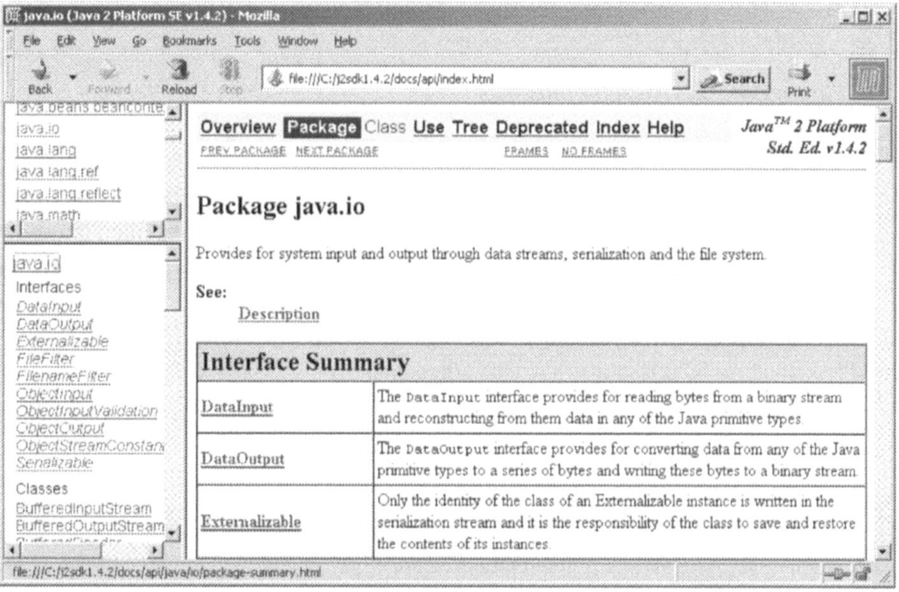


*Figure D-3.* `java.io` ***package description***

You can now locate information about the `File` class by clicking the appropriate link in either the bottom left or the main frames, which takes you to the documentation for that class, as shown in Figure D-4.

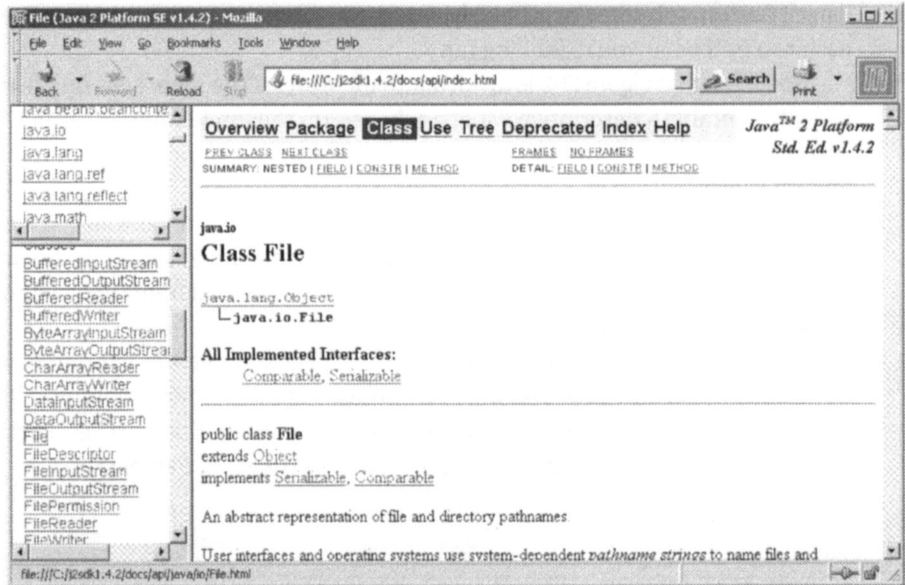


*Figure D-4.* `java.io.File` *Javadocs*

The documentation for each class is divided into a number of sections. At the top, there's a summary showing the tree of classes that has been extended and the interfaces that have been implemented to get you to `java.io.File`. Below this is a textual description of the class.

Scrolling down, you start to get to the "meat," as shown in Figure D-5.

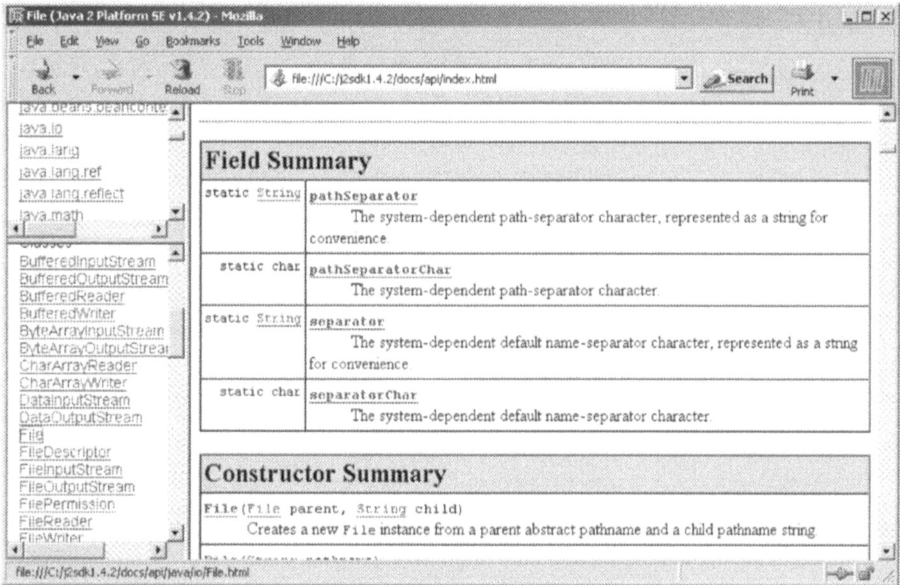


*Figure D-5. Details of* `java.io.File` *fields and constructors*

As you can see, you're given summaries of the fields, constructors, and methods declared for this class, with links to fuller descriptions farther down the page. There's also a section listing methods inherited from the parent class.

Finally, toward the bottom, you'll see detailed descriptions of each field, constructor, and method, as shown in Figure D-6.

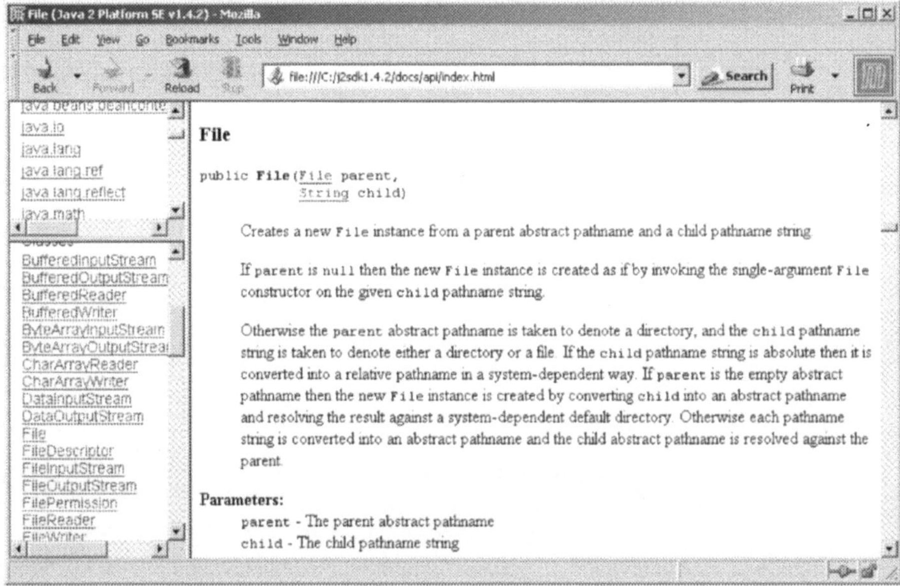


*Figure D-6. Details of a* `java.io.File` *constructor*

The whole set of API documents is liberally hyperlinked, and it's actually very easy to find your way around the documentation.

## Tomcat and JSP/Servlet Documentation

You should know about the documentation that comes with Tomcat. When you installed Tomcat 5.0, you may have seen the page shown in Figure D-7.

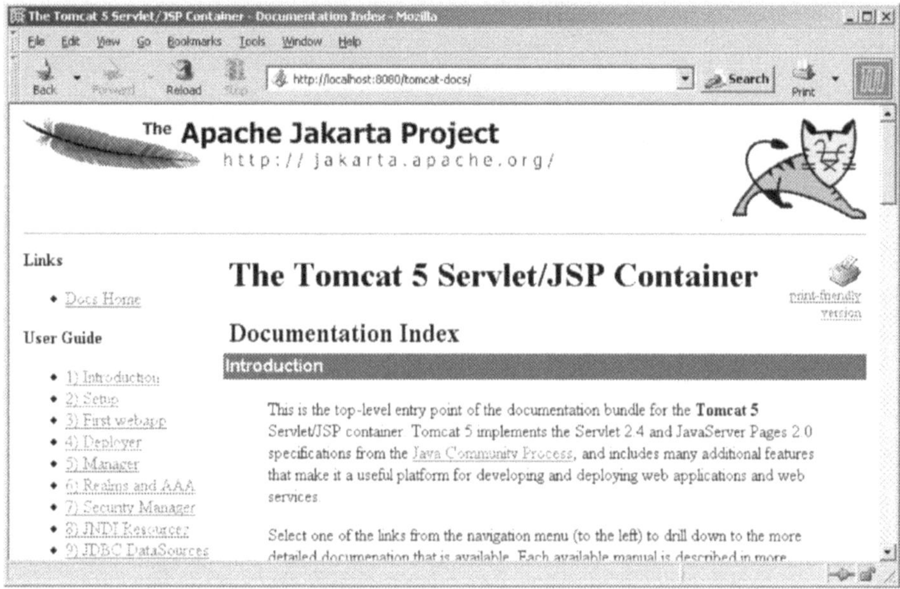


*Figure D-7. Tomcat's documentation page*

The documentation index has been greatly improved from previous versions, and it now maintains a collection of related documentation, making it very easy to find basic startup information.

The two sections of this that are particularly important are the User Guide section, which contains great startup configuration guides, and the Reference section, which includes the API documentation for the servlet 2.4 and JSP 2.0 packages.

The servlet API contains the Javadocs for `javax.servlet`, `javax.servlet.http`, `javax.servlet.jsp`, and `javax.servlet.jsp.tagext`. You'll find these documents (shown in Figure D-8) to be a handy supplement to the information on JSP implicit objects given in Appendix B.

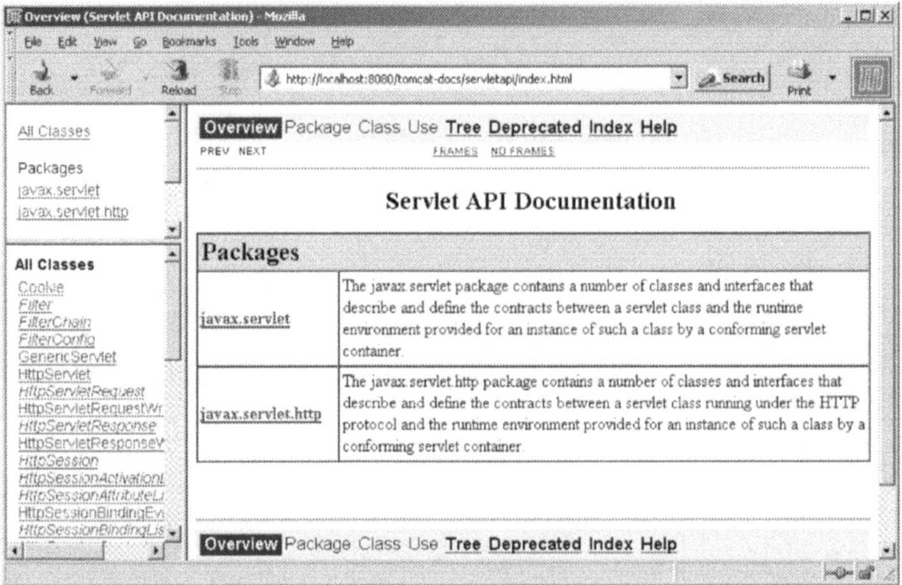


*Figure D-8. The servlet API Javadocs*

Furthermore, the JSP API documentation contains the Javadocs for the `javax.servlet.jsp`, `javax.servlet.jsp.el`, and `javax.servlet.jsp.tagext`, as shown in Figure D-9.

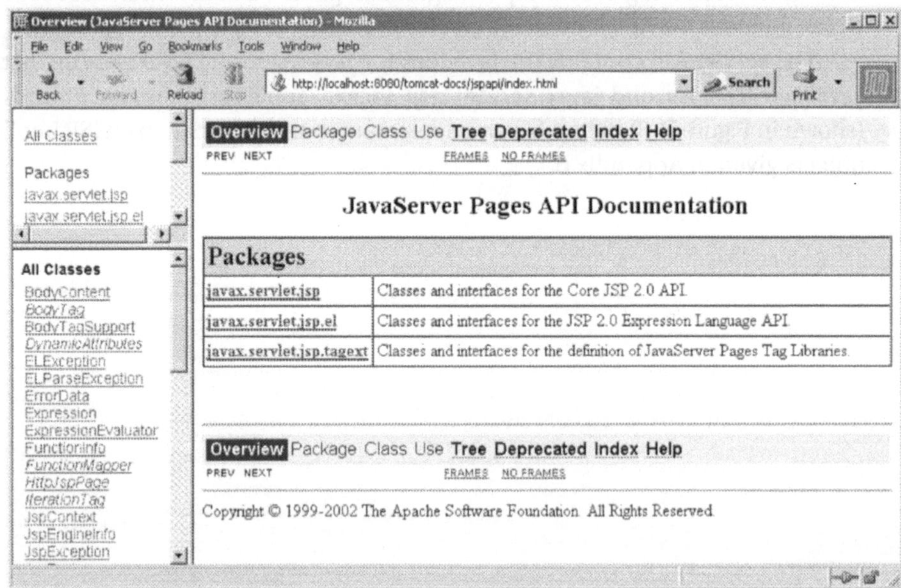


*Figure D-9. The JSP API Javadocs*

## Other Resources

This section lists some other resources you may find helpful as you continue to learn about JSP and Java.

A couple of Apress books will help you to take forward from what you've learned in this book. You may be particularly interested in the following:

- *Beginning Java Objects: From Concepts to Code* by Jacquie Barker (Apress, 2003) teaches object-oriented programming in Java from the ground up by introducing you to the concepts of object orientation and how to model your system as a set of objects. It then shows you how to translate this into Java sources.

- *Pro JSP, Third Edition* by Simon Brown, Sam Dalton, Daniel Jepp, Dave Johnson, Sing Li, and Matt Raible (Apress, 2003) takes you beyond what has been covered in this book with extensive coverage of advanced topics such as using Extensible Markup Language (XML) with Java, implementing servlets, generating nontextual types of Web content such as images and Portable Document Format (PDF) files, and using the Struts framework.

- *JSP Examples and Best Practices* by Andrew Patzer (Apress, 2002) takes basic JSP and applies sound architectural principles and design patterns to give the average developer the tools to build scalable enterprise applications using JSP. This concise, to-the-point book concentrates on the patterns needed for effective servlet- and JSP-based enterprise development.

- *J2EE FrontEnd Technologies: A Programmer's Guide to Servlets, JavaServer Pages, and Enterprise JavaBeans* by Lennart Jorelid (Apress, 2001) is a concise, to-the-point book that concentrates on the patterns needed for effective servlet- and JSP-based enterprise development.

- *Pro Jakarta Struts, Second Edition* by John Carnell and Rob Harrop (Apress, 2004) covers version 1.1 of Jakarta Struts, which provides new functionality in areas such as presentation and error handling. This book acts as a roadmap to demonstrate how to use the Jakarta Struts framework to solve everyday Web application development challenges.

- *Pro JSF: JavaServer Faces* by Kim Topley (Apress, upcoming) begins by describing the JavaServer Faces Hypertext Markup Language (HTML) tag library. It approaches JSF by treating it as a technology for building JSP pages that create HTML, and only much later in the book, when the reader is comfortable with JSF, does it introduce the details of the lifecycle, UIComponents, and renderers.

Next, here are a few Web sites that may be of use:

- Sun Microsystems' official Web site provides information about JSP and servlets at `http://java.sun.com/products/jsp/` and `http://java.sun.com/products/servlets/`, respectively. This site is particularly useful for official information such as the JSP specification, servlet specification (hard reading, though), and occasional articles.

- The Jakarta project, `http://jakarta.apache.org/`, has many useful subprojects offering useful (and free) server-side Java software. Particularly notable are Tomcat, the JSP/servlet container you've been using throughout this book (`http://jakarta.apache.org/tomcat/`), the Struts framework (`http://jakarta.apache.org/struts/`), and the Taglibs project (`http://jakarta.apache.org/taglibs/`), which offers a host of ready-made JSP tag libraries ready for you to download and use.

- JSPInsider, `http://www.jspinsider.com/`, offers a host of JSP-related information including the helpful articles and useful (free) JavaBeans and tag libraries.

Lastly, you may find mailing lists helpful if you run up against problems in your code:

- The Jakarta project has mailing lists for their projects; each has a "user" list for questions about using the product, and each has a "developer" list where the people who created the projects live. You'll probably be mainly interested in the "user" lists; see `http://jakarta.apache.org/site/mail.html` for more information.

# Index

## Symbols



## A

## B



## C

## D

## G

## H

## I

## J

## K



## L

## M



## N

## O



## P

# Q



# R

## S

## T

## X



## Y